Religious Politics in Turkey

Since the elections of 2002, Erdoğan's AKP has dominated the political scene in Turkey. This period has often been understood as a break from a secular pattern of state building. But in this book, Ceren Lord shows how Islamist mobilisation in Turkey has been facilitated from within the state by institutions established during early nation building. Lord thus challenges the traditional account of the Islamist AKP's rise that sees it either as a grass-roots reaction to the authoritarian secularism of the state or as a function of the state's utilisation of religion. Tracing struggles within the state, Lord also shows how the state's principal religious authority, the Presidency of Religious Affairs (Diyanet), competed with other state institutions to pursue Islamisation. By privileging Sunni Muslim access to state resources to the exclusion of others, the Diyanet has been a key actor in ensuring persistence and increasing salience of religious markers in political and economic competition, creating an amenable environment for Islamist mobilisation.

Ceren Lord is a British Academy Postdoctoral Research Fellow with Middle East Studies at the Oxford School of Global and Area Studies, at the University of Oxford. She is also Associate Editor of the *British Journal of Middle Eastern Studies*.

D1113154

Cambridge Middle East Studies

Editorial Board

Charles Tripp (general editor)
Julia Clancy-Smith
F. Gregory Gause
Yezid Sayigh
Avi Shlaim
Judith E. Tucker

Other titles in the series can be found after the index.

Religious Politics in Turkey

From the Birth of the Republic to the AKP

Ceren Lord

University of Oxford

CAMBRIDGE
UNIVERSITY PRESS

CAMBRIDGE
UNIVERSITY PRESS

University Printing House, Cambridge CB2 8BS, United Kingdom

One Liberty Plaza, 20th Floor, New York, NY 10006, USA

477 Williamstown Road, Port Melbourne, VIC 3207, Australia

314-321, 3rd Floor, Plot 3, Splendor Forum, Jasola District Centre, New Delhi - 110025, India

79 Anson Road, #06-04/06, Singapore 079906

Cambridge University Press is part of the University of Cambridge.

It furthers the University's mission by disseminating knowledge in the pursuit of education, learning and research at the highest international levels of excellence.

www.cambridge.org
Information on this title: www.cambridge.org/9781108458924
DOI: 10.1017/9781108638906

© Ceren Lord 2018

First published 2018
First paperback edition 2020

A catalogue record for this publication is available from the British Library

Library of Congress Cataloging in Publication data
Names: Lord, Ceren, 1982– author.
Title: Religious politics in Turkey : from the birth of the Republic to the
   AKP / Ceren Lord, University of Oxford.
Description: 1 [edition]. | New York : Cambridge University Press, 2018. |
   Series: Cambridge Middle East studies | Includes bibliographical references
   and index.
Identifiers: LCCN 2018022547| ISBN 9781108472005 (hardback : alk. paper) |
   ISBN 9781108458924 (pbk. : alk. paper)
Subjects: LCSH: Islam and politics–Turkey–History. | Islam and state–Turkey–
   History. | Religion and politics–Turkey–History. | Religion and state–
   Turkey–History. | AK Parti (Turkey) | Turkey. Diyanet İşleri Başkanlığı. |
   Turkey–Politics and government–1980-
Classification: LCC BP63.T8 L67 2018 | DDC 322/.109561–dc23
   LC record available at https://lccn.loc.gov/2018022547

ISBN   978-1-108-47200-5   Hardback
ISBN   978-1-108-45892-4   Paperback

Contents

Figures

Tables

Preface

On the night of 15 July 2016, the imams of more than 86,000 mosques, legally overseen by the Presidency of Religious Affairs (Diyanet İşleri Başkanlığı, from here on referred to as the Diyanet), the Republic of Turkey's principal religious authority, were called upon in a text message sent by Mehmet Görmez, the Diyanet's former chief, to mobilise against an ongoing coup attempt. Görmez called for imams, as the 'spiritual guides' of the people, to read the *sala* prayer and encourage citizens to take to the streets to counter the putschists. Throughout the night, an endless cacophony of *sala* prayers could be heard, punctuated by battle cries from the mosques, to which people gathering in the streets responded with exclamations of the Takbīr, involving the chants of 'Allahu Akbar' ('God is great'). Over the following days, Görmez declared proudly that 'with the *sala* prayer in its ears, Takbīr in its mouth, and the flag in its hand, the nation defeated the traitors'. Underscoring the importance of this mobilisation through the Diyanet were the comments by Hizb ut-Tahrir's media bureau chief, Mahmut Kar:

The call to resist against the coup against the terror was not made from the loudspeakers of the municipalities, but from the mosques to the public. The role of Diyanet against the coup attempt is crucial, because from midnight till dawn we heard the *sala* prayers from the mosques. In no city can you see people screaming 'democracy' and marching towards the tanks, the believers courageously stood against bullets chanting 'Allahu Akbar.' Although media may try to portray this as a "victory of democracy," thanks be to God they did not succeed, because the impact of the calls from the mosques is potent on the people. (Tremblay 25 July 2016)

The Diyanet, housing the majority of Turkey's *ulema* (Sunni Muslim religious scholars), long ignored and dismissed as a marginalised actor and an apparatus of the secular Kemalist state for controlling religion, took centre stage on the night of 15 July, cementing its rising status and expanded role in the so-called New Turkey of the Justice and Development Party (Adalet ve Kalkınma Partisi, AKP). Yet, one journalist's remark that 'observant Muslims and Islamists find comfort and encouragement in knowing that Diyanet is now out of the closet' (Tremblay 25 July 2016) appeared to be an acknowledgement of an open secret about the role played by the institution during the lifetime of the Republic.

I first began to think about the Diyanet's role in the mid-2000s when trying to make sense of the increasingly polarised public debate about secularism and Islam that had followed the ascent to power of the Islamist AKP in 2002. Some were accusing the party of having a hidden agenda of Islamisation, while others promoted it as a democratising force. In my attempt to better understand the institution, I began by examining the Diyanet's public discourse, focusing on its publications and particularly its monthly magazines distributed to all its personnel. The state body was established in 1924, taking over from the Ministry of Shari'a and Pious Foundations (Şeriye ve Evkaf Vekaleti, ŞEV), which was set up in 1920 by the nationalist government in Ankara in place of the Ottoman office of the Sheikh ul-Islam (Şeyhülislam), the chief Islamic authority. Having absorbed the Ottoman *ulema*, the Diyanet has been legally tasked with carrying out 'affairs related to the beliefs, worship and moral foundations of Islam, enlighten[ing] society about religion and manag[ing] places of worship': it has a monopoly on over-seeing religious life of Muslims and activities in the Republic. Since its establishment, and particularly with the transition to multi-party politics in 1946, its influence, remit and power have grown together with its size: it comprises around 120,000 personnel and has an expanding presence beyond Turkey's borders.

Over the years, my efforts turned into extensive historical research that went beyond the Diyanet, with time spent in archives, libraries and elsewhere, collecting a variety of materials. I was beginning to discover that the Diyanet had an institutional identity and agency of its own (but by no means monolithic or in an essentialist sense) and realised that this did not fit easily into the theories and narratives prevalent in studies on Turkey. For one, the country was classified as a secular state even if the very nature of what this meant – separation, accommodation or control of religion– was the subject of a long-standing controversy. The Diyanet, if mentioned at all, was typically treated as an anomaly or testament to the secular state's control of religion. The state thereby appeared to be a highly monolithic actor, one that has oft been conflated with what was typically described as a staunchly secular military, strictly controlling religion through a passive Diyanet. In part, this reflected the lingering influence of the analytical framework of modernisation theory but, more so, a captivation by the *idea* of the state, which has resulted in efforts to understand the state's nature through its own terms – such as laic and democratic – rather than through the practices of its different elements.

As a result, many previous studies adopted a binary framework of analysis in which Turkish history was narrated as being marked by a confrontation between an authoritarian secular Kemalist state and a Muslim society. This emerged as the 'master narrative' (Kandiyoti 2012: 515) on which the widespread portrayals of the AKP's rise as a process of democratisation, a 'Turkish model', fundamentally rested and were justified. In this vein, the early years of the AKP period were associated with moderation, democratisation and Europeanisation. This narrative had gained ascendancy, particularly in the aftermath of the attacks of 11 September 2001 and the emergence of the democracy promotion agenda in the United States, as well as the rise to power of the AKP in 2002. Indeed, in some ways, it resembled the projection of Turkey during the 1960s and 1970s as a paradigmatic case for modernisation theory in asserting a positive relationship between capitalist economic development and democracy, which had gained prominence during the Cold War in the context of US anti-communism policies. By the 2000s, with the identification of Islamism as a major challenge to the West, Turkey became repackaged as an example of moderate Islam and was promoted to other (nominally speaking) Muslim-majority contexts as a model Muslim democracy by policy bodies and scholars alike. By then, although modernisation theory was supposedly long buried, it still pervaded thinking on Islamism through assertions that moderation had been achieved through bourgeoisification and capitalist development in Muslim countries.

At the same time, this master narrative of Turkish politics was attractive to those who wanted to rebut the essentialist/culturalist explanations – of which Samuel Huntington's is the classic example – that blamed 'Islamic exceptionalism' for the lack of democratic politics in Muslim-majority countries. According to these accounts, as an authentic bottom-up grass-roots challenge to the secular authoritarian state, it was the Islamists who would lead democratisation. Indeed, the first decade of the AKP was described by analysts as marking an era of change and transformation as they pointed to the (presumed) pacification of the military, which had long exercised tutelary power over the political system, the launch of the Kurdish peace process (subsequently scrapped), expansion of the religious field (i.e. religious education) against the ostensibly secular state and adoption of Europeanisation reforms, such as the scrapping of capital punishment. These were, in turn, mirrored in the self-representation of the AKP in its narratives of 'New Turkey'. It was from around 2011, but especially from 2013 onwards, that these ideas began to show cracks as analysts became less enthusiastic about the Turkish model. Nationwide protests that erupted in the summer of 2013, triggered by government plans to demolish Gezi Park in İstanbul, and the violent crackdown against peaceful protestors clearly revealed the increasing authoritarianism of the regime. At this point, analysis began focusing on Turkey's 'democratic backslide' and the accumulation and centralisation of power in the hands of the former prime minister and current president, Recep Tayyip Erdoğan. These domestic developments, together with the increasingly hostile turn of events in the Middle East (including the fall of AKP allies such as the Muslim Brotherhood in Egypt following a military coup in July 2013 and the radicalisation of Islamist actors), were to hasten the demise of Turkey's so-called Muslim democratic model status. Yet assessments of the AKP's building authoritarianism, with the exception of those within the Marxist tradition, have tended to blame contingent events, Recep Tayyip Erdoğan's personality, international developments or the so-called Kemalist-secularist state.

Over the course of my research, therefore, my questions became broader than simply the nature of religion and state relations. On the one hand, the trajectory of the AKP, particularly in its later years, appeared to undermine the assumptions of the master narrative, the problematic nature of which was clearly exposed in July 2016 when the struggle within the state and between the Islamists erupted under the full gaze of the public. At the same time, I could see that, contrary to common wisdom, the Diyanet was a formidable institution that adopted multiple strategies in order to pursue its goals and that the boundaries between the official *ulema*, the Islamist movement and various other religious groups, such as the *tariqa* orders, were clearly highly fluid. Consequently, I began to consider the wider relationship between the state and the Islamist movement and the rise of the AKP in the Turkish case – in particular, how institutions can shape more amenable environments for certain types of mobilisation. Yet existing works that drew attention to the importance of the state for Islamist mobilisation chiefly portrayed it as a strategic decision by the secular state to utilise or control these movements. On the other hand, what I was observing through the case of the Diyanet was a far more differentiated state in which different factions, actors and currents were competing to impose and pursue their own political projects.

In a bid to bridge the gap between the theory and what I was observing, I therefore adopted an eclectic approach, drawing on different theoretical traditions, specifically (but not exclusively) historical institutionalism, and nationalism and ethnicity studies. This proved useful in two ways. Historical institutionalism focused my attention on the mutually constitutive manner in which institutions shape the nature of political struggles and also agents. Meanwhile, nationalism and ethnicity studies, particularly the modernist school that emphasises the constructedness of identity, helped to underline the importance of not taking the identity politics of Islamists for granted. In other words, it should not be assumed that Islamist mobilisation is a natural outcome within a nominally Muslim majority context. After all, we do not expect political mobilisation to occur automatically along religious lines in a Christian, Buddhist or Hindu majority setting. At the same time, helping me to break with the master narrative of Turkish state–society relations were a series of works spanning different disciplines, including Yael Navaro-Yashin's anthropological study *Faces of the State* (2002), which uses a post-structuralist framework to examine secularism as a discourse of state; political economists within the Marxist tradition, such as Galip Yalman, who have drawn attention to the changing hegemonic strategies of the Turkish state; and a new generation of revisionist historians who are challenging the accounts of early republican history as a purely top-down modernisation project. Consequently, this text builds on these theoretical frameworks and perspectives in understanding the state not as a monolithic actor that is autonomous from society, but rather one that is an arena of struggle between different actors, factions and currents (or, following Bob Jessop (2007: 37), an ensemble of competing power centres), with blurred and fluid boundaries with society.

This book offers both an alternative historical interpretation and an analytical framework that I call 'religious majoritarianism' to understand two interconnected questions:

- Why has Islamist politics arisen and become viable and successful in the Turkish case?
- More broadly, why have some contexts proved to be more conducive to this religious identity politics compared with others?

Resting on a two-level analysis involving a reconceptualisation of state–religion–society relations, the prism of religious majoritarianism refers to the political structures through which a religiously defined group's monopoly over political and economic resources is legitimated on its numerical majority in the nation. The extent to which a nation-state becomes religious majoritarian is determined by two factors:

- the degree to which majority–minority boundaries were defined along religious lines during early nation-state building; and
- whether these boundaries were subsequently reflected in state institutions.

These institutions, in turn, trigger path-dependent effects which impact the salience of religious markers for political and economic competition and, thereby, patterns of group mobilisation. In the Turkish case, nation-state building was fundamentally affected by the Ottoman legacy in terms of both the importance of religious communal boundaries and the intertwined nature of religious institutions and the state. Despite the diverse nationalist coalition in the early Republic, therefore, Sunni Muslim-Turkish identity became elevated as the basis of the nation-state and was institutionalised in various ways, including by the establishment of the Diyanet to the privileging of a 'Muslim bourgeoisie'. These in turn had path-dependent effects because institutions enable social groups and identities to be carried over the generations, building coalitions within and outside the state with those that have overlapping political visions. Institutions such as the Diyanet meant that, far from being eliminated, conservative and Islamist currents and the *ulema* had remained part of the state, albeit subdued for a time. What tipped the balance of power increasingly in favour of these factions within the state were contingent events such as the Cold War-related anti-communism policies alongside the neo-liberal restructuring policies adopted from the 1980s, which facilitated the expansion of the infrastructure behind religious mobilisation, including the Diyanet, religious education, charities and business associations. The Diyanet, together or in coalition with other factions within and outside the state, in turn, played a critical role in providing a more favourable environment for Islamist mobilisation.

In short, the main proposition of this book, therefore, is that the rise and success of religious identity politics in Turkey did not result from a break in secular nation-state building. Rather, it should be situated as the outcome of a dynamic struggle within the state, the terms of which have been shaped by the path-dependent processes related to the longer-term dynamics of nation-state building mediated by contingent events. Yet the aim is not to deny the contributions, value or truth of existing works but rather, by extensively drawing and building on these with my own research, to offer a window into another dimension of the story that has been neglected, and has, as a result, distorted our understanding of religious identity politics. Accordingly, rather than extensive discussions of secularism or Kemalism, or how religion has been 'used' by the 'secular' state, this book focuses on the other side of the coin. Factions of the state, such as the military, may have tried to control religion, but how has the Diyanet responded, what strategies has it adopted and to what extent has it been successful? This book shows that this is by no means a one-way relationship and that the Diyanet has strategically

manoeuvred to expand its domain and authority by seizing on these very
opportunities in order to push for the Islamisation of public space and
morality in a manner that has been largely neglected within the literature.
In this way, the text also offers an alternative account of the rise of the
Islamist movement and of the AKP.

Acknowledgements

My research and writing of this book has been generously supported by grants from the London School of Economics (LSE) and Sasakawa Peace Foundation (SPF). I have been able to write and complete this book thanks to the SPF fellowship programme at Oxford University. I also thank the manuscript reviewers for the incredibly detailed feedback; I hope I have been able to address all of the points raised.

This book could not have been written without the guidance, generous support and, importantly, patience of many people over the years. I owe my deepest gratitude to my PhD supervisor, Bill Kissane, who has played a formative role in my academic work and development. I am also thankful for the insights and input provided by my advisor, John Hutchinson, who supported my application for doctoral studies at the LSE. I owe special thanks to Deniz Kandiyoti for always being such a source of immense inspiration and support during the most critical of times. I am also grateful to Besim Can Zırh for his intellectual guidance in opening me up to new avenues of inquiry.

It is difficult to list all of the generous people who have crossed my path during my research and who have provided invaluable input into my work. I am grateful to the immensely helpful staff at the Turkish Grand National Assembly Library and Archives and, in particular, Faruk Nafiz Ertürk for his expert guidance in navigating through dense historical materials. I would like to thank the various members of the Diyanet who have been so kind with their time and who provided me with important resources, and I am grateful to have met Hicret Toprak at the Diyanet Vakfı, who was wonderful and extremely generous in sharing her own archival research and thoughts with me. During my research, I had the opportunity to meet and discuss my work with many scholars who helped me shape my ideas and to whom I am thankful. I am especially grateful to Menderes Çınar, whose insights and generosity with his time and resources while I was conducting research for my masters' thesis on the Diyanet has left an imprint in my mind as an example of the type of academic that I aspire to be. I want to express my warm thanks to Eric Kaufmann for his support and my colleagues at the LSE and Oxford University (the Oxford School for Global and Area Studies, and the Middle East Centre) and particularly to Philip Robins.

I am indebted to all my wonderful friends and family for their love and support, but also owe them an apology for my neglect during the long and fraught journey in producing this book. I am deeply grateful in particular to my friend Melis Kobal for her goodwill and for helping me to keep sane and positive. I thank Mesut Akbaş for his generosity in providing a home during my fieldwork in Ankara. I also owe a special thanks to my friend Tuncay Gürhan, whose intellectual probing and guidance have been so invaluable. Last, not but least, I am thankful to my mother, who raised me and made me the person I am today. She has unconditionally believed in me and supported me wholeheartedly throughout my life and in all my career choices.

This book is dedicated to my husband James, whose patience, support and intellectual input has been beyond words. I cannot thank him enough for giving me the strength and ability to pursue my dreams.

Abbreviations

AKP	Adalet ve Kalkınma Partisi (Justice and Development Party)
ANAP	Anavatan Partisi (Motherland Party)
AO	Aydınlar Ocağı (Hearth of the Enlightened)
AP	Adalet Partisi (Justice Party)
AUK	Anayasa Uzlaşma Komisyonu (Constitution Reconciliation Commission)
BCA	Başbakanlık Cumhuriyet Arşivi (Prime Minister's Republic Archives)
BDP	Barış ve Demokrasi Partisi (Peace and Democracy Party)
BJP	Bharatiya Janata Party (Indian People's Party)
CHP	Cumhuriyet Halk Partisi (Republican People's Party)
CKMP	Cumhuriyetçi Köylü Millet Partisi (Republican Villagers Nation Party)
DİTİB	Diyanet İşleri Türk-İslam Birliği (Turkish–Islamic Union for Religious Affairs)
DİYK	Din İşleri Yüksek Kurulu (Religious Affairs High Council)
DoA	Dernekler Dairesi Başkanlığı (Department of Associations)
DoF	Vakıflar Genel Müdürlüğü (Directorate General of Foundations)
DoS	Mezhepler Müdürlüğü (Department of Sects)
DP	Demokrat Partisi (Democrat Party)
DPT	Devlet Planlama Teşkilatı (State Planning Organisation)
DSP	Demokratik Sol Parti (Democratic Left Party)
DV	Diyanet Vakfı (Turkish Religious Foundation)
DYP	Doğru Yol Partisi (Right Path Party)
EIA	environmental impact assessment
EU	European Union
FETÖ	Fethullahçı Terör Örgütü (Fethullah Gülen Terrorist Organisation)

FP	Fazilet Partisi (Virtue Party)
HSYK	Hâkimler ve Savcılar Yüksek Kurulu (Supreme Board of Judges and Prosecutors)
IHH	İnsani Yardım Vakfı (Humanitarian Relief Foundation)
IHS	İmam Hatip Okulları (Imam and Preacher Schools)
INC	Indian National Congress
ISI	import substitution industrialisation
ISIS	Islamic State of Iraq and Syria
ISO	İstanbul Sanayi Odası (Istanbul Chamber of Industry)
ITC	İttihat ve Terakki Cemiyeti (Committee of Union and Progress)
İYC	İlim Yayma Cemiyeti (Association for the Dissemination of Science)
KCK	Koma Civakên Kurdistan (Union of Communities in Kurdistan)
KMD	Komünizmle Mücadele Derneği (Association for Fighting Communism)
KPSS	Kamu Personeli Seçme Sınavı (Public Personnel Selection Examination)
MBK	Milli Birlik Komitesi (National Unity Committee)
MEB	Milli Eğitim Bakanlığı (Ministry of National Education)
MGK	Milli Güvenlik Kurulu (National Security Council)
MHP	Milliyetçi Hareket Partisi (Nationalist Movement Party)
MİT	Milli İstihbarat Teşkilatı (National Intelligence Organisation)
MNP	Milli Nizam Partisi (National Order Party)
MP	Millet Partisi (Nation Party)
MSP	Millî Selâmet Partisi (Islamist National Salvation Party)
MTTB	Milli Türk Talebe Birliği (National Turkish Students Union)
MÜSİAD	Müstakil Sanayici ve İş Adamları Derneği (Independent Industrialists' and Businessmen's Association)
NATO	North Atlantic Treaty Organization
PKK	Partiya Karkerên Kurdistani (Kurdistan Workers' Party)
PR	proportional representation
RP	Refah Partisi (Welfare Party)
ŞEV	Şeriye ve Evkaf Vekaleti (Ministry of Shari'a and Pious Foundations)
SHP	Sosyaldemokrat Halk Partisi (Social Democratic People's Party)
SMEs	small and medium-sized enterprises
SoE	state of emergency

SP	Saadet Partisi (Felicity Party)
TBMM	Türkiye Büyük Millet Meclisi (Turkish Grand National Assembly)
TBP	Türkiye Birlik Partisi (Turkish Unity Party)
TIS	Türk-İslam Sentezi (Turkish–Islamic Synthesis)
TMMOB	Türk Mühendis ve Mimar Odaları Birliği (Union of Chambers of Turkish Engineers and Architects)
TOBB	Türkiye Odalar ve Borsalar Birliği (Union of Chambers and Commodity Exchanges of Turkey)
TOKI	Toplu Konut İdaresi (Mass Housing Association)
TRT	Türkiye Radyo ve Televizyon Kurumu (Turkish Radio and Television Corporation)
TRY	Turkish lira
TSK	Türk Silahlı Kuvvetleri (Turkish Armed Forces)
TÜRGEV	Türkiye Gençlik ve Eğitime Hizmet Vakfı (Foundation of Youth and Education in Turkey)
TÜSIAD	Türk Sanayicileri ve İşadamları Derneği (Turkish Industry and Business Association)
TUSKON	Türkiye İşadamları ve Sanayiciler Konfederasyonu (Turkish Confederation of Businessmen and Industrialists)
UMNO	Pertubuhan Kebangsaan Melayu Bersatu (United Malays National Organisation)
USD	US dollars
YİE	Yüksek İslam Enstitüsü (High Islamic Institutes)
YÖK	Yüksek Öğretim Kurulu (Council of Higher Education)

Introduction

The rise of Islamism in the Republic of Turkey has come to be a taken-for-granted phenomenon. This is in large part owing to the near-hegemonic status of what Kandiyoti has described as the master narrative (2012: 515) of secularism. According to this master narrative, Turkish politics is defined by a clash between centre and periphery, as elaborated by Mardin (1973) in his highly influential classical formulation, or put in another but similar manner, a struggle between a sharply distinguished authoritarian secularist Kemalist state and the Muslim majority that makes up society.[1] Within this context, Islamism is perceived largely as a bottom-up reaction to the top-down authoritarian or 'assertive' (Kuru 2009) secularism of the Kemalist regime (e.g. Aktürk 2015; Ayata 1996; Delibaş 2015: 15; Göle 1997; Gülalp 2005; Heper and Toktaş 2003; Kadıoğlu 1996; Kuru 2009; Sunar and Toprak 1983: 427; Taşpınar 2004; Yavuz 1997, 2000, 2009).[2] This perspective tends to regard the secularising reforms adopted particularly since 1924, including the closure of the *medreses* (religious schools), the enactment of a secular civil code (Türk Medeni Kanunu, which basically adopted the Swiss Civil Code), the removal of Islam as a state religion, the replacement of Perso-Arabic script with Latin script, the abolition of the caliphate, and the restriction of the *ulema*'s role as a break from the Islamic Ottoman past. In this vein, the Islamist AKP's success in 2002 has been commonly depicted as a process of democratisation of the 'assertive secularist' Kemalist regime (e.g. Barkey and Çongar 2007; Cizre 2008; Demiralp 2009; Heper 2013; İnsel 2003; Kalaycıoğlu 2007; Kuru 2009: 200; Kuru

---

[1] According to Mardin (1971, 1973), religion increasingly became identified with the periphery following the creation of the secular Republic, having been placed on the border of both sides during the Ottoman Empire.

[2] The wider literature on secularism and constitutional studies has also treated Turkey as the archetypal example of separatist secularism (Stepan 2011) or a paradigmatic case of conflict between state secularism and popular support for religion (Zucca 2009). Similarly, for Lerner (2013: 629) the 'Turkish constitution represented a revolutionary model of imposed secularism'.

1

and Stepan 2012; Mecham 2004; Öniş 2009; Özbudun 2006: 547, 554–555; Patton 2007; Sayari 2007; Somer 2007; Taniyici 2003; Yavuz 1997, 2000, 2009).

This is because, the argument goes, 2002 marked the year the Muslim majority society, or 'periphery', represented by the AKP (re)gained its rightful place in the state, or the 'centre', formerly inhabited by secular Kemalist elites. One of the main proponents of this narrative, Hakan Yavuz (1997: 64), argues that 'secularization imposed from above alien- ated Turkish society from the state. The history of Turkish politics, therefore, is the story of a complex tension between these two world- views and identities. Over time, the state-centric republican elite and its supporting groups have identified themselves as secularists, commonly known as *laikler* [laicists], and the large masses as "backward Muslims."' However, there are seemingly alternative narratives that admit a degree of continuity with the Ottoman Empire, and particularly the policies of the Young Turks – regarded as forefathers of the 'Kemalist' regime – since 1908. These accounts question the nature of the secularism of the Turkish state by arguing that rather than separating religion and state, the secularist Kemalist regime has tried to control and instrumentalise religion through institutions such as the official religious authority, the Presidency of Religious Affairs (Diyanet İşleri Başkanlığı, Diyanet) (Davison 2003; Sakallıoğlu 1996). An extension of this account includes efforts to show how secular state elites created opportunities and the space for Islamist entrepreneurs after the 1980 coup d'état, when the military regime adopted an Islamisation programme (Eligür 2010). Nevertheless, regardless of the different readings of history and the transition from empire to republic underpinning these narratives, in general, both accounts have essentially relied on a dichotomisation of state and society, and consequently narrate Turkish history as a 'struggle between the values of a secular Kemalist state elite and a traditional Muslim society' (Kandiyoti 2012: 515).

Consequently, largely based on this master narrative, in the early years of the AKP, scholars pointed to the list of reforms introduced by the Islamist government, including a series of laws to align the country with European Union (EU) membership criteria, the reconfiguration of civil- military relations and the opening of dialogue about the Kurdish ques- tion, alongside the pro-market economic policies, as testament to the party's democratic orientation. As to the explanation of why an Islamist party was leading this alleged democratisation of politics, many pointed to a dynamic of moderation underpinned by a combination of (i) inte- gration with global capitalism and the rise of a so-called conservative/ pious or pious 'Muslim bourgeoisie' acting as a liberalising class force against what is described as the authoritarian and monopolistic state-dependent traditional bourgeoisie; (ii) political learning and pragmatism catalysed by the 1997 military intervention; (iii) Europeanisation and (iv) electoral participation and the processes of becoming a mass party (e.g. Barkey and Çongar 2007; Cizre 2008; Demiralp 2009; İnsel 2003; Kalaycıoğlu 2007; Mecham 2004; Özbudun 2006: 547, 554–555; Patton 2007; Sayari 2007; Somer 2007; Taniyici 2003; Yavuz 2009; see also Kuru and Stepan 2012). As a result, despite being recognised as a 'culturally conservative movement', the AKP was, at times, accorded a leading or even revolutionary role as an 'initiating force for a normalized regime of democracy' (see Barkey and Çongar 2007; İnsel 2003). The AKP, it was argued, would end the authoritarian 12 September regime enshrined in the 1982 constitutional framework whether it liked it or not, and thereby democratise despite a lack of democrats (İnsel 2003; Patton 2007: 342; Tepe 2005: 71–73). This master narrative therefore rested, often unquestioningly, on a combination of modernisation and historical sociology theories of democratisation in assuming a deterministic positive link between economic development with democratisation and transition theories in its focus on electoral politics and taking for granted that a move away from military tutelage would necessarily involve a transition to democracy.[3]

Following the AKP's strong performance in the 2011 general elections, its third consecutive general election victory since 2002, analyses had begun to point to the increasing electoral hegemony of the AKP, absence of effective opposition, slowing progress on liberal reforms (Turam 2011), and the establishment of a predominant party system (Gümüşçü 2013; Müftüler-Baç and Keyman 2012; Musil 2015), although faith still remained that, overall, the AKP was 'deepening democracy' (Göle 2012). By 2013, with the outbreak of the Gezi Park protests, the direction of politics grew difficult to ignore and the atmosphere grew more pessimistic. Scholars began to highlight Turkey's 'democratic reversal or backslide' after a 'major wave of democratisation' (Öniş 2013), the centralisation of power under a populist leader (Aytaç and Öniş 2014; Kalaycıoğlu 2015) and illiberal democracy. Others pointed to the AKP's drift towards a highly majoritarian conception of democracy and, more recently, have underlined its transition to a

---

[3] The tenets of both theoretical approaches remain a matter of intense debate and criticism. The basic premise of the transition paradigm in terms of comprising the assumption of a unilinear development and the conception of democratisation as involving a series of set stages has been widely questioned (Carothers 2002), and scholars have found little evidence for a strong link between the emergence of democracy and that of capitalism (e.g. Przeworski et al. 2000).

competitive authoritarian regime type (Esen et al. 2016; Kalaycıoğlu 2015; Özbudun 2014). Blame was placed partly on the lack of strong opposition (Müftüler-Baç and Keyman 2012; Öniş 2014; Özbudun 2014), while others pointed to the role of Erdoğan as a leader, arguing that his 'tendency to reduce democracy to elections' had ended the 'Turkish model' (Taşpınar 2014). For some, explanations bordered on the essentialistic in claiming that the AKP and Erdoğan had been captured by the undemocratic 'DNA' of the secular Kemalist regime (Cizre 2017). The more sophisticated proponent of Islamist moderation told from a Gramscian perspective, Tuğal, (2016) argues that Turkey's 'Islamic liberalism' under the AKP had been contingent on the external context, with its downfall precipitated by the contradictions of neoliberalism and by the Arab uprisings since 2011. In short, therefore, explanations of the current state of affairs have simply been that it was the AKP or Erdoğan that had changed, shedding their democratic character over time owing to changing circumstances or their being corrupted by power. The exception to this near-hegemonic approach are the Marxist accounts that have instead underlined authoritarian persistence under the AKP (e.g. Bedirhanoğlu and Yalman 2010).

However, the unfolding events have shown that the commonly held understanding of the rise in Turkey of the AKP, or Islamism more generally, as encompassing a process of democratisation of the Kemalist regime – resting on the master narrative that equates religious expansion with democracy – and its subsequent, largely circumstantial, sidetracking has been a mistaken one. Most clearly underlining this narrative's deficiencies has been the failed coup attempt of 15 July 2016, which the AKP blamed on its former Islamist allies, the Gülenists.[4] Previously, the AKP–Gülenist alliance had been credited with helping to weaken the military's hold on politics and expanding the Islamists' control over the state bureaucracy. However, with growing competition between the two sides, evidenced by the launch of the December 2013 corruption investigations against AKP officials, the AKP government denounced the Gülenists as having established a parallel state and subsequently designated the Gülenists as a terrorist organisation.[5] The eruption since 15 July of a violent struggle within the state between different factions and among Islamists, together with the increasing visibility of the Diyanet (housing the Turkish *ulema*) in the mobilisation of popular opposition to the coup attempt, clearly demonstrates that the binary picture of a clash between a secular

---

[4] See Chapter 5 for a detailed discussion of the Gülenists.
[5] See Chapter 6 for a detailed discussion of the struggle between the AKP and the Gülenists.

Kemalist state and religious society drawn for us by the master narrative is not only simplistic; it has distorted our understanding of reality and the actual practices of politics. Indeed, one can ask, if the Gülenists have been infiltrating the state, and particularly the military, the self-designated guardians of the Republic and secular order since the 1980s, how can we base our analysis of Turkish politics on the under-standing of the Turkish state as a highly monolithic secular Kemalist actor? What should we make of the rapidly expanding role of the Diyanet, to date treated as a marginal actor or anomaly within the secular state?

This book, therefore, tackles this disjuncture between theory and the reality that has arisen in the Turkish case by considering the rise of political Islam and the AKP's ascent to power. Accordingly, it answers one case-specific question: What accounts for the political salience and persistence of religious identity over time in the ostensibly secular Turkish Republic, resulting in the rise and success of Islamist politics, particularly under the AKP? This, in turn, relates to a question of broader relevance: What does the Turkish case tell us about why certain contexts prove more conducive to the politicisation of religious iden-tities than others?

The literature on the Turkish case, which has underpinned a mis-guided perception of the AKP and the rise of Islamism, has reflected gaps in the understanding of the global phenomenon of what has been described as a 'religious resurgence' underway since the 1970s.[6] This has referred to essentially two interrelated but separate phenomena: the rise in religiosity and the emergence and spread of politicised religious move-ments. Politicised religious movements, including Islamist movements, the focus of this book, have been described by Keddie (1998) as 'religio-political' movements to emphasise their inherently political nature and to distinguish this from conservative religiosity or piety. Importantly, what sets religio-political movements apart from a simple rise in religiosity or purely religious organisations is the focus on gaining power to effect a transformation of government and society to reflect what are proclaimed to be the principles of that particular religious tradition. Religio-political movements, therefore, differ from conservative religiosity or piety in being inherently political and, ultimately, a type of identity politics geared towards political action. In this vein, Islamists, for example, appeal to, mobilise and legitimise their politics with reference to a

---

[6] Critics of secularisation theories have questioned the 'myth of past piety', arguing that there is nothing unique or exceptional about religious resurgence (Stark 1999). However, equally problematic is the assumption of the depiction of resurgence which seems to suggest that it was a natural development.

reinterpreted, homogenised Islam and its symbolic universe and idioms (Keddie 1998: 697; White 2002: 6). Such movements pursue Islamisation (the precise content of which can be highly varied between different groups and over time) through the state and civil society networks such as Islamic charities, including by expansion of religious education and adoption of conservative social policies (e.g. restrictions on alcohol and on women). Likewise, the Hindutva movement in India has promoted policies such as Hindu prayers in schools and has attempted to enforce religious norms and morality codes. Crucially, both movements recognise only members of their respective religious communities, either Muslim or Hindu, as the rightful rulers and owners of the state.

A key impact the rise of religio-politics has had on the literature since the 1970s is triggering a reassessment of modernisation theory and the assumptions that economic development and bourgeoisification bring, in the long run, secularisation of society.[7] In turn, this rethinking has produced, broadly, two main strands of analysis of religio-politics: the culturalist and functionalist/reaction-based approaches. The initial response to the conundrum posed by the rise of religio-politics was to point to its geographic concentration in predominantly Muslim majority countries and blame non-Western cultures for being unable to adjust to the secular nation-state and modernity. Rather than admitting a failure of the secularisation thesis, analysts pointed to 'Islamic exceptionalism' and the alleged (but mistaken assumption of) lack of separation between state and religion. These essentialist or culturalist arguments have been extensively contested as being orientalist and challenged for presenting religions and cultures as being highly segmented, discrete and closed systems (Halliday 1995; Said 2001, 2003; Zubaida 2011). Religio-politics is not confined to Muslim majority or non-Western contexts, and the emphasis on the autonomous influence of religious traditions on political action is also problematic. Doctrine may be important, but how individuals subjectively interpret and act on it will be influenced by existing political-economic power structures (Halliday 2000: 134). Despite the discrediting of these types of explanations, derivatives of the culturalist approach can be observed in the multiple modernities school, which, in seeking to discredit orientalist conceptions of Muslim politics, has sought to emphasise that despite cultural distinctions, there is no inherent incompatibility between non-Christian traditions and modernity. A key proponent of this perspective in the Turkish case, Göle argues,

---

[7] For an overview of the debate, see Calhoun et al. (2011), Casanova (1994), Fox (2004), Gorski and Altınordu (2008), Martin (2007), Stark (1999) and Stark and Bainbridge (1980).

for instance, that Islamist movements present a 'counter-cultural model of modernity, and a new paradigm for self-definition that has led to the formation of Islamist counter-elites' (1997; see also Çınar 2005). Yet, as Zubaida has pointed out, multiple modernities arguments are open to the same charges of essentialism in 'describ[ing] and implicitly justif[ying] the ideological projects of identity politics – defined as "alternative", presumably, to Western modernity, which is assumed to have some uniformity deriving from a Western essence' (2011: 4). In short, these approaches also reduced complex socio-political and economic struggles to culture and ideology alone.

The second and most prevalent approaches within the literature are functionalist explanations – that is, those that describe religio-politics as a reaction or as the articulations of grievances. These are also a response to the problems of modernisation theory and culturalist approaches. According to these accounts, the rise of Islamism was not a reflection of the fact that Muslims could not be secular but, rather, was because Muslims were reacting to actual or perceived social, economic, political or identity-related crises generated by modernisation or 'post-modernity' and also colonial domination. Analysts have identified a whole host of variables related to modernisation, including secularisation, capitalism, neoliberalism, economic crisis, migration, increasing rights of women, education, urbanisation, cultural homogenisation, population growth, corruption and disaffection with established institutionalised religious bodies, as contributing to the rise of religio-politics (e.g. Antoun and Hegland 1987; Bruce 2003; Ehteshami 2004; Göle 2000; Gülalp 2005; Haynes 1995; Juergensmeyer 1993, 2011; Keddie 1998; Kepel 1994; Madan 1987; Nandy 1988; Sahliyeh 1990: vii; Tehranian 2007; Tibi 2001; Tuğal 2007: 11–12; Voll 1987). In this vein, Juergensmeyer, among others, argues that religio-politics is an ideology of protest against the secular states of religious societies and is driven by the failure of secular nationalism and ideologies in the face of multifaceted crises of modernity (1993, 2011). This tendency to view religio-politics as a grass-roots or bottom-up phenomenon has, in turn, underpinned analyses that have portrayed these movements as potential democratisers.

A more recent permutation of these arguments includes accounts that seek to historically contextualise secularism as a specific political project that demarcates religion as an autonomous sphere in the nation-state by emphasising 'multiple competing secularisms' (Casanova 2011; Martin 2007; Stepan 2011; Van der Veer 2011). These reflect efforts to take into account different institutional patterns of religion–state relations, differentiating between the experiences of Western Europe, where established churches are common, along with French laicism and US secularism as a 'wall of separation', as opposed to Turkish laicism, which incorporates religious authority within the state (Fox 2008; Stepan 2011). In particular, Kuru distinguishes between passive (inclusive) and assertive (exclusionary) secularism, in which states are friendly or hostile, respectively, towards religion depending on the particular configuration of relations and the perceptions of political elites towards religion during the process of nation-state formation (2009: 22–23; Kuru and Stepan 2012: 5). However, Kuru (2007, 2009) also understands the politicisation of religion as a reaction to the 'assertive secularism' of the state. Yet, cases such as Malaysia and India suggest that religio-politics could flourish in less restrictive environments. In India, the state arguably adopts a less assertive secularism that is considered to comprise a 'principled distance' (Bhargava 2011) of the state from religion, which has involved maintaining personal religious laws. This suggests that politicisation is not solely a reaction to authoritarian secularism.

Overall, the broad approaches outlined here have generated important insights into the different political and socio-economic contexts that religio-political movements have thrived in, as well as the responses and strategies of actors within them. The fact that religio-politics arose as an important phenomenon around the 1970s in both Muslim and other contexts across the globe underlines the importance of universal structural factors such as modernisation (including capitalist development and secularisation) together with democratisation, economic deprivation and Cold War anti-communism. There is, nevertheless, a growing criticism of approaches that treat religio-politics purely as a reaction to colonialism or to modernisation and its effects (Cesari 2014; Eligür 2010; Gill 2001). Since these factors have impacted contexts that have not developed religio-politics, these variables alone do not provide answers as to why some settings proved more conducive to the emergence of religio-political movements than did others. Gill notes that modernisation has been utilised as the variable to explain both secularisation in some parts of the world, such as Western Europe, and the rise of religio-politics and religiosity in others (2001). This reasoning becomes tautological because whether communities secularise or turn to religio-politics is based on whether these movements are already present in that community, and thus, the 'dependent variable is linked to the definition of the independent variable' (Gill 2001: 126). That said, the contention here is not that structural factors such as modernisation or the experience of colonialism did not generate important grievances that subsequently produced religio-political mobilisation. Nor is the importance of factors such as the instrumentalisation of religion by political actors, grass-roots mobilisation, the role of contingent events such as economic crises, or the ideological or emotional commitment of actors or their resistance to phenomena such as modernity denied. Rather, this book underlines the gap in our knowledge that has resulted from our analytical frameworks. And, as the literature drawing on social movement theory has also demonstrated, grievance alone is not a sufficient condition for the mobilisation of actors (Eligür 2010). The literature has left unanswered the question of why some contexts have been more amenable to the transformation of this reaction into the rise of religio-politics than have others. Turkey represents a good case study to test the reaction thesis, being an ostensibly secular state and a relatively more open political system as compared to many other more authoritarian Muslim majority contexts, which typically incorporate Islamic law within their constitutions and where all political avenues and identity claims outside religion are restricted.

This text argues, however, that there is a more fundamental problem with the conceptual framework that has resulted in a gap in the understanding of why religio-political movements have emerged and become more successful in some contexts than others. It has been pointed out by Calhoun et al., among others, that 'many of us are unconsciously affected ... [by] a grand narrative involving secularism in the spread of modernization' (2011: 16). Indeed, while in general, modernisation theory has been rejected and heavily criticised, our analytical framework has nevertheless often remained epistemologically rooted in the secularisation/modernisation paradigm (Vertigans 2003). In Kandiyoti's words, 'The dead hand of the modernization paradigm ... is clearly evident in these accounts' (2012: 516). In the literature, this has meant that the notion of a secular state sharply demarcated against a religious society has been taken for granted in many analyses. More recently, Cesari (2014: 276) has also critiqued prevalent explanations of the politicisation of Islam as operating on a dichotomy of state and religion, and this work draws on these new approaches.

One consequence of this is that the secular state, considered to be exogenous (having presumably originated outside religious society), is treated as a monolithic, autonomous and unitary actor. This has resulted in a frequent tendency to neglect the role of state institutions in structuring politics, regarding them essentially as dependent variables and autonomous discrete units (i.e. church and state) that are transformed by actors. Different institutional actors and factions within the state that may have political visions allied with religio-politics are simply ignored. However, as this book will show, contrary to conventional wisdom, the Diyanet, which houses the Turkish *ulema*, despite being commonly regarded as a marginal actor within the state that is utilised by the secular elites to control religion, has, in fact, played an important role in the Islamisation of public spaces and in delimiting the boundaries of the nation. Where attention is paid to the role of institutions, it has chiefly been within studies of religio-politics that adopt rational choice or supply-side perspectives. A criticism of these approaches is that they tend to be Western-centric (particularly the United States) and that they assume a high degree of flexibility in the adoption of religion, neglecting the ways it can act as an ethnic marker. Purely instrumentalist accounts have a difficult time accounting for why religiosity or religious identities may persist despite adversity or for the intensity of those emotions. They are also less concerned with the reasons that they have become prevalent in the first place.

Additionally, even where the importance of states is acknowledged, it has typically been in the context of characterising accommodative policies towards religion as its instrumentalisation by secular elites for electoral gain, legitimacy or fighting communism. For instance, both Hibbard (2010) and Eligür (2010) have identified gaps in the reaction thesis and have drawn attention to the role of the state in supporting religio-political mobilisation. While acknowledging the importance of factors such as grass-roots mobilisation, Hibbard (2010: xi–xii) nevertheless adopts a top-down approach, arguing that the changing strategies of (secular) state elites towards 'illiberal religion' to bolster their populist legitimacy is an important factor in bolstering (illiberal) religio-politics. A closer look at both Muslim majority Turkey and Hindu majority India suggests that accommodative policies of states regarding the demands of religio-politics have often preceded these movements becoming significant political actors or electorally successful, which begs the question of why these state elites chose religion.

In the Turkish case, it has been argued that the 1980 military coup was a turning point in which the secular Turkish state adopted an Islamisation programme – the Turkish–Islamic Synthesis (Türk-İslam Sentezi, TIS) – to absorb and head off an Islamist challenge and fight against communism. However, despite indications of the greater salience of religion and religiosity in Turkey following the move to multi-partism in 1950, this did not translate into a popular mass Islamist movement or electoral success, with votes for the Islamist National Salvation Party (Millî Selâmet Partisi, MSP) peaking at 11.8 per cent in the 1973 parliamentary elections. A fluid and enmeshed relationship, collaboration and cooperation between the Islamist, conservative and rightist actors within and outside the state before and after 1980 also suggest that the description of a fundamental clash between the two sides is misleading. Similarly, in India, the 'secular' Indian National Congress's adoption of communalist policies pre-dated the rise of the Hindutva movement in the 1970s and its electoral success in the 1990s (Gupta 1991). India's religio-political Hindutva organisations in the 1960s and 1970s enjoyed weak electoral performance and limited popular support, as evidenced by the electoral defeats of the far-right Shiv Sena party. Accordingly, even if we accept that secular elites acted tactically to instrumentalise religion, the question remains as to why this strategy was chosen.

Drawing on social movement theory, Eligür (2010) and Yavuz (2003) adopt bottom-up approaches but underline the importance of the changing strategies of the state in providing 'political opportunity spaces' for Islamist mobilisation. However, both analyses, while drawing attention to the state's role, maintain the problematic dichotomy and assumption of the secular state. Indeed, Eligür considers the collaboration of secular elites with Islamists a 'malfunction of the state' (2010). An important exception is Cesari's (2014) work, which moves away from a dichotomous analytical framework by underlining the ways in which nation-state building resulted in the embeddedness of Islam within the state in Muslim majority contexts, thereby resulting in its politicisation. Yet Cesari (2014: 83) also argues that post-colonial states – which appear to be considered unitary actors – incorporated Islam as a means to shore up legitimacy and suggests that the politicisation of Islam was an inevitable outcome of the construction of Islam as a modern religion (279). This does not explain why, for instance, Islamism became emergent in the modern era only in the 1970s and a viable force only in the 1990s. I build on the later, more critical, literature and some of the more nuanced conceptualisations of the state and Islamist politics in Turkey that have stemmed from scholars adopting Marxist perspectives, including Yalman (2002) and Şen (2010), who have stressed the problems with the dualistic conceptions of society and state and the importance of institutions and emphasised the continuities of the authoritarian state form under the AKP (Bedirhanoğlu and Yalman 2010).

Second, the binary frame of reference within analyses has resulted in a tendency to conflate social categories (e.g. a Muslim majority in Turkey) with a politicised group identity (Islamism). This is in the sense that these accounts typically take 'groupness' for granted, treating groups as natural, timeless, homogenous and as a monolithic unit with a common purpose (Brubaker 2002: 164). As a result, analyses can overlook the ways in which identities are contested and how they shift over time. Additionally, such approaches can take for granted the politicisation of identity as a natural or authentic reaction (e.g. Muslims becoming Islamists), without deconstructing the extent of groupness as a contingent political project and questioning how and why certain group boundaries become politically significant while others do not. Part of the problem with the existing literature, therefore, is the leap made from a social category to a group that has identified and recognised its common interests and organised a political movement for their realisation (Kalyvas 1996: 11). Religion may well be an important basis of solidarity and political mobilisation, but the mere existence of a nominally Muslim, Christian or Hindu population does not imply that its members organise themselves on the basis of religious identity or the emergence of a political movement based on these religions. The question of why actors choose to mobilise based on religion when faced with a number of different choices (e.g. communism) remains unanswered. Some analyses can therefore be implicitly essentialist or guilty of ontological collectivism by accepting the claims of identity politics without problematising them and in assuming the politicisation of religious identity to be natural, as if these identities are primordial and ready to be awakened (Wimmer 2008: 981). As Gupta (1991: 574) argues, 'even though ethnic identities and cultural markers have always characterised human social existence, they cannot independently construct macro-ethnic political identities. Thus, while ethnic awareness is a ubiquitous aspect of social life, its political manifestation is not.' In short, the binary frame of reference can misconstrue historical development, the nature of change, and continuity, neglecting more complex patterns of interaction between religion, society and the state.

The Alternative Prism of Religious Majoritarianism

To address the growing gap between theory and reality, I adopt a theoretically eclectic approach (Sil and Katzenstein 2010) that draws on elements of different research traditions to explain empirical observations.[8] I thereby seek to offer a richer historical perspective and nuance that is often lacking in the existing works by avoiding efforts to fit and explain empirical observations within one framework of analysis and concepts within a single research paradigm, which has resulted in the development of important blind spots or a tendency to neglect important aspects of empirical phenomena. In this manner, I draw on the insights of and extract from different literatures on the state, democratisation, social movements, nationalism and secularism, alongside diverse theoretical approaches, including (but not limited to) historical institutionalist, constructivist and Marxist approaches.

---

[8] Within the literature on Islam and state relations, such an approach is also employed by Cesari (2014), reflecting growing recognition of gaps within our analysis.

Consequently, this book develops and moves beyond the existing literature by arguing that the growth of religio-politics in Turkey has been facilitated from within the state as the outcome of a dynamic struggle and competition between different factions, the terms of which have been determined by long-term path-dependent processes related to nation-state building. However, this focus on the state does not involve the adoption of a top-down approach to understanding the politicisation of religion. Instead, the state is considered both as an arena of struggle and collaboration between different actors that compete for power to implement their political visions and as having fluid borders. In this way, the book shows how the configuration of institutions that emerged during early nation-state building, together with contingent events since the 1940s that shifted the balance of power within the state, opened up space for Islamist mobilisation, precipitating its eventual success. In particular, it focuses on the state's principal religious authority, the Diyanet, and shows how this has played a key role in Islamising public space, negotiating the boundaries of national identity and shaping political and economic competition along religious lines, thereby reinforcing the privileging of Sunni Muslim Turks as the basis of the nation-state and the owners of its resources, to the exclusion of other groups. From this viewpoint, the rise of the AKP is considered to be neither a break with an authoritarian secular pattern of state building nor a democratisation against the secular Kemalist state. To operationalise this argument, the prism of 'religious majoritarianism' is developed to describe a more complex and intertwined relationship between state, religion and society, compared with the concept of secularism, which has resulted in a binary frame of reference.

Likewise, this book purposefully avoids the use of the term 'Kemalism' which is used pervasively in Turkish studies. Kemalism is widely considered to be the constitutive or hegemonic ideology of the Turkish Republic (at least until the AKP period) that was officially defined and adopted as part of the party programme of the Republican People's Party (Cumhuriyet Halk Partisi, CHP) during the period of one-party rule in 1935. It comprises the six arrows (as depicted on the CHP party emblem), or principles, including republicanism, nationalism, statism (or etatism), populism, laicism and reformism/revolutionism, the precise meanings and translations of which remain a matter of intense controversy. The extent to which Kemalism constitutes an ideology, as argued by some (see Parla and Davison 2004), or a coherent set of ideas is challenged by numerous accounts which emphasise its lack of coherence and changing and flexible content (Hanioğlu 2012; Zürcher 2004: 181–182). Hanioğlu (2012) equally notes that attempts by Mustafa

Kemal's followers to construct a doctrine in the 1930s which came to be known as Kemalism were themselves not necessarily original, but rather were rooted in the policies of the Committee of Union and Progress (İttihat ve Terakki Cemiyeti, ITC) and debates in the late Ottoman Empire as well as the post-war totalitarian regimes. Nonetheless, there has been general agreement that, owing at least in part to the transformative vision of nation-state builders in this period, Kemalism transpired as authoritarian politics. This, in turn, has underpinned the common characterisation of Kemalism as an elitist ideology or approach that was behind a top-down modernisation, reflective of a tutelary democratic view or an authoritarian/Jacobin fundamentalist project.

Yet, the historically contingent politics of this period has been generalised and essentialised within the literature. There has been a tendency to describe Kemalism in ways that it appears as an unchanging attribute or essence of the Turkish state, even when its reformulation over time (as Atatürkism, following the 1980 coup; Oran 1999) or appropriation by opposing political factions (left and right Kemalism) are acknowledged.[9] Consequently, while appearing as a potentially useful shorthand for summarising policies – which at best lacked coherence (Zürcher 2004: 181) – by a particular faction of the state during a particular period in time, its pervasive use to explain politics across the ideological spectrum and the nature of the Turkish state throughout the entire life of the Turkish Republic has resulted in conceptual overstretching. In this sense, such designations have become 'empty signifiers and tropes mobilized by contending political actors in their search for hegemony and the consolidation of their power' (Kandiyoti 2012: 528) and are of little use as analytical categories. More broadly, the fixation on such designations which are so often used and taken at face value have distorted our understanding of the state by focusing on the image of the state rather than its actual practices (Migdal 2001) and the nature of power struggles within it. The approach of this book to analysing the state therefore involves a shift in focus from its preferred terms of self-representation (e.g. secular, democratic) to its practices. The following section expands on the two levels of analysis that underpin the analytical prism of religious majoritarianism that support the argument of this book.

---

[9] A recent example of this is the depiction of the AKP as 'Islamist Kemalists' (Altan 2014; Bulaç 12 April 2014). For debates about the nature of Kemalism, see for example, Bora and Gültekingil (2002), Can and Bora (2004), Copeaux (2000: 306–307), Kadıoğlu (1996), Kandiyoti (2012), Köker (2007), Oran (1999), Parla and Davison (2004), Taşkın (2002), Tunçay (2005) and Zürcher (2002, 2004).

Deconstructing the Secular State: A Historical Institutionalist Approach to Religion, State Relations and Politicisation

Central to the argument developed in this book is an institutionalist approach that considers the state as endogenous and institutions as being determined by society through struggles among different dominant actors or factions. This, therefore, departs from the tendency of the literature on religio-political movements to consider the state as a secular and/or monolithic actor. Institutions, as defined by North, are the 'rules of the game in a society or, more formally, are the humanly devised constraints that shape human interaction [...] In consequence they structure incentives in human exchange, whether political, social, or economic' (1991: 3). The plethora of institutionalist approaches have demonstrated the ways in which institutions play a fundamental role in shaping political life, contestation and conflict, and the organisational capacity and strategies of actors. Social movement theorists, too, such as Kitschelt (1999), have long argued that institutions are 'a critical component of the environment in which actors shape their strategies of adaptation', rather than a dependent variable.

The importance of institutions for the political saliency of religion or religio-politics is highlighted by a world survey of religion and state relations compiled by Jonathan Fox (2008). According to his study, while most states display some involvement in religion and restrictions on minority religions, government involvement in the majority religion (and support of established religions) is greatest in the Muslim majority countries of the Middle East and North Africa, followed by the former Soviet Muslim majority Central Asian countries and Asian Muslim majority and Hindu countries, with the least involvement in the Western, predominantly Christian majority countries as well as in Latin America.[10] Religio-political movements are far more limited in the regions where there is less government involvement in the majority religion.

This book's view of institutions and the idea of a more differentiated state as an arena of struggle and competition borrow from historical institutionalist, (neo-)Marxist and political economy approaches. What distinguishes historical institutionalism from other institutionalist approaches is not just its focus on how institutions can constrain the actions of actors and shape outcomes but also its emphasis on how they have a constitutive impact on actors and interests. Institutions that are

---

[10] Fox (2008). Keddie (1998: 700–701) argues that religio-politics differs in substance from liberation theology in Latin America, which does not seek to transform state and society on the basis of religious doctrine.

created reflect the contestation and contributions of differently motivated actors (Mahoney and Thelen 2009). While historical institutionalism is inherently structuralist in its focus on the constitutive role of institutions, various works have sought to overcome dualistic approaches to structure and agency by emphasising the 'mutually constitutive character of structures and agents' (Hall and Taylor 1998; Hay and Wincott 1998). In this way, we can

> examine the relationship between political actors as objects and as agents of history. The institutions that are at the center of historical institutional analyses [...] can shape and constrain political strategies in important ways, but they are themselves also the outcome (conscious or unintended) of deliberate political strategies, of political conflict, and of choice. (Thelen and Steinmo 1992: 10)

In this manner, despite comprising a diversity of approaches, the two essential building blocks of historical institutionalism are the claims that (i) institutions are the outcome of and structure political struggles defined by asymmetries of power, which in turn shape and contain the actions of actors and (ii) historical processes, including timing, sequences, unintended consequences and policy feedback, matter (Hall and Taylor 1996; Ikenberry 1994: 2; Thelen and Steinmo 1992: 2–3).

Within this framework, state institutions, in particular, have 'a special influence, for [...] [they are] the agent of separation and the defender [...] of the social map' (Walzer 1984: 327). They fundamentally affect political outcomes, strategies and competition by privileging some actors, some identities, some strategies, some spatial and temporal horizons, and some actions over others (Jessop 2004) through the distribution of political and economic resources. In the literature on the nature of the state, the assumptions of autonomy (Krasner 1984; Poggi 1990; Skocpol 1985), its monolithic and unitary nature, as well as the sharp demarcation between state and society have been challenged by the institutionalist turn and neo-Marxist as well as critical theory approaches that deconstruct the notion of the state (Abrams 1988; Gupta 1995; Jessop 1990; Mann 2003: 50; Mitchell 1991; Navaro-Yashin 2002; Nugent 1994; Wells 1981). These have also highlighted a need to distinguish between the state system or practices and the idea or image of the state which is an ideological effect that gives the impression of a coherent state entity (Abrams 1988; Migdal 2001), which acts as a means of legitimating coercive apparatuses and results in reification of the state, distorting relations of power. This is important because, as Bourdieu (1994: 1) has observed, 'to endeavour to think the state is to take the risk of taking over (or being taken over by) a thought of the state, i.e. of applying to the state categories of thought produced and guaranteed by the state and hence to misrecognise its most profound truth'. Akin to methodological nationalism and its naturalisation of the regime of nation-states (Wimmer and Glick Schiller 2002), many analyses can be guilty of what can be called 'methodological statism' by taking the state as a natural unit and seeking to understand its nature through the ideology and language of states and statesmen.

Accordingly, drawing on the insights of the literature on the state, this book conceptualises the state as comprising a number of persisting institutions or, in the words of Jessop,

an ensemble of power centres that offer unequal chances to different forces within and outside the state to act for different political purposes. How far and in what ways their powers [...] are actualized depends on the action, reaction, and interaction of specific social forces located both within and beyond this complex ensemble [...] It is not the state that acts; it is always specific sets of politicians and state officials located in specific parts and levels of the state system. (2007: 37)

At the same time, this argument takes seriously the fluidity of the boundaries between state and society, underlining the ways in which different parts or factions of the state can ally not only with one another but with groups outside the official boundaries of the state and the ways in which society and state construct and transform one another (Migdal 2001). Accordingly, the state is understood as a social relation, thereby not completely autonomous from society, and as both the outcome and an arena of struggle of differentially endowed factions or institutional actors, such as the *ulema* or the military, with competing political visions.

This conceptualisation of the state as a differentiated entity also has consequences for how we can view continuity and change within a historical institutionalist framework where there is an emphasis on the path-dependent nature of political outcomes. Path dependency does not necessarily have to be a deterministic idea that emphasises the causal importance of initial conditions (Mahoney and Schensul 2006). Instead, initial conditions can be viewed as being only indirectly causal in limiting the range of alternatives in path-dependent sequences as opposed to constituting a causal condition. Therefore '"Choice is real but it is also constrained." Choices are strategic and the constraints are path dependent' (Hausner et al. 1995). Within this framework, continuity and persistence are explained by the fact that once established institutions become self-reinforcing and sticky, they generate path-dependent effects. Moving beyond discontinuous or gradualist models of change (Mahoney and Thelen 2009; Thelen 1999), it is possible to consider a dynamic of change as being built into institutions (Mahoney 2000) in the context of a differentiated state that takes agency and contingency seriously in understanding how change occurs despite persistence. Within institutions, change can result from both internal (actors' intended or unintended strategies) and external factors that create windows of opportunity for actors to shape policy options and shift the balance of power in their favour, generating new political trajectories. In this manner, it is possible to conceptualise what emerges as sudden shifts or leaps – that is, regime change – through the mechanism identified by Hegel as the 'transformation of quantity over quality' (Carneiro 2000), how gradual changes by actors within the state beyond a certain point result in a dramatic transformation of the very nature of the state itself. This is why even during critical junctures, moments of heightened contingency, antecedent conditions delimit the number of available paths for change. Whether and what type of change occurs then depends on the actors, their institutional capacity and position, and the extent to which existing institutions constrain (or not) their ability to utilise the window of opportunity (Cortell and Peterson 1999). Based on this reconceptualisation, rather than perceiving the Turkish state as being comprised purely of a monolithic and unitary Kemalist/secularist bloc armed with a timeless Kemalist ideology until the AKP period, this book argues that the state established in the 1920s encompassed competing actors (such as the *ulema*) with different endowments of power that shifted over time in a manner that facilitated the rise and success of Islamism.

Identity Politics and Deconstructing 'Religious Society'

Together with a reconceptualised state as a more differentiated entity, this book takes a second step by deconstructing the other half of the binary, the notion of 'religious society', which finds reflection in assumptions that Islamism or Hindu majoritarianism is somehow the natural or authentic reaction of a Muslim/Hindu majority society to modernisation or other developments. It recognises religio-political movements first as being inherently about an identity claim similar to politicised ethnicity that has emerged and gained electoral success in contexts where religion arose as, and has been, a dominant ethnic marker. This is in the sense that such movements elevate a particular understanding of religious identity and regard members of this group as the rightful and legitimate rulers of the polity. They are, like politicised ethnicity or nationalist movements, ultimately a means of understanding oneself against others and the world, functioning as a 'principle of vision and division of the social world' (Brubaker 1998) that make similar types of claims for political and economic resources and symbolic recognition (Brubaker 2012).

Accordingly, this book draws on theories of nationalism and ethnicity, and in particular, it grounds its analysis on the modernist school. In contrast to primordialist/perennialist arguments that assert the unchanging nature and antiquity of nations, the modernists emphasise ethnicity and nations as (modern) inventions and, thereby, constructed as well as contested (or as 'zones of conflict' [Hutchinson 2004b]).[11] Given this constructedness and highly subjective and fluid nature of ethnic identity, a key focus of this literature since the work of Barth has been on ethnic boundaries as opposed to the cultural stuff (1969). This is a reflection of Barth's and others' observation that boundaries between ethnic groups tend to persist despite changes in membership, cultural features of the collectivity, assimilation and social interaction that may result in significant changes in the content.[12] While not all boundaries are politically salient, nation building is a key mechanism of boundary creation through the politicisation of ethnicity and the elevation of ethnic unity. A key reason for this is that, unlike pre-modern universalistic multi-ethnic empires based on dynastic rule where ethnic borders were permeable and blurred, the nation-state possesses an ethnic logic (Wimmer 2008) that 'like should rule over like' and the 'principle that any nation-as-people should have their nation as state', which is a byproduct of nationalist thought and principles of popular sovereignty that arose with the French Revolution (Billig 1995: 24; Gellner 2008; Hobsbawm 1990: 9; Wimmer 1997). The establishment of the nation-state therefore involves the creation and privileging of an ethnic majority, whereby 'modern institutions of inclusion (citizenship, democracy, welfare) are systematically tied to ethnic and national forms of exclusion' (Wimmer 2002: 4–5).

---

[11] See also Calhoun (1993: 227) and Özkırımlı (2000). Smith proposes ethno-symbolism as a means of addressing the differences between modernist and primordialist accounts that assert the antiquity of nations, arguing along with modernists that nations are modern and constructed, while maintaining that the nation is based on a pre-modern ethnicity or 'ethnie'. Ethnicity is still regarded as socially constructed and not primordial, but it is argued that, once formed, it proves durable and slow to change, accounting for long-term continuity (Smith 1986). Modernist critics counter that while pre-modern loyalties and sentiments may be used as bricks and mortar to forge cultural unity, this occurs in novel and particular ways which are transformative and selective, while some myths are simply invented (Calhoun 1993; Özkırımlı 2000). Arguably, the differences between the ethno-symbolists and modernists are overstated, and ultimately, both consider nationalism to be a novel form of group identity (Calhoun 1993: 229).

[12] However, in later years, Barth's analysis has been modified to allow that content can play a bigger role than acknowledged, emphasising historical processes and effects (see Jenkins 1994).

Particularly in countries where religio-politics has become forceful, such as India, Turkey, Malaysia and in the wider Middle East, a strong relationship between religion, politicised ethnicity and nation has arisen because of the role of religion in the respective nation building projects. Within these contexts, religion has been deeply intertwined with and has contributed to the origins and development of ethnic identity formation, but it has also acted as a carrier of identity, ensuring its reproduction and persistence over time. Religion acted as a symbolic resource (Zimmer 2003) by offering a rich repertoire of myths, metaphors and symbols, which can be used as building blocks in the process of national identity construction (Asad 1999; Brubaker 2012; Smith 2003). It is in this manner that religion became an ethnic marker (Zubaida 1993) in delineating the boundaries of the nation and in involving a subjective belief in common descent. Indeed, in the Ottoman Empire, religion was both a communal marker and the basis of a system of ethnic segmentation (Göçek 1993) under the *millet* system, comprising a hierarchical social structure in which Muslims were positioned at the top and religious delineated non-Muslim communities were given a degree of autonomy. Religion was, therefore, a key component of boundary delineations between groups within the Ottoman polity.

Crucially important for ensuring the reproduction and persistence of these ethnic boundaries over time, however, is the fact that religion also acts as a resilient container for the persistence and cultural preservation of ethnic groups, since religious groups possess formal organisational bodies that contrast with loosely organised ethnic groups (Conversi 1999). In this respect, therefore, in this book, religion is not considered purely as a belief or cultural system that is an independent, transhistorical and uniform religious domain but rather as a 'field structured by its own institutions, authority relations, instilled dispositions (habitus) and means of production, accumulation and representation' (Sidel 2007). Accordingly, in the Turkish Republic, the *ulema*, through the Diyanet, acted as the carriers and protectors of not just Islamic teachings but also of Sunni Muslim identity, underpinning continuity with the Ottoman polity. This is revealed, for instance, by the Diyanet's politics towards Alevis, which is discussed in detail in Chapter 3.

Having recognised religio-politics as being akin to politicised ethnicity and nationalism, this book argues, moreover, that it is the product of the dynamics generated through a process of social closure inherent in nation building. Social closure refers to the process by which social collectivities with various levels of 'groupness' come together to ensure the monopolisation of (usually economic) resources and opportunities by constructing boundaries against those seen as outsiders or competitors (Parkin

1974: 3–4; Weber 1978; Wimmer 2008). In other words, it is a way of thinking about the process of ethnic group formation (Wimmer 2008: 980). Boundary construction involves an emphasis on any group attribute, such as religion, language or race, and which attribute is then chosen depends, in turn, on the hierarchies of power established by the institutional order (Parkin 1974: 3–4; Wimmer 2008: 993). The concept of social closure therefore provides a framework for understanding how social groups are constructed and how they mobilise to become 'groups with the potential to recognize and act upon collective interests to generate social change' (Loveman 1999: 897).

Since nation-state building inherently involves boundary building, both citizenship (Brubaker 1992) and the nation-state involve a form of social closure (Wimmer 2002: 52–64). Being embedded within the very project of the nation-state itself, the processes of social closure define the identity of the legitimate rulers or owners of the new state at the foundational stage, and as such, the forms of inclusion and exclusion become institutionalised (Wimmer 2004). According to Wimmer (2008), the prevalent forms of social closure are, in turn, determined by three structural constraints on the construction of boundaries by actors during the stage of nation building, including institutions, power endowments and political alliances. Institutional frameworks structure the field in which the specific types of boundary construction occur and 'provide incentives for actors to draw certain types of boundaries ... and to emphasize certain levels of ethnic differentiation rather than others'; while free, choice is therefore constrained. In addition, institutions play a central role in embedding processes of social closure in a path-dependent manner, while differentiated endowments of power affect which projects will ultimately be more successful. Here, the state has a privileged role, given its power resources, which place it in a uniquely powerful position to enforce particular boundaries; 'only those in control of the means of violence will be able to force their ethnic scheme of interpretation onto reality' (Wimmer 2012: 94).

The prevalent form of social closure within a nation-state is indicated by the configurations of institutions, including the particular definition of the nation and its approach to majority and minority communities, the legal framework and the distribution of resources. Under conditions of politically salient boundaries, high levels of social closure and cultural differentiation (precipitated and exacerbated by social closure) can generate path-dependent processes that underpin the persistence and stability of boundaries over time (Wimmer 2008). Democratisation, too, can further enforce boundaries by encouraging competition for the resources of the nation-state and appeals to the people, often based on the majority ethnic group (Kaufmann and Haklai 2008; Wimmer 2002). The competition for state resources hardens boundaries, reducing multiple ethnic categories to a single ethnic dimension (Wimmer 1997). In sum, the dominant forms of social closure within the nation-state crucially underpin what types of boundary become politically salient. Here, the role of the state is critical. Which boundaries are developed and persist, and how salient they are, depends on how social closure is reflected in state institutions (Brubaker 1992; Wimmer 2002, 2008). For instance, Malaysia demonstrates higher levels of social closure based on religious delineations when compared with Turkey, owing to the status of Islam as the official religion of the federation and the privileges granted to Muslim citizens. In other words, higher levels of social closure based on religious identity increase the political salience of those boundaries.

Religious Majoritarianism and the Turkish Case

To describe the multifaceted manner in which religion can become embedded in the nation-state building project, this book develops the prism of religious majoritarianism. This describes the extent to which a religiously demarcated group dominates and has a monopoly over political and economic resources, legitimating its power based on its numeric majority within the nation. All nation-state building projects, by their nature, involve majoritisation (Kaufmann and Haklai 2008) that also involves the elevation of an ethnic group(s), which may be demarcated by religion, as the owners of the state. What transforms these processes and dynamics into religious majoritarianism in some cases and not others is the degree to which they result in particular institutional configurations within the state. The degree to which a nation-state establishes a religious majoritarian structure is determined by the extent to which

- majority–minority boundaries are defined along religious lines (and how sharpened and politicised these boundaries have become, or rather, the extent of social closure), and
- these become reflected in state institutions during the foundational period of the nation-state.

This institutionalisation can, in turn, trigger long-lasting, path-dependent and self-reinforcing effects, leading to the persistence of religious boundaries over time, thereby affecting the possibility of their politicisation. In contexts where social closure hardens boundaries to the extent that political and economic competition proceeds based on a religious–ethnic dimension, nation-states are likely to emerge as highly religious majoritarian. While path dependency inherent to institutions ensures the persistence of these dynamics, such structural patterns can also change over time through internal and external interventions that alter the nature of the boundaries. Boundary blurring, which may result from a state's efforts to overcome ethnic policies, and boundary expansion or inversion, whereby it becomes more or less encompassing, are just some strategies (Wimmer 2008) that can shift the extent to which a state is religious majoritarian.

In sum, the prism of religious majoritarianism involves a conceptual redescription of the state–society–religion relationship compared with the dichotomous notions of secularism that have a homogenising impact on variables such as state and society. Moving beyond examining religio-politics as a reaction, this book argues that the possibility of religio-politics needs to be understood and situated within the longer-term dynamics of nation-state building and the level of religious majoritarian-ism that it incorporates. Consequently, I argue not that the contextual arguments of the prevalent functionalist/reaction-based approaches are necessarily wrong but that the combined analysis of the shaping of group boundaries along religious lines and the way state institutions play a role in their reproduction leads to a more complete understanding of the contexts that make the rise of religio-politics more likely. Specifically, this is not a 'linear' (Abbot 1988) deterministic argument in which a variable has only one causal outcome regardless of the specific contexts and sequencing. I am not arguing that politicisation is necessarily and deterministically caused by the dynamics of majority–minority relations at the formative period of the nation-state. Instead, the argument is rather a probabilistic one in that it claims that 'a cause increases the likelihood of an outcome and/or the magnitude of a (scalar) outcome' (Gerring 2004). Accordingly, I argue that

- variance in variable A (majority–minority relations) can lead to certain processes (institutionalisation) that generate path-dependent effects which limit the range of future paths or constrain/shape the boundaries or actions that particular agents can take; and
- this, in turn, can influence the possibility of the development of religio-politics.

In this sense, the argument can be categorised as a generative explan-ation, given the focus on describing 'processes that generate the form' (Fredrik Barth, quoted in Cederman 2005: 869).

In the Turkish case, the Ottoman legacy crucially shaped the strategies and choices of nation-state builders during the foundational stages of the Republic. In the 1920s, the Turkish state emerged through the efforts of a diverse coalition of groups, among which ideological boundaries were, on certain levels, fluid and overlapping. The faction led by Mustafa Kemal had gained prominence from 1923, resulting in the consolidation of one-party rule, but this did not mean that Islamist and other conservative actors or the *ulema* were eliminated from the state. Instead, Islamist actors and factions, together with the *ulema*, who were more reconciled with the nation-state, were absorbed within the republican state, while more pan-Islamist or traditionalist actors were pushed to go either underground or into exile, and some adopted direct confrontation. However, at this critical juncture, two key antecedent conditions limited the range of paths available for elites, which included the high levels of social closure along religious lines involving the delineation of a Muslim majority and the minority of non-Muslims and the intertwined nature of religious institutions with the state. Accordingly, reflecting the predominant forms of social closure at the end of an empire, one common denominator among the diverse power-holders and factions that comprised the nascent state was their Muslim identity. These dynamics thereby ensured important dimensions of continuity between the Ottoman polity and the Republic concerning identity and religious institutions, albeit in a significantly reconfigured manner. This intertwined nature of religion and nation, together with the continuity in religious institutions, meant that the Turkish nation-state building project was significantly religious majoritarian in nature. Hence, despite the state's ostensibly secular designation, in the Turkish case, the project of secularism, rather than marking a separation or neutrality of the state, was fundamentally linked to nation building. This meant that it involved a process of delineating the boundaries of the majority religion and the privileging of Sunni Muslim identity, but moreover, its institutionalisation marked a power struggle in which certain factions of the state, including Islamists and the *ulema*, were, for a period at least, subdued. In this sense, Turkish secularisation in the early period was not the decline of religion but the declining scope of religious authority (Chaves 1994: 750, 756), which did not end there; instead, through the continuation of the power struggle, it began to be reversed over time.

In turn, it was these particular institutions established during these founding years that underpinned path dependency because they provided a means for social groups to organise and perpetuate themselves through the generations, which underpins the salience of religious markers in political and economic struggles. One critical case was that of the *ulema*, the guardians of Sunni orthodoxy in the Ottoman state, which, having comprised just less than a fifth of the 1921 Turkish Grand National Assembly (Türkiye Büyük Millet Meclisi, TBMM) in Ankara, were absorbed by the Republic under the Diyanet umbrella. Without doubt, the disestablishment of Islam and the secularisation of law has meant that the Turkish *ulema*'s domain is significantly constricted compared with that of other Muslim majority contexts. Yet, the Diyanet is far from a passive actor that functions as an apparatus of the secular state to control religion. In part owing to the dimensions of continuity with the Ottoman *ulema*, it has been actively pursuing its own agenda of Islamisation (the content of which varies across different groups and shifts over time), while – because of the conflation between nation and religion – delineating the parameters of inclusion and exclusion of citizenship and articulating national identity as Sunni (Hanefi[13]) Muslim Turkish, to the exclusion of Alevis.

Nevertheless, according the Diyanet agency does not mean understanding the body as a monolithic and unitary actor or according it an unchanging essence. Nor is the Diyanet the only religious political actor in Turkey, where there is a diverse and heterogeneous set of Islamic and Islamist actors, communities and groups, including tariqa orders. The *ulema* employed by the Diyanet also reflects and comprises this heterogeneity and is an umbrella institution under which these diverse currents and groups come together and also compete with each other. Indeed, this book emphasises the fluid boundaries between Islamists and *ulema*, state and society. However, this does not mean that the Diyanet as an institution cannot formulate strategic interests and vision, just like any other bureaucratic state institution. That state bureaucracies can develop different types of policy behaviour, through interaction with other bodies, for instance, is well established within the political science literature on bureaucracies. Dunleavy (1985), for instance, has argued that bureaucrats adopt 'bureau-shaping' strategies at both the individual and collective agency levels to raise their and the bureau's status and centrality to power, improve the work environment and maximise welfare. It is in this sense that the Diyanet, like other arms of the state, including the military, has adopted multiple strategies against other factions and bodies within the state, which has also included coalitions with Islamist and other rightist currents within and outside the state. What makes the Diyanet a unique case, on the other hand, is that it is at the same time positioned as an Islamic authority responsible for preserving, interpreting and transferring Islamic knowledge: the body itself roots its mission and lineage with the Ottoman Sheikh ul-Islam. It is this role, and the lines of continuity with the Ottoman *ulema*, that have shaped the Diyanet's institutional identity and goals and its pursuit of Islamisation of state and society.

---

[13] The Hanafi School comprises one of the four schools of Sunni Islamic jurisprudence, alongside Maliki, Shafi'i and Hanbali.

Nonetheless, the precise content of this Islamisation is the matter of contestation, and it evolves.

Over time, the balance of power within the state shifted between the different factions and currents with their varying political visions. These shifts were driven by both the endogenous strategies of agents within the state and exogenous factors, including the Cold War anti-communism drive, neoliberal restructuring and political liberalisation, which provided opportunities for different actors to reshape the institutional milieu and thereby establish new paths. This opened up windows of opportunity for rightist, conservative and Islamist factions within the state to push an expansion of the religious field, including the infrastructure behind religion which encompasses the Diyanet; religious education; and Islamic finance, charity and business organisations, thereby providing a favourable environment for Islamist mobilisation, with the ultimate goal of the Islamisation of state and society. Accordingly, the rise of the Islamist movement and subsequently the AKP did not just mark a reaction of religious society – which is underpinned by an essentialist understanding of Muslim society – but was facilitated from within the state owing to the long-term path-dependent dynamics of nation-state building. Having ascended to power in 2002, the AKP has been able to engage in path-dependent path-shaping for a path-breaking transformation of the regime, thanks largely to the significant benefits of incumbency offered by the highly majoritarian political system it inherited.

Sources and Methods

The empirical foundation of this book is the product of more than a decade of research and collecting of several kinds of data on the Diyanet and on religion and state relations in Turkey. I extensively use and build on previous works, but based on my research, I not only offer a different emphasis and more details but have also sought to provide a different interpretation of the phenomenon in question. In particular, I undertook extensive historical research, collecting and examining official constitutional and legal documents, parliamentary deliberations, parliamentary committee reports (such as those published by the Committee for the Investigation of Military Coups and Memorandums established in 2012), party and government programmes, draft constitutional proposals and internal government correspondence and memos. Key sources included (i) parliamentary records from the Turkish Grand National Assembly Library and Archives (Türkiye Büyük Millet Meclisi Başkanlığı Kütüphane ve Arşiv Başkanlığı), which are digitalised and available online; (ii) the Prime Minister's Republic Archives (Başbakanlık

Cumhuriyet Arşivi, BCA), where I accessed the archives of the Diyanet and the CHP government records of the one-party period – I have been lucky to benefit from the willingness of Diyanet officials to share various materials and documents with me; (iii) the official gazette for laws, decrees and regulations; (iv) official bodies such as the Turkish Statistical Institute (Türkiye İstatistik Kurumu, TUIK) and Ministry of Finance (Maliye Bakanlığı) for data on election results and economic variables; (v) published archival documents such as the minutes of the 1960 military cabinet meetings, the regional inspectorate reports from the one-party period, military reports prepared in the 1930s on the state's Dersim policies and the archives of the one-party period (Dersim/ Tunceli province) lawmaker Necmettin Sahir Sılan; (vi) memoirs and biographies of various actors, including members of the *ulema* and key Islamist actors; (vii) the writings of various prominent regime historians, ideologues, lawmakers and bureaucrats of the late Ottoman Empire and Republic, such as Ziya Gökalp and Hasan Reşit Tankut; (viii) a broad selection of media sources, including Islamist journals and newspapers and (ix) interviews with a range of actors, including members of the Diyanet, journalists, business representatives and academics. Alongside these sources, I scoured second-hand bookstores in Turkey, which are a treasure trove of rare historical documents, and also spent some time at the Centre for Islamic Studies (İslam Araştırmaları Merkezi) and the National Library (Milli Kütüphane), collecting official documents, Diyanet publications and other (particularly Islamist) periodicals and media sources. It was a deep dive, going through the entire digital archive of the Diyanet at the BCA, which, for instance, led me to identify Alevism, rather than other minority groups, as the primary concern of the Diyanet. Hence, through an adaptive approach to my research, I was able to constantly hone my theoretical framework in conjunction with my data collection.

Based on this material and the insights provided by the secondary literature, I was able to trace the concerns of and constraints faced by different political actors, including lawmakers and bureaucrats, during different constitutional periods and the ways in which institutional structures and the interpretation of key principles changed or persisted over time. I was able to trace the evolution of the Diyanet's institutional identity, agency and role. Such a 'moving pictures' (Koinova 2013: 6) approach, where attention is paid to the timing and sequencing of events, is invaluable in tracing path dependency, along with continuity and change, over time. It helps to produce a more holistic picture in comparison to a snapshot approach that bases analysis on a particular moment in time, which can result in static analyses. For instance, focusing purely on the current codified principles of the Turkish constitution, such as laicism, can stabilise a historically contingent understanding of the principle and the battles involved, missing its evolution and underlying power struggles. Using multiple sources of data was critical from this perspective, since it enabled me to demonstrate that there are other dimensions and motivations behind various historical events that have been neglected in existing approaches.

The key limitation of the archives was that Diyanet documents from the 1970s onwards were not available, partly reflecting a thirty-year rule that restricts access to state documents. A further constraint on historical research of Turkey is the lack of transparency and consistency in enforcing procedures. I was unable to gain access to the Diyanet's in-house archives containing documents that had not been transferred to the BCA. To my knowledge, these archives are not systematised, and entrance is highly restricted. This is an important limitation, which I have tried to address by using multiple sources. In addition, following an official request under transparency laws, the Ministry of the Interior (İçişleri Bakanlığı) refused to provide historical statistical information on the number of associations and foundations. Although the work was time-consuming, I compiled the information myself through the online *Official Gazette* (*Resmi Gazete*) archives. Neither did I find interviews particularly fruitful, except to alert me to the existence of various data sources. This was partly because of the ways in which the 'master narrative' has become ingrained in how historical events are now presented and particularly because of the increasingly authoritarian turn in Turkish politics, which meant access to sources (and those willing to talk openly) became more difficult.

Outline of the Book

The overarching historical narrative and argument developed in this book are supported by the chapters, each of which explores a specific dimension of the phenomenon in question. For this reason, the structure of the book combines both a chronological and a thematic approach, beginning with the impact of the Ottoman legacy on nation-state building in the Republic and ending with the nature of regime change under the AKP along with thematic chapters on the role of the *ulema*, religious education and organisations and the growth of Islamism. Given the breadth of time under examination, a selected chronology of events and junctures spanning from the late Ottoman Empire to the AKP era can be found below in Figure 1 to guide the reader throughout the book.

Selected Chronology of Events

Ottoman Era

1514	Battle of Chaldiran between Ottoman and Safavid Empires
1683	Battle of Vienna
1768–1774	Russo-Ottoman War, Treaty of Küçük Kaynarca following Russian victory
1787–1792	Russo-Ottoman War, Russian victory
1789	Sultan Selim III launches New Order (*Nizam-ı Cedid*) reforms
1806–1812	Russo-Ottoman War, Russian victory
1821–1832	Greek independence war against Ottoman Empire
1826	Mahmud II's abolition of janissary corps (*Vaka-i Hayriye*) and replacement with modern army
1828–1829	Russo-Ottoman War, Russian victory
1838	Anglo-Ottoman commercial Treaty of *Balta Limanı* opens up Ottoman markets to Britain and its allies
1839–1871	Tanzimat, period of reforms including i) taxation; ii) conscription; iii) establishment of guarantees for life, honour and property; iv) legal equality
1876–1909	Reign of Sultan Abdulhamid II
1853–1856	Crimean War, victory of Ottoman, British, French and Italian alliance
1856	Reform edict promises non-Muslim subjects equality
1865	The society of Young Ottomans was established
1869	Nationality Law codifies equality and Ottoman citizenship irrespective of religious or ethnic divisions
1876–1878	First Constitutional Era following promulgation of first constitution of the Empire
1877–1878	Russo-Ottoman War, Russian victory
1889	Ottoman Unity Society founded by opposition with aim of reinstating constitution and parliamentary government; roots of Young Turk movement
1908	Young Turk revolution and beginning of Second Constitutional Era following restoration of constitution of 1876
1909	31 March Incident
1909	Constitutional reforms adopted and Sultan Abdulhamid II deposed
1912	ITC wins in the 'election with the stick' (*sopalı seçim*)
1912–1913	Balkan wars, followed by efforts to establish national economy and bourgeoisie
1913	ITC seizes power through coup d'etat (*Bâb-ı Âli Baskını*)
1914–1918	First World War
1915	Armenian Genocide
1919–1923	Turkish War of Independence, followed by the Treaty of Lausanne in 1923
1920	Treaty of Sèvres, imperial powers carve up Ottoman Empire

Turkish Republic – One-party Era

23 April 1920	Opening of the TBMM in Ankara by opposition movement
1921	Koçgiri rebellion
1921	The first constitution (Teşkilat-ı Esasiye) promulgated by Ankara government formed by independence movement
November 1922	Abolition of the sultanate by the TBMM
1923	Treaty of Lausanne
29 October 1923	Declaration of the Republic, and Islam as state religion incorporated in constitution
3 March 1924	Unification of education, abolition of caliphate, abolition of office of Sheikh ul-Islam and Ministry of Religious Affairs and Pious Foundations, establishment of the *Diyanet*
20 April 1924	New constitution promulgated, remains until 1960
1925	Sheikh Said rebellion
1925	Law on the Maintenance of Order declared against 'reactionary' threat following Sheikh Said rebellion
1926	Adoption of secular civil code

Figure 1: Selected chronology of events

1928	Constitutional amendment removing provision declaring Islam as the religion of the state
1929	The start of the Great Depression
1937	CHP's 'six arrows' including laicism incorporated in constitution
1937–1938	Dersim campaign against Alevis by state
1946–1991	Cold War
1946	Beginning of transition to multipartism
1948	Founding of Associations for Fighting Communism (*Komünizmle Mücadele Dernekleri*)

Turkish Republic – Multiparty Era

1950	DP elected in first free election
27 May 1960	**Military coup d'etat**
1961	New constitution adopted through referendum, establishment of military tutelage, return to civilian government
1962	Saudi Arabia's *Rabita* established for propagation of Islamic teaching
1969	Islamist National Outlook (*Milli Görüş*) movement founded
1970	Islamist Necmettin Erbakan founds MNP, associated with National Outlook, emerges as MSP in 1972 following closure after 1971 military coup
1970	Hearth of the Enlightened established by rightist circles
1971	Establishment of TÜSİAD, Turkey's leading business association for largest companies
12 March 1971	**Military coup d'etat, constitutional amendments**
1973	Global oil crisis following Yom Kippur War leading to jump in oil prices
1978	Maraş massacre targeting Alevis
1979	Iranian Islamic revolution
1980	Çorum massacre targeting Alevis
12 September 1980	**Military coup d'etat, adoption of Turkish-Islamic Synthesis, neoliberal economic restructuring**
1982	Promulgation of new highly majoritarian constitution following a referendum under continued military rule
1983	Return to electoral politics, election of ANAP government
1983	ANAP government decree approving opening of Islamic banks
1984	PKK launches armed insurgency
1986	ANAP government establishes Fund for Social Cooperation and Solidarity
1987	Turkey applies for membership of European Community
1990s	'Alevi revival'
1990	Establishment of conservative business association MÜSİAD
1993	Sivas massacre targeting Alevis
1994	Islamist RP wins 19% in local elections, Istanbul and Ankara municipalities
1995	Islamist RP wins 21% of vote in general elections, forms coalition government
1996	Susurluk scandal reveals ties between government, military and mafia
28 February 1997	**Military intervention through memorandum forcing resignation of Islamist RP led coalition**
1998	Islamist RP closed by Constitutional Court
1999	İzmit earthquake resulting in thousands of deaths
1999	PKK leader Abdullah Öcalan arrested
1999	Turkish candidacy granted by European Council
1999–2004	Declaration of ceasefire by PKK
2000–2001	Major financial and economic crises

Turkish Republic – AKP Era

2002	AKP wins general election with 34% of vote, forms single party government, first since 1991
2004	EU agrees to start accession negotiations on Turkish membership
12 April 2007	**Military issues e-memorandum against AKP and efforts to elect AKP candidate to presidency**
July 2007	AKP wins general election with 46.6% of vote, AKP's parliamentary majority elects AKP's Abdullah Gül as president

Figure 1: (*cont.*)

21 October 2007	Constitutional referendum introducing directly elected presidency
2008	Closure trial against AKP
2008	Ergenekon trials launched against members of the military following investigations started in 2007. Balyoz trials begin in 2010.
2009–2011	AKP government organises 'Alevi opening' meetings
12 September 2010	Constitutional referendum by AKP, including judicial reforms
2010	Mavi Marmara incident and crisis with Israel
2011	AKP wins general election with 49.8% of vote
2011	Start of Arab uprisings
2011	Negotiations between MİT and PKK leaked, prelude to launch of Kurdish 'solution process'
2011–2012	(Unsuccessful) civil constitution making efforts by an all-party commission
2013	Gezi protests
17 December 2013	Corruption investigations target AKP government, associated businessmen, signalling intensification of struggle with former Gülenist allies
2014	Recep Tayyip Erdoğan wins Turkish presidential election with 51.8% of vote
June 2015	AKP loses majority in general election, gaining 40.9% of vote, pro-Kurdish HDP passes 10% threshold
2015	End of Kurdish 'solution process'
November 2015	AKP regains majority in general election winning 49.5% of the vote
15 July 2016	**Coup attempt, triggers declaration of State of Emergency, opposition crackdown, mass purges**
16 April 2017	Constitutional referendum resulting in regime change with adoption of authoritarian presidential system.

Owing to the interconnected nature of each dimension, various events, policies, formations and actors, such as the TIS programme adopted by the 1980 junta regime or the anti-communism associations, emerge in multiple chapters. The treatment of the AKP and Islamism coming later, in Chapters 5 and 6, may appear counter-intuitive or seem to indicate an inevitable outcome. On the contrary, it follows from the overall argument that while religio-politics has to be situated within the longer path-dependent processes related to nation building, it was not inevitable or natural but rather the outcome of a dynamic struggle within the state, the course of which was influenced by contingent events.

Chapter 1 provides a historical background with an examination of the Ottoman legacy and its impact on nation-state building and institutional design in the Republic. Through a comparative historical analysis of Turkish constitution making, examining deliberations of constitutional framers on the principle of laicism and Turkish nationalism, it traces both continuity and change with respect to their operationalisation over time. Its main proposition is that the institution of secularism was closely linked to the nation-state building process and, thereby, involved the elevation and privileging of the Sunni Muslim Turkish majority rather than involving the separation or neutrality of religion. This has, in turn, embedded a religious majoritarian logic into the nation-state, which has persisted as a fundamental element of 'constitutional identity' (Jacobsohn 2010), rather than laicism or Kemalism, in Turkey. On the other hand, struggles within the state have resulted in change over time, augmenting the religious majoritarianism of the state, particularly since the 1980s.

Chapters 2 and 3 shift the focus, considering on a more detailed level the different factions within the state. They analyse the role of the Diyanet as a state institution and Islamic authority housing the official *ulema*, which has commonly been ignored and considered as a passive and marginalised actor utilised by the secular Kemalist state to control religion. Departing from these approaches, these chapters show not only continuity between the Ottoman *ulema* and the Diyanet but also in the institution's agency in adopting multiple strategies, from cooperation to struggling against other state factions in the pursuit of its own agenda. The chapters demonstrate that the Diyanet has played a crucial role in providing a more favourable environment for Islamist mobilisation and has delimited the nation's boundaries along religious lines through its engagement with and rejection of Alevism. In addition, they underline the fluid nature of the boundaries between state and society, *ulema* and Islamist, tracing how Islamist and conservative groups form coalitions both within the state and outside its official borders, promoting causes that may at the same time conflict with other factions within the state.

Chapter 4 thematically tackles the emergence and expansion of religious education, religious associations and foundations (*waqfs*), Islamic finance and the self-styled Muslim or conservative business organisations. Its main argument is that the growth of religious education and organisations were facilitated from within the state owing to two key contingent events that opened up windows of opportunity to shift the balance of power within the state: The Cold War-related anti-communism and the neoliberal economic transformation of the 1980s. The *ulema* and Islamist actors within and outside the state were then able to utilise these resources made available by the state to further the cause of Islamisation and to construct a distinct habitus through which a new generation of Islamists were raised. This was a crucial dimension, accounting for the emergence in the 1990s of Muslim business associations, indicating a fragmentation of the bourgeoisie. But the persistence of the notion of Muslim bourgeoisie and its utilisation in political and economic competition in the Republic was also a product of the path-dependent effects that relate to processes of social closure during nation building, which included the continued policies of advantaging a Muslim Turkish bourgeoisie. This was in the sense that the articulations (Muslim majority versus minority) of group boundaries in the late Ottoman Empire, which had been polarised by the bifurcation of the bourgeoisie, despite their shifting contents (with the elimination of non-Muslims) in the Republic, were transposed onto new distributional conflicts in the multi-party era.

Chapter 5 situates the AKP by tracing the history of both the varying intellectual currents and the experiences of political party mobilisation of the Islamist movement in Turkey. It does this by focusing on the emergence and expanding power of the coalitions between Islamist, conservative and nationalist currents and factions within and outside the state. Together with the establishment of the nation-state, the 1980 and 1997 interventions crucially shaped the trajectory of the Islamist movement, facilitating first its integration with Turkish nationalism and second, its re-articulation within a decisively pro-capitalist neoliberal framework. In addition, the chapter points to the different and competing strands of the movement, focusing on the rise of the Gülenist movement as an example. In sum, it underlines the symbiotic relationship between the Islamist movement and the state, together with the webs of cooperation between rightist actors, including the Islamists within and outside the state.

Chapter 6 traces changes and continuity under the AKP, demonstrating the ways in which the party has been able to engage in path-dependent path-shaping (Hausner et al. 1995) to effect path-breaking regime transformation. Drawing on Lijphart's (1999) typology of democratic regimes, it shows how Turkey's highly majoritarian political system inherited by the AKP structured political life, shaping party political competition and facilitating system capture owing to its unitary and centralised institutional character, weak separation of powers and the disproportional effect of an electoral system that favours large parties. The chapter considers the two main challenges to the AKP's and President Erdoğan's efforts to monopolise power within the state, the military and the Gülenists, concluding with a discussion of the evolution and transformation of the regime following the 16 April 2017 constitutional referendum.

The Conclusion of the book considers how the prism of religious majoritarianism may be operationalised and used to understand the rise of religio-politics outside of the Turkish case. A comparative discussion of the cases of Malaysia, India and Ireland show how different levels and forms of social closure have resulted in the embedding of varying levels of religious majoritarianism in these states. The highly religious majoritarian Malaysian state, which is the product of both high degrees of social closure along religious lines and institutional legacies of the colonial era, has made certain that religious identity remains important in gaining access to state resources, thereby ensuring an ethnicisation of political and economic competition. Somewhat similar to the Turkish case, in India, the project of secularism was tied to nation-state building, resulting in the elevation of the Hindu identity, which was supported by accommodative institutional structures over time. Yet the comparatively decentralised and pluralistic political system, and the fact that social closure has cut along other lines, including caste, language and region, have imposed some limits on the ability of religio-politics to monopolise politics in India in the same way as has happened in Turkey. The Irish case, which started as a religious majoritarian one, demonstrates how both the struggles within the state and contingent events, such as EU membership, can shift politics another way, with religious boundaries lacking salience in political competition. This concluding chapter therefore proposes that religious majoritarianism can be used to trace both the contexts that are more amenable to religio-political mobilisation and also the dynamics of continuity and change in earlier phases of nation building.

1 How Religious Majoritarianism Was Institutionalised in the Early Republic

This chapter first provides a historical background of the legacies of the Ottoman Empire and then discusses the ways in which they influenced institutional design during nation-state building with respect to religion. In demonstrating how the role of religion in the Ottoman Empire impacted its role and institutionalisation in the Turkish Republic, it also contributes to and builds on recent studies that have shown how the nature of the old order impacted the state–religion relationship in the states that emerged out of them (Kuru 2009; Lerner 2014; Rubin 2013).

Zürcher (2014: 247) has distinguished between two trends in Turkish historiography with respect to the Ottoman legacy: (i) the official so-called Kemalist historiography and early sympathetic scholars, which posited a clean break between the Ottoman Empire and the Republic in line with Atatürk's outline of events in 'Nutuk', his 1927 speech and (ii) a later generation of scholars from the 1950s, such as Niyazi Berkes and Şerif Mardin, who acknowledge the importance and influence of Ottoman modernisation and Committee of Union and Progress (İttihat ve Terakki Cemiyeti, ITC) reforms for the new Republic which underline dimensions of continuity. Some of this later generation, focusing on ideology and national identity, have tended towards narrating the history of modern Turkey as being between progress and reaction, stretching back to the Tanzimat era (Ahmad 1993: 77; Berkes 1964; Heper 2000; Mardin 1971: 210). Displaying a somewhat parallel logic is Findley's argument that 'modernity generated two major currents of change, one radical in the sense of favoring rapid change and Westernization, the other Islamically grounded and more conservative' (Findley 2010: 416). While agreeing on the continuity and without dismissing the transformative changes in the Republic, others have challenged these narratives as being a simplification of 'historical reality by depicting two imaginary camps upholding the contending banners of scientific progress and religious obscurantism', pointing instead to the 'oppressive weight of circumstances, which inhibited the freedom of realistic policy makers who sought to innovate' (Hanioğlu 2010: 2).

Indeed, this later scholarship, which has sought to depart from the modernisation paradigm on which earlier historiography rested, has drawn attention to the fluidity between ideological currents in the transition from empire to republic. In particular, it has shown the manner in which events made and remade coalitions and the contours of the different intellectual currents (Bein 2007: 614; Çetinsaya 1999; Deringil 1993b; Dressler 2015; Hanioğlu 2010), drawing attention to institutional and elite-level continuities, most apparent in Zürcher's (1992, 2010) periodisation of the Young Turk era as stretching from 1908 to 1950. In more recent years, historiography, influenced by Islamist discourse, has turned both the early break and continuity historiography on its head to develop a narrative of victimhood in which the institution of the republic is considered to be 'a clean break from Islam and the Ottoman legacy' or a 'critical juncture' (Kuru 2007), whereby Islam was excluded from the public sphere under an authoritarian Kemalist regime oppressing the Muslim masses (Göle 1997: 50; Kadıoğlu 1996: 186; Kuru 2007: 585; Yavuz 2003: 47).[1]

However, both the prevalent continuity and break accounts have nevertheless converged on the master narrative of a monolithic authoritarian secularist Kemalist state, driven by a principle of secularism that evinces a timeless message and vision vis-à-vis religion as involving neutrality, control or separation. In more recent years, revisionist accounts have begun to challenge this master narrative in two ways. First, they have pointed to the contested and far more dynamic nature of state building in the early Republic, moving away from a top-down process to a fluid interaction and relationship between state and society (Adak 2016; Akın 2007). Second, they have underlined the highly heterogeneous structures and groups that comprised the ruling bloc in the early Republic against the prevalent tendency to treat it as a homogenous Kemalist bloc rooted in an 'Enlightenment movement that had its roots in the secular-rationalist tradition of ideological positivism' (İrem 2002: 87).

This chapter builds on these works and traces how the legacy of the Ottoman Empire had consequences for the choices made by elites at the

---

[1] A 2013 statement by the AKP's Ahmet Davutoğlu, the former foreign minister (2009–2014) and prime minister (2014–2016), in an interview on foreign policy in the Middle East (and the imposition of borders by imperial powers following the First World War) that the government would close the 'hundred year old parenthesis' has been seen by their critics as an open admission of the disdain by Islamists of the Republican project and their mission to reverse the break with the Ottoman legacy (Karagül, 1 March 2013; Mumcu 9 August 2017). Similar discourse has been adopted by other AKP members, including one who described the Turkish Republic as a '90-year ad break' (*Hürriyet* 16 January 2015).

early stages of nation-state building and how this had path-dependent effects. In particular, the three structural constraints that shaped the dominant forms of social closure – identified by Wimmer (2008) as institutional legacies, power of the ethnic elites, and political networks – are examined. Accordingly, the first section of this chapter outlines two key antecedent conditions: (i) the institutional legacies of the Empire, including the intertwined relationship between religion and state involving the *ulema*'s integration within the bureaucracy, which further includes external constraints on institutional reform and design by imperial powers and (ii) the increasing political salience of religious delineations of community boundaries in the late Ottoman Empire, together with rise of Turkish nationalism. These were connected to major demographic changes that resulted in the Muslimisation of the lands, particularly from the late eighteenth century, driven by territorial losses and migration resulting from wars (e.g. the 1877–1878 Russo-Ottoman war and the 1912–1913 Balkan Wars) as well as demographic engineering and ethnic cleansing by the state (including the 1915 Armenian Genocide). These two factors were of importance particularly in terms of religion becoming a dominant marker of group boundaries and its growing salience in political and economic struggles, together with the rising currency and power of Turkish nationalism among Ottoman elites, especially since 1908. The second section examines how the institution of secularism and nationalism as key pillars of the constitutional order were essentially shaped by these antecedent conditions together with political alliances during this period. Here, the analysis adopts a more differentiated understanding of the state (compared to some of the prevalent literature) as a site of struggle and contestation in which different actors with different endowments of power vie to implement their differing visions for the polity. Accordingly, the emerging power struggle within the fairly heterogeneous nationalist coalition is underscored along with the importance of Islam as a common denominator of identity.

Just how these structural constraints shaped the available policy paths and institutional choices made regarding the role of religion in early nation building, generating path-dependent effects, is revealed through a comparative historical analysis of constitution making and deliberations in the 1920s, 1961 and 1982 and the unsuccessful attempts at drawing up a new constitution in the late 2000s.[2] Constitutions specify the locus of sovereignty within a given territory and thereby say something about

---

[2] Here, the analysis draws inspiration from the notion of 'constitutional identity' within constitutional studies (e.g. Jacobsohn 2010; Rosenfeld 1994) and how nationalism relates to constitution making (Kissane and Sitter 2010a, 2010b).

the identity of the national construct and the codified political vision of the nation from the viewpoint of the framers or nation-state builders (Jacobsohn 2010). However, constitutions are not only 'the products of political and ideological struggles and negotiations' (Bayar 2016b: 4) but also structure the nature of those struggles by establishing a framework of politics and the rules of the game and generating path-dependent effects.

In the early phases of this case of nation building, since the prevalent forms of social closure involved the salience of religious boundaries, national identity, state institutions and economic policies constructed and elevated a (Sunni) Muslim Turkish majority as the base of the nation-state and as the legitimate owner of its resources. This institution-alised a religious majoritarian logic of operation of the state. The third section on constitution making in the multi-party era reveals both path dependency effects of the early choices and also how the conceptualisa-tion of secularism and the role of religion with respect to the state and national identity evolved over time as the balance of power within the state shifted towards more conservative factions. Religious majoritarianism, involving a focus on and concern with the Muslim Turkish majority has been a persistent feature of the state and the fundamental logic of constitutional identity in Turkey, as opposed to just laicism or Kemalism.[3] On the one hand, the institution of secularism was closely linked to nation building and was constructed in a manner that implicitly and explicitly privileged and delineated a Muslim Turkish majority on which the nation-state was to be based. On the other hand, change to the role of religion and the operationalisation of this secularism has occurred over time because of the shifting balance of power within different factions of the state, resulting in the augmentation of religious majoritarianism since the 1980s. The fourth section reflects on this experience of consti-tution making by summarising and situating it against the current litera-ture and relates it to the different practices, struggles and strategies adopted by state actors in the forthcoming chapters.

The Ottoman Legacies

Religion as a Pillar of the Ottoman Order and as an Ethnic Marker

The Ottoman legacy fundamentally shaped the contours of Turkish nation building in a manner that was to give rise to the possibility and

---

[3] Analyses of Turkish constitutional identity typically emphasise Kemalism and laicism; see, for example, Jacobsohn (2010: 12–13), who argues that the Turkish constitution defines the nation's identity according to the '(extreme secular) principles of its founder'.

eventual success of religio-politics in the Turkish Republic. The high levels of social closure and the delineation of majority–minority boundaries along religious lines during the establishment of the Republic in 1923 can be traced to the Ottoman Empire's political and social structure and the dynamics unleashed during its transformation from the eighteenth century, which was followed by its eventual disintegration. The Empire was multi-ethnic and multi-religious, but Islam, and thereby, the *ulema*, alongside the military class, were key pillars of the semitheocratic monarchy (Zürcher 2004: 11–13). This dual system of legitimacy based on both Islam and the state is encapsulated in the notion of *din-u-devlet* (religion and state) (Azak 2010: 2–3). One reflection of this in the late Ottoman Empire was the sultan's status as the head of the Ottoman state and caliph,[4] making him the leader and protector of the faith and *ummah* (the Muslim community). Second was the existence of imperial laws (*kanun*) sourced from the sultan, which stood alongside Islamic law (Azak 2010: 2–3; İnalcık 2001: 333–336; Imber 2002: 244; Keddie 1972: 42; Sunar and Toprak 2007: 4). Third, the institutionalisation and integration over centuries of the *ulema*, the Islamic religious authority, into the Ottoman state had resulted in the increasing prominence of the role of the Sheikh ul-Islam (Toprak 1981: 30–31). As chief of the *ulema*, the Sheikh ul-Islam emerged as a key actor in decision-making, second only to the sultan (as his appointee) and on a par with the grand vizier. In theory, laws and decisions had to comply with Islamic law (*shari'a*), which empowered the *ulema* and raised their standing. In practice, disobedience of the sultan was rare, and he ruled through a combination of religious laws and sultanic decrees based on customary law and practices (Toprak 1981: 1–2). In fact, by the eighteenth century, the ensuing modernisation drive had largely resulted in confining Islamic law to matters of family law and ownership (Zürcher 2004: 10).

Alongside this symbolic and legal weaving together of Islam and the state, the social structure was highly stratified, and within it, religion was a communal trait that 'demarcated ethnic groups and defined these as religious communities' (Göçek 1993: 513). This 'ethnic segmentation' (Göçek 1996: 114) was operationalised in the *millet* system, which had emerged as a practical arrangement of rule over diverse populations as the Empire expanded (Barkey 2005; Karpat 1982). Based on Islamic

---

[4] While the Ottoman claim was strongly contested, the title of caliph only began to be used more actively sometime around the late eighteenth century. It was utilised in reaction to European imperial penetration and was particularly emphasised by Sultan Abdülhamid II in line with his pan-Islamist politics. It was also included in the 1876 Constitution.

principles, this framework was systematised only during the Tanzimat reforms in the nineteenth century, but never fully codified (Barkey 2005; Braude 1980). Within a hierarchical social structure in which Muslims (the *millet-i hakime*, or 'sovereign nation') were positioned at the top and ruled the lands, the *millets* comprised religiously defined communities (only non-Muslims who were recognised by Islam as 'people of the book') in which each enjoyed a degree of administrative autonomy over areas pertaining to personal law, religion, education and judicial matters (Göçek 1993: 513; Karpat 1982; Ortaylı 2001). This segmentation and stratification on the basis of religion was reinforced by various legal and social codes and restrictions, including different dress, different taxation and a system of privileges and exemptions that not only enforced 'a cognitive sense of their difference in relation to other communities' but also restricted interaction between communities (Göçek 1993: 513, 1996; Karpat 2001). Being a Muslim (by birth or conversion) was also a requirement for statesmen wishing to climb to higher ranks (Toprak 1981: 1–2).

The Growing Salience of Religious Markers in the Late Empire

The polarisation of this system of ethnic segmentation, heightening the levels of social closure, was spurred on by a confluence of developments, including growing economic and political European imperial penetration following successive Ottoman military defeats and the ongoing loss of territories following the Battle of Vienna (1683). For instance, in 1774, significant concessions were granted to Russia by the Treaty of Küçük Kaynarca, which included ceding greater rights over the Greek Orthodox subjects of the Empire (Ahmad 2000: 2–3). Likewise, in return for British help to thwart the challenge posed to the Empire by the governor of Egypt, Mehmet Ali Pasha, the Porte had fully opened up Ottoman markets to British merchants (and its allies, including France) with the 1838 Anglo-Ottoman commercial Treaty of Balta Limanı.

Consequently, from the eighteenth century onwards, increasingly focused on the issue of how to save the state, the Ottoman state sought to counter the rising military, commercial and industrial strength of Europe with a modernisation and centralisation drive that went beyond mere reform of the military. Starting with the New Order (Nizam-ı Cedit) programme of Sultan Selim III (1789–1807) and continuing with the Tanzimat era (1839–1871), the Ottoman state undertook a series of extensive reforms that resulted in a transformation of the structure and the basis of legitimacy of the state. Common to empires of continental size comprising multi-ethnic and multi-religious communities, in an age marked by rising nation-states and the diffusion of the concept of popular sovereignty following the French Revolution, the Ottoman state was increasingly faced with a legitimacy crisis, particularly beginning in the second half of the nineteenth century (Deringil 1998: 166). The state's efforts to develop ideological legitimations to address the legitimacy crisis during this period were subsequently summarised as Ottomanism, pan-Islamism and Turkism (discussed further below) by one of the key ideologues of Turkish nationalism, Yusuf Akçura, in his 1904 essay entitled 'Üç Tarz-ı Siyaset' ('Three Ways of Politics'). In reality, all three currents, which proposed different legitimating constructions of a reliable social base, were intertwined, with different elements being stressed at different times and, as Bein (2007: 614) argues, 'hardly any Ottoman thinker argued for one of these referents to the exclusion of others. Instead, major controversies revolved around what should be the prevailing component in the state's official ideology.' Equally, Hanioğlu (2010: 4) has remarked that 'Young Ottoman constitutionalism, rooted as it was in Islamic principles, and later Young Turk constitutionalism, grounded in an intensely secular outlook, are greater than many would care to admit'.

Emerging in the early nineteenth century, Ottomanism involved efforts to constitute a territorially based Ottoman national identity by unifying different communities within the Empire based on the equality of all subjects regardless of religious affiliation or ethnic origin. The aim was to stem the tide of nationalism and was also driven by the desire to eliminate the privileges enjoyed by non-Muslim communities (under the capitulations regime) in order to undermine the basis of imperial penetration which had become a key policy goal of the Sublime Porte (the central government) by 1839 (Ahmad 2000: 1; Zürcher 2004: 56). Such ideas were reflected during the Tanzimat era, when a series of modernising reforms, including the military, central bureaucracy and education, in part continuous with previous efforts, were promulgated between 1839 and 1871. Hanioğlu (2010: 87) notes that the 1839 edict 'revealed the wish to establish a single system for all subjects; it indicated a change in the official ideology of the state [...] the imperial edict was a significant first step toward the transformation of the hitherto Muslim, Christian, and Jewish subjects into *Ottomans*'. Reformist bureaucrats tried to address the legitimacy question by various means. Following this, the 1856 reform edict granted non-Muslim subjects legal equality for the first time, which was codified in the Ottoman Nationality Law of 1869. In 1876, the first Ottoman constitution (Kânûn-i Esâsî, Fundamental Law) was adopted, comprising equality of non-Muslims (Article 8) and establishing a parliament for which both Muslims and non-Muslims were elected following polls in 1877.[5] This experience was to prove brief, however, as the sultan, who remained the ultimate power in the land, ended the first constitutional period in 1878, proroguing the elected parliament for thirty years until the 1908 revolution.

However, these reforms and the underpinning ideas of Ottomanism were at odds with the existing social structure underpinned by the *millet* system. Neither the imperial powers nor the non-Muslim subjects necessarily wanted to forego their privileges or relative autonomy under the *millets* (Zürcher 2004: 56). Since the eighteenth century, in particular, imperial penetration had reinforced the economic ascendancy of non-Muslim subjects of the Empire (Göçek 1996; Karpat 2001; Kuran 2004). Over time, increasing numbers of non-Muslim subjects employed by foreign powers in different capacities were incorporated within the remit of the capitulations regime, which referred to various economic and political privileges and concessions granted to foreign powers. This enabled them to gain significant privileges (e.g. tax exemptions) and, eventually, protection by Western powers that placed them in a preferential position compared with that of Muslim merchants (Ahmad 2000: 5; Göçek 1996: 93, 97). Göçek (1996: 96) notes that, owing to the rise of Western trade and the Europeans' exclusive association with the non-Muslim minorities of the Ottoman Empire, Ottoman merchants therefore increasingly came to 'differentiate their fields of activity according to religion'.[6] Ethnic and social segmentation had also been reinforced by the modernisation reforms, including the introduction of Western-type education and the exposure to Enlightenment ideas, as well as Muslim migration from the Balkans and Russia together with the Ottoman state's migration and settlement policies. Together, these dynamics resulted in the bifurcation of the bourgeoisie (Göçek 1996; Karpat 2001: 93–97), whereby class divisions and factions increasingly became delineated along religious lines. These reinforced communal boundaries between Muslims and non-Muslims and resulted in their heightened political salience in the late Empire.

---

[5] Article 8 of the Ottoman constitution of 1876 (Kânûn-i Esâsî) states that 'All subjects of the empire are called Ottomans, without distinction whatever faith they profess; the status of an Ottoman is acquired and lost according to conditions specified by law.' The matter of equality of non-Muslims has been traced to the declarations of Sultan Mahmud II (1808–1839) to his foreign guests that, for him, there was no difference between his Muslim and non-Muslim subjects (Akyol 1998: 102–107; Bozkurt 2010: 45–51). As Hanioğlu (2010: 97) argues, these domestic reforms were tied with the efforts to gain international recognition and protect the territorial integrity of the Empire.

[6] According to Göçek, statistics from 1885 show that minorities comprised 60% of the merchants and artisans in Istanbul, with fewer than 5% being employed by the state.

Consequently, the granting of equality also met with resistance from the Empire's Muslim subjects, alongside factions within the bureaucracy itself (Hanioğlu 2010: 88; Zürcher 1984: 4, 2010: 277). For instance, Akçura notes that the failure of Ottomanism was partly owing to the negative views of equal citizenship held by Muslims and Turks, who were reluctant to give up '600 years of sovereignty', as well as Islamic doctrine which would not accept the equality of non-Muslims (1976). The trauma and polarisation caused by the Tanzimat reforms and the granting of equality, at times leading to violent reactions by Muslim subjects (Göçek 1993: 517, 1996: 114; Kara 2007; Taştan 2012), was also described in 1872 by the Ottoman statesman Ahmed Cevdet Pasha (related by Göçek 1993: 517) in his memoirs:

According to this decree, Muslim and non-Muslim subjects had to become equal before law. This affected the Muslims particularly hard. Many of the Muslims started complaining, saying, 'Today, we lost our sacred rights as a religious community, [those rights] which had been won by the blood of our fathers and forefathers. The Muslim community, which had been the dominant community, has been deprived of such a sacred right. This day is a day of mourning and despair for the Muslims.' For the minority subjects [instead], this was a day of joy.

Neither had the declaration of legal equality been enough to end the capitulations regime, and the continued imperial economic penetration and capitalist integration with Europe extended the economic demise of Muslim subjects vis-à-vis non-Muslims. Consequently, the granting of equality to non-Muslims came to be perceived by Muslim subjects not only as the loss of their politically privileged status but also as involving the expansion of the (political and economic) privileges of the non-Muslims (Kara 2007: 164–165). Indeed, Zürcher (2010: 276) has argued in this manner that:

the roots of the CUP [ITC] were to be found in the resentment felt by young Muslim bureaucrats and officers at the change in the balance of power between on the one hand the Christian bourgeoisie and the European powers who were perceived as being hand in glove with them and the Ottoman state and its servants on the other.

The Tanzimat reforms, together with previous efforts, had resulted in lasting transformation of the state bureaucracy, education and judicial systems, but Ottomanism, in short, was unsuccessful in stemming the spread of nationalisms in the Empire whereby the religiously defined *millets* had already begun to form the basis of nascent ethno-national communities (Berkes 1964: 96).

The increasing propagation of pan-Islamism during the reign of Sultan Abdülhamid II (1876–1909) was in part a response to rising nationalism, the Russian expansion into Muslim lands which saw the loss of vast non-Muslim populations during the 1877–1878 Russo-Turkish War and the politicisation of Muslim identity catalysed by the sense of loss of privileged status and competition over resources (see Chapter 5 for further discussion on the impact on Islamism). Until this period, despite the importance of Islam, identity and doctrine had been fluid in the Empire's more than 600 years of existence across different territories (Ergül 2012: 631). Indeed, the Empire had emerged at the end of the fifteenth century with a Christian majority population. Subsequent Muslimisation of the population and an emphasis on Sunni doctrine had followed the conquest of Arab lands during the reign of Selim I (1516–1518), the seizure of the caliphate by the Ottoman dynasty with the conquest of Egypt and the Battle of Chaldiran in 1514 against the Shi'a-dominated Safavid Empire. By the late nineteenth century, war, migration and Russian expansion into the Crimea had resulted in pronounced demographic changes and mass Muslim migration into the Empire. The Muslim population had risen from 59.6 per cent in the 1820s to 76.2 per cent by the 1890s (Dündar 2011: 56; Karpat 1985). This was to be followed by the near elimination of the non-Muslim populations by the establishment of the Republic, through, among other cases of ethnic cleansing, the Armenian Genocide in 1915, involving the massacre of an estimated million people. These demographic shifts occurred at a time when there was an increased focus on the numerical size of the various communities in the Empire which gained importance for claims of national and territorial rights. Indeed, it was only in the last decades of the Empire that the term *ekalliyet* ('minority') was introduced (Ortaylı 2012: 16) and the very rise of modern nation-states made the categories of majority and minority relevant (B. T. White 2011: 27).[7] Indeed, the development of national consciousness or nation building involves not just a process of majoritisation in which there is an attempt to homogenise heterogeneity, but an attendant emergence of minorities or minoritisation of elements that do not fit this constructed majority bloc and who are marginalised and viewed as suspect (Williams 1989: 435; Wimmer 2002: 62–63). Consequently, not only did the elites become cognisant of the majority–minority numerical balance, but also,

---

[7] B. T. White (2011: 22–23) notes that 'the use of the word "minority" in the modern sense – meaning a culturally defined group within a polity whose members face legal, political, or social disadvantages because of their cultural belonging – is relatively recent'. Connected to the rise of the modern state with the spread of nationalism and ideas of popular sovereignty following the 1789 French Revolution, the word appeared in the mid-1800s and gained global currency around the First World War (B. T. White 2011: 22–23, 27).

the delineation of these boundaries along religious lines was augmented through demographic changes and the spread of nationalism (Kale 2014: 256, 259; Karpat 1985).

Within this context, the Hamidian period marked the first self-conscious drive to construct a homogenous social base, involving an emphasis on (Hanefi) Sunni Islamic doctrine and identity alongside a focus on Turkish identity, which was propagated particularly in military schools (Alkan 2009: 64–66; Deringil 1998: 48; Zürcher 2010: 274). As Zürcher (2010: 274) notes, 'In order to increase solidarity and unity on the basis of Islam, a single, standardized and controlled form of "national" or Ottoman Islam had to be promoted.' However, while the 1912–1913 Balkan Wars and loss of Christian lands had largely undermined Ottomanism, subsequent revolts and loss of (Muslim majority) Arab lands played a role in weakening pan-Islamism.[8] Consequently, there was a greater shift towards both Islamism (Kayalı 1997: 8) and Turkish nationalism with the ascent of the Young Turk movement as the ITC (Hanioğlu 1995; Kushner 1977) began to assert greater power following the restoration of the constitution in 1908, eventually seizing power in 1913. Yet even if pan-Islamism as a political project became less desirable by the end of the First World War, Islam and Muslim identity remained constitutive elements of Turkish nationalism. As Ziya Gökalp, a major nationalist ideologue of the ITC and later the Republic, declared, 'I belong to the Turkish nation, the Islamic *ummah*, and Western civilisation.' His focus on synthesising what he identified as the necessary processes of Turkification, Islamisation and modernisation to save the state and 'catch up' with the West epitomised the ITC's ideology during the second constitutional period, effectively reversing Abdülhamid's Islamic–Turkish synthesis into a Turkish–Islamic synthesis (TIS) and subsequently underpinning nation building in the early Republic (Alkan 2009: 64; Davison 1995). According to Tunaya, the ITC was as Islamist as it was Turkish nationalist (Tunaya 1952).

Indeed, the dynamics of class bifurcation and ethnic segmentation based on religion fundamentally shaped the evolving nationalist consciousness and movement. For the ITC, the construction of a 'national bourgeoisie' (Toprak 1995) came to be regarded as a vital element of nation building given the disintegrating Empire and an economy dominated by non-Muslim subjects, whose interests were seen to be beholden to their external sponsors and partners under the capitulations regime. However, Turkification of the economy or creation of a national

---

[8] The Balkans comprised 69% of the population and 83% of Ottoman territory in Europe (Çağaptay 2006).

economy essentially involved state efforts to expand and advantage a Muslim bourgeoisie and to create a Muslim Turkish majority based and dominated economy. These policies accelerated in the second constitutional period and particularly following the Balkan Wars (Koraltürk 2011: 30–31, 56; Toprak 1995: 19), supported by campaigns such as the Muslim boycott in 1913–1914 of non-Muslim businesses accused of supporting the enemy side (Toprak 1995: 5). The ITC gained an opportunity with the outbreak of the First World War to push ahead with its efforts to establish a national (in effect, Muslim) bourgeoisie and abrogate the privileges of non-Muslim subjects enjoyed under the capitulations regime. In large part, however, Muslim domination of the economy (see Chapter 4 for further discussion) was achieved by war and demographic engineering, including migration, population exchanges, genocide and ethnic cleansing which together enabled the (violent) transfer of wealth from non-Muslim to Muslim subjects of the Ottoman Empire and, later, citizens of the Republic (Koraltürk 2011: 56). Around a million orthodox Christians had migrated to Greece by 1922, while the population exchange agreed upon at the Lausanne Convention in 1923 led to the transfer of a further 1.5 million Orthodox Christians to Greece in exchange for around 0.5 million Muslims sent to Turkey (Kolluoğlu 2013: 536–539).

The Establishment of the Turkish Republic as a Critical Juncture

Following the subsequent dissolution of the Ottoman Empire and the Turkish War of Independence (1919–1923), nation-state builders arrived at a critical juncture. In other words, it was a moment of heightened contingency when elites could either enact significant changes by adopting brand-new institutions and generate new patterns of path dependency or simply maintain existing institutions and thereby entrench the status quo (Lerner 2014: 387). Thanks in large part to the success of the independence struggle, nation-state builders enjoyed a large degree of freedom to enact new institutional arrangements. Yet, the available paths were delimited by two antecedent conditions – the intertwined nature of religious institutions and the state and heightened levels of social closure – which increased the political salience of religious boundaries between the Muslim majority and the non-Muslim minority and saw the rise of Turkish nationalism. At the same time, elements of continuity with the late Ottoman state were ensured by the leading role of ITC cadres in the independence struggle and the fact that the state apparatus in the Republic largely maintained the imperial bureaucracy and army, subject to some purges, as well as the educational institutions that produced them (Zürcher 2010: 144–146). Some 83 per cent of the Empire's civil servants and 93 per cent of staff officers had retained their positions in the new Republic (Rustow 1981: 73). On the other hand, nation-state builders also proceeded with revolutionary steps such as the declaration of a republic and the abolition of the sultanate and caliphate. Accordingly, there has been a tendency to emphasise that religious institutions underwent the greatest change in the Republic (Zürcher 2010: 144–145; Kuru 2009). Focusing chiefly on the secularisation reforms and the constitutional principle of laicism adopted during the early years of the Republic, accounts have typically presented Turkish secularism as what Charles Taylor has described as 'subtraction stories' in which religion, having filled a certain space, contracts and becomes replaced by secular norms (Taylor 2011). Thus a grand narrative of authoritarian secular modernisation has been taken for granted and understood in zero-sum terms as involving a subtraction of religion and its replacement by secular Turkish nationalism with the relegation of Islam to the private sphere. According to this narrative, the move to multi-party democracy in the 1950s subsequently reversed these trends owing to the failure of Kemalism to fill this space as an emotional equivalent (Findley 2010: 256; Kalaycıoğlu 2005: 55–56; Lewis 1968; Mardin 1971: 197–211).

Yet during this period of nation-state building, the project of secularism and constitution making also involved, implicitly and explicitly, privileging one religion. Beyond delineating relations between state and religion, it therefore also involved constructing the nation as a (Sunni) Muslim Turkish majority. As Kaufmann and Haklai (2008) argue, the advent of popular sovereignty in parallel with the emergence of the nation-state involved a shift from dominant minority rule to dominant majority ethnicity. Since the 'state embodies the idea and political practice of *national* sovereignty', the perceived ethnicisation of the state meant that competition for resources would appear to be determined on the basis of belonging to that particular majority, and as such, it can lead to contestation and a sense of discrimination (Wimmer 1997). The project of secularism can reinforce this process. This is because, rather than simply drawing the boundaries between the private and public roles of religion, it can involve a process of drawing boundaries of national identity, especially in cases where religious identities perform the function of ethnic markers. As Calhoun et al. (2011: 16) highlight, this is in the sense that 'the secular realm is sometimes constructed in a manner that implicitly privileges one type of religion while more or less expressly delegitimizing other sorts of religious engagement'. By delineating the borders of the majority and minority religious populations of the nation-state, it therefore facilitates group-making and the politicisation of religio-ethnic identities. Consequently, 'in a secular, democratic state whose citizens are seen, by religious as well as secular-nationalist observers, to be divided into "the majority [religious] community" and "religious minorities," there will tend to be an elision between the politically representative character of government on the one hand and the state's national presentation of itself on the other. Assisting this elision will be the dominant nationalist discourse which identifies the history of "the nation" with the history of "the [religious] majority"' (Asad 1992: 11). How this came about in the Turkish case is revealed by constitution making in the early Republic.

Constitution Making, Religion and State in the Early Republic

The 1921 Constitution

When the first constitution of the Republic was adopted in 1921, questions about the precise nature of the nascent nation-state, fundamental principles and the role of religion had largely been left untouched or postponed. This was because the Teşkilat-ı Esasiye (Law of Fundamental Organization, or 1921 Constitution) had been adopted by the nationalist movement in the midst of the independence struggle (1919–1923) to establish a new executive authority and parliament based in Ankara, against the Ottoman government in İstanbul that was subjugated by occupation forces. As a result, it was a short document, reflecting the need to hold a diverse coalition together during a time of war. While the independence struggle (which came together as the defence of rights associations) was largely mobilised by the ITC cadres, they had also co-opted ITC army officers, members of the *ulema* and other local elites into the national movement (Zürcher 2004: 148; 2010: 221–222). Consequently, the first parliamentary period (1920–1923) and the 1921 constitutional drafters were relatively pluralistic, comprising a coalition of different factions, actors and movements with different political visions for the new state, from Bolshevism to Islamism and conservatism (Akın 2001: 52–53) and with different ethnic and religious backgrounds (such as Kurdish and Alevi), who had joined forces during war. Out of 380 lawmakers, 18 per cent were members of the *ulema* and *tariqa* sheikhs, which does not include Islamists such as Mehmet Akif, who were also in the assembly (Akın 2001: 49–50; Aktürk 2015: 789; Akyol 2008: 145), while soldiers comprised 13 per cent, civil servants and retirees 30 per cent, farmers 12 per cent and merchants 10 per cent

(Aydemir 1976: 365).[9] The nationalist coalition, as Bein notes, was a 'big tent' under which diverging ideological and sociocultural groups came together (2011: 105). Still, boundaries between them were fluid and overlapping rather than polarised, and crucially, Islam was a common denominator of this political alliance.

During this period of constitution making under conditions of war, lawmakers were focused particularly on immediate matters, such as establishing the basis of representation and the extent of local government. Where there was disagreement, the matter was temporarily resolved through a fudge, or compromise. Indeed, several lawmakers resisted the introduction of the concept of national sovereignty, arguing that sovereignty could only rest with God and that the nationalist assembly could not contravene the 1876 constitution, which placed sovereignty in the 'sacred' person of the sultan-caliph. This had resulted in various revisions to the final document, including a reference to the enforcement of *shari'a* (Article 7), which outlined the legal remit of the TBMM, the replacement of the word *meclis* ('parliament') with *shura* in order to reflect what some lawmakers described as the Muslim character of the population, and a direct link to the 1876 constitution (Özbudun 1992: 37). Equally controversial was the matter of the caliphate's future after the Constitutional Commission removed an article referring to a commitment to the rescue and reinstatement of the sultan-caliph following independence. The lawmakers had only dropped their insistence on a direct reference to the caliph after reassurances by Mustafa Kemal and his supporters that the primary goal of the TBMM was the protection of the sultan-caliph and that it would be unwise to abandon the office given its importance to the Islamic world. Consequently, the 1921 Constitution emerged to some extent as a contradictory document in comprising both the principle of national sovereignty and *shari'a* (Özbudun 1992: 37) alongside the continued reference to the 1876 Constitution.

Despite this diversity in the first assembly, there was, nevertheless, consensus on the people whom the constitution addressed. For one, a common denominator was that all of the members were Muslim, as required by the electoral rules prepared by the Committee of Representation (Heyet-i Temsiliye), which was the executive of the independence movement, despite the fact that non-Muslims still comprised around

---

[9] These numbers vary owing to poor records and the fact that some of the elected lawmakers were unable to join the assembly (Akın 2001: 49–51). According to Demirel (2010: 231), the *ulema* comprised 11.8% of the assembly, while Tunaya (1957: 231) notes that fourteen muftis, thirteen mudarris and ten sheikhs represented the different *tariqa* orders (Mevlevi, Bektashi and Naqhibandi).

one-tenth of the population (Aktürk 2015: 789; Okutan 2004:148). While no reference was made to Turkish national identity in the constitutional debates or the final codified 1921 document, nation-state builders clearly conceptualised their role as representatives of Muslim subjects remaining in the Ottoman territories. An explicit reference to the 'Islamic majority' was inserted into the 1921 parliamentary declaration outlining the duties of the TBMM (Özbudun 1992: 22), which was conceived as the embodiment and representative of the Muslim community. As Zürcher notes, the political and military leaders of the independence struggle were motivated by what he has described as a type of Ottoman–Muslim nationalism – 'the nationalist programme is based on an ethnicity whose membership is determined largely by religious affiliation' (Yavuz 2003: 45; Zürcher 2010: 229–231) – which also meant minimising the number of non-Muslims within the remaining territories. Indeed, this was a reflection of the high levels of social closure at the end of the Empire, and as such, the approach towards non-Muslim minorities was dismissive and exclusionary. This was spelt out by a prominent Turkish nationalist member of the Constitutional Commission, Mahmut Esat (Bozkurt) Bey, who declared that the fears relating to Christians entering parliament were misplaced because Muslims constituted the majority and Christians had lost their rights since 'they resigned from citizenship owing to their betrayal [during the late Ottoman Empire]' (ZC 7 November 1336: 43).[10] This concern with the construction and elevation of the Sunni Muslim, and later, Turkish, majority was to remain a key concern of decision-makers and political actors in subsequent periods of constitution making.

Nationalising State Building and Constitution Making in the 1920s

Nation-state builders waited until after the end of the War of Independence and declaration of the Turkish Republic in 1923 to tackle fundamental questions about the shape and nature of the nascent state. As Zürcher (2010: 223) notes, the principle of self-determination of the 'Turkish parts of the Ottoman Empire' articulated in President Woodrow Wilson's Fourteen Points outlined in 1918, had been a crucial reference point for the resistance movement. Indeed, Turkish nationalism had been gaining currency among Ottoman elites and politics from the early 1900s. By the end of the war and the negotiations at Lausanne

---

[10] Bozkurt later served as justice minister and is regarded as a prominent Turkish nationalist and is also known for his statements about the superiority of the Turkish race.

in 1923, the Ankara government was keen to overturn the 1920 Sèvres Treaty which had partitioned Ottoman lands between the imperial powers and included the creation of an independent Armenian Republic in major concessions to Greece and a Kurdish entity. The decisions made in this period would prove consequential for the nature of religion and state relations. Even during periods of heightened contingency, however, antecedent conditions and institutional and political legacies are important in influencing the range of options and paths available for actors (Koinova 2013). In this vein, nation-state builders in the 1920s faced two crucial antecedent conditions with respect to religion. First, they confronted the intertwined relationship between Islam and state, symbolically and legally, as well as the integration of the *ulema* within the Ottoman state, which had evolved over centuries. The second legacy was the emergence of religious categories as ethnic markers owing to a confluence of developments, including the polarisation of ethnic segmentation under the *millet* system, war, the dynamics of class formation influenced by imperial penetration and demographic shifts involving the devastation of the non-Muslim population and the Muslimisation of the land (Karpat 2001). This underpinned the high level of social closure in the late 1920s, which was further exacerbated by ongoing international pressure (the Treaty of Lausanne on the treatment of minorities) and historical memory (including the traumas relating to the break-up of the Empire, minority nationalisms and the so-called Sèvres mentality – fear of the designs of Western powers to divide the country; see Robins [2003: 103–105]). Consequently, the prevalent forms of social closure by the establishment of the Republic in 1923 were based on religious delineations.

The ways in which nation building influences constitution making and how national identity is codified reflect the specific legacies faced by state builders. Kissane and Sitter (2010a, 2010b) have differentiated between the earlier European constitutional tradition whereby constitutions represented a contract between different actors regarding the distribution of power, and the later constitutions adopted following the collapse of empires in the aftermath of the First World War, which drew a more explicit link between national identity and the constitution. The Turkish constitutional experience reflected the latter tradition in being explicitly nationalist and majoritising rather than a liberal effort to constrain and set bounds on the exercise of power. Accordingly, the Turkish state which emerged in the 1920s was not just a national but also a 'nationalising' one, concerned with establishing a core nation that involved the elevation and construction of a dominant majority ethnicity that was to be the owner of the state (Brubaker 2011). Additionally, owing to the prevalent forms of social closure in this period, this involved the construction and claim to primacy of a Sunni (Hanefi) Muslim Turkish majority. This, in turn, was reflected in the construction of the principle of laicism and the manner in which state–religion relations were institutionalised.

From the establishment of the Republic on 29 October 1923, the parliament adopted sweeping reforms. To begin with, Islam was explicitly included in the constitution as the state religion, together with the declaration of the Republic. This was greeted by the prominent Turkish nationalist and writer Mehmet Emin Yurdakul with, 'Today the Turkish nation has established at Ankara what Prophet Muhammed established fourteen centuries ago within the walls of Mecca' (ZC 29 October 1339 [1923]: 96). This was followed by chants of 'long live the Republic' within the assembly and a statement by Sheikh Saffet Efendi (a prominent member of the *ulema* and a deputy[11]) that the inclusion of Islam had only made explicit the underlying principle of the Teşkilat-ı Esasiye, which he declared was more Islamic than the 1876 Constitution (ZC 29 October 1339 [1923]: 96–97). However, on 3 March 1924, three major constitutional amendments significantly altered the nature of the state–religion relationship by undermining the socio-legal status of Islam through a significant narrowing of the role of the *ulema*. This included the unification of education (Tevhid-i Tedrisat, Article 430), resulting in the closure of the *medreses*; the abolition of the ŞEV (Article 429), which was replaced by the Diyanet; and most controversially, the abolition of the caliphate (Article 431). With the exception of the latter, these amendments generated little debate in parliament. By this period, oppositional voices had been silenced to a great extent with the increasing hold on the national assembly of Mustafa Kemal's First Group – from which he would form the People's Party (Halk Fırkası, which was subsequently renamed as the CHP) – following the 28 June 1923 elections and his manoeuvrings that limited the participation of opponents during the vote on the amendments (Demirel 2013: 66–67). Moreover, in a somewhat shrewd move, the bills for the abolition of the caliphate and the ŞEV were proposed by members of the *ulema*, who argued that the caliphate was not an Islamic requirement, noting that, in any case, other schools

---

[11] Also known as Saffet Kemaleddin Yetkin, Efendi was a Halveti tariqa leader, a politician who served as a deputy in the Ottoman parliament and in the Turkish Republic. In 1918, he was appointed to the head of the Ottoman Council of Sheikhs (Meclis-i Meşâyih), where he served until 1919. He was one of the deputies to propose the law abolishing the caliphate.

of Sunni Islam had not generally recognised the claim to the caliphate of the (Hanefi) Sunni Ottoman rulers.

Subsequently, the adoption of the Swiss Civil Code in 1926 had left no further dominion for *shari'a*, and in 1928, what remained largely as a symbolic reference to Islam was removed from the constitution, while at the same time, the alphabet was also Latinised. The principle of laicism, previously incorporated into the CHP's programme in 1931 as part of six main principles – republicanism, nationalism, populism, statism and revolutionism (or reformism) – that comprised the six arrows of the party logo, was finally incorporated into the constitution in 1937. The six arrows came to represent what was called Kemalism, or Atatürkism, in the 1930s, forming 'the basis for indoctrination in schools, the media, and the army' (Zürcher 2004: 128). Lawmakers reasoned that these amendments were necessary to respond to the needs of the times and the desire to reflect the political programme of the state to legally express the nation's commitment to Atatürk's principles and 'not rest the state and nation's administration in mystical and dogmatic principles' (ZC 5 February 1937: 60). Evincing anti-clericalism, lawmakers blamed the *ulema* for the 'disasters' that had befallen the Turks (ZC 5 February 1937: 60). This was the contention of Interior Minister Şükrü Kaya, who declared:

Since we are determinists in history, and since we are pragmatic materialists in execution, then we have to make our own laws [. . .] only this will save the material state of the country. The development of the Turks' pure morality will help their spiritual state. This is why we declared our laicism first. We do not intervene in individuals' freedom of conscience or freedom to belong to any religion. What we want is freedom, what we mean by laicism is to avoid religion influencing or motivating country matters. (ZC 5 February 1937: 60)

Yet the emergence of laicism had been reflective of a power struggle within the state, which involved the elevation of one faction of the independence struggle coalition over others. Indeed, as Calhoun et al. argue,

The assertion of secularism may often seem to be no more than an assertion of neutrality vis-à-vis religion or religions. But when it is written into a constitution, it typically reflects events that are not in any way neutral: the ascendency of a new political party, a revolution, or an interstate conflict. So there is always a kind of political context, and it needs to be asked of particular secular regimes what they express in that political context and how they shape distributions of power and recognition. (2011: 16)

Using Chaves's (1994: 750, 756) depiction, secularisation reforms in this period can therefore be characterised as a decline in the scope of religious authority rather than a decline or 'cleansing' of religion, which was

crucially subject to change over time. In this vein, marking the dominance of Mustafa Kemal's faction, the composition of the second national
assembly following the 1923 election was far less pluralistic compared to
the first one between 1921 and 1923. Yet, while this essentially involved
the sidelining of what has typically been considered to be the more
conservative Second Group of the first assembly, Koçak notes that it
would be misleading to conclude that there was much difference between
the two assemblies (2005; Akın 2001: 59). However, debate and divisions remained, becoming pronounced in the 1930s with the emergence
of socialist-oriented (e.g. the Kadro intellectuals[12]) and traditionalist-
socialist circles within the elites and extraparliamentary groups
(Çetinsaya 1999: 366; İrem 2002: 96).

In any case, the unfolding of secularisation laws from 1924, together
with the adoption of martial law in March 1925 in the wake of the Sheikh
Said Rebellion, had facilitated the ascent and consolidation of power of
the First Group, which became the CHP after 1923, through the disestablishment of religion and by constraining factions within the ruling
elite, including the *ulema*. Matters such as the abolition of the caliphate
reflected the concerns of nationalists regarding not only its transnational
links with Islam and becoming an alternative centre of power and opposition, but also a power struggle within the elite, with some seeing the
caliph as the only counterweight to the growing dominance of Mustafa
Kemal (Deringil 1993b: 177; Earle 1925; Zürcher 2004: 166–167).[13]

Similarly, during the 1924 constitutional debates, drafters were more
concerned about resisting the expansion of Mustafa Kemal's presidential
powers than the future of religious institutions. Such divisions, as well as
strategic, and to some extent ideological, differences, resulted in the
establishment in late 1924 of the Progressive Republican Party (Terakki-
perver Cumhuriyet Fırkası). This experiment was to prove short-lived,
and increasingly in the second half of the 1920s, the distribution of power
within the government had shifted, resulting in the ascendancy of a more
anti-clerical and positivist faction of the ruling coalition.

A visible sign of this struggle was the reduction in MPs drawn from the
ulema or educated in religious schools, while those with a military background increased. In the second parliamentary period, the number of
ulema in the national assembly dropped to 4.2 per cent of the total from

[12] The Kadro (Cadre) circles were so named after the journal *Kadro*, which was published
by leftist writers in the early 1930s. Sanctioned by the regime, they were committed to
the Republic and sought to propose an alternative development strategy in the wake of
the 1929 Global Economic Depression. See Türkeş (2001).

[13] Historian Mete Tunçay (2005: 216) has also alleged that a consideration in the abolition
of the caliphate was the existence of Alevi communities.

18 per cent prior to the 1923 elections, whereas the number of soldiers rose to 19.8 per cent from 13 per cent (Demirel: 2010: 328). Similarly, the number of lawmakers with religious education dropped from 24.5 per cent in the 1920–1923 parliament to 3.3 per cent in 1943–1946 (327). Yet despite the domination of government by the 'Kemalist' faction since the late 1920s, this had not meant that the state was completely overtaken. Conservatives, Islamists and the *ulema* remained and formed other institutional arms of the state. While subdued during the one-party era, given the suppression of all types of politics, including religious (Islamic and Alevi) practices that the regime feared could pose a threat to the Republic, the balance of power was to shift with the move to multi-partism and contingent events. The fate of the Ottoman *ulema*, which were absorbed by the Diyanet, and its strategies of struggle and compromise with other factions of the state will be examined in more detail in Chapters 2 and 3.

The project of secularism was not only an ideological project by positivist or military-bureaucratic Kemalist elites. It also heralded the construction and ascendancy of a Muslim majority from the perspective of nation-state builders. Debate about the nature of the relationship between religion and state, including the question of the extent to which Western constitutionalism was in line with the Islamic tradition, and indeed many of the reforms of the early Republic, were certainly not novel and can be dated to the late Empire. One of the first explicit references to and defences of the principle of laicism is traced to Ali Suavi (Bozkurt 2010: 54), a Muslim intellectual (and an early Islamist or Turkist, according to some accounts) who was a prominent member of the Young Ottomans (Yeni Osmanlılar), established in 1865 in reaction to Tanzimat reforms and to push for constitutional government based on Islamic principles (Hanioğlu 2010: 103; Karpat 1972: 262–270; Zürcher 2010: 68). The edict of the Tanzimat had initiated debate about the adoption of a civil code, pitting different factions of the Ottoman bureaucracy against each other, with one side arguing for the French Civil Code to provide equality between Muslims and non-Muslims, and the other arguing that the Ottoman Civil Code should be compatible with Islamic law (Bozkurt 1998: 292–293). This matter was finalised in the Republic with the adoption of the Swiss Civil Code. With the ascendancy of the positivist and Westernist-oriented ITC during the second constitutional period, the matter of laicism and women's rights were also increasingly being debated in the public realm (Bozkurt 2010: 95–96). These debates, which had particularly intensified during the Tanzimat period and led to the increasing push by Ottoman intellectuals and bureaucrats for the adoption of Western legal codes, related not just to the diffusion of European and Enlightenment ideas, however. They were crucially linked to concerns about ensuring the unity of the Empire following nationalist agitation among non-Muslims and imperial penetration, which had also been a key trigger to the modernisation drive of the Ottoman state. Secularism was thereby discussed within the context of debates about how to prevent imperial penetration on behalf of the various non-Muslim communities that enjoyed privileges and protection from Western powers.

In the late Ottoman Empire, the debate about the secularisation of the legal framework had not only emerged as a result of the engagement with and penetration of positivist and Westernist ideas but was also fundamentally tied to the national question. Both for the Ottoman authorities and for the founders of the Republic, the status of non-Muslims was used as a pretext for imperial penetration and undermined state sovereignty, as experienced under the capitulations regime. Therefore, in the early Republic, laicism also came to be perceived as essential to eliminating the privileges of non-Muslims. Following the War of Independence and during the Lausanne Convention in 1922 to 1923, the status of non-Muslims and capitulations had emerged as a key sticking point among the imperial powers and the representatives of the nascent Turkish Republic. For the republican elites, the lifting of the capitulations regime could be secured and further future intervention on behalf of non-Muslims prevented if the equality of non-Muslims could be granted under secular laws. Consequently, the promise of the adoption of a secular civil code was given during the Lausanne negotiations in order to avoid the continuation of privileges for non-Muslims on the basis that they were not protected under *shari'a*, which was still in force at the time (Aktar 2000: 109–110; Akyol 1998; Bozkurt 2010). Similarly, Aktar (2009: 37) also argues that the enactment of the civil code was not 'just "a step leading to the level of contemporary civilization," since this law provided the Kemalists also with the magic key that let them not just be in power, but also made them capable of exerting unlimited power over the citizens of the Turkish State'.[14] The capitulations regime was thereby officially abolished by the Lausanne Treaty, having been abrogated by the ITC with the outbreak of the First World War. These considerations were reflected in the debates about the adoption of a secular civil code in 1926, when constitutional drafters reasoned that its adoption was necessary for 'national sovereignty [...] because if laws are based on religion, a

---

[14] Minority representatives were forced to renounce rights granted to them under the Lausanne Treaty, including maintaining their own personal status laws, just before the enactment of the civil code (Aktar 2009: 38).

state that accepts freedom of conscience will have to enact different laws for different groups of subjects, and such a state of affairs is completely discordant with the political, social, and national unity required by contemporary states' (Aktar 2009: 37; Bozkurt 2010: 193).

The stipulations of the Lausanne Treaty had also acted as a constraint on definitions of the Turkish nation and citizenship during the drafting of the 1924 Constitution. In fact, this had parallels with the circumstances preceding the introduction of a more inclusive definition of the Ottoman subject during the Tanzimat era and the granting of equality to non-Muslims, which were partly an outcome of external pressures. While the 1921 Constitution had introduced the concept of national sovereignty, the 1924 version established the concept of the Turkish nation. Compared with its complete absence from the 1921 Constitution, there are nineteen references to 'Turk', 'Turkish' and 'Turkishness' in the 1924 Constitution, alongside a significant focus by lawmakers on the need to 'Turkify' the language of the constitution away from Arabic. Together with the Turkification of the constitution, there had also been the continued Turkification of place names to make them in line with Islam and Turkishness, a move traced to ITC policies in the Ottoman Empire (Bayır 2016: 105–106; Üngör 2012: 240–245).[15] Yet, together with this emphasis on Turkishness, religion remained a clear marker of what comprised a Turk, and being Sunni Muslim continued to be a constitutive element of national identity.

Crucially, during the 1924 debates, nationalising constitutional framers had clearly differentiated between what constituted the nation and citizenship, a demarcation that was largely based on religion. The initial proposal for the article on Turkish citizenship had treated it as congruous with nationality: 'all people in Turkey without distinction of race and religion are Turks'. This was chiefly based on the Ottoman constitution of 1876 (and the Ottoman Nationality Law of 1869), which had declared that 'all subjects of the empire are called Ottomans, without distinction whatever faith they profess' (Article 8). Nationality was to be achieved, therefore, on the grounds of either *jus soli* (right of soil, including those born in the specified territory) or *jus sanguinis* (right of blood, including children of subjects/nationals). However, such a formulation was objected to by lawmakers in 1924 as they argued that there should be

---

[15] Turkification measures continued with steps such as the 1932 Law on Reserving Certain Professions, Trades, and Services to Turkish Citizens; the 1934 Law of Family Names; the 'Citizen, Speak Turkish!' campaigns launched in the late 1920s; and the various economic Turkification measures which restricted or ended the employment of non-Muslims by the state. For discussion of these policies, see Aktar (2009), Bali (2006) and Bayır (2016).

a distinction between a Turkish national and a citizen of Turkey. In a telling exposition on Turkish national identity, a Constitutional Commission reporter declared during constitutional debates that:

Our genuine citizens are those that are Muslim, of the Hanefi sect and speak Turkish [...] there used to be the title of Ottoman which was inclusive. We are abolishing this title. In its place, a Turkish Republic has come to exist. Not all of the individuals in this Turkish Republic are Turkish and Muslim. What are we going to do with them? There are Greeks, Armenians, Jews, there are all sorts of elements. Thankfully they are a minority. If we do not give the title of Turk to them what do we say? (ZC 20 March 1340 [1924]: 910)

While the reporter's words were met with noises from the chamber of Turkey, it was not possible to adopt a more exclusivist definition of Turkish citizenship. The Constitutional Commission reporter warned that this was restricted by the terms of the Lausanne Treaty.[16] Following further discussion about how to restrict the definition of Turk without contravening the Lausanne Treaty, Article 88 was revised in a manner that sidestepped the issue of defining the substance of a Turkish nation: 'All people in Turkey without distinction of race and religion are Turkish *citizens* [my emphasis]'. Consequently, despite the adoption of a putatively inclusive concept of citizenship, for the constitutional framers, religion remained a clear marker of what comprised a Turk, as demonstrated by their resistance to including non-Muslims as nationals. Equally, this reveals how nation building involves a process of minoritisation or the emergence of 'minorities' – including Kurds, Alevis, Armenians, Jews and Christians – who become stigmatised and marginalised as falling outside of the (constructed) majority.

This distinction made by nation-state builders was reflected in different practices of the state, such as refugee and immigration policies, which were biased in favour of Muslims with Turkish descent and of Sunni Hanefi background (Kirişci 2000: 4) as well as economic policies. To ensure the monopolisation of the economy by the Muslim Turkish majority, the Republic continued the Turkification, or rather, Muslimisation, efforts of the ITC adopted from 1908 to 1922. Examples of these policies include the displacement of the Jewish population with the Thrace Incident in 1934; the discriminatory Wealth Tax of 1942–1944; the adoption in 1932 of Law No. 2007 reserving certain professions only for Turkish citizens; and the Turkish language campaigns from 1937. Businesses were instructed by the central government to replace non-

---

[16] Article 37 of the Treaty of Lausanne states, 'The Turkish Government undertakes to assure full and complete protection of life and liberty to all inhabitants of Turkey without distinction of birth, nationality, language, race or religion.'

Muslim workers with Muslim Turks during the early Republic. Bracketing the question of Alevi identity (see Chapter 3), estimated to comprise some 15 to 20 per cent of the population according to official censuses that categorise Alevis as Muslims, by 1927, the Republic's first census showed that the non-Muslim share of the population had declined to just 2.64 per cent from 20 per cent in 1912 (over the same territory) (Çağaptay 2002; Koraltürk 2011: 26–27). Following the 5–6 September 1955 attacks against minorities involving the violent appropriation of their wealth, non-Muslims had fallen to less than 1 per cent of the population. Thus, contrary to analyses of Turkish nationalism that differentiate between its ethnic and civic (territorially defined and inclusive) forms (e.g. Bora 2003a: 437; Parla and Davison 2004: 68–69), Islam remained the defining marker of identity, alongside language. Aktürk (2009: 906) has, in this vein, underscored the 'continuity between the Islamic *millet* as an Ottoman legacy and the formulation of Turkish nationhood'.

Constitution Making after the Transition to Multi-Partism: Continuity and Change

The 1961 Constitution

Compared with nationalising constitution making in the 1920s, the 1961 document was prepared after the struggle within the state had culminated and was – temporarily – subdued by a military coup. The balance of power within the state had begun to shift towards rightist traditionalist-conservative Islamist factions, especially by the 1940s, as the one-party regime came under growing internal and external pressure. At the seventh congress of the CHP held in 1947, the split between the different factions became especially apparent in the debate about laicism, with one side arguing for the reform of religion by the government and the other that it should be left to the *ulema* (Tunaya 2007: 171–175). According to Çetinsaya (1999: 366–367), the traditionalist-conservatives developed 'four philosophical and political lines during this time: anti-collectivism/societalism; cultural nationalism; modernist Islam; and anti-positivist modernism', which overlapped on some levels with Islamism. This faction within the state had argued during 1947 that religion was important both for public morality and as a bulwark against communism. Based on this, they called for the expansion of religious education and the Diyanet, arguing that the latter should either be made autonomous or be given greater resources. However, another more radical faction disputed the role of religion as an antidote to communism, arguing that the survival of the Turkish nation depended not on religion but on the Turkish race. Instead, they saw the expansion of religious infrastructure as compromising laicism.

Together with intra-regime struggles, of equal importance was the impact of increasing class differentiation, the prominence of a domestic bourgeoisie cultivated by the state and, externally, the emergence of the Cold War in the aftermath of the Second World War. The transition to multi-partism in 1946 therefore addressed both intensifying intra-elite divisions and growing discontent at home and was also viewed by the regime as a means of extracting political and economic support from Western powers, including protection from Soviet demands. Meanwhile, from the perspective of Western powers, Turkey was emerging as a critical element of anti-communist strategies and the encirclement of the Soviet Bloc (Angrist 2004: 239; Zürcher 2004: 208–209), which was marked by its inclusion in the North Atlantic Treaty Organization (NATO) in 1952. These contingent events were to have a lasting impact on the balance of power between different elements of the Turkish state, empowering more rightist, traditionalist-conservative Islamist elements and policies. For one, the Cold War related anti-communism drive from the late 1940s was important for the expansion of religious infrastructure, including religious education and the role of the Diyanet, along with creation of anti-communist associations by state actors in cooperation with Islamist and rightist actors such as the Association for Fighting Communism (Komünizmle Mücadele Derneği, KMD). In 1949, the CHP had even appointed as prime minister (1949–1950) Şemsettin Günaltay, an Islamist who was a frequent writer for Islamist journals such as *Sebilürreşad*, which was also closely associated with the senior *ulema* within the Diyanet.[17]

The Democrat Party (Demokrat Partisi, DP), established by former members of the CHP, ascended to power in 1950 and became the dominant party of the decade. It had employed a combination of populist appeals, politics and patronage to build its support, appealing particularly to the peasantry in a still largely agrarian society of small producers (Sunar 2004: 124–128). Initially, the party had continued the loosening of restrictions on political life and religious activity that the CHP had initiated in the late 1940s, but it had become increasingly authoritarian towards the end of the decade as economic crisis and mismanagement precipitated a declining vote share. The drift towards authoritarianism

---

[17] It is widely thought that the CHP's decision to make an Islamist and *medrese* graduate, Günaltay, prime minister during the transition to multi-partism was driven by electoral concerns.

was facilitated by the highly majoritarian political system (in Lijphart's sense; see Chapter 6) established by the 1924 Constitution, which reflected the majoritising and nationalising concerns of state builders. In this vein, the Turkish system comprised a highly centralised government with no checks and balances in the form of a separation of powers constraining the sovereignty of the parliamentary majority and, thereby, the concentration of power in the executive. The subsequent transition to multi-party politics in 1946 was achieved with only small changes in the media, electoral and association laws and without an overhaul of the unconstrained majoritarian political system (Özbudun 2000: 53).

Together with this, the growing socio-economic crisis and political contestation in the 1950s formed the backdrop to a military takeover in 1960, which resulted in the closure of the DP. The 1961 Constitution was prepared under the auspices of the military – which was itself deeply divided and comprised various competing factions (Jacoby 2003: 674; Ulus 2010: 15) – and drafted by a Constituent Assembly composed of the National Unity Committee (Milli Birlik Komitesi, MBK), comprising the military junta leaders and the partially indirectly elected Assembly of Representatives, which was largely dominated by the CHP or its sympathisers, with no representation of the DP.[18] A key concern of constitutional framers in the Constituent Assembly was the moderation of the unrestrained majoritarianism of the political system founded by the 1924 Constitution, which also partly underpinned the DP's increasing authoritarianism, through the introduction of separation of powers, judicial review, a proportional representation (PR) electoral system and a bicameral parliament (Tanör 1995: 309–313). However, together with the constitutional framers' efforts to impose checks and balances against majoritarian government, the military was also moved to position itself as a tutelary actor, an alternative power centre to civilian government, through the establishment of the National Security Council (Milli Güvenlik Kurulu, MGK) as a constitutional body in 1961.

The draft constitutional proposal in 1961 defended the principle of laicism in similar terms as when it was first adopted in 1937, stating that 'the Turkish Republic is laic; it rejects the interference of religion in state

---

[18] The task of drawing up a preliminary proposal was given to a commission of law professors. Two proposals were produced. According to Tanör (1995: 309–313), both were anti-majoritarian in content, but the first proposal by professors from Istanbul and Ankara University evinced a distrust of political parties, while the second proposal by academics from the Ankara University Faculty of Political Science was less distrustful and sought not to weaken executive power. The final document was closer to the second Ankara proposal (Weiker 1963). For a more detailed discussion on the preparation and content of both proposals and commission members see Tanör (1995: 309–313).

matters and the influence of irrational sources on law. Without doubt this does not mean that religion is denied but that religion is left to individuals' consciences.' Yet, constitutional drafters in 1961 were also concerned with clarifying what this involved in practice, and compared with 1937, there was a plurality of approaches. Despite the military's involvement and the lack of a (democratic) representative element during the constitution making, however, there was active debate on different political sides and, significantly, in contrast with other periods of constitution making, inclusion of non-Muslim representatives. Several drafters argued that laicism meant a separation of religion from state matters, objecting to the role of the Diyanet within the state apparatus, while others focused on the principle of freedom of conscience and worship, positing that the state should give equal treatment to or be neutral in the provision of religious services for both the majority and the minority. In this manner, Hikmet Kümbetlioğlu, a representative of the judiciary in the Constituent Assembly, opined that it was contrary to laicism to make other religions and denominations fund the Diyanet through taxes, which represented only one denomination of one religion (Islam): 'In this country where 99% of the population are Muslim, there has to be the same respect for the beliefs of the members of the 1%' (Öztürk 1966a: 721). From this standpoint, it appeared that elements of the 1961 Constituent Assembly regarded laicism as involving 'private' religiosity alongside the restriction of religious authority to ensure 'public' secularity. Conversely, some members argued that the nature of the Turkish nation required the state to support religious affairs and revitalise religion. At the same time, Assembly members were keen to emphasise that laicism should not be understood as irreligiosity or as being an enemy of religion, thereby responding to the criticisms, particularly from conservative circles, of reforms and restrictions on religious activity adopted during the one-party period.

What emerged in the final document was a compromise between these diverging currents. Alongside objections to the Diyanet's role within a laic state, one group of constitutional framers also protested about the inclusion of a clause on the state provision of religious education (in Article 19). Two dissenters among the ten members of the original İstanbul University Committee that had prepared the first draft of the constitution argued that the provision of such services, even if to the majority religious group, was contrary to laicism and democracy. It is also clear that the 1961 constitution making involved an anti-majoritarian (but not necessarily pluralistic) impulse, as framers were keen to prevent the accumulation of power allowed by the 1924 Constitution through the introduction of checks and balances. Consequently, despite the fact that an overwhelming majority appeared to support state intervention in religion, the clause was removed from the final draft, and religious education was left to individual choice. The other tendency was related to concerns that if religion was not kept under state control then it would either take over the state or organise itself outside the state. According to some constitutional framers, therefore, this made Turkey a unique case in contrast to the West. They were equally afraid of the exploitation of religious sentiment by political actors to bolster their power, which was the accusation faced by the DP government in the 1950s.

Elements of the junta regime were motivated by similar thinking, and at that point, exerted their influence on the side of this group. Consequently, in the 1961 Constitution, the Diyanet was incorporated as a constitutional body for the first time on the directives of the military (the implications of this are further discussed in Chapters 2 and 3), having not been previously mentioned in the constitution or the proposals prepared by the designated academic commissions. On the one hand, this meant that the constitution essentially (re)constructed laicism by linking it explicitly with the majority religion through the inclusion of the Diyanet in the constitutional order. On the other hand, as the following chapters will show, this association did not simply involve control of religion by the state since the relationship between religion and state was not a one-way relationship; in turn, the religious authority – the Diyanet – was also able to expand its power and domain of action.

While the nature of laicism came under greater scrutiny following the transition to multi-partism, a key aspect of continuity with previous periods of constitution making was the enduring concern with the Muslim Turkish majority during 1961. Many constitutional framers were more concerned about expanding the religious freedom of the Muslim majority, which they commonly referred to as comprising between 90 and 99.5 per cent, and as 'our religion', than about ensuring equal protection of rights and freedoms for minorities.[19] They argued, therefore, that religious freedom required the ability to organise and carry out religious education (whereas the constitution guaranteed only belief and worship). Religious education was supported and justified by most members who spoke based on the Muslim majority, the so-called 90 to 99 per cent Muslim character of the Turkish nation, alongside what

---

[19] For a selection of these arguments, see the parliamentary records in Öztürk (1966b: 1346–1347, 1350–1352, 1358, 1364–1365, 1378–1379). Only a few contradicted this line of reasoning. For example, Hıfzı Veldet Velidedeoğlu, a law professor, argued that while it was necessary for the state to provide religious education to combat 'ignorance', it would only be able to maintain its laic character if it was provided for both the majority and the minority (Öztürk 1966b: 1372–1373).

they believed to be a need to teach true and correct religion to enlighten the population. Somewhat telling with regard to a continued suspicion of non-Muslims are the comments by Constitutional Commission speaker Muammer Aksoy,[20] who, in responding to the protests regarding the unequal treatment of minorities, rejected the existence of discrimination, referring to 'mistakes in implementation' and 'precautionary measures' against minorities owing to 'painful' past experiences impacted by 'external players' (Öztürk 1966b: 1263–1264).

Nevertheless, despite this consensus and concern with the 'Muslim majority', one of the longest debates among constitution framers was about the nature of Turkish nation identity and nationalism.[21] In general, there was consensus on the definition of Turkish nationalism as not being racist (or inspired by Turanism) or pan-Islamist (ümmetçilik, the unity of the Islamic community, or ummah). The aim was, rather, to distinguish between Turkish Islam and transnational pan-Islamism. Consequently, framers underlined the failure of pan-Islamism and Ottomanism to save the Ottoman Empire. A pertinent example is the words of Şemsettin Günaltay:

Albanian, Arab and Turk are all Muslim. Pan-Islamism lost its power. When we say Turkish nation it is the beginning of a completely new era. The Empire was wrecked. This country was established on the wreckage of the Empire [...] Atatürkist nationalism has tied individuals living in this country, has bound on language, history and fate regardless of their race. Consequently, our nationalism is not racism, it is cultural unity. (Öztürk 1966b: 1032)

Nationalist Abdülhadi Toplu stated similarly that

since 1070 [...] up to the Tanzimat, religion filled the inside of our society. All the sacrifices were made for being a Muslim and to remain Muslim [...] the Ottoman Empire which was established over our motherland, maintained the ideal of Islam in its world view within its Ottomanism consciousness which started with the Tanzimat [...] However, the 1912 Balkan War was the clear blow to this ideal and opened the eyes of our nation like an earthquake [...] at the last point the real owners of this country also accepted the ideal of nationalism and embraced political Turkism. (Öztürk 1966b: 979–980)

---

[20] Aksoy was a prominent professor of law, CHP politician and columnist, characterised as an Atatürkist (Atatürkçü) given his defence of the secular reforms and principles of the Republic. He was the target of a political assassination in 1990, allegedly by a radical Islamist organisation. Aksoy's murder was one of a series of similar political assassinations of secularist, social democrat or leftist intellectuals, journalists and politicians such as Ahmet Taner Kışlalı, Bahriye Üçok and Uğur Mumcu that took place in the 1990s. See Tarih ve Toplum (29 March 2013).

[21] See also Bayar (2016b) for a detailed discussion of the principle of nationalism in the 1924 and 1961 constitutions and the continuities between them.

Yet, contrary to other periods of constitution making, there were currents that emphasised Turkishness as distinct from Islam. For instance, Cemal Gürsel, the head of the MBK, argued that 'Islamism is the biggest element that ruined our nationalism. The Islamic creed made us forget our nationalism, due to ignorance our nation couldn't have a Turkish spirit' (Öztürk 1966b: 1086–1087). He went on to add that if a citizen in Anatolia is asked what they are, they will first say they are Muslim, not a Turk (Öztürk 1966b: 1079–1080). Other members of the assembly, such as Kasım Gülek (former CHP general secretary between 1950 and 1959), emphasised Turkish national identity in apparently more inclusive language:

The principle of the Turk, since the time of Atatürk, has been to see as a Turk and treat as a Turk whoever says he is a Turk, says and feels he is a son of this soil [. . .] We recognise the equality of those belonging to another religion. As long as they remain committed to the nation, see themselves as a Turk and consider the country's interests as their own interests. (Öztürk 1966b: 1265)

The 1982 Constitution and Augmentation of Religious Majoritarianism

The 1961 Constitution failed to deliver political stability to Turkey, however. Not unlike developments elsewhere in the world, the country witnessed an intense polarisation between leftist and rightist politics, which became increasingly violent in the lead-up to the 1980 coup. On 12 March 1971, the military intervened, issuing an ultimatum that outlined the need for the political authorities to address 'anarchy' in the country. Yet the 1971 coup was also a product of the intensifying divisions within the military as exemplified by the failed coup plot by a leftist faction prior to 12 March (Hale 1994: 186; Ulus 2010; 52–63). While the struggle within the military itself intensified, catalysing an ongoing purge of leftist currents, the successive coalition governments were unable to reverse the tide on the civilian side as the executive and legislative body became increasingly paralysed, partly as a result of polarisation and in-fighting. Political violence continued to build while taking on sectarian undertones, with massacres of Alevi citizens in Maraş in 1978 and in Çorum in 1980 alongside the assassination of prominent political actors. Meanwhile, the import substitution strategy had begun to falter, particularly after the 1973 to 1974 oil shocks, and Turkey was becoming increasingly engulfed by a growing economic crisis.

On the other hand, Cold War anti-communism policies continued to have an impact on Turkish political life. Since the 1960s, Saudi Arabia, supported by the United States, had been using Islam as a means to counter Arab nationalism and leftists (Ahmad 1988: 761). Following the 1973 to 1974 oil embargo, the prominence and influence of the conservative Arab monarchies were further raised. In turn, the growing wealth of these monarchies enabled increased funding for religious and Islamist actors and organisations in Turkey through bodies such as the Saudi-based Muslim World League (Rabita al-Alam al-Islami, Rabita). Within this context, Turkey emerged as a critical actor that was 'considered to be at the heart of a[n Islamic] "green belt" fighting against the "red belt" of communism' (Ergil 2000: 54–55).[22] Such geopolitical developments, together with domestic factors in Turkey, played a role in creating new opportunity structures for conservative and Islamist actors, particularly during the rightist Islamist National Front coalition governments of the 1970s.

The 1982 Constitution emerged within this milieu following the 12 September 1980 military intervention, which has commonly been regarded as a turning point in the history of the Republic concerning the state's relationship with religion (Atasoy 2009: 95; Çarkoğlu and Kalaycıoğlu 2009: 10; Eligür 2010; Sakallıoğlu 1996; Toprak 1990: 10; Tuğal 2007: 11; Yavuz 2003). Rather than a radical break or 'a highly controlled opening to religious groups' to control and suppress the Islamist movement through its absorption into official ideology, the 1980 intervention underscored the decisive shifting balance of power within the state. Most revealing as to the nature of this was the junta regime's adoption of what has been designated the TIS, which was an Islamisation programme developed by the Hearth of the Enlightened (Aydınlar Ocağı, AO; see Chapter 5), a small organisation comprising around 150 anti-communist, rightist Islamist-conservative-nationalist intellectuals working closely with state actors, which was in part aimed at stemming intense social contestation and polarisation in the 1970s and ensuring national unity (Can and Bora 2004: 150–189; Taşkın 2007; Toprak 1990).[23] The National Culture Report, prepared in 1983 by the State Planning Organisation (Devlet Planlama Teşkilatı, DPT), including members of the Hearth of the Enlightened, is an exemplary document in terms of the TIS programme, with its vision of reorienting society around 'the mosque, barracks and the family', regarded as the

---

[22] For a more comprehensive account of Saudi Arabia's influence on Turkish Islamism and political life since the 1970s and the importance of petrodollars, see Köni (2012).

[23] See also Can and Bora (2004) for the international context, the project of 'green belt' comprising Saudi Arabia, Turkey, Pakistan and Kuwait against the Soviet Union from 1977 and also Mumcu (1993) for the funding of Islamist organisations and *ulema* by Saudi Arabia.

three pillars of Turkish national culture that were undermined by Westernisation. Islam was defined by the report as the most important aspect of national culture within the context of a country characterised as 99.8 per cent Muslim. The political crises of the preceding years and 'regionalism', identified as a by-product of democratisation, were described as being damaging to national culture and integrity. In this manner, 'national culture planning' was embraced as a weapon against ideological movements. A comprehensive strategy of cultural engineering was proposed, including the creation of a 'model human' and a pious (*dindar*) Turkish nation through the expansion of religious education (including compulsory lessons) in schools, hospitals, prisons and workers' associations, as well as the promotion of Islam by the Diyanet (e.g. by teaching families how to provide religious education to their children) and the state public broadcasting organisations (DPT 1983). This Islamisation programme also targeted Alevis, which faced rejuvenated efforts at systematic faith-based assimilation that included forcing Alevi children to attend Sunni religious schools (Kenanoğlu 11 April 2013; *Radikal* 26 October 2012) (see Chapter 3).

The TIS doctrine also defines the spirit of the 1982 Constitution, promulgated during the period of direct military rule (1980–1983), which was at heart a nationalising programme that paralleled the majoritising constitution making of the 1920s. Indeed, Yavuz (2003: 77) notes that the Constitutional Preparation Committee comprised two members of the Hearth of the Enlightened. The bicameral Constituent Assembly, which prepared the constitution, in comparison with that of 1961, was considerably less pluralistic, as evidenced by both the limited debate and the lack of minority representatives.[24] Reflecting this, the 1982 Constitution clearly steered the political system back towards the unconstrained majoritarianism of the one-party period by further eroding the checks and balances introduced by the 1961 Constitution, which had also been tapered following the 1971 coup. This included strengthening the executive branch at the expense of parliament, introducing a 10 per cent national electoral threshold to facilitate one-party government and further curtailing the powers of the Constitutional Court. With respect to religion, the article on laicism was untouched, while its irrevocability was introduced for the first time, together with an expressive preamble, which declared that 'laicism requires that sacred religious feelings should never interfere in state matters and politics'. More in keeping with the 1920s, however, laicism became more explicitly linked to the majority religion as

---

[24] With the MGK comprising one chamber, the second chamber, the civilian Consultative Assembly, was composed purely of MGK-appointed members.

framers conceptualised the article as involving a natural partiality towards the Muslim majority Turkish nation. As one member of the Constituent Assembly stated,

the reality is that the Turkish nation is a Muslim nation. The synthesis of Turkishness and Islam is the source of life of the unity and strength of our great nation. This source can never be neglected. The natural duties of the laic state therefore include servicing the needs of the nation that it has emerged from. (Mahmut Nedim Bilgiç in DM 1 September 1982: 300)

Drafters emphasised that laicism did not mean 'irreligiosity' ('*dinsizlik*', to be without religion) or being an infidel (*gavur*) but, instead, the protection of religion through the Diyanet.[25]

More significantly, it was the expansion of the Diyanet's role outlined in the constitution (examined in Chapter 2) and the introduction of compulsory religious education – essentially the propagation of Sunni Islam – as part of the article on the freedom of religion and conscience that clearly privileged Muslim Turkish identity.[26] Compulsory religious education was one of the most debated items by the MGK and the Consultative Assembly, even though the outcome had already been determined: the leader of the 1980 junta regime, General Kenan Evren, had announced its introduction in 1981. Accordingly, just two objections were raised during the debates. In 1982, as in 1961, constitutional framers were concerned about teaching 'correct religion', and they saw religious education as a means of preventing the exploitation of religion or the influence of reactionary forces. However, in 1982, religious education was also conceptualised and highlighted as being essential for the attainment of national unity and solidarity, providing an antidote or 'national cement' against anarchy, communism, reaction and nationally divisive currents.[27] A common sentiment voiced was the desire to raise an anti-materialist faithful (*imanlı*) generation (Recai Dinçer in DM 12 August 1982: 478). As one member stated, 'Let's remember what preceded 12 September. It came about because of irreligiosity in high

---

[25] For a selection of examples of these types of arguments, see Mehmet Velid Koran in DM (12 August 1982: 502), İsa Vardal Aynı in DM (9 August 1982: 250); Feyzi Feyzioğlu in DM (12 August 1982: 519); Bekir Tünayin in DM (1 September 1982: 289); Turhan Güven in DM (4 August 1982: 40); Doğan Gürbüz in DM (1 September 1982: 273).

[26] Article 24, which is otherwise largely based on Article 12 of the preceding 1961 Constitution.

[27] For a selection of examples see: Evliya Parlak in DM (5 August 1982: 116; 1 September 1982: 289); Fuat Yilmaz in DM (1 September 1982: 215); Nihat Kubilay in DM (1 September 1982: 287); İ. Doğan Gürbüz in DM (1 September 1982: 299); Mahmut Nedim Bilgiç in DM (1 September 1982: 297); Mehmet Velid Koran in DM (12 August 1982: 502–503); Beşir Hamitoğullari in DM (1 September 1982: 278).

schools and universities, which underpins anarchy' (Î. Doğan Gürbüz in DM 1 September 1982: 299).

The elevation of and focus on a Muslim Turkish majority as the base of the nation-state was naturally reflected in the reconfiguration of national identity, which was more in keeping with the early periods of constitution making. The drafters envisaged an explicit synthesis of Turkishness and Islam. As one member of the Consultative Assembly pointed out,

In Turkey there is only one society that is of Turkish origin [...] Every Turk of Turkish origin is Muslim. The language of our Prophet is Arabic, and despite the fact that the Koran is Arabic, not all Arabs are Muslims. In contrast to this all those of Turkish origin are Muslims. (Nuri Özgöker in DM 11 August 1982: 424)

Based on their conception of the nation as '90 per cent'/'95 per cent'/ '99 per cent' majority Muslim, the framers voiced concern chiefly for the freedom of the Sunni Muslim Turkish majority and its needs and were less interested in neutrality or the protection of minorities. This senti-ment was pithily summarised by the declaration of one member of the assembly, who said that 'the vast majority of the Turkish nation is Muslim. Given this, it is required that the Islamic religion should be the focal point of [the laws pertaining to] freedom of religion and con-science' (DM 1 September 1982: 273). Based on similar reasoning, many framers objected to Article 24 on grounds of religious freedom, arguing that it gave too much protection to non-believers, with one member stating that the article 'gives the impression as if this has not been prepared for the Turkish nation which is 99.14 per cent Muslim' (Mehmet Pamak in DM 10 August 1982: 294).

And, again, like the earlier periods of constitution making, but in contrast to 1961, there was a significantly more hostile and exclusionary approach towards minorities in 1982. Any expression of 'denominational differences' (an implicit reference to Alevis) was considered to be grounds for the Constitutional Commission to impose restrictions on religious freedom. Meanwhile, a reference to the educational rights of minorities, or even use of the word 'minority',[28] was rejected by the assembly, with minorities being merely tolerated, at best: 'We will not force anyone towards *our* [my emphasis] religion' (DM 1 September

---

[28] For examples of the disdain for the word minority and concept of minority rights, see M. Fevzi Uyguner's comment that there is no such thing as a minority: 'Everyone is a Turk' (DM 1 September 1982: 275). Another member, Beşir Hamitoğullari, objected to the word 'minority', arguing that 'in Atatürk's Turkey there is no minority; there are citizens' (DM 1 September 1982: 292), while Mustafa Alpdündar rejected mentions of inclusion of a mention of minority rights in the constitution (DM 1 September 1982: 295).

1982: 283). In sum, the approach of the 1982 constitutional drafters towards religious freedom can be summarised in the sentence of one member: 'Thank God, we live in a country that is 99.9 per cent Muslim' (Mustafa Alpdündar in DM 1 September 1982: 295).

The re-emphasis on the synthesis between Islam and Turkishness in 1961, and more so in 1983, was just as much a reflection of the fear of the transnationalism of religion. During the 1960s, Islamists in Turkey were coming under the influence of movements in other Muslim majority contexts, such as Egypt, and questioning whether nationalism was an alien ideology (Çetinsaya 1999: 371). For the constitutional framers, therefore, Turkish identity, while being deeply intertwined with Islam, had to be distinguished from the wider *ummah*, or Islamic community, as much as communism. Such thoughts echoed the debates in the late Ottoman Empire and the concerns of nationalists that pan-Islamism and pan-Turkism (Turanism) were insufficient to secure national unity. This situation was articulated by Mustafa Kemal in Nutuk in 1927 – that pan-Islamism and pan-Turkism had never been successful and that the rational choice suggested by history was the adoption of national politics. A similar attitude can be observed in the official military documents from the 1997 coup unearthed by the parliamentary commission investigating coups in 2012: there, pan-Islamists are seen to be emboldening Kurdish separatism.

Constitution Making and Change in the Post-1980s Period

The military-led redesign of the rules of the game in the 1980s resulted in expanding military tutelage over the political system; increasing restrictions on political life, including the closure of political parties and associations such as trade unions; and the strengthening of religious majoritarianism. With the TIS programme, the religious field was privileged and endowed with significant organisational and material resources and networks that were not afforded to alternative currents and formations. This was reflected in all levels of social life, from the expansion of religious education to the proliferation of Islamic associations. Islamic charities providing social welfare services increased following the neoliberal restructuring of the economy, also facilitated by petrodollars from the Persian Gulf monarchies. On the other hand, the leftist movement, regarded by the junta leaders as the biggest danger, was decimated owing to both the widespread political repression after the coup and to the retreat of socialist ideology globally with the decline and collapse of the Soviet Union.

As political life was liberalised beginning in the late 1980s, the left–right polarisation of the 1970s was supplanted by the rise of identity politics, involving the emergence of a secular–Islamist fault line, sectarian violence against the Alevi community and the oppression of Kurdish citizens by the state engaged in a violent conflict against the Kurdish nationalist movement. The highly majoritarian and executive-heavy political system introduced by the 1982 Constitution was not effective in mitigating the extreme fragmentation of the party system that followed in the 1990s. The series of short-lived and unstable coalition governments were unable to address, and instead exacerbated, the recurrent economic and financial crises during this period, further creating a general sense of crisis.

Following success in the municipal elections in İstanbul in 1994, the Islamist Welfare Party (Refah Partisi, RP) was catapulted to countrywide success in the general elections of 1995 by gaining 21.4 per cent, the biggest vote share achieved by the Islamist movement at the time. On the one hand, relations between the RP-led coalition government and the military appeared to deteriorate on the back of allegations that the party had become the centre of reactionary activity and was seeking to undermine Turkey's Western orientation. On the other hand, perhaps a more significant event during this period was the unravelling of the so-called deep state with the Susurluk incident in November 1996, exposing the links between politicians, rightist mafia and the security forces. In reaction, a highly popular nationwide campaign, One Minute of Darkness for Permanent Light (Sürekli Aydınlık İçin Bir Dakika Karanlık), was launched, but it was soon to be supplanted by a renewed focus on Islamist–secularist polarisation. On 28 February 1997, Turkey experienced its fourth military intervention, a so-called post-modern coup. Military elites targeted the Refah-Yol coalition government composed of the RP and the centre-right True Path Party (Doğru Yol Partisi, DYP). The government was issued a memorandum tasking them with fighting against 'reaction' (a reference to Islamist activity in Turkish politics). Ultimately forced to resign, the RP was subsequently closed down by the Constitutional Court for violating the constitution by engaging in anti-secular activity. By the end of the 1990s, therefore, the sense of crisis was palpable, with continued political instability, the state's inability to cope with a major earthquake in 1999 that left thousands dead and major economic and financial crises in 2001 to 2002. It was within this context that the Islamist AKP ascended to power in 2002, marking a turning point in Turkish history.

In parallel with these developments, political liberalisation was catalysed by the ideological hegemony of democracy in the post-Cold War period (Diamond 2002) and Turkey's bid to join the EU. Turkey applied for membership to the European Community in 1987 and joined the Customs Union with the EU in 1995. Turkish candidacy was granted by the European Council in 1999, and in 2004, agreement was finally reached with the EU to start negotiations on Turkish membership. Major reforms catalysed by the Europeanisation process during this period most notably included the role of the military in politics; the Turkish Penal Code and its articles on freedom of expression and association; the death penalty; the transparency of the public sector; and human rights legislation (Müftüler-Baç 2005). Despite the waning of the Europeanisation process, particularly since 2007, when the AKP successfully staved off a challenge to its rule from the military, Turkey was promoted as a model of 'Muslim democracy' both domestically (by the AKP) and by external actors, overlooking growing authoritarianism and the augmentation of religious majoritarianism.

In particular, in the period 1983 to 2004, the 1982 Constitution was amended eight times, and these included some substantial changes. In 1995, the debate about changes to the preamble of the 1982 Constitution turned into a dispute over the last clause of Article 24 on religious freedom and, by extension, laicism, delaying the amendment process.[29] The constitutional amendment proposal by the DYP–ANAP–CHP (DYP–Anavatan Partisi [Motherland Party; ANAP]–CHP) coalition was accepted by a cross-party consensus in the committee, but no agreement was reached on the fate of Article 24. The SHP rejected any changes to the article, while the RP refused to accept any constitution that did not include a revision of it. The right-wing conservative ANAP and Islamist RP argued that this clause had resulted in the oppression of the Muslim majority. In fact, the article remained symbolic to the extent that in 1991, the ANAP government had already scrapped Article 163 of the Turkish Penal Code, which criminalised anti-secularist activity. More interesting in some sense was what these debates revealed. As with the previous constitutions outlined above, lawmakers interpreted democratisation and fundamental rights and freedoms as being the fulfilment of the freedom of religion and conscience of the Sunni Muslim majority (Doğanay 2007: 398). Indeed, consider the following defence of Article 24 and laicism at the time by Bülent Ecevit, the centre-left Democratic Left Party (Demokratik Sol Parti, DSP) leader:

---

[29] Article 24: 'No one shall be allowed to exploit or abuse religion or religious feelings, or things held sacred by religion, in any manner whatsoever, for the purpose of personal or political interest or influence, or for even partially basing the fundamental, social, economic, political and legal order of the State on religious tenets.'

It is a great injustice to present the last clause of Article 24 and laicism as it has been implemented in Turkey as anti-religious. The Muslim-Turkish people have only been able to learn its religion, access its sacred book, possess the sacred book and have it in their home thanks to the laic and democratic Republic [. . .] in the Ottoman period where *shari'a* reigned [. . .] many of our villages did not have mosques, but in the laic Republic there are hardly any villages without mosques. (TBMM TDb 14 June 1995: 389)

Constitution Making in the AKP Era

Efforts to draw up a new civil constitution prepared by elected representatives rather than under military rule were to wait until October 2011. The early years of the AKP had witnessed an increasing struggle between different parts of the state and the government. Elements within the military and Constitutional Court had manoeuvred to prevent the election of the AKP's representative to the presidency in 2007, while in a highly controversial decision that some saw as overstepping its remit, the top court rejected constitutional amendments to lift restrictions on the headscarf in 2008.[30] At the same time, the AKP narrowly escaped a party closure case launched by the public prosecutor of the Court of Cassation, based on one vote of the members of the Constitutional Court. The AKP had responded by holding referendums on constitutional amendments in 2007 in which the public voted for a directly elected president, and following September 2010, the judiciary was restructured significantly. However, the AKP did not deem the amendments sufficient to alter the 'soul' of the constitution. In October 2011, the government launched a Constitution Reconciliation Commission (Anayasa Uzlaşma Komisyonu, AUK) comprising the four main parties, which was tasked with drawing up a new constitution. The need for a new civil constitution to replace the current version imposed (through a plebiscitary referendum) by the 1982 junta regime had been one of the central calls across the party divide during the 2011 general election. The AKP's AUK representative and lawmaker, Mustafa Şentop, declared:

[Sixty per cent] of the constitution has changed, but it is still not sufficient. According to the bureaucratic oligarchy, the constitution has first [a written] expression and also a soul. You make a law, it is not unconstitutional, so there [should be] no problem; but the authorised institutions then say 'it is against the soul of the constitution' and reject it. They call upon and ask the spirit [of the

---

[30] The judiciary had long been an ideological battleground, with the Constitutional Court held up as a 'bastion of secularism'. The move to strike down the headscarf bill has been described as a 'usurpation of power' by the judiciary for violating Article 148 (see Özbudun and Gençkaya 2009: 108–109).

constitution], if that spirit does not deem [the law] fit, they reject it. This is why we have to bury the soul of the constitution. (*Mynet Haber* 17 March 2013)

As a civil attempt, and owing to the range of actors and political parties of different ideological backgrounds, the 2011 to 2012 constitutional deliberations were some of the most open, diverse and representative in modern Turkish history.[31] At the same time, they revealed a deep level of polarisation. The major political parties held different constitutive visions for the polity, not just on the nature of government (parliamentary vs. presidential, majoritarian vs. consensus models) but also, fundamentally, on national identity and the relationship between religion and state. According to the Peace and Democracy Party (Barış ve Demokrasi Partisi, BDP) representative Altan Tan, Kurds were included in the Muslim majority during the establishment of the Republic but were never given the rights that minorities were granted. The pro-Kurdish BDP and Nationalist Movement Party (Milliyetçi Hareket Partisi, MHP) stood at polar ends of the debate about the nature of citizenship and Turkish national identity. For the BDP, the constitution should contain recognition of Kurdish language rights along with what it regarded as a more neutral and inclusive reference to citizens of the Turkish Republic rather that to Turkish citizens, which is seen as an exclusive ethnic identity. This reformulation of citizenship, albeit more narrow, was supported by the AKP, for which Muslim identity was emphasised as the primary identity of Turkish citizens. The CHP, too, was emphatic in its argument that inclusivity was not achieved by forcing Kurds to define themselves as Turks, but the party maintained the reference to 'Turkish citizen' in the article. From the MHP's perspective, however, 'Turk' referred not to an ethnic label but to a culture and civilisation that spoke Turkish. The constitution was being written for and addressed to the 'founding' Turkish nation within the Turkish Republic, and the recognition of Kurdish identity or ethnic difference could result in the dismantling of Turkey. Accordingly, the MHP insisted on Turkish remaining the language of education, while the BDP sought education in the Kurdish language.

On the principle of laicism, rightist and conservative parties upheld a religious majoritarian logic. The AKP and the MHP argued that laicism should be about ensuring toleration and freedom of belief, while also insisting that it was normal for a state to be partial to, and serve, the majority religion. The CHP did not necessarily reject this stance,

---

[31] The deliberations referred to in this section are sourced from the Constitutional Reconciliation Commission, which are available online. See AUK (2012–2013a, 2012–2013b).

supporting the maintenance of the Diyanet, while insisting on the importance of laicism for the protection of citizens and to prevent the interference of religion in state matters. In contrast to the AKP and the MHP, both the CHP and the BDP argued that the state should be equal in its treatment of other religions and sects (*mezhep*), such as the Alevis. Only the small leftist parties interpreted laicism as state neutrality to all faiths, pushing for the abolition of the Diyanet. Accordingly, both the AKP and the MHP defended compulsory religious education, while the CHP pushed for a more pluralistic and critical teaching of religion.

Equally, the AKP focused on the majoritarian 1921 and 1924 constitutions as points of reference and emphasised unrestricted religious freedom and the sovereignty of the parliamentary majority. Its target was, therefore, the 1961 Constitution, as the party's head of the Constitutional Commission, Mustafa Şentop, outlined:

In my opinion, Turkey's fundamental problem is with the new state ideology established following the 27 May [1960 coup] [. . .] In terms of continuity, we are against a mentality of tutelage, a bureaucratic, oligarchic mentality, a mentality that bases political power with the constitution rather than the nation [. . .] But, if by continuity it is meant the philosophy that has been since the Ottoman [Empire], since the establishment of the republic, the state's correct ideology, then we accept it, we can maintain this continuity. But, we are for abandoning the break in between, the break that arose with 27 May [19]60. (AUK 2012–2013a: 310)

This contrasted with the stress placed by the CHP on what it viewed as the fundamental achievements of the Republic, including laicism, republican reforms and checks and balances on parliamentary majorities. As such, the AKP and the CHP in particular were fundamentally divided on the irrevocability (Article 4) of the first three articles of the current 1982 Constitution, which outline (i) the form of the state as a republic (Article 1); (ii) the characteristics of the republic as including 'Atatürkist nationalism' and laicism (Article 2) and (iii) the integrity, official language, flag, national anthem and capital of the state (Article 3).

The cross-party efforts to draw up a new constitution between 2011 and 2012, based on a negotiated consensus, subsequently failed. In 2014, Erdoğan was elected president and has continued to progressively amass significant powers relative to the other arms of the state, which has, in turn, equipped him with extensive informal power through his domination of patron–client relationships. With the declaration of a state of emergency (SoE) after the 15 July coup attempt, any remaining checks on presidential power were undermined by executive decrees and unprecedented purges within public institutions, including the judiciary. Following the 16 April 2017 constitutional amendment, Turkey has not only come full circle to its one-party era majoritarianism by ending the separation of powers but also gone beyond it by establishing the grounds for a highly personalised autocratic rule (see Chapter 6).

Conclusion

In his work on state formation, nation building, and mass politics in Europe, Stein Rokkan (1999: 135) argued that the structuring of mass politics cannot be understood without 'going far back in history, without analysing the differences in the initial conditions and the early processes of territorial organisation, of state building, of resource combination'. In this manner, understanding the components of a particular nation-state project sheds light on why some boundaries become more salient compared to others in political and economic struggles. In the Turkish case, nation-state building involved the construction and elevation of (Sunni) Muslim Turkishness as the marker of the national majority to which sovereignty belonged.

To come back to Wimmer's (2008) framework, this was the result of three structural constraints – institutions, power and networks (see Introduction) – that determined the prevalent forms of social closure, namely the choice and salience of particular boundary delineations during the early stages of nation building. First was the institutional legacy of the Ottoman Empire, which included the incorporation of religious institutions within the state. However, just as Ottoman modernisation was shaped by the interrelated internal impetus for reform and external interventions, in the 1920s, nation-state builders had been faced with constraints imposed under the Treaty of Lausanne. Such considerations had played a role in the decision to secularise the civil code. Second, for Ottoman state elites, the polarisation of ethnic segmentation between Muslims and non-Muslims in the late Empire, together with the rise of ethnic nationalism and the ascent of the Young Turks since 1908, had underpinned the rise of Turkish nationalism for which Islam was a constitutive element. Third, in terms of political networks and alliances, despite the diverse nature of the coalition brought together by the independence struggle and their differing political visions, Islam was the common denominator of the nation-state builders of the early Republic. These three elements of the Ottoman legacy thereby meant that religion became a primary factor in social closure.

Turkey's constitutional experience outlined above shows that the decisions taken by nation-state builders during these foundational years proved to be robust over time, demonstrating path dependency effects. Constitution making in the 1920s was not solely the reflection of a positivist ideology and a Westernising project driven by Kemalists as emphasised in the scholarship. It was equally the product of the rise of a particular faction of the state over others which had involved the sidelining of the *ulema* – formerly a key pillar of the Ottoman order and, therefore, important competitors – but not its elimination (see Chapter 2). At the same time, as nationalising constitutions, they were concerned chiefly with the construction and elevation of a majority base for the state. The increasing domination of the DP in the 1950s had intensified the struggle within the state, and against a backdrop of this experience, the 1961 Constitution comprised an anti-majoritarian thrust in establishing checks and balances against executive power as well as the establishment of military tutelage. In this sense, it was to some extent an outlier in comparatively more pluralistic interpretations of the principle of laicism among constitutional framers, although, significantly, it was the ostensibly secularist military which had insisted that the Diyanet become a constitutional body. Turkish secularism thereby continued to reflect the privileging of Sunni Islam.

In comparison, the 1982 Constitution had more parallels with the constitutions of the early 1920s in its level of majoritarianism and emphasis on a Turkish–Islamic synthesis as conservative factions within the military and the state gained the upper hand. With the augmentation of this formulation under the Islamist AKP, the privileging of the Sunni Muslim Turkish majority has been a persistent feature in the Republic, making religious majoritarianism a fundamental element of the constitutional identity and operational logic of the state. There are various ways in which this found reflection in state practices, including in the institution of citizenship, where Muslim Turks have been accorded a privileged position, including in the economy (see more discussion in Chapter 4) and compared to minorities (for the case of Alevis see Chapter 3), as well as the incorporation of the Ottoman Sunni *ulema* within the Republican state (examined in Chapter 2). Equally, what the above discussion on constitution making illuminates is the gap between codified law and state practices. Despite its civic face and promise, there was in practice an ethnicisation of the state in which 'ethnic ties are reinforced and politicised' (Wimmer 2002: 66). As Bayır has argued:

The 'civic' language used in the legal description for citizenship in the Constitutions is misleading if one takes into account the heavily loaded ethno-cultural and religious references in the constitutions, legislation, and […] the jurisprudence of the courts. In fact, the state's official stance of 'civic' and 'territorial' nationalism has in practice been used to justify the promotion of 'Turkishness' and the 'Turkification' of 'others' in Turkey. (Bayır 2016: 1)

The same logic applies to the principle of laicism codified in the constitution. Beyond control, neutrality or separation, the project of secularism in Turkey came to be constructed in a manner that implicitly and explicitly privileged and delineated a Muslim Turkish majority as the base of the nation-state. It has evolved and reflected a power struggle within the nascent state and the nationalising concerns of state builders. The prevalent understanding of secularism in Turkey – either as an 'assertive' (Kuru 2009) authoritarian imposition on a religious society that involves cleansing religion from the public space and/or as an *a la turca* secularism in which, rather than a separation, religion becomes subservient to and controlled by the secular state – is therefore misleading or incomplete. Many of these narratives not only continue to be influenced by the epistemological framework of the modernisation paradigm but also have a tendency to focus on codified principles such as laicism, as if they evince a timeless message. As a result, not only do they conceive of the state in the state's own terms, but they have a tendency to retrospectively read current conceptualisations of secularism and polarisation into earlier periods of the Republic. Rather, as the power balance within the state shifted over time towards more conservative factions, so too did the conceptualisation of secularism, together with the manner of its institutionalisation, as the infrastructure and role of the Diyanet and state-administered religious education were expanded. Meanwhile, other types of Islamic/Islamist organisations were also granted support and resources. Chapters 2 and 3 focus on the *ulema*, tracing the evolution of these dynamics over time.

2   The Struggle within the State
The Diyanet and Islamisation

This chapter shifts the focus on the role of the Diyanet to show how this state institution established in 1924 played an important role in facilitating an environment more conducive to the mobilisation of religio-politics. Despite being the country's religious authority and the primary institution for formulating and channelling policies on Islam, scholars have minimised the Diyanet's role, characterising it as a passive and marginal actor and primarily an instrument of the Kemalist/secular state for controlling religion. Certainly, the *ulema* were significantly curtailed during the one-party period, alongside other Islamist and conservative groups within the founding coalition of the Republic. Secularisation of the legal framework and the unification of education were manifestations also of the new balance of power within the state, which shifted after 1923 in particular towards factions coalescing around Mustafa Kemal, at least until his death in 1938. Yet this did not mean that the *ulema* was altogether eliminated from the state or the Diyanet completely disempowered; they remained an organic part of the state. Contingent events such as the Cold War and related anti-communism policies, alongside the neoliberal restructuring in the 1980s, opened up opportunities for rightist conservative and Islamist factions within the state. As a result, they were able to tilt the balance of power within the state in their favour, thereby further strengthening conservative and Islamist actors within and outside the state, which included the expansion of the Diyanet.

Given significant intertwining and blurred boundaries between the Diyanet *ulema* and the Islamist movement through their common cause and actors, this ultimately meant that their religio-politics was empowered as the product of a struggle within the state. This is because the state, as an ensemble of persisting institutions and competing power centres, has a direct impact on the dynamics and types of mobilisation that take place by providing differential access to, or control of, state resources and capacity (Brass 1985; Jessop 2004, 2007: 37). Consequently, in contrast to depictions of the Diyanet as a tool of the secular state, this chapter demonstrates the Diyanet's agency and the ways in which the body has developed multiple strategies, from cooperation to active struggle, resulting in degrees of reciprocity and subversion against other actors within the state. It thereby shows how, like other bureaucratic institutions, it has utilised windows of opportunity to expand its authority and jurisdiction. Given its status as an Islamic authority, this has involved pursuit of the Islamisation of public and private spaces, including morality, thereby also helping to (re)shape a more favourable institutional environment for Islamists.[1]

To situate the body over time, the first section of this chapter elaborates the Ottoman legacy and dimensions of continuity between the Ottoman *ulema* and the Diyanet which have underpinned its specific mission and identity as the carrier of Sunni-Hanefi orthodoxy. The second and third sections trace the institutionalisation of the *ulema* within the Diyanet in the Republic, how the dimensions of continuity shaped the ways in which the Diyanet dealt with the diminution of its authority and jurisdiction following the establishment of the modern nation-state and how it subsequently sought to expand its domain and power. The fourth section reflects on how this understanding of the Diyanet differs from prevalent accounts and the role played by the Diyanet in ensuring the persistence and increasing salience of religious boundaries in political and economic struggles.

---

[1] Some of the main units of the Diyanet include (i) The DİYK, an advisory committee comprising sixteen elected distinguished religious scholars on the highest decision-making body. Its main duty is to research religious issues, answer religious questions and issue fatwas. (ii) The Board for the Investigation of Copies of the Qur'an, charged with examining and ensuring the accuracy of copies of the Qur'an published by Diyanet or others. (iii) The Department of Religious Services, tasked with 'enlightening' and educating Turkish citizens about religion, giving religious guidance and spreading Islamic teaching (*irşad* and *tebliğ*), as well as organising conferences on religious issues, including family guidance bureaus established in 2003 'to support healthy family life'. It also determines the correct times of prayer, sacred days, worship and mosque-related services such as the maintenance of mosques, the administering of Ramadan programmes and preaching services, Friday sermons and funeral services. The content of sermons has been centrally controlled, but in 2006, the Diyanet relaxed the rules, enabling *imams* to prepare and deliver their own sermons provided they are approved by muftis. (iv) The Department of Religious Education, responsible for the educational and professional development of religious functionaries as well as running Qur'an courses and religious education centres for the wider public. (v) The Department of Pilgrimage, charged with organising services related to citizens performing pilgrimage. (vi) The Department of Religious Publications, responsible for published material intended for 'enlightening' society about religion. (vii) The Department of External Relations, which provides religious services to Turkish citizens abroad (Erdem 2008: 209–210). See also Gözaydın (2009b) for a comprehensive legal overview. See the Diyanet's website (www.diyanet.gov.tr/tr-TR/Kurumsal/TeskilatSemasi/4) for a map of the organisational structure.

Reassessing the Role of the *Ulema*

The *ulema* (plural of *'alim*), religious scholars, or 'men of knowledge', trained in Islamic jurisprudence have been described as the guardians of the Islamic faith (Hatina 2003; Metcalf 1982; Moustafa 2000; Zaman 2002; Zeghal 1999). Since there is no formal designated institutional authority in Islam equivalent to the church in Christianity (Metcalf 1982: 16), as Berkey (2001: 89) explains, the authority of the *ulema* was essentially constructed following a series of struggles between different actors. The emergence of the *ulema* as an institution and their bureaucratisation (for some, 'clericalisation' [Berkey 2001: 89; Winter 2009: 25]) are dated to sometime around the eleventh century, with the centralisation of political authority in the Abbasid Dynasty (749–1258), during which there was an expansion of Islamic institutions, including *medreses* (Berkey 2001: 89; Hatina 2003: 51; Keddie 1972: 1–3; Winter 2009: 25). Accordingly, the emergence of the *ulema* as a distinct social group, and what Zilfi (1983) has described as its aristocratisation within Ottoman Muslim history, was concomitant with the *ulema*'s institutionalisation and their greater integration with the state apparatus and the ruling authority by essentially joining its payroll rather than with the establishment of an autonomous or independent authority. While sovereigns enhanced and bolstered their authority and legitimacy through this association with religion, the *ulema* gained access to state power and resources through which they could shape the community along Islamic lines (Hatina 2003: 63–64). Essentially, the *ulema* acted as a conservative force that could reinforce and protect the authority of the Muslim sovereigns through the propagation of adherence to the principle of prohibition of revolt against the ruler in order to avoid civil strife (*fitna*) (Hatina 2003). In this vein, the *ulema* have also been characterised as the guardians of tradition and transmitters and protectors of Islamic learning – which they play a fundamental role in shaping and defining – thereby constituting a key pillar of the social order within Muslim populations (Bein 2009: 68; Hatina 2003: 51, 2009b: 3; Imber 2002: 218; Kara 2005: 163; Metcalf 1982; Zaman 2002; Zeghal 1999).

The collapse of traditional empires and the transition to modern nation-states resulted in the reconfiguration of the status and role of the *ulema*. Indeed, the emergence of the nation-state comprised a transformation of the locus of sovereignty, new forms of power and territorial centralisation, as well as the introduction of rationalised bureaucracies (Mann 2003: 56–57) that sought to penetrate all aspects of social life, resulting in increasing encroachments on the traditional domains of the *ulema*. Earlier accounts of how the *ulema* coped in the modern period tended to regard them/the institution as both a marginalised and an anachronistic actor within the nation-state. This was a reflection of two key factors. First, under the influence of the modernisation paradigm, scholars considered the *ulema* to be a relic of traditional society and, as such, doomed to marginalisation in the modern period. The *ulema*, it was argued, had been confined to the mosque or *medreses* owing to the secularisation policies of nation-state builders (Hatina 2009b: 4–5; Keddie 1972: 7). Second, scholars pointed to the pluralisation of Islamic knowledge and the challenge to the authority of the *ulema*, particularly following the emergence of religio-political movements in the 1970s. To some extent, this mirrored the criticisms made by Islamist actors of what they regarded as the *ulema*'s quietist and submissive stance against secularising regimes. These approaches were underpinned by the presumption of a sharp demarcation between the secular state and society on which the status of the *ulema*, integrated within the state machinery, sat uncomfortably. Overall, these two tendencies within the earlier literature resulted in the neglect of the role of religious institutions and the dominant perception of the *ulema* as a marginalised and passive institution under the control of secular elites and as being clearly differentiated from Islamists.[2] Consequently, in the study of Islamist movements, the focus stayed on grass-roots or bottom-up Islamisation, considered to be the natural result of traditional society reacting to the secularising modern state.

In recent years, on the other hand, revisionist works on religious establishments across other Muslim majority contexts have demonstrated that in three key aspects, the reality of the role played by the *ulema* is more complex than reductionist approaches have allowed. First, the institutionalisation and integration of the *ulema* within the modern nation-state, despite being transformative with respect to functions and status, represents a degree of continuity with Islamic history. Second, recent studies, including those on the Egyptian *ulema* at al-Azhar and the Pakistani *deobandi ulema*, have demonstrated that the decline of the authority of the *ulema* has been relatively less than was previously assumed (Hatina 2003: 52). Accordingly, M. Zaman (2002: xx) argues that the question is not whether the authority of the *ulema* has declined or increased but 'how that authority is constructed, argued, put on display, and constantly defended'. Rather than a passive acceptance by the *ulema* of attempts within the modern nation-state to control and subordinate

---

[2] For example, Olivier Roy argues that, unlike the 'anticlerical' Islamists, the *ulema* accepted modernity and allowed for positive laws in areas not covered by *shari'a* (Keddie 1972: 13; Roy 1994).

the religious field, a far more dynamic relationship of conflict and cooperation has been observed (Hatina 2003; Moustafa 2000; M. Zaman 2002; Zeghal 1999). At the same time, what was lost in terms of status and autonomy following the rise of the nation-state was subsequently supplemented by gains, including the access to the resources of the modern state. This involved the creation of a religious monopoly that, in turn, enabled the *ulema* to expand and reassert themselves when opportunities arose, particularly following the liberalisation of politics. Scholars have shown that in the case of Egypt's al-Azhar, this meant a reassertion of the *ulema* in the post-Nasser era (Hatina 2003; Moustafa 2000; Zeghal 1999). The *ulema* of al-Azhar were able to take advantage of Islamisation under Sadat while bargaining with state elites to expand the institution's domain of action and monopoly over religious life in return for defusing the challenge to the state by radical Islamists. Third, these studies have shown that the line between the *ulema* and Islamists is more blurred than previously assumed, involving a greater degree of cooperation than conflict. Compared with binary perspectives that emphasise bottom-up reaction/Islamisation by religio-political movements, the complex relations and blurring of the line between the *ulema* and Islamists, state and society, shed light on the ways in which state actors, together with non-state or civil actors, are equally implicated in Islamisation, the politicisation of religious identities and the emergence and sustenance of religio-politics. As Hatina (2009b: 264) states, in fact, 'the struggle of the "ulama" to set moral limits to the national impetus in Arab societies, prevent the erosion of the Islamic ethos in the public sphere, and delegitimise the foreign culture and missionary activity had the effect of preparing a more responsive environment for the Islamists in which to promote their cause'.

Yet the new revisionist literature on the *ulema* has commonly concluded that their revival, particularly after the initial period of diminution following the establishment of nation-states, was the unintended outcome of the (secular) state's efforts to control religion and use it as a legitimating tool. Moustafa (2000: 17–18) thus argues that state policies appear to be 'schizophrenic'. Similarly, Zeghal (1999: 396) states, 'Unexpectedly, once the political arena liberalized, the modernization policy which the political elites had imposed earlier on the religious sphere backfired on the state', giving 'al-Azhar its best chances for political revival and prov[ing] that secularization is a self-limiting process'. Moving beyond this conceptualisation of the secular state as an overly unitary and monolithic actor, the case of the Diyanet demonstrates that the *ulema* should be considered as one among other persisting institutions, such as the military, that comprise the state and are engaged in a dynamic struggle for influence and power to implement their different visions of the polity.

Despite the reappraisal of the role of the *ulema* within Muslim contexts in recent years, in Turkish studies, there has been a predominant tendency to overlook or consider marginal the *ulema* housed within the Diyanet. The typically dismissive and negative treatment within Turkish historiography of the Ottoman *ulema*, presented as reactionaries and as opposed to reform and modernisation, is one factor in this.[3] By the 1930s, the word '*ulema*' had been consciously abandoned by the one-party regime (Bein 2011: 106), and it is rarely used in studies of the Diyanet. Another factor is the ostensibly secular nature of the Turkish state, which has meant that the roles and status of the Turkish *ulema* differ in some significant ways from those of their counterparts in other Muslim contexts. Unlike in most other Muslim majority countries, where the *ulema* have the power to issue legally binding judgements based on Islamic doctrine, the *ulema* in Turkey lost their jurisdiction following the secularisation of the legal framework in the 1920s. The Diyanet's role is, therefore, comparatively more limited and constrained. Reflecting these dynamics and binary perspectives of state–religion–society, the literature on the Diyanet and more general Turkish state–religion relations have conceived of the institution as an apparatus of the 'secular Kemalist' state.

According to this hegemonic paradigm, the Diyanet's establishment constituted a break from the Islamic Ottoman heritage and was driven by the secular state's desire to control and utilise it as a legitimising mechanism and to transform and nationalise religious life, while the *ulema* were pacified and marginalised (Aktay 2000; Azak 2010: 9–14; Davison: 2003: 337–338; Gözaydın 2009a; Hassan 2011; Kara 2012; Koylu 2005; Mardin 1982: 171–198; Norton 1988: 403; Seufert 2006: 137–138; Sunar and Toprak 1983: 426; Toprak 1981: 46; Yavuz 2003: 48–49; Zürcher 2004: 233). This has been the common theme for both earlier work on Turkish religion–state relations underpinned by modernisation theory, such as that of Berkes (1964: 490), for whom the Diyanet was a means for modernising state builders to lead religious reform, and for later studies. Compared to these earlier works, which largely mirrored official historiography in focusing on the modernising impulse accorded to the republican state, later works have emphasised the secular state's *control* of the Diyanet as a facet of the master narrative. In this vein, for Kuru (2009: 166–168), the Diyanet is a part of the 'assertive secularist

---

[3] Bein notes that Islamists, on the other hand, have depicted the *ulema* more favourably as the victims of an anti-religious attack, chiefly by the ITC (2011).

agenda to keep Islam under control', while Hassan (2011: 455) argues that it is a 'state institution commissioned to manage and redefine "religion" and its appropriate domains'. In her more extensive work on the Diyanet, Gözaydın (2009a: 273–275) concludes that the institution is a 'means of "securing" the secular nature of the state in Turkey', and this has parallels with Axiarlis's (2014: 49) argument that the body serves the purpose of 'perpetuating the dominant political ideology of Turkey: Kemalist secularism'. For Çakmak (2009: 825), beyond 'exploiting religion in the interests of legitimising itself, the intention is to restrain religion in order to inhibit its potential capacity for challenging the state and its efforts at modernization'. A prominent scholar of Turkish Islamist thought, İsmail Kara (2012: 77–79), has advanced similar arguments, emphasising that the Republic constituted a break with the Ottoman past. He argues that the secular state, through the Diyanet, has attempted to confine, dominate and oppress religion; sought to transform religious life to establish a 'national and modern religion'; and to also use it as a legitimating tool. Analyses of the Diyanet under the AKP have largely echoed these lines of argument in portraying it as an 'imposer' of the AKP's Islamist ideology (Öztürk 2016). In a more nuanced discussion, Gürbey (2009: 395) argues that through the Diyanet, the state has been exercising a theological function that involves a 'policy to provide Muslims with a true knowledge of Islam'. An important exception, which the current study builds on, is Amit Bein's (2011) study of the Ottoman *ulema*, which traces elements of continuity between the late empire and the early Republic.

The Transition from the Ottoman *Ulema* to the Diyanet

Indeed, to understand the Diyanet's evolution and the ways in which its establishment involved the embedding of religious majoritarianism in the nation-state project, a consideration of the Ottoman legacy is required. In its heyday, the Sunni *ulema* in the Ottoman Empire constituted a vast network of institutions headed by the Meşihat-i İslâmiyye, office of the top religious authority, the Sheikh ul-Islam. They comprised judicial (as *kadı* and *kazasker*) and educational (at the *medreses*) institutions alongside the muftis (*ulema* charged with giving Islamic legal judgements: *fatwas*), the *imams*, preachers, Sufi sheikhs and *waqf*s (religious charities) (Kara 2005: 163; Yakut 2005: 33–38). The *ulema* were a key pillar of the social order in the Ottoman Empire, comprising a dual system of legitimacy based on both Islam and the state, as outlined in Chapter 1. At the same time, greater centralisation and supervision of the *medrese* system under the Ottoman state, particularly from the sixteenth century onwards, enhanced the integration of the *ulema*, with many becoming the state's salaried officials over time.

As a result, the extent of the Ottoman *ulema*'s power and its autonomy from political authority has remained a contested issue. In theory, the Sheikh ul-Islam, who was ultimately an appointee of the sultan, could refuse to issue a fatwa, acting as a constraint on the sovereign. Despite cases of the *ulema* playing a role in the dethroning of sultans, contravention of the sovereign's authority was, in reality, rare, although the *ulema* tended to enjoy greater power if the political authority was weak (Gibb and Bowen 1963: 85–86). As a result, some have pointed to a tension between Islamic values and bureaucratic rule (Sunar and Toprak 1983; 194). A case in point was the existence, alongside *shari'a*, of secular law, or *kanun*, initially derived from custom and later importing sultanic decrees that pertained to areas such as those that were not covered by sacred law but, in theory, had to reflect the spirit of Islamic law (Imber 2002: 244; Keddie 1972: 42; Sunar and Toprak 1983: 4). Nevertheless, as Ottoman historian Colin Imber (2002: 218) points out, no ruler could alter the substance of the sacred law, the interpretation and transmission of which was always in the hands of the *ulema*. It was because of this religious authority and the institution's elevation as a key pillar in the Ottoman state that the *ulema* could carve out a sphere of authority and criticise the sultan (Winter 2009: 33).

Modernisation reforms beginning in the nineteenth century certainly presented the Ottoman *ulema* with a number of challenges to their power and role, including but not limited to (i) the abolition of the Janissary Corps in 1826, robbing the *ulema* of their military allies; (ii) the centralisation and expansion of the state and the reorganisation of the civil bureaucracy and (iii) the decline of the *medreses* and the emergence of educated elites from the new military schools, who had begun to outperform *medrese* graduates (Chambers 1972: 35–36). The establishment of Nizamiye courts and new Western-style schools, as well as institutions such as the Charitable Foundations Administration (Evkaf-ı Hümayun Nezareti) in 1826, had begun to encroach on the powers and domain of the *ulema*, curbing their administrative autonomy and economic power. However, against the thesis of decline, Kushner (1987: 55) argues that the *ulema* nevertheless resisted challenges to their authority with flexibility, while in some cases, their remit and monopoly on religious life were accentuated as the central state sought to both impose greater control over the institution and facilitate reform schemes. Bein (2011) further notes that modernisation expanded the size and reach of the official religious establishment, particularly as the centre tried to absorb unofficial *ulema* and Sunni sheikhs and extend its network to the peripheries.

An example of the (official) *ulema*'s expanding monopoly was the creation in 1866 of the Council of Sheikhs (Meclis-i Meşâyih) to supervise and make appointments to the Sufi brotherhoods or *tariqa* (religious orders). In addition, the *ulema* played an active role in modernisation reforms and the promulgation of the 1876 Constitution, and they often filled positions within the new so-called secular/modern educational and legal institutions that had been established in parallel with the traditional religious ones. Dressler (2015: 513) notes that while the establishment of Nizamiye courts narrowed the remit of the *shari'a* courts, they were neither 'purely secular [n]or Western, but rather were a hybrid amalgamation between Islamic and Ottoman legal traditions and borrowings from France'. In this sense, modernisation also created new spaces and opportunities for the *ulema*.

At the same time, the Ottoman *ulema* were by no means a monolithic body and were not only stratified by rank and geography. While many in the *ulema* had supported the restoration of the constitution by the Young Turks in 1908, by the Second Constitutional Period (1908–1918), there were two distinct schools of thought within the *ulema*. These divisions had crystallised in the creation of two organisations, the traditionalist anti-ITC Ulema Association and the reformist pro-ITC Ulema Committee (Bein 2009, 2011). The traditionalists advocated a defensive strategy with incremental change, while the reformists not only pushed for extensive reforms, including the rapid overhaul of the *medrese* system to adjust to the forces of change, but also sought greater influence in the management of changes under way.[4] Relations between the traditionalist *ulema* and the ITC, which had become powerful following the 1908 restoration of the constitution and assumed direct power in 1913, had deteriorated following the 1909 anti-ITC rebellion that had been supported by parts of the religious establishment. On the other hand, some of the reformist *ulema*, such as the Sheikh ul-Islam Musa Kazım Efendi (1910–1911, 1916–1918), who had allied with the ITC, also gained the opportunity to implement the more radical reforms that he had advocated.

With the onset of the First World War, the struggle between the two currents within the *ulema* had gathered momentum. At this time, the ITC's policies, shaped by the prominent ideologue of Turkish nationalism, Ziya Gökalp (1876–1924), created new opportunities for the reformist camp. Gökalp distinguished between the *ulema*'s remit

---

[4] The designations of 'traditionalist' and 'reformist' do not necessarily translate into ideological or theological interpretations or differences but rather indicate varying political positions and strategies.

regarding matters of belief (*itikad*) and worship (*ibadet*) and proposed an ending of their legal authority (*muamalat*) by according legislative functions to secular authorities, effectively ending their involvement in politics (Erşahin 2008: 189; Yakut 2005: 199–201). According to Dressler (2015: 515–516), Gökalp's argument was structurally similar to that of Islamic reformers such as Muhammad Abduh (1849–1905). This engagement of the ITC with 'reformist' Islamic currents and the *ulema* arose in *İslam Mecmuası* (1914–1918), a journal established by the ITC to rival another reformist periodical, *Sebilürreşad*, which duly became highly critical of the ITC and was closed (Dressler 2015: 515–518). Such engagement with reformist Islamic currents and contestations over the nature of Islamic reform and authority continued within religious institutions and the state in the Republic. In 1916, the ITC gained the opportunity to implement Gökalp's proposals following the outbreak of the First World War and the suppression of the opposition. The Meşihat's role would be confined to belief, worship and the supervision of the *medreses*, *tekkes* (lodges) and mosques, while in 1917, jurisdiction over the *shari'a* courts was transferred to the Ministry of Justice.

Undoubtedly, the ITC reforms resulted in a narrowing of the domain of action of the *ulema*. This pushback against religious authority was not dissimilar to the modernisation reforms of Muhammad Ali in Egypt (in power from 1805 to 1848) to assert greater centralised state control over al-Azhar (M. Zaman 2002: 60) and, more broadly, were influenced by and paralleled the attack on church power and anti-clericalism in Europe (Bein 2011: 5). Yet, on the other hand, some factions of the *ulema* who allied with the ITC also learnt new ways to adapt and survive in order to protect their position of influence in a period of profound turmoil and transformation, which would come in handy during the early phase of nation building in the Turkish Republic. With the end of the First World War and the subsequent collapse of the ITC government, the traditionalist wing of the *ulema* gained the upper hand, marked by the appointment of a new Sheikh ul-Islam, Mustafa Sabri Efendi, who was a staunch critic of the nationalists and reversed many of the ITC reforms. Still, ITC policies were to become the building blocks of the republican regime beginning in 1923, facilitating continuity between the Republic and the Empire in the birth of the Diyanet. With the establishment of the Republic, a new spell of institutionalisation for the *ulema* had begun under the body of the Diyanet, which incorporated the relations developed between the *ulema* and the state following the ascent of the ITC. However, as Bein (2011: 165) concludes, 'When it comes to the relations between religion and state in general and the Diyanet in particular, the legacies of the late

Ottoman *ulema* and their institutions, as well as the debates and struggles surrounding them, did not dissipate with the end of empire'.

The Evolution and Expansion of the Diyanet

The Diyanetification of the Ottoman Ulema *in the Republic: Institutionalisation and Centralisation*

As scholars have shown, the role of the *ulema* in nation building in Muslim majority contexts has varied (e.g. Hatina 2009b). Nationalising and, at times, anticlerical state builders in Turkey or Egypt sought to curb the power of religious authority. Meanwhile, in the more conservative monarchical regimes in the Persian Gulf and North Africa, the *ulema* played a more fundamental role in the legitimation of national struggles and state building, ensuring a more prominent place within the power matrix (see Hatina 2009b: 1–20). In the Turkish case, particularly after 1924, it is clear that the dominant faction within the nation-state building elites were keen to limit the role of religion as an alternative power centre but were not willing to challenge or reject it altogether. While anti-clericalist and positivist elements amongst the nation building elites had regarded the *ulema*'s conservatism as contributing to the decline of the Ottoman state, there was also broad consensus on the constitutive role of Islam in Turkish national identity, as outlined in Chapter 1. In 1920, the nationalist government in Ankara had established the ŞEV. Despite its narrower official remit, the ŞEV was still a significant authority, encompassing both the fatwa authority of the Sheikh ul-Islam and control of the charitable foundations. The minister's status was similar to that of the Sheikh ul-Islam in being second after the prime minister, and as head of the Shari'a Committee (Şeriye Encümeni) within the legislature, he was expected to give his opinion on all matters. Since 1924, the emerging one-party regime began to push ahead with the reform of the *ulema*, influenced by the ideas of Gökalp, who was in the parliamentary commission that prepared the law on the Diyanet (Dressler 2015: 522). The abolition of the ŞEV had been proposed as part of a bill that also sought to restrict the military's involvement in politics, which was justified with the argument that the interference of religion and the military in politics 'is objected to by most civilised nations and regarded as disadvantageous'.[5]

---

[5] See, for the proposal, ZC (3 March 1340 [1924]; 21); for discussions relating to the bill, see ZC (3 March 1340 [1924]; 23–26).

The series of reforms adopted on 3 March 1924, including the establishment of the Diyanet in place of the ŞEV, the unification of education (Tevhid-i Tedrisat) resulting in the closure of *medreses* and the abolition of the caliphate, have commonly been regarded as an important breaking point in state–religion relations. These reforms kick-started a phase that included the secularisation of the legal framework and family law and the removal from the constitution of the article declaring Islam as the state religion, resulting in a major diminution of the power and role of the *ulema* compared with both the previous Ottoman administration and other Muslim majority contexts. Compared with the Ottoman Sheikh ul-Islam, which had extensive powers over education and law, the foundational law (Law 429) of the Diyanet tied the institution to the prime minister's office while it delineated its domain narrowly as 'faith and worship' and the administration of all religious organisations, transferring all lawmaking powers to the TBMM.[6] The *ulema*'s financial autonomy was lost as control over the *waqfs* was transferred to another state department, the Directorate General of Foundations (Vakıflar Genel Müdürlüğü, DoF).[7] Another significant development in this period that substantially narrowed the Diyanet's remit was the transfer of the management of all mosques and their personnel to the DoF, in 1931, which was reversed only in 1950. A selected chronology of events and laws marking this diminution of authority and its subsequent reversal is highlighted in Figure 7.

However, the view that during this period of a break and secularisation, the *ulema* were transformed into a passive and impotent actor with the establishment of the Diyanet, regarded merely as an apparatus to control religion, is deficient and one-sided. Such an assessment overlooks not only the continuity between the Ottoman *ulema* and the Diyanet but also, related to this, the possibility that the Diyanet has a unique mission and institutional identity as an Islamic authority, comparable to other *ulema* bodies in Muslim majority contexts. Comparable to the ITC era, the real break, therefore, occurred in the grounds of legitimacy and configuration of the state within which the *ulema*, or subsequently the Diyanet, resided,

---

[6] Kara (2012: 62–63) argues that the choice of the word Diyanet as opposed to Din (religion) also reflected the *ulema*'s narrower role in the Republic.

[7] Article 6 of Law 429. See ZC (3 March 1340 [1924]: 22). This marked a process that had begun with the modernisation reforms in the late Ottoman Empire. The Charitable Foundations Administration was established by Mahmud II in 1826 as part of the modernisation reforms of the era, centralising the organisation and administration of the charitable foundations. A key driver behind the reform was the wish to utilise the economic potential of the foundations, which was significant, to channel resources to other parts of the state and, importantly, to constrain the power of the religious establishment by curbing their financial autonomy (M. Kara 1992).

not in the religious scholars themselves. With the establishment of the Diyanet in 1924, a new republican *ulema* corps did not suddenly come into existence. Rather, the Republic absorbed the Ottoman *ulema* into the newly reconfigured state, with religious scholars either joining the bureaucracy and becoming employed by the Diyanet or the ministries of Education and the Interior (as judges or teachers), or being given the right to retirement, regardless of their years of service or age. Whether or not the scholars continued to be employed by the state, those who had lost their jobs as a result of the closure of religious institutions such as *medreses* continued to receive their retirement salary (Kara 2000, 2008: 109). At least until the 1960s, the Diyanet consisted of religious scholars who had been raised and educated in the Ottoman era, and subsequently, their relatives or children who had been trained under the traditional *medrese* system, which continued to exist illegally underground despite having been closed by the one-party regime in 1924 (Bali 2011: 39; Kara 2012: 109). The Diyanet's preference for hiring the relatives of existing and former officials, the *ulema* of the banned *tariqa* orders and the closure of the *imam-hatip* (prayer leader and preacher) schools in the 1930s (Yanardağ 2012: 251–257) equally meant that the now illegal *medrese* system continued to be the main source of religious education, together with Qu'ran schools, until the reopening of *imam-hatip* schools and theology institutes with the transition to multi-partism in 1946.

This element of continuity with the Ottoman *ulema*, the continuation of traditional religious education together with the Diyanet's status as an Islamic authority concerned with preserving and transmitting religion, had a bearing on the formation and development of the Diyanet's institutional identity and strategies. This is not unlike how the Turkish military – again, far from monolithic – has also developed an institutional identity through military academies and high schools (at least until the 15 July coup attempt) and changing strategies over time in pursuit of varying interests. Just like the state at the macro level, the struggles within the Diyanet among different factions, *tariqa* orders and groups has also resulted in the evolution of its identity and strategies, which is discussed further in the remainder of this chapter. Nonetheless, the pursuit of Islamisation has remained the common denominator despite contestation and change over how this is interpreted. Equally, as a Sunni Islamic authority, the Diyanet has acted as a carrier and preserver of Sunni-Hanefi orthodoxy in continuity with the Ottoman *ulema*, which has manifested in the institution's resistance and rejectionist stance towards demands for equal citizenship made by the Alevis, the second largest faith community after Sunni Muslims in Turkey (see Chapter 3). It is significant in this vein that the Diyanet itself currently (and in the past) articulates itself within continuity with the Ottoman *ulema* and describes its role as carrying out the mission of the Sheikh ul-Islam.[8]

Survival and Damage Control in the Early Republic

These dimensions of continuity were, in turn, important in how the *ulema* as an institution survived the diminution of its power and jurisdiction during the early Republic and shaped the struggle within the state between the Diyanet – which was by no means monolithic itself – and other state actors. In the drive for power over and influence of public and private morality and communal boundaries, the Diyanet adopted multiple strategies. These included accommodation for damage control, direct resistance, subversion, and strategic cooperation in areas where it shares an 'overlapping consensus' (Rawls 1987) with other actors, such as the military. This is understood in the sense that, while both sides may hold different (but not mutually exclusive) conceptions of the nation, political union or the purpose of life, the same conclusions by actors may still be reached and, consequently, 'essential elements of the political conception, its principles, standards and ideals, are theorems ... at which the comprehensive doctrines in the consensus intersect or converge' (Rawls 1987: 9). As a result, over time, and particularly following the transition to multi-party politics, the Diyanet could manoeuvre to use opportunities arising from internal developments and external events to expand the institution's role and power.

Alongside the challenges to its authority following the collapse of the Ottoman Empire, the new Republic nevertheless offered opportunities for the *ulema* corps. First, the dynamics of centralisation inherent to nation-state building facilitated rather than eroded the institutional capacity of the Diyanet to develop and pursue its interests over time and supported continuity by strengthening the forces at the centre of the institution which themselves represented continuity as the inheritors of Sunni orthodoxy. In fact, this paralleled the ways in which processes of centralisation during Ottoman modernisation had expanded the official *ulema*'s monopoly, such as through the creation of the Meclis-i Meşâyih in 1866 to expand the centre's control over *tariqa* and Sufi brotherhoods.

---

[8] For the Diyanet's own description of its mission from its website, see 'Diyanet İşleri Başkanlığı' ('Establishment and a Brief History'), www.diyanet.gov.tr/en-US/ Institutional/Detail//1/establishment-and-a-brief-history (accessed 7 June 2018). This is not necessarily a new definition and it is frequently elaborated in this manner, see, for example, Coskun (2005) and discussions that the Diyanet's First Council on Religion (Birinci Din Şurası) held in 1993. A retired member of the Diyanet's Religious Affairs High Council (Din İşleri Yüksek Kurulu, DİYK), Recep Akakuş, states that at the root of the Diyanet lies the Meşihat-i İslâmiyye and that one must keep in mind the notion of 'continuity of the state and nation' (Akakuş 2003: 402).

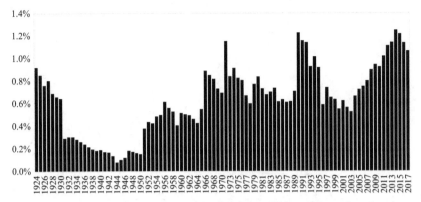

Sources: Maliye Bakanlığı Bütçe ve Mali Kontrol Genel Müdürlüğü (Ministry of Finance General Directorate of Budget and Fiscal Control, BUMKO)

Figure 2: The Diyanet budget as a percentage of the total budget

In this vein, the closure of the dervish lodges and orders in 1925 by the one-party regime following the Sheikh Said Rebellion effectively supported the Diyanet's monopoly on religious life, whereby Sunni *tariqa* orders continued their existence under the umbrella of the state, with many embedded in mosques (Çakır 2008; Günay 2006: 146–147; Kara 2012: 112; Zarcone 1993: 99–105).[9] A corollary of centralisation for the institutionalisation of the Diyanet was that similar to the other cases, such as al-Azhar, despite the loss of political and economic assets, the *ulema* had gained access to new, modern forms of power and budgets. Indeed, the Diyanet's resources have grown considerably since its establishment in 1924, as can be seen in the growth in its budget (Figures 2 and 3) – which has outpaced the general budget – personnel and mosque infrastructure (Figures 4, 5 and 6). These correlate to a degree with the waves of expansion (Şen 2010) of the Diyanet's role since the transition to multi-partism, but the declines in the budget (Figure 2, as a percentage of the total) and the annual change in the number of personnel (Figure 6) also reflect the broader fiscal constraints of the state, not just the influence of changing governments or political factions. Second, the

---

[9] *Tariqa* orders (Islamic Sufi brotherhoods), which remain technically illegal under the Turkish Law of 1925 (Law 677) closing all dervish lodges and orders, have played an active role in politics. In particular, the Naqshbandi and its various offshoots, particularly the Khalidi branch, inspired by the 'revivalist' Naqshbandi teachings of Mevlana Halid (1776–1777/1827), have been among the most active *tariqa* orders during both the Ottoman Empire and the Republic. The most prominent of these are the Menzil, Erenköy, İskenderpaşa, İsmailağa, Işık and Süleymancı *cemaats* (communities). The Süleymancılar has an extensive network of Qur'an courses and dormitories, estimated at around 2,000, housing 250,000 students. See Karpat (2001), Mardin (1989: 57–59) and Yavuz (2003: 133–150).

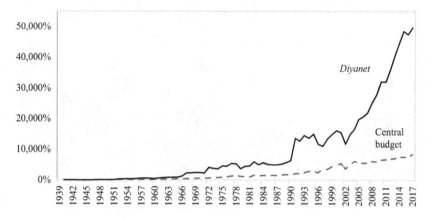

Sources: Author's calculations based on data from Maliye Bakanlığı Bütçe ve Mali Kontrol Genel
Müdürlüğü (Ministry of Finance General Directorate of Budget and Fiscal Control, BUMKO);
Türkiye İstatistik Kurumu

Figure 3: Cumulative growth in the real central budget vs. the
Diyanet budget

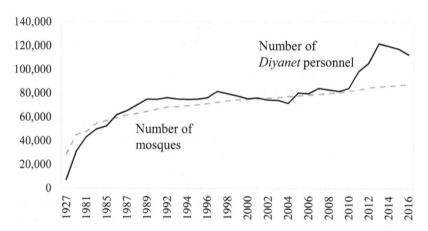

Sources: (DİB; Çakır and Bozan 2005).

Figure 4: The number of mosques and personnel over time

ongoing relevance of the Diyanet within the Republic was bolstered by
the conflation of nation and religion during the process of nation-state
building, which involved the elevation of Sunni Muslim and (from 1924)
Turkish identity. Since the Diyanet, as an institutional site of Islam, has
the authority to define what is Islamically acceptable, this conflation
means that the institution's judgements have a bearing on national and
communal boundaries (see Chapter 3 on Alevis) and thereby the

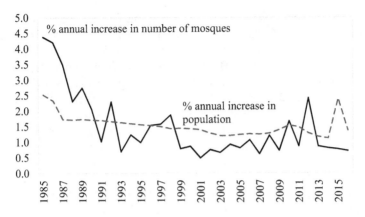

Sources: (DİB; TUIK).

Figure 5: Annual increases in mosques and population

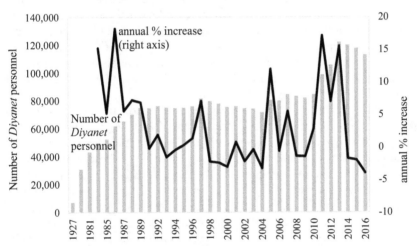

Sources: (DİB; Çakır and Bozan 2005).

Figure 6: The number and annual increases of Diyanet personnel

reproduction of religious majoritarianism. Finally, the Diyanet was empowered by the continuity of practices. Not unlike the Ottoman period or the Nasser regime's efforts to gain al-Azhar's endorsement for radical policies and messages (Moustafa 2000), the ostensibly secular Republic continued the practice of turning to the *ulema* to bolster support for reforms and state policies. Even during the one-party era (1923–1946), the CHP elites sought endorsements from the Diyanet, which involved giving sermons on praying for the nation following the abolition of the Caliphate in 1924 (BCA 7 March 1924), issuing statements on the permissibility of praying while wearing a hat or without a head covering in 1926 (BCA 10 April 1926) and encouraging private savings and domestic consumption (BCA 20 February 1939). A 1944 circular to muftis illustrates how the Diyanet propagated the new nationalist and republican values while demanding loyalty and submission to the state. After describing sorcery and fortune-telling as superstitious beliefs that have no place in Islam, the Diyanet declared Islam a rational religion that dictates the love of the fatherland (*vatan*) as well as willingness to give one's life for God and the fatherland. Being a Muslim, it concluded, meant obeying the orders of the authorities, respecting elders and obeying and loving God and the Prophet (BCA 16 February 1944). Indeed, Diyanet officials and chiefs have often criticised the demands placed on the body, even in routine matters such as traffic rules, which they argue diminish the body's authority (Altıkulaç November 2013; Yazıcıoğlu 2013). Yet the continued reliance on the Diyanet for bolstering support of government policies, and the Diyanet's accommodation of these demands, has not been a one-way street. Instead, as state actors such as the military pushed expansion of the Diyanet or attempted to assert themselves over the body, these again provided opportunities for reciprocal exchanges, giving the Diyanet leverage to negotiate further broadening of the body's role and power.

Within this context, the early period of nation building involved a phase of 'qualified accommodation' (Bein 2011: 114) of damage control and lying low for the Diyanet, much like in other Muslim majority contexts. On the one hand, various reformist *ulema* and Islamist-conservative circles, and particularly those associated with the journal *İslam Mecmuası*, were party to and supported the new regime's reforms (108–109). On the other hand, while open critics were designated as reactionary and so went into exile or underground, as Bein (110–113) notes, the majority of the *ulema* 'neither enthusiastically supported the regime and its policies nor were diehard opponents unwilling to offer any cooperation. Instead, they opted for middle-of-the-road approaches that entailed various levels of qualified cooperation and low intensity resistance' that involved a 'pragmatic engagement with the Republic'. That the *ulema* were far from declaring total submission is indicated by the writings of a prominent and leading Islamist figure of the time, Necip Fazıl Kısakürek. He wrote in his memoirs that when he questioned Ahmet Hamdi Akseki (1947–1951), the former chief of the Diyanet, as to why he took the opportunity to work there, the response was that he wanted to 'prevent further harm' to religion (Kara 2002: 30–37).

Even under the restrictive conditions of the early Republic, faced with an onslaught of reforms, the Diyanet 'used its spiritual authority and implemented the duties given to them by the political centre by loosening or widening their content and boundaries', and primarily with mosques, they ensured the survival and opening of new religious institutions (Qur'an courses, *imam-hatip* schools, charitable organisations) (Kara 2002: 30–37, 2012: 109–110). In the 1930s, the first president of the Diyanet, Rıfat Börekçi (1924–1941) expanded religious services by issuing a decision to enable, for the first time, Friday prayer services to be held in all village mosques. During the Ottoman period, this had been subject to permission and not widely practised. Likewise, Börekçi's predecessor Akseki's strategic rapprochement with other state actors, enabled him to make important contributions to Islam in the period 1924–1945 by, among other things, using the state budget to publish major Islamic works for religious education (BCA 8 February 1938; Kara 2002: 34). Even in this period, however, the Diyanet continued to push for an expansion of its role and infrastructure, demonstrated by an organisational law proposal prepared by the body in 1942 that pressed for the establishment of religious schools to 'spread [...] the Islamic religion as far as the villages' (BCA 4 April 1942).

In addition to damage limitation and cooperation in this period, particularly outside the centre, Diyanet officials acted to resist the centre's orders, including muftis spreading propaganda against the government (BCA 7 March 1929a, 7 March 1929b) and issuing unauthorised *fatwas* (BCA 22 May 1923) and preachers criticising uncovered women in opposition to the central government (BCA 21 February 1929, 24 January 1936, 19 August 1944, 5 September 1944). A document sent from the Ministry of Interior in 1930, for example, warns the Diyanet that it should take the necessary measures during Ramadan to avoid mosque functionaries preaching against reforms adopted by parliament (BCA 6 January 1930). Similarly, as Azak (2010: 54–60) notes, in this period, Diyanet officials defied the Turkification of the *ezan* (call to prayer) in 1932, with some refusing to implement the policy and reciting the Arabic *ezan*, while others employed someone else to do it in their place or used both Arabic and Turkish versions.[10]

---

[10] Similar to other reforms of the early Republic, the matter of the Turkification of the *ezan* can be traced to debates in the later nineteenth century Ottoman Empire with the rise of Turkish nationalism. One of its strongest advocates was the prominent ideologue of Turkish nationalism, Ziya Gökalp, who declared in a poem, 'In one country in the mosque the Turkish call to prayer is read, The villager understands the meaning of the namaz prayers, Young and old everyone knows God's command' (McPherson 2011).

The Diyanet's Expansion and Reproduction of Religious Majoritarianism in the Multi-Party Era

While the institution of the Diyanet had marked a major diminution of the role of the *ulema* within the state and power nexus, beginning in the late 1940s, a reversal was under way, which was followed by successive waves of expansion with the transition to multi-partism. The four waves of expansion (see also Şen 2010 for waves of enlargement of the Diyanet's role) can be distinguished in the multi-party period, marked by (i) the transition to multi-partism starting in 1946; (ii) the 1960 military coup and adoption of a Diyanet organisational law in 1965; (iii) the 1980 military coup and the Diyanet's role in the Islamisation drive and (iv) the ascent to power of the Islamist AKP in 2002, which is outlined later, in the section, 'The Diyanet's Golden Era under the AKP'. A selected chronology of events can be seen in Figure 7.

The First Wave of Expansion Following the Transition to Multi-Partism

From the 1940s on, Cold War related anti-communism politics, together with lobbying by the Diyanet, meant that the dynamics of centralisation and continuity in state practices increasingly evolved into those of institutional expansion. On the one hand, concerns over and identification of communism as a national security threat by the one-party regime, particularly in the 1940s, had catalysed the expansion of the religious field. This included the relaxation of restrictions on religious activity alongside the introduction of religious education in primary schools, the establishment of theology faculties, the opening of Qur'an courses and the reopening of tombs and shrines closed since 1925. Within this context, the governing CHP, which was also mindful of the upcoming free elections, again turned to the Diyanet, seeing its institutional centralisation and expansion as necessary to combating not just the 'danger of communism' but also the propagation of an 'enlightened version of Islam'. The Diyanet thereby continued to be regarded by regime elites as a means to tackle superstition by teaching 'true' Islam and enlightening the so-called 95 per cent Muslim population on religious matters (TBMM TDa 27 December 1947: 420–421; TBMM TDa 23 February 1949: 446, 449). The CHP government accordingly undertook policies to create new Diyanet units and returned the management and personnel of mosques to the Diyanet. For the first time, previously independent mobile preachers were incorporated into the Diyanet. Additionally, local elections for muftis were scrapped, with future appointments granted by the Diyanet's

Selected Chronology of Events and Laws

Ottoman Era

1826	Charitable Foundations Administration established, encroaching on ulema's economic power
1866	Creation of Council of Sheikhs tied to Sheikh ul-Islam
1877	The *Mecelle* (Shari'a based civil code) enters force, replaced in 1926 by secular Swiss civil code
1914	Reformist ulema introduce *medrese* reform programme
1917	Jurisdiction over *shari'a* courts transferred to Ministry of Justice
1920	ŞEV formed by Ankara government, assumes duties of *Sheikh ul-Islam*

Turkish Republic – One-party Era, Diminution of Authority of Ulema

3 March 1924	*Diyanet* established in place of ŞEV, domain restricted to 'faith and worship'; unification of education results in closure of medreses, abolition of caliphate
1930	Closure of *imam-hatip* schools which were established as vocational schools following the closure of medreses in 1924
1931	Responsibility for management of mosques and personnel transferred to Directorate General of Foundations
1932	Ban on Arabic call to prayer
1935	First organisational law of *Diyanet*

First Wave of Expansion Following Transition to Multipartism

Late 1940s	One-party regime decision to expand religious education, lifting restrictions on religious activities, re-opening tombs and shrines
1949	Launch of *imam-hatip* courses
1950	Responsibility for management of mosques and personnel returned to *Diyanet*
1950	DP ends ban on Arabic call to prayer
1951	Re-establishment of *imam-hatip* schools by DP
1959	High Islamic Institutes established by DP
1959	Launch of religious services in prisons

Second Wave of Expansion Following 1960 Military Coup

1961	Diyanet incorporated in constitution for the first time
1965	New organisational law (633), expands Diyanet's role as 'carrying out affairs related to the beliefs, worship, and moral foundations of Islam, to enlighten Turkish society about religion and to manage places of worship', introduces *imam-hatip* school requirement for personnel
1971	*Imam-hatip* middle schools closed, restrictions on graduates imposed
1973–1974	Restrictions on *imam-hatip* schools lifted, middle schools re-opened
1978	*Diyanet* begins religious services abroad

Third Wave of Expansion Following 1982 Military Coup

1980s	*Diyanet* given leading role in TIS programme
1981	*Diyanet* establishes Religious Guidance Department established with aim of fighting Kurdish nationalism
1984	Establishment of *Diyanet*'s external arm DİTİB
1993	*Diyanet*'s First Council on Religion specifies areas of 'religious services outside the mosque' as including 'education centres, Qu'ran courses, hospitals, prisons, youth detention centres, work places and families'
1994	*Diyanet* cooperation with Ministry of Health to provide religious services in hospitals
1997	Military drives introduction of 8 year compulsory education, leading to closure of middle sections of *imam-hatip* schools

Diyanet's Golden Era Under the AKP since 2002

2003	Launch of family guidance bureaus
2009	*TRT Diyanet* TV launched
2010	New *Diyanet* organisational law (6002)
2010	Legal change allowing *Diyanet* to request to censor religious content on internet
2011	*Diyanet* chief performs part of religious ceremony in Kurdish in Diyarbakır
2011	*Diyanet* announces plans to form special guidance team to fight against (Kurdish) 'separatism', hire 1,000 Kurdish ulema
2012	*Diyanet* raised in state's protocol list from fifty-first to tenth place
March 2012	New education system introduced, known as (4+4+4), paving way for re-opening of *imam-hatip* middle schools
2012	Lifting of age restrictions for Qu'ran courses
2014	*Diyanet* tied directly to prime minister
2015	*Diyanet*-Ministry of Health protocol on religious services and provision of moral support in hospitals
March 2016	*Diyanet*-MEB cooperation agreement, *Diyanet* publications on MEB's online education platform
2017	Law allowing muftis and imams to perform civil marriages passed
2017	*Diyanet* establishes Department of Migration and Moral Support Services, for provision of religious services during crises, emergencies, and to refugees drug addicts, prisoners, seasonal workers and child care centres

Figure 7: The Diyanet – selected chronology of events

head office, and it became a requirement for all village *imams* to obtain permission from the muftis to operate.

At the same time, the Diyanet's budget was substantially increased (Figures 1 and 2), reversing the period of decline since 1929 (which had affected other budget items as it was the beginning of the Great Depression). During the 1946 to 1950 period, the Diyanet's budget increased by an average 38 per cent annually in real terms (adjusted for inflation) – including a 107 per cent increase in 1946 – compared with a –12 per cent contraction between 1938 and 1945. And following the ascent to power in 1950 of the conservative and populist DP, the budget jumped by 172 per cent in 1951, with overall growth averaging 23 per cent during the 1950s, while restrictions on the Diyanet were eased further with the lifting of the ban on the Arabic call to prayer (Turkified since 1932 by the one-party regime). During this period, the expansion of religious education also broadened the Diyanet's manpower base, which had been eroded during the one-party era. Reports of American diplomats at the time also note that the rise of the DP resulted in the 'restoration to positions of power of the village Imams and Hojas', with the latter being particularly identified as reactionary or opposed to the Republic (Bali 2011: 40–41, 94, 101).

These developments in turn created new windows of opportunity for the Diyanet to manoeuvre and tilt the balance of power in the struggle with other actors within the state. Essentially, the overlapping consensus with other state actors such as the CHP or the military – that is, in the fight against communism and the preservation of the Diyanet's monopoly as the highest Islamic authority – could be utilised by the Diyanet to push for an expansion of its role in much the same way as Moustafa (2000) shows al-Azhar in Egypt had capitalised on the tensions between the government and Islamists to gain concessions. Indeed, in his account of the 'Islamic revival' in Turkey in the 1950s, Bernard Lewis (1952: 42) notes being struck by the 'growing self-assertiveness' of the Diyanet:

For a long time they had been very quiet and did not dare to raise their voices, certainly not in the towns [...] The survivors of the ulama have become more ambitious. They are openly demanding control of religious education, and they have begun, in a tentative way, to intervene in politics.

Indicating this growing confidence of the institution and revealing the bargaining process with other state bodies is an internal report prepared for the government authorities in 1950 by the Diyanet chief at the time, Ahmet Hamdi Akseki (1997). Akseki had essentially proposed strategic cooperation and reciprocal exchanges in areas of overlapping consensus, lobbying for not just an expansion of the Diyanet's role but also for religious education and *imam-hatip* schools. He espoused the republican discourse of the Diyanet's role as a propagator of an 'enlightened version of Islam' (for other examples of this discourse, see DİB 1962) – presenting itself as an authority of 'true Islam' against 'superstition' and bulwark against communism – and as a means through which to pursue its own prerogatives and to protect its religious monopoly from alternative challenges. Akseki claimed that restrictions faced by the Diyanet and the inadequate capacity of religious institutions in the country had resulted in an increase in superstition and 'false' beliefs as well as the spread of *tariqa* orders, sectarian movements 'with foreign roots' and non-Muslim missionaries. To combat these 'harmful currents', he argued, it was necessary to expand the Diyanet. On this basis, he outlined demands for greater autonomy, the return of control of the General Directorate of Foundations and its financial resources to the Diyanet, the expansion of religious education under the auspices of the Diyanet and the introduction of compulsory religious education in all schools, which he maintained had prevented the youth from becoming communists.

Akseki's call for the greater autonomy of the Diyanet, also made by prominent Islamists, did not reflect a desire for the secularisation of the state, or rather separation of religion and state. Instead, similar to strategies adopted by the *ulema* in other Muslim majority contexts, it reflected a strategy to both limit the encroachment of other state actors onto the *ulema*'s territory and to expand their authority. In addition, the Diyanet's differentiation of itself from the (banned) *tariqa* orders, as can be seen in Akseki's report, reflected a strategy to protect the official *ulema* body's religious monopoly and its authority rather than offering a negative view of *tariqa*. Indeed, as outlined above, the *tariqa* orders have not only survived under the institutional umbrella of the Diyanet but have also been involved in the institution in different capacities, including as *imams* and preachers, as detailed by various former Diyanet members. This strategy of exaggerating the threat of *tariqa* orders and non-official religious formations by the Diyanet, as Kara argues, typically reflects an effort to gain concessions from other state actors to further expand its role and preserve its monopoly in the face of alternative challenges to its authority. Accordingly, even if the Diyanet's actions and aims are in line with those of these unofficial religious groupings, it claims to go about things in the 'correct' way (Kara 2002: 58–60). In short, Akseki argued, Islam was the best antidote to communism.

The upshot of this bargaining process was the galvanisation of the Diyanet's pursuit of the Islamisation of public space and morality, thereby reinforcing the religious delineation of community boundaries. How the Diyanet negotiated the greater Islamisation of public and private space and the expansion of its role in return for supporting the maintenance of social order is revealed, for instance, by the internal correspondence between a Diyanet official and the prime minister's office in 1957. Here, the official asserts that

protecting the social order is in essence the primary aim of our religion [...] It is clear that [the Diyanet's] function is wider than the implementation of all provisions concerning faith and worship of the religion of Islam and concerned with the country's spiritual and material development [...] Thanks to men of religion, we can achieve many things by taking advantage of religious input and as such making them more attractive so that they [the public] adopt them, and we can get rid of elements that we perceive to be harmful to our existence. (BCA 8 August 1957)

Religious scholars, according to the official, could be useful in tackling everything from literacy to smuggling and crime. The response from the prime minister's office that the Diyanet could be useful in reducing crime and seeking public consent on policies demonstrates the nature of the bargaining process between the different state actors.

Turkey's First Military Intervention and the Beginning of the Second Wave of Expansion

Nevertheless, the major instances of enlargement of the Diyanet's infrastructure in the multi-party period, at least until the AKP era, typically took place following military interventions, despite the prevalent tendency within scholarship to attribute a secularist orientation to the military in Turkey. Indeed, the military, the self-designated guardians of the secular Republic, also turned to the Diyanet to bolster legitimacy. The coup on 27 May 1960, widely considered to be one of the most ideologically secularist military interventions in republican history, was celebrated in Diyanet sermons. Muftis during the period were encouraged to preach and deliver sermons to communicate the 'great meaning' of the 27 May 'reforms' (inkılab) to the public and villagers through the use of religious verses and hadiths, because 'to support our government is a sacred duty' and because 'our religion orders us to be united and disapproves of any dissention and factionalism' (BCA 28 September 1960).

Such declarations by the Diyanet and the parallel expansion of its infrastructure under junta regimes have typically been seen in the literature as proof of its submissive nature and the instrumentalising of the institution by the secular state. Yet, as in previous periods, these developments not only posed challenges but also opened up opportunities for the Diyanet. The relationship between the Diyanet and other state actors is not a one-way street. While the 1960 junta leaders sought to use it to enhance its legitimacy and pursue a re-engineering of the political landscape, this in turned involved (i) recognition of the Diyanet as an Islamic authority and of its position as determining the bounds of public morality and nation and (ii) augmentation of the reach and monopoly of the Diyanet through concomitant centralisation and expansion of its infrastructure.

Essentially, therefore, the relationship involved a two-way bargaining process and a struggle. Efforts by the military, alongside other state actors, including governing political parties, to assert itself over the Diyanet chiefs reveal the extent of that struggle. Following the 1960 coup, the Diyanet chief, Eyüp Sabri Hayırlıoğlu (1951–1960), who had been against the Turkification of the *ezan*, was removed by junta leaders and replaced by the mufti of İstanbul, Ömer Nasuhi Bilmen (1960–1961). Hayırlıoğlu's words to Bilmen, which have been related by the former president, Görmez, are reminiscent of Akseki's words to Akif Ersoy in the late 1940s – 'this is an age of disorder, not an age of goodness. We will live through difficult days [...] you will protect our state and nation like other periods in the Diyanet's history, and dissuade wrongs' – indicating strategies of tactical accommodation for damage control.[11] Yet Bilmen was also removed after serving just nine months because he resisted pressure by the junta regime to issue a sermon legitimising the prosecution of the DP leaders and to sign a negative report on the influential Islamist Nurcu movement (see Chapter 5 for further details on this group), with whom he had a close relationship. Bilmen's successor, Hasan Hüsnü Erdem (1961–1964), resigned after a retired general (and *tariqa* member), Sadettin Evrin, was appointed vice-president to the Diyanet and tried to pressure him into publishing (under his own name) a booklet against the Nurcu movement. The booklet was subsequently published by the Diyanet with the Diyanet as an author (DİB 1964a). Ultimately, the pushback from the Diyanet and conservative circles meant that the efforts of the MBK leader and the subsequent president, Cemal Gürsel, for the 'reform' and 'modernisation' of Islam through measures that included reintroducing the Turkification of the call to prayer were fruitless.

In one sense, the legal changes adopted in the 1960s simply formalised what was already being practised and were therefore playing catch-up with the Diyanet's conception of its role as shaping public and private morality. The changes introduced were chiefly in line with a 1935 draft

---

[11] Said Nursi also relates that, while he had initially criticised Akseki for joining the Diyanet, he subsequently realised that Akseki had accepted the role as a lesser of two evils (*ehven-us ser*) to limit the damage to religion (Okur 2011: 69–74).

bill prepared by the Diyanet outlining its function as 'the enlightenment of the public on religious and moral matters directly or through preachers'. Following the 1960 coup, the Diyanet was incorporated as a constitutional body by the 1961 Constitution written under the auspices of the junta regime, and in addition, a military-sponsored organisational law (Law 633) widened the Diyanet's jurisdiction in 1965. The foundational 1924 law on the Diyanet had narrowly delineated its domain as 'faith and worship' and the administration of religious activities (e.g. regulation of all mosques), while conferring all legal authority to the TBMM. However, under Law 633, the Diyanet's role was now more broadly defined to include the provision of moral guidance to the nation: its responsibilities were 'to carry out affairs related to the beliefs, worship, and moral foundations of Islam, to enlighten Turkish society about religion and to manage places of worship'.[12] In fact, the final draft of Law 633 referred to the Diyanet as the 'spiritual leader of the Muslim Turkish public', charged with handling three of the four domains defined by Islam–belief, worship and morality–with the fourth - law - being the domain of parliament. Lawmakers reasoned that the Diyanet had an important role in developing the spirituality of the nation, arguing that religion was necessary to secure social order and material development. This official widening of the Diyanet's role brought with it a major enlargement of its provincial organisation and an undertaking to hire 2,000 personnel annually to meet the needs of town and village mosques, thereby considerably increasing the presence and reach of the institution (Şen 2010).

An important aspect of the new organisational law involved further centralisation and bureaucratisation of the Diyanet, which was facilitated by the introduction of new educational qualifications and skills requirements for religious personnel alongside the absorption of around 12,000 religious scholars educated in the banned *medreses* that did not meet these new minimal criteria. Yet the new requirements, which stipulated that Diyanet personnel had to be graduates of the expanding state-administered *imam-hatip* schools, was to catalyse a shift of balance in the Diyanet and struggles in the Islamist movement more generally. Until the adoption of the 1965 organisational law, the Qur'an courses established by the traditionalist and conservative Naqshbandi *tariqa* order, the Süleymancılar, had been since the relaxation of restrictions

---

[12] For a discussion of these changes from a legal perspective, see Gözaydın (2009a: 108–119, 163–164) who interprets these developments as 'a reflection of the altering politics of religion in Turkey over 40 years, starting with attempts to "reform Islam" and come to grips with it' (April/July 2008: 221).

in 1949 an important source of trained religious personnel who occupied many top posts in the Diyanet.[13] According to Yavuz (2003: 146), this domination of various levels of the Diyanet resulted in a 'symbiotic relationship with the state'. Partly owing to the breaking of its monopoly in 1965, therefore, the Süleymancılar adopted an active campaign against *imam-hatip* schools, accusing their graduates of spoiling the religion, and their campaigns resulted in, at times, violent struggles between the two sides (see Chapter 6). Since the 1970s in particular, a new generation of *ulema* with *imam-hatip* school and High Islamic Institutes (Yüksek İslam Enstitüsü, YİE) backgrounds, who were more reformist and, to some extent, closer to the 'neo-Salafi' tradition, gained prominence in the Diyanet (Kara 2016: 566). This included prominent Islamists associated with the Nesil group (or Nesil Hareketi, as related in the section titled 'The Diyanet's Golden Era under the AKP' in this chapter and in Chapter 4), including, for instance, the former Diyanet chief Tayyar Altıkulaç (1978–1986). These developments were an important aspect of the attacks against the Diyanet by the more traditionalist currents within the Islamist movement, including from within the MSP and *tariqa* orders such as the Süleymancılar. With the rise of Nesil group associates in the Diyanet, the institution also came to be attacked as being reformist (in the footsteps of early Islamist thinkers), subverting religion and being 'without sect' (*mezhepsiz*) and thereby not protecting Sunni Islam. The representation of the Diyanet as being 'above sect' was indeed to gain currency in later years in self-representations of the institution. Meanwhile, the conflict between these currents intensified further in 1971 following the nationalisation of Qur'an schools and their handover to the Diyanet by the junta regime, and it only began to defuse in the 1980s. Yet the Süleymancı–Diyanet battle was also revealing of the contestation within the Diyanet itself, among different factions and levels of the hierarchy.

At the same time, the stipulation of Article 7 of the 1965 law that the Diyanet was responsible for 'taking precautions to protect Muslim citizens' loyalty to national ideals and prevent[ing] the exploitation of belief and differences in belief' also highlights the extent of the overlapping consensus between different state actors regarding the Muslim character of the nation and the Diyanet's role in maintaining and defining national

---

[13] The Süleymancılar is a *tariqa* order that formed around a conservative member of the *ulema*, Süleyman Hilmi Tunahan, which is claimed to have between 2 million and 4 million followers (Eligür 2010: 57; Yavuz 2003: 145). The Süleymancılar are traditionalists, concerned with protecting Sunni-Hanefi Islam against what they see as deviant currents, such as Wahhabism and Shi'ism, and they focus on developing traditional religious teaching (see Yavuz 2003: 145–149).

and citizenship boundaries. Indeed, strategic cooperation on this matter can be observed in the deployment of *tariqa* on the initiative of the Diyanet for the surveillance of non-Muslim citizens. The Ticani (Tijaniyya) *tariqa* had attracted official ire after it came to prominence in the 1950s following a series of attacks on Atatürk statues, and its leader, Kemal Pilavoğlu, was sentenced to fifteen years in prison under a 1951 law to penalise anti-Atatürk conduct. Official correspondence from the 1960s (BCA 1 April 1964) reveals that when a CHP government minister, İbrahim Saffet Onay, approached the Diyanet for its views on the Ticanis and how to handle them, the Diyanet responded by first emphasising the importance of dialogue with the *tariqa* orders rather than using oppressive means. The Diyanet then advised that the Ticanis could be useful given their anti-communist nature, and their leader could be made a (Diyanet) mufti on the island of Bozcaada, which is populated by Turks of Greek origin, to watch over non-Muslim citizens and impede efforts to achieve enosis. How a similar distrust of Alevi citizens by different state actors and the Sunni-Hanefi Diyanet's historically rejectionist stance towards Alevis has ensured the reproduction of the nation's boundaries as a Sunni Muslim Turkish majority is outlined in Chapter 3. Yet, beyond the areas of overlapping consensus, the expanding role of the Diyanet following the liberalisation of politics meant that it became more active in opposing pluralistic culture and the Islamisation of public morality. One such case was the Diyanet's battle with the state-owned Turkish Radio and Television Corporation (Türkiye Radyo ve Televizyon Kurumu, TRT) in the 1960s. In response to TRT's airing of programmes about other religions, such as Baha'ism, several warnings were issued by the then president of the Diyanet, İbrahim Elmalı, who argued that TRT had been 'established with 100 per cent Muslim Turkish money' and should be careful given the '99.5 per cent Muslim' population and the nation's religious feelings, which were that 'the Islamic religion is the world's most eminent and advanced religion' (Bedir Yayınevi 1966: 3–7).

The Diyanet and the TIS in the 1980s

The highly polarised political environment of the 1970s intensified the struggle for, with and within the Diyanet. Following the 1971 coup, the military appointed another retired colonel as vice-president of the Diyanet, but according to the former vice-president (1971–1976) and chief (1978–1986), Tayyar Altıkulaç, the body was otherwise largely left alone, as compared to other parts of the state. At the same time, the Islamist MSP, a small but nevertheless key player in three-party coalition government between 1974 and 1978, had made its influence felt on the Diyanet, including through the appointment of Süleyman Ateş (1976–1978) to head the institution.[14] Despite this, the series of unstable and short-lived coalition governments during this period meant that the various efforts to restructure the Diyanet, including a proposal to introduce electoral elements into the selection of its head, had failed to gain approval or were subsequently rejected by the Constitutional Court. Consequently, from 1965 until the adoption of a new organisational law in 2010, the Diyanet has been described as a 'legal oddity', with its institutional growth achieved, according to Gözaydın (2008: 221) without a 'technically legal basis', enabled by cabinet decrees and other administrative regulations. On the other hand, despite these challenges, the continuity in the sense of self and identity of the Diyanet alongside increasing public confidence is highlighted by Ateş's announcement during this period that frock coats worn by Diyanet chiefs would be remodelled to be the same as those worn by the Ottoman Sheikh ul-Islam (*Milliyet* 22 August 1977).

Nevertheless, the 1980 military coup marked a new wave of centralisation and expansion of the Diyanet's role. The Diyanet was seen by the junta regime as a mechanism through which to implement the TIS programme. This re-emphasis on Islam in national ideology involved enlarging the institution's capacity and personnel to create a 'pious' Turkish nation by undertaking the expansion of religious education and guidance for youths, families, prisoners, hospitalised citizens and civil society organisations, such as trade unions, and increasing Islamic media broadcasts and publications (DPT 1983). For instance, in 1981, the military General Staff (Genelkurmay Başkanlığı) ordered religious and moral knowledge (Din ve Ahlak Bilgisi) lessons to be given in prisons, and these were prepared by the Ministry of Justice with the input of the Diyanet (Özdemir 2007: 164). In 1983, 214 Diyanet preachers were appointed to give religious services in prisons (Erol 2008: 657).[15] The purpose of the religious lessons was to instil religious and nationalist values, loyalty to the state and nation. While these lessons were given for two hours a week between 1982 and 2001, in 2001, this was expanded

---

[14] The former Diyanet chief, Altıkulaç (2011a: 481–489), has argued that the MSP was particularly interventionist. Necmettin Erbakan, while in government in the 1970s, sought to pressure the Diyanet into promoting the party's cause through various means, such as in mosques, and to investigate the Süleymancı *tariqa* in order to declare it un-Islamic if necessary.

[15] Cooperation between the Justice Ministry and the Diyanet over prisoners has been dated as extending back to an agreement in 1950 (İğde 2010: 126). Religious services in prisons included the start of conferences being held beginning in 1959. In 1974, the Diyanet began to appoint personnel for the first time to provide religious services in prisons (Erol 2008: 656–657).

through a new protocol between the Diyanet and the Justice Ministry (Özdemir 2007: 164, 167).

Furthermore, following the 1980 intervention, prayers and sermons were centralised and standardised in an effort to reassert central control and maintain the Diyanet's monopoly. This effort to reorient society towards the mosque, barracks and family, regarded as a means to achieve a 'disciplined' society (Toprak 1990: 11), also involved increasing the propagation of Islam within the military, including the introduction of courses on Islam in all military academies (Yavuz 2003: 288). These courses underlined the importance of Islam from a Sunni Hanefi Muslim perspective for the development of a moral society and to ensure dutiful citizens. Accordingly, the Political Parties Act (2820, Article 89), which was adopted following the coup, barred parties from campaigning for the abolition of the Diyanet, while the 1982 Constitution, written under the auspices of the junta regime, also reaffirmed the Diyanet as a constitutional body, adding that it would 'implement its duties as outlined by its law in accordance with the principles of laicism, remaining outside all political views and thoughts and with the aim of national solidarity and integrity'. In a sense, the new article in the constitution made explicit what was already the case: that owing to the conflation between nation and religion, the words and actions of the Diyanet necessarily concerned the boundaries of the nation and not just Islam. As Yavuz (2003: 70) argues, the Diyanet 'tried to expand its power and legitimacy within the state by becoming the bastion of Turkish nationalism. It defined itself as the institution that was to "protect and preserve Turkish national identity" and protect the new generation against "communist and atheistic" ideologies.' There was thus a reciprocity between the Diyanet and the military, as the former 'used nationalism to consolidate and expand its position within the state', while the latter 'used religion to expand its legitimacy within society and enhance Turkish nationalism' (Yavuz 2003: 70).

This expansion of the Diyanet's role was welcomed by the *ulema*. In the words of the former Diyanet chief Altıkulaç (2011: 559), the period following the 1980 coup was the mildest and most harmless compared with other interventions, which he relates to his observation that the actors were 'moral' and 'believers'. Indeed, Altıkulaç adopted various approaches, including strategic cooperation, and even under the junta regime, did not refrain from refusing requests that they did not agree with (*Radikal* 31 October 2011). For instance, the efforts of some members of the MGK to interfere in the content of a book of sermons (*hutbes*) for religious functionaries was successfully resisted by the Diyanet (Altıkulaç 2011b: 564–575). At the same time, not only did lawmakers continue to seek the views of the Diyanet on matters such as abortion, but the Diyanet actively sought to influence policies by, for example, lobbying the Ministry of National Education (Milli Eğitim Bakanlığı, MEB) against teaching evolutionary theory in a majority Muslim country (Altıkulaç 2011a: 422–428, 431–432).

However, a key area of contestation between the Diyanet and other state actors that emerged in this period was the matter of the headscarf. The Diyanet came under periodic pressure, particularly from the military and the Council of Higher Education (Yüksek Öğretim Kurulu, YÖK) to issue *fatwas* stating that covering the head was not a requirement of Islam. Yet the complexity of the military's stance is indicated by the fact that the Islamist Gülenist schools (see Chapter 5) appear to have expanded during this period under one of the proponents of the headscarf ban, Hasan Sağlam, vice-general secretary of the MGK, who was to also join the Islamist association actively involved in expanding religious education, the İYC, in 1986. Opposing Sağlam's support for a ban was Mehmet Özgüneş, one of the prominent leaders of the secularist 27 May junta regime, who incidentally had signed off on the Diyanet's cooperation with the Saudi Rabita organisation. In this sense, the matter cannot be considered as only a secularist imposition. Since an official ban was first introduced in universities in 1982, the Diyanet has responded by repeatedly ruling that covering is a requirement of Islam, including during the 1997 military intervention.[16] Indeed, Diyanet officials are typically proud to point out how the institution has 'resisted the state' and has not shied away from stern statements such as those by the former Diyanet chief Mehmet Nuri Yılmaz in 1998 that 'the Turkish citizen should not be left face-to-face with a need to make a serious choice between the commands of God or the principles of Atatürk' (*Sabah* 1 March 1998). There is, therefore, a limit to how much political authorities or other state actors can manipulate or use the Diyanet, which stands as an Islamic authority. Hence, despite the overlapping consensus on various matters such as the Sunni Muslim character of the polity, non-Muslims and communism, there was nevertheless a struggle over

---

[16] The first Diyanet and headscarf controversy dates back to 1955, when the Diyanet issued a circular stating that women working for the body should have their heads covered. The headscarf was banned by the Council of Higher Education (Yüksek Öğretim Kurulu, YÖK) in universities in 1982. The ban was lifted in 1984, but the headscarf was subsequently banned again in 1987. The ban was lifted by the ANAP government in 1988 through a legal change, but this was overturned in 1989 by a Constitutional Court decision on referral by the 1980 junta leader and president General Kenan Evren. Following the lifting of the ban in 1990, another was introduced with the 28 February 1997 military intervention. The ban was again lifted by the AKP government in 2008 (for a summary see Hür 24 October 2010).

different visions of the state and society. In other words, there was a boundary, albeit a changeable and moving one, between those who might, for instance, advocate for the TIS and those seeking an Islamic state.

The Diyanet certainly became bolder in this period, emphasising the continuity between the institution and the Ottoman office of the Sheikh ul-Islam. A typical example of this is the comments of the former vice-president of the Diyanet Hamdi Mert during a Diyanet seminar on religious education and services in 1988 (DİB 1988: 413–415, 418). According to him, the Turkish nation had seen the Diyanet as the heir of the Meşihat and was longing for it to play such a role, yet the Republic had imposed restrictions on its ability to take a more active role in current affairs. Again underlining the *ulema*'s strategic bargaining to pursue their own agenda, the expansion of the Diyanet's role and religious education were important, Mert warned, in fighting against radical Islamists and efforts by neighbouring countries (including Iran) to export these currents into Turkey, as well as for national unity against ethnic agitation.

At the same time, despite the renewed emphasis on Islamisation following the 1980 coup, many of the TIS policies marked a continuity with previous practices. For instance, a 'book of religion for the military' (*Askere Din Kitabı*) had been prepared by the Diyanet in 1925 for all military academies and units. Even before the military intervention on 12 September, the Diyanet frequently championed the role of Islam as an antidote to anarchy on the streets, and certainly its expanded role after the coup offered new opportunities for the pursuit of the Islamisation of public space and morality, such as through increasing religious education and Qur'an courses. Ultimately, the Diyanet emerged as a more expansive institution with an international presence involving a growing network of branches abroad (established under the Turkish-Islamic Union for Religious Affairs (Diyanet İşleri Türk-İslam Birliği). What was new, however, was the increasing shift in the balance of power between different state actors towards more conservative elements, as outlined in Chapter 1. This shift was not unrelated to geopolitical developments and the Cold War, which included the propagation of Islam as a means of fighting communism, influenced by the newly enriched (from oil) conservative Persian Gulf monarchies. Indeed, the global nature of this situation is revealed by the fact that the Saudi-based Rabita, established in 1962 and known to propagate a highly strict understanding of Islam (Wahhabism), had been building links with the Turkish *ulema* and Islamists. A key interlocutor in the Islamist movement was Salih Özcan (1929–2006), who was a member of Rabita. He was a disciple of Said Nursi, who had been active as a member of parliament in the MSP in the

1970s and was the owner of the Islamist *Hilal* journal and publishing house, which had translated important works by the Egyptian Muslim Brotherhood (Kara 2016: 517–523; Çağatay 1972). On the Diyanet side, a key point of contact with Rabita was the former vice-president of the Diyanet (1965–1971), Yaşar Tunagür (1924–2006), who was known as a Nurcu and also one of the leading members of the Gülen movement (Kara 2016: 523). In 1975, at the request of Mehmet Özgüneş, Tunagür's activities were examined by a Senate committee in a twenty-nine-page report (CSAK 17 February 1975) that reveals his connections with, and those between, the Nurcus, the KMD (see Chapters 4 and 5), nationalist Turkish Hearths (Türk Ocağı), the Muslim Brotherhood and Rabita. According to the report, Tunagür had become the leader of an extremist rightist faction, engaging in 'anti-secular activities', such as attacking the regime in sermons and mobilising Islamists against the Republic, translating radical Islamist Sayyid Qutb's works, privileging building Nurcu cadres within the Diyanet and engaging with Kurdish nationalists. His activities were contested within the Diyanet, which is also revealing of the struggles within the organisation. İbrahim Elmalı (1965–1966) and Ali Rıza Hakses (1966–1968), Diyanet chiefs during this period, had written to the president, Cevdet Sunay, to express discomfort at Tunagür's 'destructive and divisive' actions, asking for his removal. Yet relations between Rabita and the Diyanet expanded in the 1980s (Mumcu 1993), when the organisation began to fund the salaries of the Diyanet officials overseas with the stated aim that Turkish workers abroad would not be tainted by 'foreign ideologies' (Ahmad 1988: 762).

The Diyanet's Golden Era under the AKP

The 1980 coup and the adoption of the TIS programme not only resulted in the Islamisation of public space but also opened up opportunities for Islamist movements. This outcome was not surprising given that states have a special role in shaping the social map through their ability to influence and prohibit political activity and distribute economic and political resources. Suppression by the junta regime, together with the end of the Cold War, had largely weakened the leftist movement, significantly constraining its ability to manoeuvre and organise. On the other hand, as rightist, Islamist and conservative currents gained an upper hand within the state, more spaces were opened up for Islamist mobilisation with the TIS project and expansion of religious infrastructure. By the 1990s, this had borne fruit with the increasing success of Islamist parties in the general elections. Yet the mounting tensions within the state had erupted in another military intervention. Compared with previous overthrows in Turkish history, the so-called post-modern coup of 28 February 1997 appeared on the surface to be the most anti-Islamist, involving not only the forced resignation of the Islamist-led coalition government and the party's subsequent closure but also a significant curbing of religious education and the targeting of Islamic capital.

During this period, the struggle with the Diyanet also intensified. Similar to previous takeovers, in renewed efforts by the military to assert itself over the Diyanet, a retired general staff officer was appointed as an advisor to the chief to teach Atatürkism to religious officials. For a brief period, these interventions had a marked effect on the Diyanet's public discourse (Coskun 2005). For instance, prior to 28 February, the institution's publications (e.g. *Diyanet Dergisi*, distributed to all personnel) and chiefs often not only emphasised continuity with the office of the Sheikh ul-Islam but also argued that the Diyanet's role should be expanded in line with its Ottoman counterpart. Equally, reference to Atatürk or praise of the Republic were absent or rare. After 28 February, references to the Sheikh ul-Islam or other Ottoman figures, such as Abdülhamid II, were replaced by praise of Atatürk's role in the Turkish War of Independence and the importance of the Republic. Meanwhile, in a highly symbolic move, the first female member (and without a headscarf) was appointed to the Religious Affairs High Council (Din İşleri Yüksek Kurulu, DİYK), the highest decision-making and consultative body in the Diyanet. The move followed the reaffirmation of the headscarf ban by the YÖK and was made despite the repeated *fatwas* and declarations by the Diyanet stating that the headscarf was an Islamic requirement. For some generals at the MGK, the Diyanet had remained too passive against the proliferation and mobilisation of *tariqa* orders and Islamists domestically and abroad. And, like previous junta regimes, these generals considered the institution to be a means of fighting radical Islamists and Kurdish nationalists. In this vein, the MGK pushed for centralisation measures that included giving the Diyanet greater control over mosques to prevent the emergence of independent mosques and *imams* outside the Diyanet's oversight. They also pushed for the dispatch of 'guidance' teams to 'enlighten' citizens.

However, these pressures on the Diyanet were to largely dissipate with the ascent to government of the Islamist AKP in 2002 and the military's push away from politics since 2007, although new types of challenges have emerged, especially since the 2016 coup attempt. Underlining the post-2002 period as a new era for the Diyanet, the former chief, Mehmet Görmez (2010–2017), frequently emphasised that the institution is no longer confined to the mosque but is fulfilling a much wider role as a moral leader for society in all walks of life. This has certainly been marked by its growing visibility in public life and its unprecedented institutional expansion. Consequently, conventional wisdom has shifted in recent years from characterising the Diyanet as a protector and complementary element of Kemalist ideology to characterising it as an imposer of AKP's Islamist ideology (Öztürk 2016). The perception of Diyanet's submission to the AKP has been reinforced by its steadfast stand with the AKP government during the 15 July coup attempt by mobilising opposition to the coup attempt, positioning itself firmly against the Gülenists in the subsequent days – though the body not only previously collaborated with the Gülenists but Gülen had himself been a former Diyanet *imam* some years earlier. Likewise, the Diyanet appeared to be aligned with the AKP even prior to 15 July. For instance, Görmez was highly criticised for his support of AKP's incendiary allegations that the Gezi Park protestors in 2013 had consumed alcohol at a mosque in a central İstanbul neighbourhood. Equally, in recent years, there has been mounting criticism alleging that Diyanet sermons have been used as a channel for pro-AKP propaganda, while *imams* have reportedly been under pressure to seek votes for the AKP, including for the constitutional referendum in April 2017 (Tremblay 12 April 2017). Despite his apparent loyalty to the AKP and amidst rumours that he was forced to resign, Görmez's resignation in July 2017, a year after the coup attempt, has been regarded as another sign of the Diyanet's deepening submission to the will and control of President Recep Tayyip Erdoğan. The AKP's, or rather Erdoğan's, increasing weight over the Diyanet is also revealed by a damning 140-page report published in July 2017 on the Gülenists, accusing them of being 'organised exploiters of religion' (DİB 2017a) – notably around the same time as the resignation of Görmez.

Even so, together with these new pressures and challenges for the Diyanet, the body has been able to take advantage of the opportunities created by the AKP and the greater degree of consensus in political visions, including the Islamisation of state and society, to pursue its own agenda and institutional expansion. Indeed, the body's steadfast support of the AKP government has borne much fruit for the institution (see a selected summary in Figure 7). A new organisation law (No. 6002) adopted in 2010 not only formalised the Diyanet's institutional expansion since 1965 but also considerably widened its jurisdiction and raised its status within the administrative hierarchy of the state (to undersecretary, second only to a minister). The Diyanet's mission was now to explicitly include (i) conducting 'studies on different religious communities and religious-social formations that are members of the Islamic religion' (Article 5, Clause c) and (ii) (more importantly) tasking the

Strategy Development Department with examining 'from a legal perspective', and giving opinions on, laws, statutes, regulations and draft laws forwarded by the Office of the Prime Minister, other ministries and the presidency (Article 7, Clause ğ, 5).

Thus, on the one hand, the Diyanet's position as a 'higher' religious authority was reaffirmed and augmented by a subsequent law to allow it to request to censor religious content on the internet by seeking a court order. On the other hand, given that the Diyanet is an Islamic authority, one can only infer that the examination of laws, traditionally the duty of the Council of State (Danıştay), is being undertaken from the perspective of Islamic law. In effect, therefore, the new law bolstered the Diyanet's role in politics and its activism in this field has become more visible over time. The Diyanet was also granted the right to establish its media sources, which gave it an opportunity to finally establish the television station – to 'inform' the public about religious matters and teach them the Qu'ran – that had been planned for some years (*Yeni Şafak* 29 December 2006).[17] Celebrated by Diyanet officials and Islamist circles, the 2010 law was described by the Diyanet as 'paving the way for religious services outside the mosque', moving out of the way anything that could be considered a constraint and enabling its personnel to serve in a suitable environment (DİB 2008).[18] The renewed focus on services outside the mosque is not new but began to be explicitly formalized during the November 1993 First Council on Religion (Birinci Din Şurası). In this meeting, the target sites for Diyanet services were specified as mosques, education centres, Qu'ran courses, hospitals, prisons, youth detention centres, workplaces and families (Başar 2008: 621; Özdemir 2007: 163). Following this, in 1994, cooperation with the Ministry of Health was expanded, with the Diyanet kick-starting efforts to provide religious and psychological services in hospitals. These services were launched in January 1995, and in 1996, a Diyanet memorandum (No. 506, 8 April 1996) 'Religious Services Outside the Mosque' ('Cami Dışı Din Hizmetleri') was a distinct, or stand-alone (*müstakil*), service area (Başar 2008: 621). Another Diyanet memorandum from 2007 which specified that, 'the responsibility of enlightening society and overseeing places of worship accorded to the presidency [Diyanet] as specified in Law 633, cannot be restricted to mosque services alone' (İğde 2010: 121) can be viewed as another attempt to

---

[17] See, for example, discussions at the First Council on Religion (Birinci Din Şurası) held in 1993, including İskurt (1995).

[18] There is also a description by the body on the Diyanet's own website at www.diyanet.gov.tr/tr-TR/Kurumsal/Detay//1/diyanet-isleri-baskanligi-kurulus-ve-tarihcesi.

specify an expanded framework for Diyanet's role. Diyanet's trade union, Diyanet-Sen has also campaigned for the appointment of Diyanet *ulema* as 'religion psychologists' to hospitals and as religious personnel to the military, with many of these demands realised under the AKP. Furthermore, underlining this increased role and visibility was the highly symbolic move in 2012 to raise the chairman of the Diyanet in the state's protocol list from fifty-first to tenth place.

Together with these new political resources and opportunities, the Diyanet also gained considerable economic resources as a result of being allocated a larger budget than in any other period. While the Diyanet's budget averaged around 0.6 per cent of the total budget over the history of the Republic – 0.4 per cent from 1925 to 1951 and 0.7 per cent in the multi-party period – it has risen to 0.9 per cent under the AKP, starting in 2002. Generally, in keeping with previous periods, its budget has also outpaced growth in the general budget in real terms (adjusted for inflation), reaching 10 per cent year-on-year compared with 7 per cent between 2003 and 2016. The Diyanet's budget increased by an average of 25 per cent year-on-year in real terms during 1951 to 1960, 14 per cent during 1961 to 1970, 10 per cent during 1971 to 1980 and 8 per cent during 1981 to 2002, compared with the growth in the central budget of 22 per cent between 1951 and 1960, 5 per cent between 1961 and 1970, 9 per cent between 1971 and 1980, 9 per cent between 1981 and 2002 and 6 per cent between 2002 and 2016. In the 2014 general budget, the Diyanet's budget spending was the sixteenth largest (as a percentage of the total), and greater than, for example, the ministries of development, foreign affairs, health, the interior and science, industry and technology. While around 97 per cent of the Diyanet's budgetary expenditures is on personnel, which totalled 112,725 people in 2016 (see Figure 6 for its evolution over time), it has access to other resources, such as income generated from arranging pilgrimages. A further important source of income is the Turkish Religious Foundation (Türkiye Diyanet Vakfı, DV), established in 1975 by the Diyanet to provide support for its activities, including the construction of Qur'an courses and mosques (which are controlled but not typically funded directly by the Diyanet). Meanwhile, the Diyanet's personnel have increased by 52 per cent between 2002 and 2016, compared with a 15 per cent increase in the number of mosques to 87,381, and 21 per cent growth in the population over the same period (see Figures 4, 5, 6). The rise in the number of Qur'an courses has also been unprecedented at 392 per cent between 2002 and 2016 to 18,021 (see Figure 14), buoyed by the relaxation of the regulatory framework, including the lifting of age restrictions, in 2012.

Certainly, in continuity with and in a manner outpacing the TIS programme, the Diyanet has emerged as a key actor in social policies under the AKP, which in turn has significantly expanded the Diyanet's capacity and opportunities to pursue the Islamisation and its bid to dominate public morality by 'stepping outside the mosque'. It was in much this vein that Görmez called on the *ulema* to take a leading role in public life, stepping outside the mosque to not just offer moral leadership, but to more actively pursue Islamization: 'No Muslim should be deprived of reading the Qur'an. For this reason, in recent years, as the Presidency of Religious Affairs, we have completely changed the curriculum, program and methodology. Previously, we taught the Qu'ran to those that came to us... now... I say we should go to those that do not come to us, we should go their homes, shops... and teach them the Qur'an. To achieve this, we will be at the service of our nation with our 120,000 personnel. *We will come to you. There should be no one that has not read the Qu'ran* [my italics]' (*TRT Haber* 15 November 2015). Likewise, the establishment of Family and Moral Guidance Bureaus (Aile İrşat ve Rehberlik Büroları) since 2003, tasking *imams* with offering moral support and guidance to families, workers, youth and particularly women, has been an important mechanism through which the *ulema* has extended its penetration of private spaces, enhancing its capacity to refashion social mores (Adak November 2015). In a 2016 report to the parliamentary commission on strengthening family unity, the Diyanet recommended that an increase in its institutional capacity was necessary for it to be able to provide services such as advice to newly married couples, and moral and religious guidance to families to protect them from superstition, anti-Islamic activities and addiction. This was further broadened by a new directive adopted in July 2017 which established a new Department of Migration and Moral Support Services (Göç ve Manevi Destek Hizmetleri Daire Başkanlığı) to provide religious services during crises and emergencies such as earthquakes and terror attacks, while assigning it new duties such as the provision of services to Syrian refugees, drug addicts, prisoners, seasonal workers and child care centres.

Accompanying this expansion has been a hitherto unseen level of explicit attacks by the Diyanet against secularism and the secular legal framework. Following a spate of jihadi terrorist attacks targeting Turkey in 2015, Görmez declared that secularism was responsible for sending the world into a total war, arguing that more religion was the antidote to conflict and radical Islamists, who have 'learned [Islam] in an incorrect way' (*Hürriyet Daily News* 14 December 2015). Likewise, during his handover ceremony, the newly appointed Diyanet Director, Ali Erbaş, underlined the *ulema*'s fight against secularism by vowing to 'work harder to reach mankind, which is wallowing in the grip of secularism [...] to deliver to mankind the eternal call of Allah and his messenger' (*Cumhuriyet* 18 September 2017). Legislation in 2017 empowering Diyanet *muftis* and *imams* to perform civil marriages, which were previously conducted only by municipal authorities, can be seen as a creeping attack against the secular legal framework, and particularly the secular civil code adopted in 1926.[19] While this legislation was first proposed in 2014 by an AKP member of parliament, with the public support of Görmez, it was also previously a key proposal put forward in 2007 by Diyanet-Sen (26 July 2017).

The Diyanet's increasing influence over education is another area that has been expanded in the AKP era, particularly through greater collaboration between the MEB and the Diyanet. This collaboration has included the Diyanet becoming more involved in shaping the delivery and curriculum of religious education and extending the body's influence through the transfer of Diyanet personnel to the MEB (Eser 12 November 2017). A cooperation agreement with the MEB in 2014 involved the inclusion of the Diyanet's publications on the MEB's online education platform, which has just under twelve million users. The Diyanet's ambitions on this front were indeed underlined by the new chief, Erbaş, in his handover ceremony, when he declared that the institution would strengthen its collaboration with the state's (Islamic) religious schools (the *imam-hatips*) and theology faculties (*Cumhuriyet* 18 September 2017).

Despite its fruitful partnership with the AKP, the Diyanet has not refrained from demanding autonomy, either. Indeed, even Mehmet Görmez, seen as one of the most politicised and compliant Diyanet chiefs, periodically demanded autonomy (*Haber 7* 24 July 2013; *CNN-Türk* 8 March 2016). In 2014, the Diyanet was attached directly to the Office of the Prime Minister rather than that of the deputy prime minister. This was defended by the prime minister of the time, Ahmet Davutoğlu, with the following words:

---

[19] The law allows for civil marriages to be performed by muftis and *imams*, whereas previously, only non-religious officials, including municipality officials and *mukhtars* (elected officials of neighbourhoods, villages and the like) were empowered to do so. Despite the fact that the law still does not recognise Islamic marriage and, thereby, officially does not undermine the secular civil law, how this will blur the lines of civil and Islamic marriages is revealed by, for example, the prominent pro-government Islamist Hayrettin Karaman (30 July 2017). According to Karaman, those who choose to get married by a mufti will 'believe that these marriage ceremonies [...] will be in conformity with Islamic law [...] thereby killing two birds with one stone', by not having to first have a legally recognised civil marriage, as was the case previously, and then a legally unrecognised Islamic ceremony.

I do not find it appropriate to confine religious authorities with bureaucratic restrictions. I was disturbed that our Presidency of Religious Affairs acted as an institution that functioned as a bureaucracy. We have removed these bureaucratic limitations by linking it directly to the Prime Minister [...] As a structure representing the vast majority of society, the Diyanet should have a prestigious position in society. It should be seen as a social authority. For the Diyanet [the need for] reform is obvious. The Diyanet organization should work in a manner that is more autonomous and appealing to all religious groups. (*Milliyet* 4 September 2014).

Following the 15 July coup attempt, the call by the Diyanet's former chief Görmez for the body to be tied directly to the presidency should not necessarily be regarded as an abandonment of the push for autonomy. This call can instead be interpreted as the formalisation of its mission and existence as an Islamic authority, in continuity with the Ottoman *ulema* – given that the institution describes itself as being rooted in the Ottoman Sheikh ul-Islam rather than just a natural extension of the programme of the political authority. Within the Ottoman system, the Sheikh ul-Islam rarely opposed the sultan but had extensive powers given the role of the *ulema* as a key pillar of the state, which in turn enabled it to enjoy degrees of autonomy. Such a role has been underlined by the critical part that the Diyanet played in the mobilisation of opposition to the attempted coup on 15 July 2016 and its support of the AKP regime. Equally, the decision by the Diyanet to hold special 'conquest' prayers in mosques across the country for the victory of the Turkish military in Syria against the Syrian Kurdish People's Protection Units (YPG) is another case in which the Diyanet can be positioning itself in such a role.

The enlargement and increasing prominence of the Diyanet in the AKP period therefore cannot be regarded as a purely one-way relationship in which the former is always used and expansion is considered an outcome of government manipulation. Such a picture is missing an important part including dimensions of continuity and the Diyanet's agency. The prevalence of the master narrative and a binary approach to the relationship between state, religion and society has meant the neglect of the ways in which the Diyanet, in parallel with the Ottoman *ulema*, have struggled and adopted different strategies to turn developments in their favour and thereby increase their power. While governments and other state actors have found it politically expedient to bolster their legitimacy through the Diyanet, this in turn has augmented the body's authority to decide what is Islamically acceptable as well as to strengthen its capacity and monopoly. Crucially, this has meant that the Diyanet is a central institution that has reproduced the religious majoritarianism of the state in terms of the continued persistence of the Sunni

Muslim (Turkish) delineation of community boundaries and has also ensured the Islamisation of public and private space and morality.

At the heart of the ostensibly secular Republic was an institution that facilitated a more conducive environment for the growth of Islamism, and in fact, the Islamist movement, far from its assumed peripheral status until the rise of the AKP, was intertwined with the Diyanet. It is therefore not a coincidence that, for instance, two Diyanet chiefs, Lütfi Doğan (1968–1972) and Tayyar Altıkulaç, were directly involved in the founding of the two most important Islamist political parties, the National Order Party (Milli Nizam Partisi, MNP) and the AKP, respectively, and that many others have also been active in Islamist politics. Underlining the fluidity of the boundaries between state and society, Islamist and *ulema*, is the case of the close relationship between the highly influential triumvirate who were the leaders of the Islamist Generation Movement (Nesil Hareketi), which played an important role in the pursuit of the Islamisation of society and the (re)production of an Islamist generation (see Chapters 4 and 5): Hayrettin Karaman, a theologian and columnist closely associated with the AKP, who openly gave his support for the party and for President Erdoğan; the theologian Bekir Topaloğlu (1936–2016), who was Erdoğan's *imam-hatip* teacher; and Tayyar Altıkulaç, who was first appointed as vice-president to the Diyanet in 1971, serving as its chief between 1978 and 1986 (Kara April 2016; İnal and Alagöz 2016; Karaman 2015a, 2015b).[20] Karaman (2015a, 2015b), for instance, relates how the three debated whether Altıkulaç should join the Diyanet and decided that it would strengthen the movement to have their man in Ankara.[21] Altıkulaç (2011a, 2011b) also notes how he discussed many policies, such as the development of training for Diyanet officials and the content of the policies, with this circle of 'friends'. This relationship between the Islamist movement and the *ulema* has become more public in the AKP period, as exemplified by the establishment of an Enlarged Consultative Board (Genişletilmiş İstişare Heyeti) in 2017, tasked with supporting the brain of the Diyanet, the DİYK, which includes names such as Hayrettin Karaman. Yet, at the same time, competition between the different currents within the Diyanet, also reflecting and related to struggles within the Islamist movement,

---

[20] Karaman has become a highly controversial figure, with opposition critics accusing him of becoming the AKP's fatwa authority, especially following his writings on the religious necessity of voting yes in the 2017 constitutional referendum. See, for example, Karaman (13 April 2017) and Mumcu (1 April 2017).

[21] Altıkulaç (2011a) claims that his decision to join was not motivated by such a discussion with friends, although he does not deny that they worked closely together during his tenure.

continues. A case in 2017 has been the uproar among traditionalist groups and *tariqa* orders such as the Naqshbandi İsmailağa community, who criticised the decision by the Diyanet to suspend İhsan Şenocak following his controversial comments about women. The Diyanet was accused of not being able to serve 'the Sunni Muslim nation' as befitting a Sunni institution, together with accusations of 'crypto' (Gülenist) groups within the institution trying to undermine it (*Milli Gazete* 31 October 2017; *Milli Gazete* 4 November 2017; *İhvanlar* 4 November 2017).

In this manner, the Diyanet may be regarded as the umbrella under which the various Islamist communities and *tariqas* have continued their existence of struggling, competing and mobilising. The leaders of the most influential *tariqa* orders, the Süleymancıs, the İskenderpaşa *cemaat* (community), the Nurcu and the Gülenists, were all Diyanet employees, and the extent of their influence within the institution has been referred to by Diyanet chiefs and raised as a concern by other state actors over the years. The Süleymancıs have comprised an important bloc within the Diyanet owing to their Qur'an courses, acting like an autonomous group within the organisation's body, according to Altıkulaç. Likewise, the influence of the Gülenists is highlighted by the purge of 3,090 (or 2.7 per cent of the total) personnel as of January 2018 from the organisation following the July 2016 coup attempt.[22] Prominent chiefs of the Diyanet, such as Ahmet Hamdi Akseki, are known to have been sympathetic to Said Nursi and the various factions of the Nurcu movement. In the AKP period, these relationships between the *ulema* and *tariqa* orders have also become more visible, with a public meeting for the first time in the Republic's history taking place between the Diyanet and some thirty *tariqa* orders in January 2017 to determine common principles in a move that also suggests an effort by the institution to reassert its authority over different religious groups and currents. Since the 15 July 2016 coup attempt, the Diyanet has been calling for greater control and authority for itself over the religious orders to adequately monitor groups such as the Gülenists (*Al Jazeera* 8 September 2016), again turning event into opportunity to expand its monopoly and remit. In fact, in 2015, a prominent Naqshbandi sheikh did not hold back from referring to the chief of the Diyanet as the order's 'army commander' (Cornell 19 October 2015). Far from having a differentiation between the Diyanet, Islamists, state and society, official or unofficial Islam, there is clear intertwining based on a common political vision. The Diyanet, through

---

[22] Just under 300 have since been allowed to return to their posts. This data has been compiled by the author from decrees published on the state's Official Gazette (*Resmi Gazete*) portal.

its legal monopoly, as a centralised and hierarchical organisational structure, was well placed to aggregate and facilitate what Bowen (2016: 231) has described as 'practical convergence' which related to 'instances of reasoning toward a shared horizon from distinct starting points' in order to achieve coordination and agreement between the different Muslim religious groups and factions.

The Diyanet's Global Expansion in the AKP Era

A further dimension of the expansion of the Diyanet in the AKP era is its growing reach beyond Turkey's borders. The Diyanet's foreign policy activism is not entirely new. Its involvement in delivering religious services in Europe under the formal structure of the Turkish-Islamic Association of Religious Affairs (Diyanet İşleri Türk İslam Birliği, DİTİB) began in the early 1980s, partly driven by the growing influence of the Islamist National Outlook (Milli Görüş) movement founded in 1969 that is associated with the MSP, and the Süleymancılar and Kaplancıs[23] (Çıtak 2010: 621–622).[24] Since the collapse of the Soviet Union in 1991, it has been engaged in Central Asia and the Balkans building mosques, sending *imams*, disseminating religious knowledge, establishing educational institutions to train religious personnel and competing for influence against Iran and Saudi Arabia. These activities have gained momentum in the AKP era (Balcı 27 January 2014) with the Diyanet's activities widening in recent years to include the targeting of the Alevi-Bektashi communities in the Balkans,[25] humanitarian aid and conducting relief activities in Africa, providing Islamic education scholarships to students around the world (*Daily Sabah* 15 June 2017) and building a growing presence in the Middle East. Equally, the Diyanet has become more involved in Syria concomitant with Turkey's growing entanglement with the unfolding conflict in its neighbour since 2011.

---

[23] The Kaplancıs was led by Cemalettin Kaplan, a former Diyanet *imam* who was an MSP candidate and had been involved in building the National Outlook movement. He fled to Germany in 1981 and splintered from National Outlook in 1983, attacking the Turkish Republic and the Diyanet. He proclaimed himself the Caliph of a Caliphate he declared in 1992 (Sunier and Landman 2014: 112–113).

[24] Korkut (2010: 121) contextualises the Diyanet's rise as a foreign policy actor within the post September 2001 environment and debates and the post Cold War environment in which religions were 'converted into a sphere of international relations'. The Diyanet began services abroad for the first time in 1978, with seventeen personnel, and as of 2015, they had around 2,000 personnel, fifty-two consultancies, thirty-eight attaches and twelve coordinating bureaus (*DİTİB Haber* 2015: 3).

[25] Alevi organisations in Turkey have accused the Diyanet of pursuing Islamisation or Sunnification strategies against Alevi communities in the Balkans. See, for example, reports by Aydın (16 July 2017).

This was revealed by the former Diyanet chief's meeting on the evening of the 15 July coup attempt with Sheikh Moaz al Khatib,[26] who is the former president of the National Coalition of Syrian Revolutionary and Opposition Forces, former *imam* of the Umayyad mosque in Damascus, and a member of the League of the Ulema of Sham (Rabitat Ulama al-Sham, established in 2012 by opposition *ulema* from Damascus and Homs, and member of the umbrella group, the Syrian Islamic Council, Al-Majlis al-Islami al-Suri), which is also ideologically close to the Muslim Brotherhood (Pierret May 2014, 25 May 2014).

In 2017, the Diyanet announced that it would begin dispatching *muftis* as emissaries and coordinators to Syrian opposition areas taken by Turkey under Operation Euphrates Shield. They are involved in repairing damaged mosques and appointing hundreds of Syrian *imams* and female Qur'an course teachers to serve both in these regions and in refugee camps in Syria. In addition, the Diyanet will now be directly involved in training Syrian *ulema* in new educational centres such as in Gaziantep, a city in south-eastern Turkey (DİB 12 June 2017). This outreach into Syria is also matched within Turkey by the provision of religious services for Syrian refugees, which includes plans for the establishment of religious advisory bureaus in refugee camps and the employment by the Diyanet of Syrian *imams*. An important aspect of this is the leading role played by the Diyanet in the education of Syrian children to 'protect' them from the 'manipulation' of terrorist organisations (*Habertürk* 7 November 2017). The Diyanet Foundation has worked together with the Ministry of Education and the Qatari Sheikh Thani bin Abdullah Foundation for Humanitarian Services (RAF) to publish four million school books for Syrian children (*Hürriyet* 21 December 2016).

More broadly, these moves represent a wider agenda by the AKP and Diyanet of positioning the institution as an Islamic authority beyond Turkey. In this vein, Görmez has underlined that 'the Diyanet has become not just Turkey's but the Diyanet of all Muslims. The Diyanet has become the organization that our brothers in Central Asia, Balkans, Africa and other geographies come to for religious services and religious education. Since 2006, it has become an organization that is serving in forty locations in Africa, providing services for seven million brothers in Latin America, and for our Muslim brothers in the Asia Pacific region' (*Yeni Akit* 26 November 2016). Likewise, the Diyanet's plans to establish centres of Islamic learning in Turkey for training *ulema* also include a

---

[26] This was the same individual who caused controversy in 2012 following his call on the United States to reconsider its decision to list Syria's Islamist Jabhat al-Nusra as a terrorist organisation (LaFranchi 12 December 2012).

project to establish an international Islamic university in İstanbul, which it has been publicly pushing for since at least 2014 and which has recently won the support of President Erdoğan. Both AKP circles and the Diyanet have presented the project as offering an alternative to the more historically prestigious Islamic centres such as Egypt's al-Azhar. This is because, they argue, al-Azhar in particular has been undermined by military pressure since the 2013 coup ousting the elected Muslim Brotherhood government. For the Diyanet's former chief Görmez, the traditional centres of Islamic learning in Egypt, Saudi Arabia, Iran, Pakistan and Malaysia are 'unable to find solutions to problems in the world' (*Hürriyet Daily News* 1 October 2014) and have 'collapsed' (*Yeni Akit* 26 November 2016). With the launch planned for 2019 or 2020, the university is envisioned to be linked to the theology faculties in Kyrgyzstan, Kazakhstan, Azerbaijan, Frankfurt Goethe University's Islamic Research Centre, Strasbourg University's Islamic Theology Faculty and the Higher Islamic Institute in Sofia (*Hürriyet* 1 October 2014). Such an international expansion is likely to further enhance the Diyanet's role and status.

However, this growing global engagement is likely to have repercussions for the evolution of the institutional identity of the Diyanet. The nature of these shifts will be influenced by both changes within the global Islamist movement, 'salafisation' and radicalisation, alongside its cooperation with and efforts to absorb exiled or displaced *ulema*, particularly those from Syria who are now based in Turkey. According to Görmez, there are around one thousand *ulema* taking refuge in Turkey from countries such as Syria, Iran, Yemen and Libya (*Yeni Akit* 30 May 2016). An important aspect of this may take the form of a deepening relationship with the Muslim Brotherhood, with which the AKP government has developed a strong affinity (*Al Monitor* 12 December 2014). Former chairman of the Muslim Brotherhood-linked Association of Syrian Scholars (Rabitat al-Ulema al-Suriyin), (Pierret May 2014, 25 May 2014) Muhammad Ali al-Sabuni, has praised Diyanet's Islamic education projects, describing Turkey as playing a leading role in training *ulema* in the Islamic world and spreading the correct version of Islam (*Yeni Akit* 21 May 2016).

Conclusion

Within the scholarship, the Diyanet has been conceived through the master narrative of Turkish secularism that pits a largely monolithic state sharply against religion and society. Only one side of the story is considered when it comes to state–religion relations: the loss of authority of

Islam with the establishment of the modern nation-state, with this 'break' in state–religion relations crowned by the establishment of the Diyanet under the tutelage of the secular state in 1924. Secularisation of the legal framework in the early Republic at the same time as the establishment of the Diyanet was viewed as reflecting only the Kemalist elites' will to control religion and the disestablishment resulting in the marginalisation of the *ulema* as an anachronism. Accordingly, the Diyanet has been conceptualised as only a passive tool of the secular state, with both the institutional expansion and the continued reference to the Diyanet by state actors to enhance their legitimacy or rally support being given as evidence of the body's subordination to and control by the Kemalist state and, more recently, by the AKP. Certainly, the establishment of the modern nation-state dealt a blow to the *ulema*, and comparatively speaking, the Turkish *ulema* were weakened significantly compared with their counterparts in other Muslim majority contexts.

Yet, this narrative misses the other side of the story, which involves dimensions of continuity with the Ottoman *ulema* that underpins the specific identity and agency of the Diyanet in terms of its capacity to formulate and pursue its own agenda. A key aspect of this continuity was the *ulema*'s absorption and, thereby, the continued integration of Islamic authority within the state. Beyond a move by factions within the nationalist coalition to control religion, this reflected two factors. First, the integration was a product of the Ottoman legacy and the high levels of social closure that shaped institutional design in the early Republic. How this involved the state assuming a Sunni Islamic colouring with lines of continuity with the Ottoman state and *ulema* is elaborated in the next chapter, Chapter 3, which discusses the Diyanet's approach to Alevis. Second, it also reflects the outcome of a power struggle within a coalition of nation-state builders, as discussed in Chapter 1, and the weakening but not annihilation of various conservative and Islamist factions, including the *ulema* themselves. Ultimately, it was this integration that embedded a religious majoritarian logic within the state, facilitating its persistence over time and a more conducive environment for Islamist mobilisation.

Contrary to the prevalent narratives outlined above, viewed from the standpoint of the Diyanet, one can see an institution that seeks to preserve continuity with the Ottoman *ulema*, pursuing its mission of Islamisation and expanding its role and power as opportunities arise. This does not mean that the Diyanet is an unchanging and monolithic entity; it is not dissimilar to other bureaucratic organisations or institutions of the state. However, what distinguishes the Diyanet from other state institutions is that it is an Islamic authority, a carrier and transmitter of religion, and that endows it with a stronger sense of identity and mission, even if the precise content of this is contested within it and over time.

Although the establishment of the Diyanet symbolised the weakened position of the *ulema*, the body has steadily been able to reinforce its authority as an Islamic institution. Against the efforts of other state actors to control and influence it, it adopted multiple strategies, including cooperation and resistance, resulting in degrees of reciprocity and subversion. The overlapping consensus shared with other state actors such as the military on anti-communism and preserving the hegemonic status of a Sunni Muslim Turkish majority (discussed further in Chapter 3 on Alevis) meant that, in particular, the Cold War and the liberalisation of politics since the late 1940s opened up windows of opportunity for the Diyanet. As a result, until the AKP era, it had chiefly been during the 1960 and 1982 military interventions that the Diyanet infrastructure saw the biggest expansions, reflecting the continued reliance by other state actors on the Diyanet to boost legitimacy and support for reforms and policies. These efforts to 'use' the Diyanet, however, provided opportunities for the body, bolstering its ability to draw the bounds of what is Islamically acceptable and to turn these policies to its advantage by strengthening and expanding its authority and monopoly in pursuing its own agenda, all done in a manner similar to al-Azhar in the Egyptian case (M. Zaman 2002: 146–147). The body was not only able to reassert itself but also widen the spaces for Islamist actors, with which it was deeply intertwined and shared a common cause.

The push for the Islamisation of public space and morality ensured the persistence of the delineation of community boundaries along religious lines. This was critical in facilitating the increasing salience of religious boundaries over time in political and economic struggles, particularly as liberalisation of politics since 1950 has accentuated distributional conflicts over the state. As the Diyanet encouraged the expansion of religious education and infrastructure (elaborated in Chapter 5), it also in turn widened its constituency and gathered allies who would support its ongoing role and mission. Indeed, as an Islamic authority, the Diyanet is likely to perceive its continuity and preservation as being ensured by Islamisation and the rise of Islamist government compared to a situation in which religiosity declines and/or secularist parties take power. Under the AKP, the Diyanet is enjoying a golden era in which it is able to seize opportunities arising from its common cause with the government to accelerate Islamization. In this manner, the increased vocal attacks against secularism are revealing of efforts to speed up the reversal of the diminution of the *ulema*'s authority experienced in the early

Republic, which has been underway since at least the 1940s. Nonetheless, despite its common cause, the Diyanet also faces new challenges and risks with the growing authoritarianism of the AKP and its evolution towards a highly personalised autocracy. On the one hand, the AKP regime will seek to bring the institution more under its control, like other state actors and the military previously. On the other hand, the AKP, just as with its predecessors, benefits from enhancing the credibility of the Diyanet – which is what makes it useful in the first place. As in previous episodes, but now at unprecedented levels, this is spurring an expansion of the Diyanet's infrastructural capacity, which in turn bolsters the body's bargaining power and authority. These dynamics are not necessarily contradictory, however, since the future trajectory of the Diyanet may further parallel the status of the office of the Sheikh ul-Islam in the Ottoman state, when it was beholden to the sultan but also enjoyed a sphere of autonomy as an Islamic authority.

In sum, the evolution of the role of the Diyanet and its politics, including the overlapping and common cause with Islamist actors; the dominant paradigm of Islamism developing purely as a bottom-up reaction to the secular state and the latter's utilisation of religion for control purposes are clearly problematic. Rather, religious politics have been facilitated not just from the bottom up but also from within the state since the dawn of the Turkish Republic, owing to institutions established during early nation building combined with contingent events that tilted the balance of power in a way that allowed religio-politics to gain currency.

3   Shaping the Nation

The Diyanet's Interventions against Alevism and the Privileging of Sunni Islam

In countries as diverse as the UK and Iran, Saudi Arabia and Ireland, Greece and Turkey, rather than a strict separation, states are associated with a particular majority religion to varying degrees. Yet despite this common intertwining of religion and state, all of these countries deal with minorities in very different ways. While in theocratic states such as Iran and Saudi Arabia, minority religious practice is either prohibited or restricted, in the UK and Ireland, religious freedom and equality is generally guaranteed by law. A telling indicator of the nature of a state's relationship with religion, therefore, is not just how it relates to the majority religion but also how it relates to minorities and draws and articulates boundaries between the majority and the minority. Chapters 1 and 2 have demonstrated the relationship between the state and the majority religion in Turkey and the ways in which the Diyanet has played an active role in the Islamisation of public space. This chapter focuses on how state actors, including the Diyanet, engage with 'minorities' such as Alevis, which is revealing of the degree of religious majoritarianism in a country.[1]

Alevis have been a key matter of concern for state actors, including the Diyanet, because while Christian and Jewish communities were largely

---

[1] The designation 'Alevi' is taken here as an umbrella term (but not necessarily synonymous) for various heterogenous communities, such as Bektashi and Kızılbaş, also differentiated along ethnic and regional lines (Erdemir 2005; Sökefeld 2008; Zırh 2012). The matter of how to approach Alevi identity is highly contested: it has been considered through ethnic, cultural, political and religious terms; as within and outside Islam; and as ethnically Turkish or Kurdish (see Erdemir 2005; Sökefeld 2008; White and Jongerden 2003; Zırh 2012a). Massicard (2007) has described the Alevi movement as an 'identity movement without an identity'. In addition, Sökefeld (2008) argues that the master narrative of Alevism employs Sunni Islam as a 'negative template' in order to define itself. Works on Alevi identity include the claims that (i) Alevis represent 'true Turkish Islam' vs. 'Arab Islam' (Şener 2003); (ii) Alevis are ethnic Kurds, within or outside Islamic tradition (Bayrak 1997; Çem 2009); (iii) Alevis represent an Islamised pre-Islamic syncretic Turkish heterodoxy (Melikoff 1998: 237; Ocak 1983) and (iv) Alevis represent a predominantly Anatolia-based heterodox Islamic tradition (Shankland 1999).

eliminated with the establishment of the Republic, Alevis comprise the second largest faith group after Sunni Muslims in Turkey – estimated at between 15 per cent and 25 per cent of the population (Erdemir 2005: 938). As a result, Alevis, like Kurds, are both necessary constituents that enable (through assimilation) the construction of the Muslim Turkish majority bloc embodied in the prevalent discourse of the 99 per cent Muslim Turkish majority and also, precisely because of this role, a threat that challenges the hegemony of this constructed bloc. What the contrasting strategies employed by different state actors discussed below reveals, however, are the ways in which the Diyanet as a state institution has locked in social closure by playing a crucial role in negotiating and reproducing communal and national boundaries along religious lines. This, in turn, has underpinned the persistence of the religious delineation of nationhood and citizenship, but as the power and domain of the Diyanet has grown, it has also meant increasing the Sunni Muslim complexion of the state. The ways in which this contributes to an ethnicisation of political and economic competition, thereby raising the salience and hardening of community boundaries, is revealed by, for instance, the Diyanet's long-running resistance to Alevi demands for equal access to state resources for their places of worship.

The first section of this chapter proceeds by contextualising republican policies with an overview of the Ottoman legacy and the relationship between Alevi identity and Turkish nationalism. While Alevism was used in the process of Turkish national identity construction, it was simultaneously not recognised within this construct, and Alevis continued to be treated as an internal enemy in the Republic despite the promise of equal citizenship under the ostensibly secular state. The second section turns to the Republic, outlining competing strategies adopted by different state actors, including the Diyanet and the military, while demonstrating how the overlapping consensus within the state has resulted in cooperation to ensure the hegemonic status of the Sunni Muslim Turkish majority bloc as the basis of the nation-state. In particular, with lines of continuity with the Ottoman *ulema*, the Diyanet has acted as a carrier and preserver of Sunni (Hanefi) Muslim Turkish identity through the generations, negotiating and delimiting the nation along religious lines, as evidenced through its resistance to the absorption of Alevism within Turkish nationalism. It is in this manner that, over time, the Diyanet has not only embedded but reproduced the religious majoritarianism of the nation-state, helping religion persist as a marker of identity in public life and ensuring the continued salience of religious and sectarian boundaries in political and economic competition. The third section examines how these dynamics have been augmented in the AKP era, focusing on collaboration with the Gülen movement as well as the sectarianisation of politics in the wake of the Syrian civil war, since 2011, that have involved the targeting of Alevis. The fourth section concludes by evaluating the different state practices towards Alevis and how these dynamics have heightened social closure, further increasing the political salience of religious (Alevi–Sunni) boundaries.

The Diyanet, Institutions and National Identity

The Diyanet's approach to the Alevi issue has typically been treated as a matter of religious freedom and related to the nature and limits of Turkish secularism, but this position has been regarded as pertaining only to an Islamic interpretation. Indeed, the Diyanet is widely acknowledged as a Sunni (Hanefi) Muslim religious authority, yet its approach to Alevis not only concerns religious doctrine but is also illuminating with regard to the relationship between state, religion and nation. In fact, in shaping the bounds of Islam, the Diyanet not only defines what is Islamically acceptable but also has an impact on the boundaries of the national community and nature of citizenship. This is the result of two dynamics that relate to the relationship between religion and nationalism.

First, as a rich 'symbolic resource' (Zimmer 2003) facilitating ethnic formation and Turkish nation building, Islam has been intertwined with Turkish national identity. Second, religion, considered here to be an institutional site rather than a 'disembodied belief system' (Sidel 2007), has acted as a carrier of identity, underpinning the persistence of Sunni (Hanefi) Muslim group boundaries. Religion can prove to be a resilient container for the cultural preservation of an ethnic community because religious entities possess formal organisational bodies and institutions that contrast with loosely organised ethnic groups (Conversi 1999). With respect to national identity, institutions can therefore act as 'carriers and preservers of collective identities' (Hutchinson 2004a; Özkırımlı 2000: 184–185; Smith 1998) which underpin their persistence, because through them, 'individuals are united into social groups that can perpetuate themselves down the generations' (Özkırımlı 2000: 184–185; Smith 1998: 69). This is not to suggest, however, that identities are primordial and unchanging; the cultural stuff, or the content, of identity can change and transform over time, even if this is limited by the menu of symbolic resources (Kaufmann 2008; Zimmer 2003). But, as Barth (1969: 14) argues, it is the boundary, 'the fact of continuing dichotomization between members and outsiders, which allows us to specify the nature of continuity'.

Third, institutions are crucially involved in the construction, reproduction and negotiation of national identity, thereby shaping the contours of the nation-state. State institutions in particular, such as the Diyanet, are uniquely positioned to build and affect the construction of ethnic categories by acting as a differentiating force that distributes privileges and resources amongst groups (Brass 1985). As described by Bourdieu (1994: 7–8), 'through classificational systems [. . .] inscribed in law, through bureaucratic procedures, educational structures and social rituals [. . .] the state moulds mental structures and imposes common principles of vision and division [. . .] And it thereby contributes to the construction of what is commonly designated as national identity'. It can be argued, therefore, that institutions underpin the persistence of identity boundaries, while the content and criteria of inclusion and exclusion are subject to ongoing negotiation and change. From this perspective, in the case of Turkey, as well as in other Muslim contexts, Islam is not just intertwined with nationalism in providing a rich symbolic resource that contributes to ethnic formation but is also a carrier of identity. Accordingly, this conflation between Islam and nation means that the Diyanet's approach to Alevism is consequential for the parameters of inclusion and exclusion of Turkish national identity. In particular, if we consider nations as 'zones of conflict' (Hutchinson 2004b) in which competing conceptions of the nation based on multiple heritages, historical cleavages and legacies 'become systemised into competing cultural and political projects', then the Diyanet, while not a monolithic entity itself, can be considered to be a highly influential state actor (amongst others) that ensures the reproduction of identity along religious lines.

At the same time, in negotiating community boundaries, the Diyanet has been helped by what can be described as an overlapping consensus within the state regarding the vision of a homogenous Sunni Muslim Turkish nation. The overlapping consensus is also facilitated by the 'overlapping systems of meaning' that connect 'self, community, polity, the highest good [. . .] [and] the totality' across religion and nationalism (Lapidus 2001: 51). Within the discourse of the Diyanet, therefore, the link between (Sunni) Islam and Turkish nationalism is 'reinforced by the symbolic construction of meaning' (Lapidus 2001: 51) seen in the framing of the nation (*millet*) with Islamic terminology. The following words of a long-time Diyanet functionary, related by Yavuz (2003: 70), are revealing of this dynamic: 'Our national and religious feelings are interwoven, the DİB seeks to consolidate and cultivate national and religious consciousness at the same time. Our task is not connected to religion only but it also includes preservation of Turkish nationalism'. Despite the adoption of competing strategies towards Alevis, therefore, there has been more collaboration than struggle within the state on this matter, while the policies have, in substance, been structurally homologous and have ultimately been concerned with the hegemony of the Sunni Muslim Turkish majority as owners of the state.

The Ottoman Legacy, Turkish Nationalism and Alevis

The Elevation of Sunni Hanefi Orthodoxy in the Ottoman Empire

The practices of the Ottoman state towards Alevis were consequential for the Turkish Republic since they served as a blueprint for nation-state builders. The Republic not only continued the policies of social and demographic engineering through coercion and assimilationist practices but also inherited the sectarian bias of the Ottoman *ulema*, which continued their existence under the Diyanet. Consequently, it is possible to distinguish notable parallels of approach towards communities loosely designated as Alevis between the Ottoman state and the Republic. Within the Ottoman Empire, the *ulema* played a key role in shaping the boundaries of the *ummah* and propagating Sunni (Hanefi) Islam against the various heterogeneous communities. The emphasis on Sunni orthodoxy has been traced by some scholars to the rivalry between the Shi'a Safavids of Persia and the Sunni Ottoman state during the sixteenth century (culminating in the Battle of Chaldiran in 1514). For the Ottoman rulers, the Safavids posed a challenge to the state's claim to be the caliph of all Muslims and, hence, Islam's universal authority (Deringil 1990: 46; Gündoğdu and Genç 2013: 17). As a result, the struggle between the two sides has been interpreted chiefly as a political rather than religious one (Deringil 2000: 555; Kehl-Bodrogi 2003: 54; Ocak 1998). Terzioğlu argues, however, that the elevation of Sunni orthodoxy dates further back and can be traced to the 'gradual process of *ulema* empowerment and the spread of . . . "Islamic literacy" in the Ottoman lands' (2013: 309). In any case, following the struggle against the Safavids, the Ottoman state began to increasingly use the designation Kızılbaş (Alevis) not just against those considered to be pro-shah loyalists but against all communities regarded as heterodox, along with the Shi'a, who were perceived as open to infiltration by external enemies and missionaries (Ateş 2012: 239; Deringil 2000; Kehl-Bodrogi 2003; Massicard 2007). The Sunni *ulema* were at the forefront of delineating these communities as a threat to the abode of Islam. In 1548, a fatwa was issued by the Sheikh ul-Islam Ebussuud Efendi in which the Kızılbaş were declared heretics and their killing was proclaimed permissible by Islamic law. Subsequently, such communities became the most

persecuted elements in the Ottoman state, while non-Muslims, considered to be the 'people of the book', were recognised and protected
under the *millet* system (Ateş 2012: 240, 251; Deringil 1993a: 13;
Kehl-Bodrogi 2003; Massicard 2007: 39).

In the nineteenth century, a renewed focus on orthodoxy emerged
owing to the legitimacy crisis of the Ottoman state resulting from the
loss of territories and the rise of nationalism. The three currents of
Ottomanism, Islamism and Turkism (discussed in Chapter 1) had
emerged to address this crisis of the state through the promotion of a
new social base and ideology of legitimation (Deringil 1993a: 3–4).
Following failed attempts to forge a territorially based Ottoman identity,
the policy of Ottomanism and state ideology under Sultan Abdülhamid
II (1876–1909) shifted towards pan-Islamism. This period was marked
by the increased propagation of the Sunni (Hanefi) School of Islamic
jurisprudence as the 'official belief' (*mezheb-i resmiye*) and the active
encouragement of conversion and coercion in order to create a (Muslim)
majority 'reliable core population who would be duly imbued with the
"correct" ideology' (Deringil 1993a: 3–4). Ateş (2012: 252) has gone
further, describing Ottoman modernisation as a process of Sunnification,
including the outlawing of the Bektashi order following the abolition of
the Janissary Corps by Sultan Murad II in 1826, followed by their
handover to the Sunni Naqshbandi *tariqa* orders. In 1826, when the
sultan called on the various sheikhs of the tariqa orders and the *ulema*
to deliberate about the Bektashis, it was the *ulema* who took the lead in
damning the order, while others held back (Maden 2016: 190), suggesting their role as the carriers of Sunni orthodoxy through the generations.
Consequently, in marking the first self-conscious drive to establish a
majority Sunni (Hanefi) Muslim social base for the state, as Deringil
(1998; 1993a) argues, this period saw the increasing pursuit of Islamisation policies targeted at communities perceived as potential fifth
columns, such as the Yezidi Kurds, Kızılbaş Alevis, Zaidi Shi'a in Yemen
and Shi'a communities in the Iraqi provinces.[2] In particular, this
involved the active encouragement of conversion and also coercion
(Deringil 1998; Gündoğdu and Genç 2013: 46). The Sunni *ulema* and
Sufi sheikhs played a leading role in the propagation of Sunni orthodoxy
through missionary activities and the construction of mosques, while
Sunni *imams*, tasked with fighting heresy, were involved in state surveillance of the various faith communities (Ateş 2012: 282; Deringil 1993a;

---

[2] Additionally, Dersim clans were perceived as being too close to Armenians, Russians and
Shi'a Iran and were a target of Protestant missionaries (Deringil 1990; Dressler 2013: 75;
Gündoğdu and Genç 2013: 21, 31–32).

Gündoğdu and Genç 2013; Küçük 2002). For instance, reports prepared by the former Sheikh ul-Islam Hüseyin Hüsnü Efendi suggest that the *ulema* not only saw non-Sunni heterodox communities as potential fifth columns to be kept under surveillance but also regarded Islamisation as necessary for the maintenance of order, as the instillation of Sunni Islam in the population would 'accomplish more by education than his illustrious ancestor Selim I did by the sword' (Deringil 1990: 51).

The ITC and Alevis: 'Sunnification' and 'Turkification'

With the drift towards Turkism under the ITC in the aftermath of the Balkan Wars in 1912 to 1913, Alevis increasingly became the target of the Turkish nationalists in their Turkification (and Muslimisation) or nation building policies. In this period, the ITC commissioned a number of ethnographic investigations of the characteristics of non-Sunni Muslim communities in Anatolia. A key motivation for these was fear that such communities were close to and coming under the influence of Christian missionaries and Armenians (Ateş 2006: 269–270; Dressler 2013: 127; Kieser 2003). In 1914 and 1915, investigations into the Alevis conducted by the ITC official Baha Said Bey posited that Alevis were of Turkish origin by drawing links between Alevi practices and central Asian shamanism. Alevis were rearticulated as 'real Turks' (*öz Türk*) who had carried and preserved Turkish customs and traditions, race, blood and language since the pre-Islamic and pre-Ottoman era. This reimagined Alevi identity was, in turn, used as an element in the construction of Turkish national identity in order to posit an ethnic continuity with Central Asia (Ateş 2006: 269–270).

Yet, while elements of this reimagined Alevi identity were then integrated into the nationalist project by being ethnicised, Alevi identity was itself not recognised and was instead consigned to invisibility. These policies can be understood through what Brackette Williams (1989: 434–436) describes as the transformist hegemony of nationalism. This refers to the process whereby a putative homogeneity is created out of heterogeneity through a process of 'appropriations that devalue and deny their link to marginalised others' contributions to the patrimony'. Thus, during the construction of Turkish national identity, Alevism was ethnicised and rearticulated in order to appropriate elements of it to create a majority Muslim Turkish bloc. As suggested by Williams's framework, this appropriation did not involve the recognition of Alevism but rather marked a process through which it would be rendered obsolete. As Williams (1989: 434–436) argues, following this process, those regarded as marginal others either continue to insist on their putative root identity and are rejected as not true members of the nation, or they adopt the new identity and are 'constantly required to show proof of their contribution to the nation as they search for a place in its political and economic structure', but they 'soon learn that such proofs are often considered by the "non-ethnics" as little more than feathers and flourishes'. In this manner, despite the reimagining of Alevis as Muslim Turks, Alevis who refused this imposition were rejected as separatist and enemies of the nation, while those who tried to assimilate into the majority bloc also continued to be regarded as suspect and as potential fifth columns.

The State and Alevis in the Republic

The Early Republic and Alevis: Continued Sunnification and Turkification

In the one-party era, the early nation-state builders were to continue the ITC's practices of Islamisation/Sunnification and Turkification of Alevis, together with brutal campaigns against those who resisted their interventions. Baha Said's works and their articulation of Alevis as 'real Turks' came to form the basis of nationalist historiography. Alevi identity, which was perceived as heretical by the (Sunni) Islamic Ottoman state, became reframed (as seen in the writings of prominent politicians and historians Hasan Reşid Tankut and Fuat Köprülü) in the ostensibly secular Republic as constituting a 'Turkish Islam' in contrast to what was described as the 'Arabised Islam' of the Ottoman past (Ateş 2012: 263; Dressler 2013; Massicard 2007: 45). Exemplifying these policies are the internal reports prepared between 1931 and 1960 by Hasan Reşid Tankut, a CHP lawmaker who had also been a key proponent of the nationalist Turkish History Thesis and Sun Language Theory[3] and the founder of the Turkish Language Association. In a 1937 report on the Alevi–Zazas of Dersim province, Tankut (2000: 30) defined Alevis as belonging to the Turkish race and related to the Sumerians, and he was subsequently to make a similar claim in his 1938 report on the Nusayris (Tankut 1938), who were characterised as Turks related to the Hittites. Alevism, he argued, had become a fusion of shamanism and Shi'ism, and consequently, owing to the Sunni–Shi'a schism, had turned into a hatred of Turks, who were identified as Sunni Muslims. He claimed Alevis bore a grudge against Sunni Muslims and therefore did not want to accept that they were 'real Turks', which, he argued, also

---

[3] These are nationalist theses on the origins of the Turks and the proposition that all other languages originated from Turkish (Copeaux 2000; Zürcher 2004: 190).

made them open to incitement by Armenian 'traitors' to 'divide' the Turks. Likewise, as Dressler (2013) shows in his study on the policies of the early Republic towards Alevis, Fuat Köprülü's works in the same period placed Alevism firmly within an Islamic framework. These articulations had become the accepted logic in various elements of the state, including the military and the MEB, as revealed by a report (Yıldırım 2011: 62) submitted to the latter in 1926 which describes 'Kızılbaş Turkcomens' as being in reality Turkish Muslims who could be distinguished from Arabised (Sunni) Muslims.

Still, the one-party regime, in continuity with the Ottoman state, continued to view Alevis as suspect and fundamentally as an internal enemy. Policies in dealing with Dersim province in eastern Anatolia, renamed Tunceli province in 1936 as part of assimiliationist practices, exemplify these perceptions. Just as for the Ottoman state, Kızılbaş Alevis and Dersim province were regarded by the nation-state builders in the early Republic as a source of trouble. The province had already become the target of military campaigns and Islamisation efforts during the Hamidian era due to the state's fears about the extent of their loyalty (Dressler 2013: 114–115). For the Republic, too, 'Kızılbaş Alevism' stood as a barrier to the assimilation of Kurds and Alevis into the Muslim Turkish bloc under construction, and the inhabitants of Dersim province had been regarded as a challenge to the domination and ultimate sovereignty of the state, who had to be subdued and brought under central government control. These concerns engaged the military throughout the 1930s, as the plethora of reports from this period reveal. The chief of staff of the military, Fevzi Çakmak, had warned in 1930 that the Kurds in Erzincan were 'using Alevism to Kurdify currently Turkish villages and spread the Kurdish language', and that 'many Alevi Turkish villages that are by custom Turkish are abandoning their mother tongue and speaking Kurdish owing to the mentality that Alevism denotes Kurdishness' (Ateş 2012: 268). Similar concerns were raised in another military document in the early 1930s, where there was apprehension that Alevis, or 'real Turks', were coming under the influence of Shi'a currents and Kurdishness and that this had led the Alevis of Dersim province to identify themselves as Kızılbaş. The development of this Kızılbaş identity, it was claimed, was what had created a 'cliff' between Alevis and Turkishness because the community equated Sunni Islam with Turks and thereby regarded them as enemies. In 1936, a briefing prepared by commander Ragıp Gümüşpala (Yıldırım 2011: 90) cautioned that the Kızılbaş in Dersim province were called Kurds because in the Ottoman Empire, religious schisms led to Sunnis being called Muslims and Shi'a being called Kurds. Such divisions were being exploited by Armenians and were ruinous for the Turkish community, according to Gümüşpala. For the nationalists, therefore, 'Kızılbaş Alevis' in particular posed a danger to national unity for purportedly driving real Turks towards Kurdishness and making them a potential fifth column of Iran (Yıldırım 2011: 62).[4] As with the Ottoman state, for the republican elites, the Kızılbaş faith had to be corrected, whether through coercion, education or missionary activity (Sunnification) (Çalışlar 2010; Dressler 2013: 115; Gündoğdu and Vural 2013: 37, 45). This was to set the stage for a systematic assimilation campaign that included a brutal policy of ethnic cleansing in Dersim province in 1937 to 1938, resulting in an estimated 40,000 deaths and with parallels to the Armenian Genocide in 1915.[5]

Despite these policies of the one-party regime, there has been a tendency, particularly amongst earlier studies and in popular works, to present Alevis as the natural allies of the Republic and a guarantor of laicism, insuring it against Sunni radicalism, albeit unappreciated by the Turkish state (Koçan and Öncü 2004; Ocak 1996: 192; Poyraz 2005; Soner and Toktaş 2011).[6] Some of these portrayals have essentially mirrored the master narrative of the battle between Kemalist secularism and religion, articulating Alevis as firmly with the former but ignoring or masking the organic nexus between the Turkish state, society and Sunni Islam. In response, others have pointed out that having faced persecution under the Ottoman state, Alevi communities generally accepted invisibility and developed an affinity with the Republic given the promise of equal citizenship (Zırh 2012a: 287). However, as the Dersim Massacre (1937–1938),[7] alongside many others, highlighted, this promise was not fulfilled. Likewise, no amount of correction or assimilation was regarded by state elites as sufficient to overcome the marginalisation of Alevis in relation to Turkish national identity. Similar to the Ottoman *ulema*, who were missionaries pursuing Islamisation and also acting as informants for the state regarding other religious communities, the Diyanet was involved in the active surveillance of Alevi communities in this period. In 1946, a circular to muftis from the Diyanet headquarters warned that

---

[4] Similarly, Naşit Hakkı Uluğ, a key member of the CHP elites, describes Alevis as coming under Safavid influence against the Ottoman Empire (2007 [1939]: 89–92).

[5] This is evidenced in various documents from the 1930s, including a confidential Dersim Report produced by the Gendarmerie General Command between 1933 and 1934 (Çalışlar 2010) and reports of the public inspectorates (Koçak 2010b: 143).

[6] For a critical approach towards these narratives, see Sinclair-Webb (2003).

[7] The numbers of killed are contested and fluctuate between 10,000 and 70,000, but equally many thousands were forced to migrate and disperse into other regions of Turkey in order for the state to implement Turkification and Sunnification of the region.

it has been observed and heard that in some areas some unknown people are making propaganda for particular purposes. Their propaganda especially is against the Hanefi sect and sometimes against the prophet's hadiths and Sunnah and aimed at forming another sect and as such is a form of tariqa and therefore illegal [...] Those that are making propaganda create factionalism amongst the public intentionally and there is no doubt that they are trying to damage national unity that we need more than ever. We must be very sensitive to this and if we hear or see anything like this, you must immediately inform the presidency. (BCA 15 April 1946)[8]

Such distrust of Alevis, amongst other state actors, including the CHP, is equally revealed by a secret report prepared for the CHP government by Tankut (2000: 110; Zırh 2012a: 134) in 1949. This warned that the Alevis, despite their affinity with the values of the Republic, harboured socialistic characteristics and, hence, were open to communist infiltration.

Competing State Strategies Following the Transition to Multi-Partism

Greater political pluralism following the transition to multi-partism in the late 1940s triggered increasing competition within the state, presenting opportunities for the Diyanet to resist and counter policies that other actors with differing political visions had towards Alevis. The Diyanet's role and interventions in Alevi identity, and the extent to which the body collaborated in the drive for Turkification and Islamisation policies of other state actors has been largely overlooked in the literature so far. In fact, the Diyanet, as a key institution of the Republic, plays a critical role in the construction of national identity, ensuring the reproduction of community boundaries along religious lines and thereby the persistence of the religious majoritarianism of the state.

In part reflecting the changing balance of currents within the Diyanet, the institution has increasingly characterised itself as the representative and propagator of a 'high Islam', cleansed of divisive sectarian rifts and superstition, as compared with more traditionalist factions such as the Süleymancı, which asserts its Sunni (Hanefi) character. As a result, the Diyanet has increasingly emphasised its authority in relation to alternative faith communities (e.g. Alevis) and hierarchies (e.g. *tariqa* orders) on the basis of being above sectarian or denominational divisions,

---

[8] This particular circular does not explicitly name Alevis. However, this can be inferred from the Diyanet's stance in targeting Alevis as sowing divisions amongst Muslims as well as the allusion to association with Shi'ism.

representing itself as the principal authority in providing 'healthy', 'true', 'correct' and objective knowledge of a universal Islam that is 'encompassing of all groups'.[9] Nevertheless, it remains widely acknowledged that the Diyanet adopts a Sunni (Hanefi) reading of Islam.[10] Indeed, having absorbed the guardians of Sunni (Hanefi) orthodoxy in the Ottoman Empire, the Diyanet became a central institutional site and a key carrier and preserver of Sunni (Hanefi) Muslim identity. Its interventions against Alevism therefore demonstrate the ways in which it has been a site of reproduction of the Sunni Muslim colouring of the nation-state and the ways in which it is actively engaged in negotiating boundaries of the nation or community. From the late 1940s until at least the 1980 military intervention, the Diyanet actively resisted and countered strategies by other state actors, such as the military or elements within the MEB, to rearticulate Alevism as 'Turkish Islam', adopting a chiefly rejectionist stance. Yet, as will be shown later in the chapter, despite the differences in their political visions, in general, these actors shared an overlapping consensus on the nation's self-definition as Sunni Muslim and Turkish and the suspicion of Alevis as an internal enemy and potential fifth column.

During the one-party era, the practice of the Alevi faith had effectively been driven underground through the closure of dervish lodges in 1925 and restrictions on worship, along with coercion. However, political liberalisation, together with industrialisation, urbanisation and migration since the late 1940s meant that Alevis, previously under the 'republican cloak of invisibility', were becoming visible again in aspects of public life (Zırh 2012a: 140–141). On the one hand, the reintroduction of religious lessons in schools, the establishment of theology faculties and the reopening of certain tombs and shrines focused attention on how the boundaries of religious activity would be drawn, particularly in dealing with any differentiation. The politicisation of identity boundaries

---

[9] There are numerous examples of this; see *Zaman* (26 February 2005), DİB (13 September 2006), DİB (13 November 2007), DİB (28 February 2006), DİB (30 June 2005), DİB (21 March 2007), DİB (30 May 2008), DİB (22 January 2014), Bardakoğlu (2006: 165), Gültekin and Yüksel (2005: 5) and Gözaydın (2014: 13).

[10] This is widely acknowledged by Diyanet representatives and scholars as well as within the media (examples include Çakır and Bozan 2005: 114; Gözaydın 2009a: 27, 2014: 13 and Yavuz 2003: 66). For instance, Gözaydın (2014: 13) relates that the highly important and significant interpretation of the Qu'ran by Elmalı Hamdi Yazır commissioned by the one-party government in 1936 was based on a Hanefi Sunni reading of Islam. However, particularly since the 1990s, the Diyanet has emphasised the institution as being 'above denominations' (*mezhepler üstü*) (Ateş 2012: 358; also see, for example, *Habertürk* 20 January 2014). This was related to the rise of a particular faction within the Diyanet from the 1970s, discussed later in the chapter.

was further spurred on by the increased political and economic competition for access to resources, which resulted in sharpening sectarian fault lines in society and eventually stoking numerous bouts of communitarian violence against the Alevis (some of which were state sanctioned).[11] Widespread sectarianism, together with the projection of Alevis as a potential fifth column, were evident even in the mainstream media's coverage of, for instance, tensions in 1951 in Hatay province following the killing of an Alevi youth. In the newspaper *Milliyet* (24 July 1951, 1 August 1951), for example, it was alleged that Alevis destroyed Atatürk's statues and burnt the Turkish flag on the direction of external forces ('Alevis' - conflated by them with Alawite - from Syria) and communists. Just how these Alevi–Sunni divisions and processes of boundary construction became intertwined with growing competition in multi-party life is brought to light by Necmeddin Sahir Sılan, a CHP lawmaker and, later, DP deputy for Tunceli province, in his internal party reports prepared between 1939 and 1953.[12] In a 1952 report to the DP, Sılan notes how following the election of a majority of Alevi Turks to the DP's administrative board in Erzincan district, they were effectively removed from their posts when other (Sunni) party members played on Turkish–Kurdish and Sunni–Alevi divisions and moved to establish a new administrative board. He described the objections and refusal of party members to work with the original elected board as owing to the members' Alevi identity and alleged commitment to communist views, but he recommended to the DP that the party nevertheless try to embrace citizens of eastern Turkey under the bond of Islam, which he claimed was the common denominator for Alevis, Zazas and Kurds (Akekmekçi and Pervan 2010: 401–405, 437, 441, 472–473). Such recommendations were to go largely unheeded as the DP's closer association with Islamist and conservative movements, such as the Nurcus, would effectively limit Alevi engagement with the party.

However, Sılan also blamed the CHP for provoking community tensions and reinterpreting history to portray the DP as being responsible for bad treatment of 'Alevi Turks', referred to as 'Kurds' in Erzincan and Tunceli provinces – a reference to the Dersim Massacre of 1937 to

---

[11] Despite minimal research on the matter, it has been argued with regard to the various bouts of ethnic violence against Alevis, as in Maraş, Sivas, Çorum and Malatya, that some of the underlying reasons were the unease of the Sunni bourgeoisie and locals who felt threatened by their economic involvement and ascendency, as well as the increased visibility of Alevis, particularly in cities that experienced significant internal migration. See Doğan (2007) and Yılmaz (2004).

[12] The archives of Sılan referred to here have been published by the History Foundation (Tarih Vakfı) (Akekmekçi and Pervan 2010, 2011a, 2011b, 2012).

1938 – in order to dissuade Alevis from joining the party (Akekmekçi and Pervan 2010: 458–459). Indeed, as the Tankut (2000) report referred to above demonstrates, the CHP sought to propagate the idea that Alevis were the natural allies of the party and the Kemalist republican project despite their continued suspicion of these communities (see also Bozarslan 2003: 6–7). Moreover, it is clear that other state elites, particularly some factions within the military, concerned about the consequences for the national security of social differentiation, saw it as necessary to refocus efforts to absorb Alevism into the nationalist project by rearticulating it as Turkish Islam. For instance, in 1948, the MEB published a book for primary schools entitled *The Muslim Child's Book* (*Müslüman Çocuğun Kitabı*), which was co-authored by Nurettin Arman, regarded as a staunch Kemalist poet, and which included references to prominent Alevi spiritual leaders such as Hacı Bektaş Veli and Pir Sultan Abdal. Subsequently, another book written by Artam, published in 1953 and entitled *Muslim Turks, Beware of Division!* (*Müslüman Türkler, Ayrılıktan Kaçının!*), warned against divisions between Alevis and Sunnis. Bayrak (2004: 63) has argued that in the 1950s, prominent Alevi figures such as Halil Öztoprak acted almost as an arm of the state in promoting the state-friendly articulation of Alevis as Turkish Muslims. For example, the publication in 1956 of an edition of Halil Öztoprak's book on Alevism was sanctioned by the MEB.

These renewed efforts to rearticulate Alevism as Turkish Islam by elements of the state met fierce criticism and resistance from the Diyanet together with Islamist and conservative circles. For instance, Artam's 1948 book was strongly attacked in the Islamist periodical *Sebilürreşad*, which was closely associated with the Diyanet, in which Alevism was argued to be a divisive and dangerous *tariqa* order, a 'Batiniyya'[13] sect steeped in superstition spread by Safavi leader Shah Ismail against the sacred beliefs of the *millet* to destroy the Ottoman state. The mere mention of these Alevi figures, it was contended, 'sows division amongst Muslims' (*Sebilürreşad* 1948: 12–16) As testament to the highly rejectionist stance of the Diyanet compared with other state actors, in 1948, the institution translated and published the treatise of an eleventh-century Yemeni Sunni jurist entitled *The Inner Face of the Batiniyya and Qarmatian* (*Batiniler ve Karmatilerin İç Yüzü*) against esoteric interpretations of the Qur'an. The publication of this treatise, including its foreword by Ahmet Hamdi Akseki (1947–1951), the former chief of the Diyanet, was

---

[13] 'Batiniyya' has been used as a pejorative term to refer to various groups condemned by Sunni orthodoxy, such as Alevism or Ismailism, which are described as distinguishing between the literal and hidden (esoteric) meaning of religious texts.

revealing as to the sectarian bias of the institution as a carrier and preserver of Sunni (Hanefi) Islamic orthodoxy. Making highly derogatory comments about Alevis, Akseki (Hammadi 1948: 3) argued that Shi'ism and its different formations, such as Batiniyya, were propagated by Iranian Zoroastrians and Jews to sow sedition within Islam in hopes of destroying its unity and corrupting its beliefs. He further declared that 'our nation must be protected from falling into the trap of these evil-spirited peoples' who are 'corrupting the pure beliefs of our people'. The book was not withdrawn despite the political fallout caused by its publication, including a great degree of public upset in Hatay province, home to a sizeable Alawite population, which was to provoke a debate in parliament. Rather, the book has remained a key reference point and formed the basis of attacks made by the Diyanet and Islamist and conservative circles against Alevi communities. In 1956, another Diyanet publication, entitled *Religion and Nationalism* (*Din ve Milliyet*), likewise declared that 'to reach the unity that is required by religion, there is a need to prevent the entry of false and Batiniyya sectarian currents' (Kürkçüoğlu 1956: 17). The Islamist press, including *Sebilürreşad*, echoed these views, frequently depicting Alevis as potential communists, atheists and heretics and also dangerous for the Muslim community. Significantly, controversy over the book was to resurface in 2004 (see Hammadi 2004), when it was reprinted with Akseki's foreword by an Islamist publishing house. In response, the Alevi Bektashi Federation (Alevi Bektaşi Federasyonu) launched a criminal complaint demanding withdrawal of the book on the basis that it contained hate speech and derogatory remarks about Alevism.

Such hostility and suspicion towards Alevism in this period did not go unnoticed by others. In 1956, one American diplomat noted in an internal memo that

this powerful minority [Alevis] has no contact with the official religion. It has no representative at the Direction [sic] of Religious Affairs; to the contrary it is there that it encounters its worst enemies and the Director of Religious Affairs, Mr Eyüp Sabri Hayırlıoğlu, did not hesitate to say to a foreign journalist some time ago that the Alevis follow a false faith. (Bali 2011: 34)

Given these perceptions, the Diyanet maintained its active surveillance of Alevis in this period also, and officials were instructed to monitor Alevis closely. For instance, a booklet of regulations circulated to muftis in 1961 contained the warning that

whatever the intentions, anyone that is seen or heard in confusing our public's minds with thoughts that are against the Sunni denomination and those that spread Shiism and Alevism propaganda by raising events that occurred

1300 years ago, and in this way can become a means for causing damage to national unity, must be reported immediately to the Presidency. (DİB 1961: 4)

Such an inimical approach towards Alevis was not just pervasive at the centre but also common amongst the peripheral Diyanet officials, and it resulted in discriminatory practices such as the refusal to conduct funeral services. That many muftis held negative views regarding Alevis, such as that one should not eat food handled by Alevis, was also noted by the former president of the Diyanet Tayyar Altıkulaç (2011: 664), and the pervasiveness of such attitudes is brought to light in more recent surveys of Diyanet officials in a study (Çakır and Bozan 2005) by a Turkish think tank, the Turkish Economic and Social Studies Foundation (Türkiye Ekonomik ve Sosyal Etüdler Vakfı), in 2005.

The 1960 Military Coup and the First 'Alevi Opening' by the State

The 1960 coup marked a new phase in the competition between different strategies adopted by state actors towards Alevis despite the overlapping consensus they shared. The junta leaders were particularly concerned with Kurdish nationalism, arguably more than the threat of Islamism, and indeed, having links with Kurdish actors was one of the accusations levelled at the deposed DP government during the trial of its leaders. It was in this context that junta leaders concerned about the relationship and links between Alevis and Kurds initiated what could be described as the first 'Alevi opening' by the state, which involved the development of the idea to establish a Department of Sects (Mezhepler Müdürlüğü, DoS) within the Diyanet. The DoS was therefore conceived largely as a means to dissolve manifestations of ethnic difference and Kurdish identity through religion (Sunni Islam), as represented by the Diyanet. In other words, Sunnification and Islamisation were conceived as means of Turkification of Alevis and to sever links with Kurdishness.

The matter was debated by junta leaders during a cabinet meeting in October 1960 (Koçak 2010a: 555–558). President Cemal Gürsel raised concerns about Kurdish nationalism, arguing that the Kurdish rebels stoked by the Russians following the First World War were, in fact, of 80 per cent Turkish origin.[14] He added:

For instance, we regard people that are Alevi as Kurds. The public also regards them this way, and [Alevis] who in turn think then that 'if this is the case' quickly learn Kurdish and become Kurds. Because, for some reason Sunnis see them as

---

[14] Prime minister between 1960 and 1961, Gürsel was appointed by the military following the 27 May 1960 coup.

enemies. For this reason, Shiis, Alevi and Bektashis have an inclination to become Kurdish [...] Whereas we have to admit that Alevis have continued the original Turkish customs [...] If we don't do serious work, teach them the truth and take possession of this country, it will certainly be a disaster for the future of Turkey. (Koçak 2010a: 556)

The minister of national defence, Fahri Özdilek, worriedly responded that 'there has been insistence on differences between Shii, Shafi'i, Tahtacı, etc. which lead to sectarian separationism [...] It is necessary to put an article in law that abolishes sectarian disputes'.[15] However, he was reassured by President Gürsel, who remarked, 'I have made them include this in the Constitution. This is an abhorrent affair. However, it is regarded as natural. From now on, this country will be free from actual divisions and animosities. Actually, I will have studies conducted and publications prepared.' One of the chief mechanisms for this policy of Turkification and Islamisation was envisaged as being the Diyanet, which the minister of state, Hayri Mumcuoğlu, asserted 'has duties with regards to this matter. We have to establish an Alevi department within the Presidency of Religious Affairs. The Alevis, like the Sunnis, will easily separate themselves from Kurdishness once they find a point of authority in the [Presidency] of Religious Affairs' (Koçak 2010a: 555–558).

The military's efforts, led by President Cemal Gürsel, to Turkify Alevism by rearticulating it through an Islamic framing subsequently proceeded with legislative efforts to institute a DoS within the Diyanet as well as attempts to co-opt selected Alevi figures. The first of the legislative actions was seen just a couple of months later, in April 1961, when the idea of a 'Department of Denominations ... to meet the needs of denominations that are included within the Muslim establishment' was proposed by the ultranationalist Republican Villagers Nation Party (Cumhuriyetçi Köylü Millet Partisi, CKMP), the predecessor of the MHP, during debates about drafting a new constitution within the Assembly of Representatives (TM 25 April 1961: 231–232). Significantly, this proposal enjoyed some support from prominent conservatives such as Ali Fuat Başgil, who had outlined a proposal that was identical to the one made by the CKMP in his column in the newspaper *Yeni Sabah* in July 1960.[16] While the proposal was rejected without further discussion in the TBMM, it continued to resurface under other propositions made by former military members or politicians close to the military leadership.

---

[15] The Tahtacı are a subgroup within Alevism.
[16] For an analysis of Başgil's stance, see Ateş (2012: 326–328).

For instance, the establishment of a Religious Cultural Matters Directorate (Dini Kültür İşleri Müdürlüğü) was proposed in January 1962 by the permanent members of the Senate (composed chiefly of former members of the junta National Unity Committee General Assembly [27 May 1960–15 October 1961]) (TC MM 28 January 1965a [22 January 1962]) and the CHP government during this period (TC MM 28 January 1965b [24 January 1962]; TİTYEDF 1962). Similar to the DoS, but with a wider remit, the Religious Cultural Matters Directorate was envisaged as a point of reference within the state for all religions and denominations. Yet again, rather than equality or recognition, the key concern for the proponents of the bill was to expand state supervision over all communities for the purposes of 'national unity' (TM 21 February 1961: 127), with the draft outlining the responsibilities of the body as being to 'report to relevant authorities and take precautions to protect the commitment to national ideals and prevent exploitation of disputes arising from divisions of faith amongst members of various religious and sects [*mezhep*]' (TC MM 28 January 1965a [22 January 1962]). In 1963, the last legislative push, led by President Gürsel, returned to the idea of a DoS only for Muslims that would 'consider the Muslim community in a completely equal manner' and would be responsible for

enlightening [*tenvir*] and showing the right path [*irşad etmek*] to followers of Sunni and Shi'i sects, which do not differ in terms of the essentials of the religion of Islam, by settling according to the Islamic creed and purifying from superstition the matters related to detail and manifestation of differences owing to the particular geography and places of residence (Article 10). (Bilimer 1963: 13)

In parallel with these legislative efforts, President Gürsel had also begun to engage with Alevi figures whom he invited to raise their concerns and demands, including their views about the idea of a DoS. In 1961, Hayri Mumcuoğlu, a serving minister within the military cabinet, even suggested bringing to the head of the proposed DoS within the Diyanet a leading Alevi figure, Feyzullah Ulusoy, part of the Ulusoy family and the hereditary representative of the Hacı Bektaş Veli lodge, suggesting his conceptualisation of Alevism was not too much at odds with the military government's.[17] It was as a result of these engagements that various Alevi associations were subsequently founded and the Hacı Bektaş lodge was reopened as a museum in 1964. The shadow of the military could also be seen in the establishment in 1966 of what was widely perceived as the first Alevi party, the Turkish Unity Party (Türkiye Birlik Partisi, TBP), which

---

[17] These events were related by Feyzullah Ulusoy to a Diyanet official, Abdülkadir Sezgin, and published by the Diyanet in January 1992. See Sezgin (7 March 2012).

was headed by a retired general and former member of the nationalist CKMP, Hasan Tahsin Berkman. Significantly, the TBP had also called for the representation of Alevis within the Diyanet and stressed the Turkishness of Alevis (Ata 2007: 48–50).

Despite these persistent efforts during the early 1960s by Cemal Gürsel – as leader of the junta regime and thereby with the Republic's most powerful institution, the military, behind him and subsequently as president – to establish a DoS, the attempts encountered significant opposition, resulting in the subsequent withdrawal of the proposal by the CHP government (Ata 2007: 51; Gözaydın 2009a: 72; Kara 2012: 99; Massicard 2007: 55; Savcı 1967: 97–102). First, the military was itself not a monolithic actor, and different factions within it were opposed to the idea of a DoS. For instance, one of the leaders of the 1960 coup, Mehmet Özgüneş, declared in 1963 that establishing a DoS would be 'murderous' (Karaman 2015a: 422). Second, equally vociferous in its rejection of the idea was the Diyanet, as indicated by articles that appeared in the Islamist *Sebilürreşad* journal, which was closely associated with senior Diyanet officials. In a 1961 piece about the DoS proposal, it was argued that there were no 'real Shi'a' in the country, and those 'associating themselves with Shiism' – insinuating Alevis – were described as an 'extremist and perverted *tariqa*' steeped in superstition and which could not be recognised as a sect (*mezhep*) by a laic state. Such writings referred to the Diyanet's 1948 publication about Batiniyye (discussed earlier) and called on the Diyanet to 'save these citizens' brains from darkness and enlighten them' as part of its 'national and religious duty'. The disquiet within the ranks of the Diyanet was equally underlined by the release of a statement by a group of unnamed preachers referring to themselves as the 'İstanbul preachers' (İstanbul Vaizleri) in 1963 (İstanbul Vaizleri 1963; Gözaydın 2009a: 72). Similarly, the İstanbul preachers emphasised national religious unity and the conceptualisation of Alevis as a fifth column of Iran:

Since today in our country there are no denominations that are openly Shi'i and they don't have a doctrine, it is well placed to ask those that defend Shiism on an individual basis: do they have a book that explains that Shiism's belief, worship and other provisions are against or in line with Ehl-i Sünnet [Sunni Islam] or, by according rights to Shiism in the proposal, are they going to import their books from Iran and in thus re-open historical wounds? It is a catastrophe to bring about for no reason Shi'a and Sunni conflict that has been extinguished for centuries and to divide into two our national and religious unity. The only elements that will benefit from this are foreign ones. (İstanbul Vaizleri 1963: 3)

Such views held by the Diyanet were mirrored by other conservative and Islamist actors. The conservative media outlets, including *Sebilürreşad* and papers such as *Yeni Sabah* (*New Morning*), *Zafer* (*Victory*) and *Adalet* (*Justice*), harshly criticised the proposal, arguing that it would reignite Sunni–Shi'a schisms and destroy national unity (*Sebilürreşad* 1961: 363–367; Zırh 2012a: 150), and they targeted Alevis by using the centuries-old Kızılbaş stigma (Zırh 2012a: 150). Recognition of Alevism was considered a 'serious threat to the spirit of unity enunciated by Islam', and equating this group to Sunnis was seen as 'tantamount to mocking 27 million Muslims' (Ata 2007: 49). A prominent Islamist, Vehbi Bilimer (1963: 13), associated with the Islamist Nurcu movement and the (state-supported) Association for the Dissemination of Science (İlim Yayma Cemiyeti, İYC), also rejected the proposal on the basis that the 'gates of discord [*tefrika*] would officially be opened' (Gözaydın 2009a: 72). In response to these reactions from conservative circles, a number of Alevi university students issued an Alevi Declaration in 1963 in support of a DoS by underlining the identity of Alevis 'as Turks by race and Muslim by religion' (Ata 2007: 47–50). Resistance by the Diyanet, as well as conservative and Islamist circles, had ultimately succeeded. The question of any accommodation or representation of Alevism within the Diyanet was to be largely abandoned by the second half of the 1960s, not to resurface until the 1990s and subsequently, under the AKP. In 1966, derogatory statements made against Alevis by the former Diyanet president İbrahim Elmalı (1965–1966) further raised sectarian tensions and were followed by numerous incidents of violence directed at Alevi communities (Ata 2007: 49–52).

This increased visibility of Alevis in public life in the 1960s in turn spurred increasing political mobilisation within the community. In the 1970s, an era of intense polarisation between left and right, this mobilisation would take place in the context of the increasing engagement of Alevis with leftist politics. During this period, the notion of the '3Ks' was developed, articulating the combination of Komünist (communist), Kızılbaş and Kürt (Kurd) as constituting national security threats to the state (Erdemir 2005: 950). This was to remain a pervasive lens through which internal security threats were viewed by the state. A handbook for the police force published in 1969, for example, claimed that different denominations were a security risk to the state within a section headed 'Internal enemies' (Şenel and Şenel 1969: 113). Likewise, just before the intervention in 1980, the military had prepared an internal report entitled 'Internal Threats Aimed at Turkey' (Türkiye'ye Yönelik İç Tehditler), in which Alevism, characterised as comprising a mixture of Bektashi Turkish customs and Sunni principles, was designated as an internal threat incited by internal (Kurdish) and external forces against the Turkish state in a context of highly polarised political and social contestation (*Radikal*

11 July 2013). Such perceptions made Alevis the target of state-sanctioned political violence, and the community faced numerous pogroms in Maraş (1978) and Çorum (July 1980).

The Turkish–Islamic Synthesis and Alevis in the Aftermath of the 1980 Coup

Following the 1980 military coup, a new wave of Islamisation efforts by state actors against Alevis was triggered with the adoption of the TIS. The 1983 National Culture Report (DPT 1983), a key TIS document (see Chapters 1 and 2), argued with reference to Fuat Köprülü's works on Alevis that there was 'no logical or rational reason' for sectarian divisions in the country and that Turkish culture and Islam had 'unified and made everyone alike'.[18] The Diyanet had been identified as a key mechanism for the propagation of the TIS and, indeed, had embraced this role since it enabled it to not only secure the expansion of its role and religious infrastructure but also to pursue its mission of Islamisation of public space and morality. The coup, therefore, also occasioned a shift from competing, but structurally homologous, strategies pursued by state actors towards greater collaboration on the Alevi matter. A systematic 'faith-based assimilation' agenda arose involving policies such as the construction of mosques in Alevi settlements[19] and the military's move to take several thousand children from their families in the Alevi majority Tunceli (Dersim) province and send them to (Sunni Islamic) *imam-hatip* schools (Kenanoğlu 11 April 2013; *Radikal* 26 October 2012).

In line with the renewed emphasis on Islam with respect to Turkish national identity and the TIS agenda, the Diyanet also adopted strategies involving the rearticulation of Alevis within an Islamic framing, in contrast to the comparatively more rejectionist stance of previous periods, partly reflecting the rise of a new generation of *ulema* within the Diyanet since the 1970s. Such a turn was evident, for example, in the efforts by a long-term Diyanet official, Abdülkadir Sezgin, who published numerous

---

[18] The report also makes references to key Alevi figures such as Hacı Bektaş-ı Veli and Yunus Emre and also the Sufi leader of the Mevlevi order, Mevlana Celaddiin-i Rumi (DPT 1983: 129, 144).

[19] Former Diyanet chief Altıkulaç (2011b: 662–663) describes mosque building in Alevi villages as being undertaken on the basis of requests from villagers. An end to mosque building is one of the key demands of the Alevi movement, which can be seen from the list of demands of the leading umbrella organisation, the Alevi Bektashi Federation (Alevi Bektaşi Federasyonu, ABF), www.alevifederasyonu.org.tr/abfhakkindadetay.php?id=5.

texts (on behalf of the Diyanet) in the 1990s claiming that Alevis were in reality Hanefi Sunnis.[20] Such a development did not mean an acceptance or recognition of Alevis, however. Indeed, even when the Diyanet began to articulate Alevism increasingly within an Islamic framework and muted its more rejectionist stance, the ongoing suspicion and depiction of Alevis as a potential fifth column – open to infiltration by Iran, communists and atheists – continued. Alevis were portrayed as impressionable and as coming under the influence of Iranian culture and 'Khomeneism', masons, Christians and atheists, while being described as the biggest danger and threat to national unity after Kurdish currents. It was the Diyanet's duty, according to this view, to enlighten Alevis so that they would not be left in darkness (Sezgin 2012: 269).

Despite these efforts, the widespread political repression of especially the left following the coup, the development of an 'Alevi diaspora' in Europe and the rise of Islamist and Kurdish nationalist movements contributed to what has been described as an Alevi revival by the end of the 1980s. Crucially, this involved a new phase of increasing political mobilisation in which the emerging Alevi movement pursued its demands for equal citizenship (Zırh 2012a: 6). However, together with the ongoing Islamisation efforts, particularly from the 1990s, when Islamist political parties began to make unprecedented electoral gains, military actors shifted towards emphasising narratives of Alevis as stalwart allies of Kemalism, protecting laicism against radical (described as Arabised) Islam. In other words, military actors were attempting to instrumentalise Alevism by fuelling a secular–Islamist divide, which would serve to patch over the increasingly bewildered image of the state after revelations of links to organised crime and widespread corruption. In particular, after the so-called post-modern coup in 1997, when the Islamist-led coalition government was pushed out of power, the military actors attempted to reshape and reconstruct Alevi group boundaries through the channelling of budgetary funds to 'state-friendly' (Shankland 1999: 162) Alevi organisations that articulated Alevism within an Islamic–Turkish framework. In 1998, the Alevi organisations Hacı Bektaş Anatolian Culture Foundation (Hacı Bektaş Veli Anadolu Kültür Vakfı) and Foundation for Republican Education and Culture (Cumhuriyetçi Eğitim ve Kültür Merkezi Vakfı, Cem Vakfı) were granted public benefit status, while another, Malatya Hacı Bektaş Veli Cultural Centre Foundation (Malatya Hacı Bektaş Veli Kültür Merkezi Vakfı) was granted this status in 2002. The allocation of

---

[20] Sezgin was based at the Diyanet for thirty-eight years, and his books were published by the DV and Ministry of Culture throughout the 1990s.

budgetary funds to Alevi organisations – the Foundation for Culture and Art of Anatolian Saints (Alevi-Turkist Anadolu Erenleri Kültür ve Sanat Vakfı) and Hacı Bektaş Anatolian Culture Foundation – was initiated by the ANAP–DSP government in 1998. In that year, out of a total of USD 1.8 million of budgetary funds allocated to non-governmental organisations, 90 per cent were destined for Alevi foundations. A further USD 0.4 million was apportioned to four civil society organisations in 1999, 85 per cent of which went to Alevi organisations. Similar budgeting was recorded for 2000, 2001 and 2002, when 84 per cent, 92 per cent and 92 per cent, respectively, of the funds went to Alevi organisations (Cangöz 2010: 138).[21]

Reflecting these efforts to rearticulate (but not recognise) Alevis as 'real' Turkish Muslims, in the 1990s, state representatives and political parties began to regularly attend the annual Hacı Bektaş celebrations. Even the leader of the ultranationalist MHP – a party that has historically been implicated in anti-Alevi violence and campaigns – called for the embrace of Alevis during an election rally in 1999 (*Habertürk* 5 June 2007). It was also in this context that the idea of a DoS, or Alevi representation within the Diyanet, re-emerged. Together with state-friendly Alevi associations such as the Cem Foundation, the policy was advocated chiefly by centre-left parties, including the Social Democratic People's Party (Sosyaldemokrat Halk Partisi, SHP) in a statement in 1991, during debates about a new constitution by the DSP in 1993 (Schüler 1999: 171) and in numerous parliamentary debates throughout the 1990s and 2000s by the SHP, CHP and DSP.

On the other hand, increased visibility of Alevis starting in the 1990s had met with characteristic suspicion by state actors, which involved surveillance and monitoring of Alevi communities as well as major bouts of state-sanctioned communitarian violence.[22] Between 1994 and 2000, a series of purportedly academic studies were commissioned by the military and conducted particularly in provinces with significant Alevi, Alawite or Kurdish communities, such as Sivas, Malatya, Diyarbakır, Tokat and Hatay.[23] In reality, the content of these PhD and master's

---

[21] The extent to which these practices have continued since the AKP's ascent to power is difficult to measure owing to changes in budgetary reporting since 2003 which removed transparency.

[22] These included the Sivas massacre in July 1993, which resulted in the killing of thirty-five individuals attending an Alevi cultural festival, and the Gazi massacre, when twenty-three citizens were killed and more than 1,400 injured.

[23] As Ata (29 December 2013) points out, this research was prepared with the involvement of Prof Şaban Kuzgun, founder of the Fırat University Theology Faculty, who died in a suspicious traffic accident in 2000. Kuzgun had established the project about Turkey's Belief Map (Türkiye'nin İnanç Haritası) (see Kuzgun 2000). See also Çakır (26 August

theses confirm that, rather than being academic studies, they were largely intended for the observation and surveillance of Alevis, comprising a standard format which recorded the number of Alevis in different locations, the extent of their religious observance compared with that of Sunni citizens and their close relations with non-Muslim communities such as Baha'i (Demirpolat 1997; Erdoğan 1996; Mustafa 1997; Tutar 1997; Ünalan 1997). Significantly, a key concern raised in the reports was the ratio of Alevis to Sunnis and the size of the Muslim majority, which was used as an indicator of the magnitude of the 'threat' that Alevis might pose. For example, the study on the city of Amasya argued that Alevis in this region had revolted against the state during the Ottoman era owing to the influence of Iranian Shi'a propaganda, but that they had been emboldened to this only because they constituted a large proportion of the population at the time (Erdoğan 1996: 53–55). Equally, the study on Van province in eastern Turkey, an area predominantly populated by Shafi'i Muslim Kurds, emphasised that there were no Alevis in the city because of the 'continued effects of the Battle of Chaldiran'. The Sunni *medreses* it noted, had played a key role in preventing 'Shi'a propaganda', and there were no Alevi cultural spaces there because Alevis had not been able to establish colonies in the city through migration (Demirpolat 1997: 53). The Diyanet officials appeared to have supported these efforts by the military, with mosque functionaries being a key source of data about the patterns of worship and levels of observation of the different faith groups (Ünalan 1997: 294). In later years, the general secretary of the MGK from 2001 to 2003, Tuncer Kılınç (later detained under the Ergenekon case), had described Alevi demands in 2003 as a separatist threat to national unity and went on to describe Islam as the most suitable religion for laicism (*Zaman* 17 May 2003).

2004). A similar project was implemented in 2013 by the Diyanet following remarks by the former chief Görmez that the religious life of İzmir – a province on the Aegean coast in western Turkey commonly identified in public discourse as more liberal and secular in orientation – is different and insufficient (*Hürriyet* 27 March 2013). Research mapping religious life in Turkey was conducted in collaboration with the Turkish Statistical Institute (Türkiye İstatistik Kurumu, TUIK). Significantly, the report which was published in 2014 by the Diyanet did not contain any reference to Alevis and appeared to be subsuming these communities under the category of Sunni (Hanefi) Islam (DİB 2014). See also discussions at the Diyanet's First Council on Religion held in 1993 on the need for a belief map of various religious communities, including Christians and Jews as well as Alevis. In particular, it is noted that this mapping of Alevism and number of Alevis is necessary to protect them from 'being exploited by internal and external centres' (Kalafat 1995: 129).

Continuity and Change in the AKP Era

2002–2011 Continuity

The AKP period since 2002 has been marked by both continuity, particularly between 2002 and 2011, and change since 2011 in the policies of state actors towards Alevis. Given the AKP's Sunni Islamist roots, the relationship with the Alevi movement was difficult from the start, as it had been with previous Islamist parties, partly owing to historical experience.[24] At least in its early years, the AKP's public discourse and approach towards Alevis were largely in line with previous conservative and Islamist parties. Accordingly, any visibility of Alevi identity was seen as instigating differentiation within the Muslim Turkish community (*millet*), sowing discord (*tefrika*), division (*fitne*) or separatism (*ayrılıkçılık*), and hence was a danger to the unity of Islam and Muslims (*tevhid*). In substance, this was not so different from centre-left parties such as the CHP and the SHP/DSP. These similarly regarded Alevi differentiation as dangerous, emphasising the need to protect the 'unity and integrity of the nation' (*birlik ve beraberlik*), but did so through a discourse that underlined the importance of laicism and the role of the establishment of the Republic in the defeat of the 'ills of sectarianism' rather than through Islamic references and terminology. In this sense, even when these parties warned of discrimination against Alevis or of sectarianism, it was not within the context of equality or religious freedom per se but rather concern about national unity. In any case, under the AKP, the long-standing demands of Alevi organisations remained unmet, and particularly since 2011, in the wake of the Arab uprisings, they had begun to report an increase in discrimination and hate crimes (*Evrensel* 7 May 2013). However, owing to the prevalence of a narrative of democratisation in the early years of the AKP regime, such developments were largely overlooked.

The launch of the AKP's Alevi opening (Alevi açılımı) had at first seemed to be not only a surprise but also a break with the tradition of animosity by (Sunni) Islamist parties towards Alevis. However, it can be considered to be the second attempt at such an 'opening' by the state since the efforts of Cemal Gürsel in the 1960s, which have been discussed earlier (Lord 2016b). Periodically revived, the AKP's Alevi opening initiative was presented as part of a wider policy of what the AKP described as a 'Democratic opening' (*demokratik açılım*), otherwise named the National Unity and Brotherhood Project (Milli Birlik ve Kardeşlik Projesi), which was purportedly concerned with addressing

---

[24] For instance, observers pointed to the involvement of many defendants of the perpetuators of the Sivas massacre in 1993 within the AKP.

the demands and problems of Turkey's various ethnic and religious communities, including Kurds and Roma. The initial stage of the AKP's first Alevi opening involved symbolic moves, such as the participation of AKP politicians in Alevi fast-breaking, and was followed by a series of seven workshops held with Alevi and non-Alevi actors from 2009 to 2010. The initiative was widely lauded as a historic step in the life of the Republic. For the current president and former prime minister, Recep Tayyip Erdoğan, who stated in the final report of the workshops, 'This is the first time that the official offices of the state have regarded Alevis as interlocutors', the opening marked a new era in the state's approach to the community. Many scholarly analyses echoed the official line in regarding the openings as heralding an important change and a liberal shift in the state's policy towards Alevis in addition to marking an unprecedented move and a turning point in relations between them and the state (Aktürk 2012: 193; Bardakçı 2015: 354–355; Borovalı and Boyraz 2015: 146; Massicard 2016: 81–82; Soner and Toktaş 2011: 419).[25] In this vein, scholars emphasised the Alevi opening policies as an example of Turkey's democratisation under the AKP, at least until its more visibly authoritarian turn in 2013, and lauded them as a move away from an authoritarian laicism, or 'assertive secularism'.

In fact, there were some important parallels between the Alevi opening launched in the 1960s by military actors and the AKP's initiative. Both were initiated in the context of rising social contestation and the perception of Alevis as a security threat and internal enemy. In part reflecting a sectarian approach, the AKP government alleged that growing opposition to the party stemmed largely from Alevis. The AKP's opening in 2007 had begun prior to the general elections in July and had followed the anti-AKP demonstrations, which pro-AKP circles had alleged mostly comprised Alevis. Similarly, the subsequent revival of the opening by the AKP preceded important general elections in 2015 and followed the 2013 Gezi Park demonstrations, which the AKP again blamed on Alevis (see discussion in the section 'The Syrian Conflict and Sectarinised Securitisation' of this chapter).

At the same time, despite the change in state actors, there was continuity between the two openings regarding the approach to Alevism. In terms of the choice of participants as well the content of the debates, both organisations suggested that the AKP's opening constituted a state intervention concerned with the rearticulation of Alevism rather than a

---

[25] An important exception was Yalçınkaya (2009), who argued that the Alevi openings did not mark a fundamental change in 'Sunni mentality' or state practices aimed at (re) shaping Alevi rituals.

democratic debate or a liberal/pluralistic turn in state policy. Indeed, as critics argued, the workshops held between June 2009 and January 2010 excluded key segments of the Alevi movement, such as the European diaspora organisations. Instead, they had been composed largely of non-Alevi participants, except in the first and seventh meetings, and even those included Alevi organisations established by the government and Gülenists against the Alevi movement (see 'The Gülenist and AKP Collaboration over Alevis', next section). As a result, criticising the opening as an assimilationist strategy of the state, major organisations of the Alevi movement, with the exception of state-friendly ones, had largely withdrawn from the process.[26]

Indeed, rather than engaging with Alevi demands for equal citizenship and access to state resources, the workshop discussions turned into theological debates that attempted to define Alevism and to decide how the demands of Alevis could be reconciled with the Sunni public. As Bardakçı (2015: 367) argues, the AKP was inclined to 'view the demands of the Alevi from a religious standpoint rather than as a human rights issue'. Such a concern with drawing the boundaries of Alevis is revealed in the final report of the workshops, which identifies the fundamental problem of Alevism as being 'how Alevism [...] will be transmitted to future generations' (Nihai Rapor 2010: 67). From this perspective, the Alevi community's allegedly highly fragmented and heterogeneous approach to Alevism was considered a negative issue that needed to be addressed. Yet the report repeatedly underlined the fact that despite the ambiguity around the definition of Alevism, 'in reality' it is a manner of thinking and living that is both within and shaped by Islamic tradition, and the approach that is widely accepted with regard to Alevism is that, above all, it is part of religious groups that fundamentally have Islam as their root, and it has particularities that are specific to Anatolia. On this basis, it was argued that the definition of Alevism could therefore be clarified with the aid of Sunni Islamic theologians, who were presented as the purveyors of objective knowledge of religion:

[Theologians who] make a significant contribution to the updating of society's conception of religion clearly can have an impact in uncovering Alevism's historical, sociological and religious roots. (Nihai Rapor 2010: 21).

Such a desire to articulate Alevism within an Islamic framework was also suggested by the comments of Necdet Subaşı, the coordinator of the Alevi workshops, when he spoke at a meeting with Alevi faith leaders. He claimed

---

[26] For a detailed review of the meetings and a summary of criticisms made by Alevi organisations, see Yalçınkaya and Ecevitoğlu (2013).

In the past six workshops, we have not seen such a strong emphasis on Islam, I am sorry to say. As someone who witnessed all six workshops until now, this enthusiastic and intensive reference to Islam catches one's attention. But let me also ask openly: 'Where are you in real life?' (Alevi Opening Report 2010: 33–34)

A similar approach can be observed in the Diyanet's 'survey on religious life', conducted by Subaşı and published in 2014, where Alevis did not feature as a separate faith group or a Muslim denomination because they were defined as Hanefi Sunnis.

On the other hand, the workshops underscored the extent to which Alevis who did not accept the reframing of Alevism in Islamic terms were approached with suspicion because they were repeatedly portrayed as marginal separationists and extremists (e.g. Nihai Rapor 2010: 20–21, 27, 32, 40, 43, 69, 141–142). As Yalçınkaya and Ecevitoğlu (2013: 65) note, the emphasis on how to ensure 'unity and brotherhood' during the theological discussions in the workshops suggests that there was a distrust of the commitment of the Alevi community to the unity of the nation and the state. The alleged oppositional character of Alevis was linked to their historical involvement with Marxist-socialist movements, and it was claimed that failure to address the Alevi issue would result in radicalisations of Alevis and thereby pose a 'security problem of multiple dimensions' (Nihai Rapor 2010: 15, 51–52). It was not just Alevis on the ideological left who were treated with suspicion, however. A critical tone was adopted when considering Alevis who were described as having a deep devotion to the founding principles of the Republic, including laicism, and thereby would allegedly be unable to question the destructive impact of republican reforms on their faith.[27] A similar stance can be observed in the discussion of Alevi approaches to compulsory education in the final report, where it is argued that, unlike Alevis, Sunnis adopt a more balanced and conciliatory approach to the state that accepts its policies for ensuring togetherness (Nihai Rapor 2010: 141–142). This precise logic was to make an appearance in the Diyanet's 2009–2013 Strategic Plan, which identified as a threat the 'efforts to show different views and interpretations of Islam as a different religion' and 'the demands by some circles to remove compulsory religious education', both of which have been linked to Alevi organisations (DİB 2008:39).

Within this context and mirroring the logic of the first Alevi opening in the 1960s, the second opening under the AKP also conjured up a

---

[27] This can also be seen in a newspaper interview with Dr Necdet Subaşı, coordinator and moderator of the workshops, who subsequently joined the Diyanet (*Zaman Gazetesi* 21 February 2010).

recommendation to establish a DoS within the Diyanet. Yet, despite the greater degree of overlapping consensus between the Diyanet's mission and the AKP, the Diyanet would maintain its resistance to such a proposal, which was subsequently abandoned. In analysing the AKP's approach, Çarkoğlu and Bilgili (2011: 361) note that 'within the Sunni establishment, there is an almost total theological disagreement that the Alevi identity is a legitimate reality to be reckoned with', which is unsurprising given the Diyanet's role as a carrier and preserver of Sunni Muslim identity. Indeed, a statement made in 2001 by the former Diyanet president Ali Bardakoğlu that a DoS would be 'completely against the nation-state and society project as aimed for by the will that established the Republic' exemplifies the institution's stance on the matter (Milliyet 18 August 2001). Outside of the 'state-friendly' organisations, the Alevi movement has also widely rejected the idea of a DoS and has advocated for the abolition of the Diyanet altogether.[28]

Similar to the DoS matter, the Diyanet has been persistent in resisting official recognition of cemevis, Alevi places of worship, a key demand by Alevis that would give them equal status (to Sunni Muslims) and the same financial benefits granted to mosques, despite the push for recognition by other state actors, political parties and government authorities.[29] Demands for the recognition of cemevis have instead been portrayed as a threat to Islam, and thereby the nation, and described as separatism. Such a view has been expressed by the former president of the Diyanet, Tayyar Altıkulaç (2011b: 660), who argues that Alevi leaders

do not want other pure Alevis to come face to face with the reality of Islam [. . .] That is why you use the issue of the cemevis to distance Alevis from the Islam which is the true religion and Alevism that is within Islam. By presenting cemevis as alternatives to mosques you are being separationist.

These discourses on Alevi separatism culminated in equating Alevis with illegal and terrorist organisations. For instance, in a book published in 1997 by the Centre for Islamic Studies (İslam Araştırmaları Merkezi, part of the DV and associated with the Diyanet), İlyas Üzüm(1997: 40) (appointed to the Diyanet's Religious Affairs High Council in 2008) argued that Alevi cemevis could not be an alternative to mosques and

---

[28] The final report of the Alevi workshops concedes that 'many Alevis have given up on their request to be represented within the Diyanet' (Nihai Rapor 2010: 131). For example, key demands made by the prominent elements of the Alevi movement can be seen on the website of a leading umbrella organisation, the Alevi Bektashi Federation: www.alevifederasyonu.org.tr/index.php?option=com_content&view=article&id=255& Itemid=264.

[29] For instance, Turkey has compulsory religious education, which is based exclusively on the Sunni understanding of Islam, while mosques are exempt from paying utility bills.

claimed that they were used inappropriately by illegal political organisations: 'Those that have been involved in armed action have their funerals conducted here [...] and open banners of foreign countries'. In turn, these allegations were mirrored in public discourse, particularly by Islamist politicians, including an AKP lawmaker, Mehmet Metiner, who declared in 2013 that 'cemevis are homes of terrorists' (Radikal 8 October 2013: 40). Despite the promises for the recognition of cemevis made by the AKP during the 2015 elections, the Diyanet has maintained its active resistance, as demonstrated by the statement of its former chief Mehmet Görmez in January 2016, which emphasised 'two red lines' for the state body: 'One of them is defining Alevism as a path separate from Islam, since its 1,000-year-old history refutes this claim. The second is presenting cemevis as an alternative to mosques and as the place of worship of another belief' (Hürriyet Daily News 2 January 2016).

The Gülenist and AKP Collaboration over Alevis

A critical actor in state policies on Alevis in the AKP era has been the Gülenist movement, at least until the deepening of the public falling out between the two sides began in December 2013. While Gülen's highly negative views about Kurds and Alevis have been documented, since the 1990s, the movement has functioned as an extension of the state in pursuing assimilationist strategies against first Kurds and then, especially since 2002, Alevis. Beginning in the mid-1990s in particular, at the height of the conflict between the Turkish state and the Kurdistan Workers' Party (Partiya Karkerên Kurdistani, PKK), the Gülenists have established educational institutions in the south-east of the country that might be perceived as part of a wider policy of Islamisation to break Kurdish nationalism and in line with state strategies adopted against the PKK.[30] Following the AKP's ascent to power, Gülenists also expanded their systematic campaign of Islamisation to Alevis. A key aspect of their strategy was the establishment of educational institutions – as in the Kurdish provinces – including in the only Alevi majority province, Tunceli, where the first Gülenist school was constructed in 2003.

Overall, the AKP collaborated in these policies and practices. The Gülenist mosque-cemevi projects, which involved constructing cemevis attached to mosques, thereby drawing Alevism firmly within Islam, were launched with the support of AKP government ministers in the face of resistance from the local Alevi communities. Likewise, since 2010, the AKP and Gülenists have collaborated to create alternative Alevi

---

[30] See, for instance, 'Gülenists relate expansion of activities in the predominantly Kurdish areas of south-eastern Turkey' (T24 20 September 2010).

organisations across the country, including the Anatolia Alevi-Bektashi Federation (Anadolu Alevi-Bektaşi Federasyonu) headed by Cengiz Hortoğlu, a former AKP provincial board member for Gaziantep. And it was these Gülenist–AKP organisations that would participate in the Alevi opening and other government initiatives, while non-associated Alevi actors withdrew or stayed away. However, this collaboration began to falter by 2015 as the struggle between the two sides deepened, leading state authorities to begin demolishing the mosque-*cemevi* projects, while Alevi associations established by the Gülenists were closed down following the 2016 coup attempt. The capital Ankara's Mamak municipality ordered the demolition of a prominent mosque-*cemevi* project in 2015 which had been launched in September 2013 with an opening ceremony attended by the AKP's former speaker of parliament (2011–2015) and deputy prime minister, (2007–2011) Cemil Çiçek; the AKP Minister of Work and Social Security, Faruk Çelik and the head of the (Alevi) Cem Foundation, İzzettin Doğan. In 2017, state prosecutors demanded fifteen-year prison sentences for five people involved in the Mamak Tuzluçayır mosque-*cemevi* – originally marketed as a so-called Alevi–Sunni brotherhood project – on the basis that it is what the state has designated as the Gülenist Terror Organisation (Fethullahçı Terör Örgütü, FETÖ) (see Chapters 5 and 6 for further discussion on Gülenists) (*Cumhuriyet* 27 February 2017).[31]

The Syrian Conflict and Sectarinised Securitisation

A shift in AKP policies from general continuity with previous state practices towards Alevis was catalysed by a confluence of geopolitical developments, including the outbreak of civil war in neighbouring Syria in 2011, alongside rising domestic opposition in events like the eruption of the Gezi Park protests in 2013. As the AKP's foreign policy in the region and towards Syria changed from zero problems to the promotion of intervention to topple a so-called Alevi dictator over the Sunni majority, there was also a shift to a sectarian nexus domestically. Since this period, there has been a sectarianised securitisation that involves not only a re-emphasis on the Sunni–Alevi boundary but also the portrayal of Alevis as a fifth column of neighbouring Iran and Syria through the conflation of Alevis with Alawites and their rearticulation as a Shi'a minority. Sectarianisation by the AKP or other state actors was not necessarily novel, but its degree and the link to evolving regional politics and foreign policy were new and unprecedented. In 2011, following anti-war

---

[31] Upon the demands of residents of the neighbourhood, the mosque-*cemevi* is expected to be turned into a health centre (*Milliyet* 4 April 2017).

demonstrations, Hüseyin Çelik, the then vice-chairman of the AKP, suggested that there was a sectarian affinity between the leader of the CHP, Kemal Kılıçdaroğlu (who is from Tunceli province and is of Alevi background), and the Syrian regime. Likewise, the former prime minister and current president, Erdoğan, highlighted sectarian identity when he remarked that 'fifty-three of our Sunni citizens were martyred' following what was one of the deadliest terrorist attacks on Turkish soil, in 2013 in the town of Reyhanlı in Hatay province, near the Syrian border. Alevi organisations also reported that, particularly since 2011, attacks against the community were becoming routine and systematic. Since 2012, there have been periodic bouts of unsolved cases of markings appearing on Alevi houses which have raised fears amongst communities of a repeat of the Maraş massacre, when homes of Alevis were marked with red crosses (*Cumhuriyet* 13 October 2014; *Cumhuriyet* 23 May 2015; *Evrensel* 22 November 2017; *Radikal* 7 May 2013; *Sabah* 29 February 2012).

In parallel with state strategies employed in the wider Middle East, such as in Bahrain, sectarianisation was utilised by the AKP regime to counter mass opposition to the government that emerged in 2013. Reflecting this, pro-government circles wrote that a police report had shown 78 per cent of the Gezi Park protestors had been Alevi (*Hürriyet Daily News* 25 November 2013). And it was no coincidence that the majority of those killed during that period were of Alevi and Alawite origin since, as Karakaya-Stump (16 March 2014) notes, the authorities 'discriminately unleashed police violence and repression' against Alevi–Kurdish working-class neighbourhoods as a strategy of Alevising the Gezi Park protests to counter and divide the opposition. Further exacerbating this sectarian turn was the July 2016 coup attempt. On the one hand, immediately following the coup attempt was the targeting of Alevis within pro-government media and the marching of anti-coup crowds into Alevi neighbourhoods, raising the spectre of sectarian civil conflict and massacre. Government sources and media propagated the allegation that Alevis were going to be used to provoke a Sunni–Alevi civil war in the country, even going as far as to claim that 50,000 Iranian-backed Shi'a militias as well as Alawites from Syria, ultimately backed by the United States, would have occupied the country had the coup been successful.[32] On the other hand, extrapolating the narrative of a wider Sunni–Shi'a sectarian schism in the Middle East region onto the domestic Sunni–Alevi fault line and portraying Alevi communities as potential fifth columns in this period served more than one purpose. First,

---

[32] See, for example, Bursalı (29 July 2016), *Star Gazetesi* (19 July 2016) and *Yeni Şafak* (22 July 2016).

sectarianisation would work as a hegemonic strategy of manufacturing consent to help solidify the AKP's base and expand it by making the Sunni–Alevi boundary more salient. Second, it would distract from the struggle in the conservative and Islamist neighbourhoods owing to a falling out with the AKP's former allies, the Gülenists. Yet, discursively trying to associate the Alevis with Gülenists would not only serve as a means for the regime to discredit its former allies but also intervene in Alevi identity-making strategies by trying to marginalise Alevis refusing to be boxed within an Islamic framework. Indeed, despite the fact that the AKP and Gülenists had pursued assimilative strategies to rearticulate Alevism within a Turkish–Islamic framework, since July 2016, the government has accused Gülenists of trying to promote 'atheistic Alevism' or 'Alevism without Ali' (*Akit* 1 August 2016). As a result, Alevis who do not accept the state's framing of Alevism are now being targeted as Gülenist terrorists as the AKP regime has expanded its crackdown on the Alevi movement by closing media organisations and detaining prominent Alevi leaders.

The Diyanet and the Kurdish Question

Compared to the Diyanet's rejectionist stance towards Alevis and their incorporation or representation within the institution, the body has adopted a more amenable stance towards Sunni Kurds and Kurdish *ulema*, the majority of whom follow the Shafi'i *madhab* (school of Islamic jurisprudence) (compared to the majority of Turks and the Diyanet, which follow the Hanefi school) (Bruinessen 1991). Gündoğan (2012: 126–129) notes that similar to the co-option of various Kurdish actors by the DP, and its successor JP alongside the MSP, the Diyanet also absorbed Kurdish religious leaders and scholars or *ulema* (referred to as *melle* or *mullah*, or *seyda* for more senior ones). This co-option of parts of the Kurdish *ulema* was an important channel of Turkification into the system in the sense that the *medreses* had played an important part as carriers of Kurdish identity (Gündoğan 2012: 126–129). This process gained further pace, particularly, with the push of the military as part of the TIS programme since the 1980s. It was in the late 1970s that Special Guidance Teams (Özel İrşat Ekipleri) were first dispatched to the south-east regions following sectarian violence (the Maraş massacre in 1978) (*Milliyet* 30 December 1978). In 1981, a Religious Guidance department (İrşat Dairesi) was established with the aim of fighting the rise of the Kurdish nationalist movement (Yavuz 1997: 68) along with efforts to absorb Kurdish *ulema* as part of attempts to address the 'terror problem' (Altıkulaç November 2013; Yazıcıoğlu 2013: 219–220;). These politics had met with some resistance in these regions and were perceived as assimilationist efforts of the Turkish state, but they were nevertheless revived following the 1997 military intervention (Yazıcıoğlu 2013: 115).[33] However, a more concerted effort can be seen in the AKP era. In its 2011 budget, the Diyanet announced its plans to form special guidance teams to fight against separatism and to ensure national unity and togetherness (*milli birlik ve beraberlik*) as well as to construct 1,362 mosques (*Milliyet* 11 November 2010). In late 2011, the AKP government announced 1,000 Kurdish *ulema*, or religious leaders, would be appointed by the Diyanet.

The fairly positive approach towards these efforts from within the ranks of the Diyanet may be deduced from a statement for expansion of Kurdish religious services and Shafi'i representation released by Diyanet-Sen, the trade union for Diyanet personnel (*Habertürk* 25 October 2010). The former chief of the Diyanet, Görmez, would go on to conduct part of a religious ceremony in Kurdish in Diyarbakır in 2011, where he affirmed the importance of Kurdish-language preaching in mosques so that 'believers could hear the message of Islam in a language they understand'[34] (*Habertürk* 6 April 2012). Likewise, one can point to the fifth annual national religious personnel symposium organised in 2014, where there was an emphasis on the role of *medreses*, the integration of Kurdish religious leaders, representation of Shafi'is for peace and to achieve peace, and a focus more on Islam as a common identity than on Turkishness or Kurdishness. As in previous periods, however, these efforts had mixed success and faced resistance. One example is the launch of the civil Friday prayers, which were not only part of a wider civil disobedience campaign kick-started by the Kurdish nationalist movement but also meant contesting the control and authority of the Diyanet as the country's chief religious authority. With the effective end of the peace negotiations with the Kurdish following the June 2015 election,[35] the AKP also stepped up the campaign against opposition Kurdish religious leaders either through arrests or closing down of Religious Scholars' Welfare Associations (Din Adamları Yardımlaşma

---

[33] For examples of perspectives from the region, see a report by the Islamist human rights organisation MAZLUMDER (2012: 121, 183, 208–209).

[34] This contrasts, for example, with the Diyanet's former chief Bardakoğlu's statement in 2009 that they 'do not have another language on their agenda apart from Turkish preaching and Turkish sermons' but also that they would be open to reviewing this (*CNN-Türk* 3 September 2009). However, although not official policy, the Diyanet has been conducting religious services such as preaching in the south-east in Kurdish and Zaza languages (*Akşam* 20 February 2013).

[35] In June 2015, the crackdown on the Kurdish nationalist movement stepped up following the election, when the AKP lost its majority in parliament as the pro-Kurdish People's Democratic Party (Halkların Demokratik Partisi, HDP) crossed the 10% electoral threshold.

Derneği, DİAY-DER) which were involved in the civil Friday prayers. Nevertheless, the Diyanet has continued its efforts in the region, particularly through the appointment of Special Guidance Teams (DİB July 2017: 28). Certainly, the Diyanet also comprises more Turkish nationalist factions, and its nationalist discourse has evolved over time, emphasising Turkish nationalism, particularly with the TIS programme of the 1980s. For instance, the Diyanet's former chief Ali Bardakoğlu (2003–2010) is known for having resisted Kurdish-language religious services on the basis that they would 'augment divisions in the mind' (*Cumhuriyet* 10 November 2010), and it is rumoured this was one of the reasons for his departure. Yet, the body's ability to develop a comparatively more open approach to Sunni Kurds reveals its role as a carrier of Sunni Islam that ensures the reproduction of religious boundaries.

Conclusion

Competition and collaboration within the state regarding the approach towards Alevis is revealing of the nature of the Turkish state's relationship with the majority religion and the degree of religious majoritarianism. A clear impulse within the state since at least the establishment of the Republic has been a nationalist one that seeks the absorption of Alevism through Turkification and Sunnification, using it as bricks and mortar in the construction of the nation and the majority bloc, while simultaneously rejecting it and rendering it obsolete. Such strategies were commonly adopted during the one-party era and by elements within the military that sought to rearticulate Alevism as 'real' Turkish Islam, especially in a bid to break any links with Kurdishness. The Diyanet's impulse, on the other hand, has been more sectarian and religious, given that the body is an institutional site of Islam and a carrier and preserver of Sunni (Hanefi) Muslim orthodoxy, in continuity with the Ottoman *ulema*.

These different factions within the state, despite competing political visions, have ultimately shared an overlapping consensus on Alevis owing to the intertwined nature of Turkish national identity and Islam. For both, the drive to rearticulate Alevism within an Islamic and/or Turkish (also intertwined with Islam) framing has been driven by fear of any signs of distinction as a threat to the constructed Sunni Muslim Turkish majority and this bloc's dominant position within the nation-state. Consequently, despite their Turkification and Islamisation efforts, these different state actors continued to regard Alevis not just as a heretical other (for Sunni Islam) but also as a security threat, evidenced by their continued surveillance and perceptions of the community as a potential fifth column. These dynamics were reinforced by the Diyanet, which, as an Islamic authority and state institution, could successfully negotiate national identity and resist the policies of absorption of Alevism.

The manner in which the Diyanet has delimited community and national boundaries along religious lines in turn underlines the institution's role in the embedding and reproduction of the religious majoritarianism of the state in privileging Sunni Muslim identity and endowing it with resources. Through its interventions against Alevism, the Diyanet has accentuated the level of social closure, resulting in the hardening of group boundaries. This has contributed over time to the ethnicisation of political competition whereby multiple identities and political associations become reduced to a single ethnic dimension (Wimmer 1997: 643). In other words, the Diyanet has played a key role in ensuring the persistence of the salience of religious markers in political and economic struggles. Accordingly, the sectarianised securitisation by the AKP government since the outbreak of the Syrian conflict in 2011 that involves the targeting of Alevis as a security threat has to be situated against this background of the Diyanet's role in sectarian boundary making and policies.

Equally, the Diyanet's rejection of recognition of Alevi places of worship, and therefore rejection of equal access to state resources and equal citizenship, highlights the importance of religious markers, particularly when compared to the body's more favourable approach towards Kurdish or Syrian (Arab) Sunni *ulema*. These underlying processes have, in turn, reinforced path-dependency effects, making it difficult to restructure the Diyanet through, for example, the attempts since the early 1960s and in the AKP era to open it up to Alevis or non-Muslims by establishing a Department of Denominations (even in the context of absorption rather than recognition). More broadly, therefore, the Diyanet's stance towards Alevism suggests that institutions can become barriers to the hegemonic practices of absorption in nation building, thereby impeding the push towards homogeneity. In this manner, the institutionalisation of identities, the very process that ensures the stability of the dominant hegemonic bloc, can eventually also harden categories in a way that forms barriers of resistance to absorption of what are perceived to be 'marginal elements'. Institutions may thus be considered a key factor underpinning the nation as a 'zone of conflict' (Hutchinson 2004b).

4   The Expansion of the Religious Field in the Multi-Party Era

---

The Diyanet was not the only institution that facilitated Islamist mobil-isation through Islamisation or enabling the reproduction of religious delineations of identity and salience of religious markers. Equally import-ant for Islamist mobilisation have been other factors, such as education, charities and associations, as well as the growth of what has been described as an Islamic economy or economic actors. The master narra-tive of Turkish politics (Kandiyoti 2012: 515) has viewed the expansion of religious education, faith-based charities, conservative business asso-ciations and Islamic banking as a revival or a bottom-up push by religious society or marginalised groups empowered by the democratisation of politics since the 1950s and neoliberal economic transformation since the 1980s (e.g. Kuru 2009: 161–201; Kuru and Stepan 2012: 104; Pupcenoks 2012: 287–289; Sunar and Toprak 1983: 428; Yavuz 2006). Connected to this conception of a religious revival enabled by political and economic liberalisation is the notion of the rise of a 'Muslim bourgeoisie', which has been a central aspect of accounts of Turkish Islamism and Islamist moderation (see discussion in Chapter 6) (e.g. Atasoy 2009; Gülalp 2001; Gümüşçü 2010; Nasr 2005; Tuğal 2009a; Yavuz 2003, 2006). Thus, the increasing differentiation in lifestyles and symbols within the public sphere have been interpreted as reflecting 'a unified Muslim habitus entering into conflict with Western modernity' (Kandiyoti 2012: 515). One influential account is from Göle (1997), who has employed a Bourdieusian perspective in describing this mobilisation in terms of cultural distinction and social stratification resulting from a 'shift from an Islamic to a Western culture', which involved a 'radical break with the local culture, under the modernizing programs of the Republicanists, [which] rendered difficult the process of identification of the rising peripheral classes with the established elites' (Göle 1997: 51–52). In this formulation, which is widely echoed in the literature, Islamisation becomes a 'counter-attack against the principles of the Kemalist project of modernization' and Islamism a form of political expression of the 'Muslim periphery' (Göle 1997: 52, 57).

First, this chapter departs from these accounts and builds on works such as by Şen (2010) on how enlargement of the religious field influenced Islamist mobilisation. It relates how the expansion of the institutional infrastructure behind religion shifted the balance of power within the state, resulting over time in a more supportive institutional framework and greater access to state resources for conservative and Islamist actors. In this manner, it underlines the webs of reciprocity and enmeshed relationship with the state that underpins Islamist mobilisation that is neglected by the master narrative. This is done by focusing on three key sites of Islamist mobilisation and Islamisation: religious education, Islamic charities and Islamic banking and conservative business organisations associated with the rise of a 'Muslim bourgeoisie'. With this, it builds on the growing literature on Islamisation in Turkey under Islamist government (Kaya 2015; Pupcenoks 2012; Yeşilada and Rubin 2011), in part concomitant with the increasing focus on AKP authoritarianism, including on religious schools and the Islamisation of mainstream education (Çakmak 2009; Coşkun and Şentürk 2012; Kandiyoti and Emanet 2017; Lüküslü 2016; Özgür 2012), the growth of faith-based associations and Islamic capital in the context of neo-liberal transformation of the economy (Buğra and Savaşkan 2014; Eder 2010; Göçmen 2014; Hosgör 2011; White 2002; Yankaya 2014) and Islamic finance (Başkan 2004). It also highlights, in line with the literature on Islamist mobilisation in Turkey, the importance of two critical contingent factors, the Cold War related anti-communism drive and the neo-liberal economic transformation of the 1980s (e.g. Eligür 2010; Şen 2010; Yavuz 2003). However, rather than viewing these episodes as resulting in the secular state's instrumentalisation of religion and Islamists, they are understood here as opening up 'windows of opportunity' to shift the balance of power and resources within the state among different factions, towards more rightist conservative or Islamist elements.

For instance, the expansion of religious education was championed and advocated by the Diyanet but also came to be regarded by other state actors as necessary in the 1940s as part of the Cold War related anti-communism drive. Once these schools were re-established in the 1950s, Islamist actors were able to utilise the state-administered religious education in order to generate and reproduce an Islamist generation. Likewise, the neo-liberal restructuring of the economy in the 1980s opened up important opportunities for Islamist mobilisation (Eligür 2010; Yavuz 2003) but also reflected strategies of conservative and Islamist actors within and outside the state. Islamic charities and Islamic finance grew as the state withdrew from welfare provision in response to its fiscal crisis and began to search for new sources of capital. These expanding networks and capital underpinned the ascendancy of the so-called Muslim bourgeoisie, manifesting in the establishment of conservative business associations together with the emergence of new patterns of consumption and lifestyles, including Islamic fashion, and restructuring of social spaces. In this sense, beyond the maintenance of religious boundaries, these habits have been tied to both neo-liberal economic restructuring and a drive for the assertion of religion in everyday life (Tarlo and Moors 2013). Significantly, Craciun (2017: 6) notes that Islamic fashion began to develop in Turkey in the 1980s, earlier than in other countries.

That the expansion of this infrastructure, particularly religious education, has been important for the reproduction of a distinct habitus, or a pious generation, and for supporting Islamist mobilisation has been noted (Lüküslü 2016; Özgür 2012). Bourdieu's concept of habitus is useful in conceptualising social stratification as Göle (1997) and others have outlined. It allows us to (i) conceptualise the differentiated effects of particular configurations of structures in shaping different actors; (ii) explain change through the incorporation of agency that leaves room for strategic action and (iii) accounts for persistence through an understanding of the reproduction of these structures, which is underpinned by the self-reinforcing dynamic of institutions. Habitus is defined as a system of internalised dispositions 'acquired through lasting exposure to particular social conditions and conditionings, via the internalization of external constraints and possibilities' (Wacquant 2006: 266). The nature of dispositions acquired depends on the particular endowment of capital, which is defined as comprising all forms of power, including material (economic), cultural, social and symbolic (Mangi 2009). The habitus can, in this manner, be conceived of as the product of the mutually constitutive means by which structure and agent shape each other and are reproduced (Wacquant 2006); it is 'the product of structure, producer of practice, and reproducer of structure' (Bourdieu 1977: 72, 1979, 1989; Wacquant 2006: 267). It defines the nature of the competition and differentiation between social groups composed of individuals who share similar dispositions which reflect their mutual conditioning and similar endowment of capital. However, unlike Göle (1997; 2013), this chapter does not relate the formation of a distinct habitus to a cultural clash or struggle between alternative conceptualisations of modernity or civilisation (1997, 2013: 12, 67, 132). Rather, social differentiation is connected to the dominant forms of social source at the point of nation-state building. This draws from Wimmer's argument that

Social closure and high degrees of 'groupness' in turn will lead, as we have learned from Max Weber [...] and Pierre Bourdieu, [...] to cultural differentiation because those who set themselves apart reinforce the boundary by adding new cultural diacritics in order to show how culturally different and inferior the subordinated groups are. This reinforces the taken for grantedness of the boundary, which leads to further and ongoing cultural differentiation, and so forth. (Wimmer 2008: 1002)

As outlined in Chapter 1, during the early phases of nation building, the construction of citizenship and institutions was the Ottoman legacy of high levels of social closure, involving the heightened salience of boundaries demarcated along religious lines. Following from this, later social differentiation and the growing salience of religious markers over time are not only related to the expansion of the religious field, particularly since the 1940s, but understood as being ontologically related to earlier forms of boundary making.

Based on this context, the first section traces the growing salience of religious markers in economic competition manifesting in the emergence of conservative business organisations in the 1990s and then situates it within the religiously coded manner of class formation during nation building. The second and third sections tackle how these religious markers maintained and increased their salience over time by focusing on the expansion of the religious field. Specifically, this involves the infrastructure behind religion, including religious education, faith-based organisations and Islamic finance, within the context of the emerging Cold War and neo-liberal economic restructuring in the 1980s. The conclusion examines the growing salience of religious markers over time and the resultant social differentiation by defining it as (i) related to path-dependent effects of processes of social closure during nation building that resulted in the continuation of policies advantaging a Muslim Turkish bourgeoisie in the early Republic and (ii) how, over time, mobilisation on the basis of religious group identity became a more attractive strategy for actors during economic and political competition because of the shifts in power relations within the state.

The Rise of the 'Muslim Bourgeoisie'

The emergence in the 1990s of what have been styled as 'conservative', 'Muslim' or 'pious' business organisations has been widely linked to and described as a manifestation of the rise of the 'Muslim bourgeoisie' (see Figure 8). Some prominent examples of this include Nasr (2005: 18–19, 24) and Yavuz (2003: 185). Commonly, the usage of this depiction is an effort to distinguish a faction of capital emphasising distinctly religious

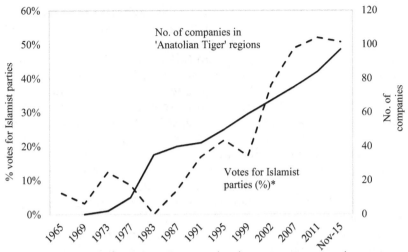

Sources: İstanbul Sanayi Odası [İstanbul Chamber of Industry, İSO]; İstanbul Sanayi Odasi Dergisi [İstanbul Chamber of Industry Magazine] 1968–2013; 'Election of Representatives Statistics' from the Türkiye İstatistik Kurumu [Turkish Statistical Institute, TUIK]. Calculations are my own. *Includes AKP, RP, SP, FP, MSP, MNP, MP, BBP

Figure 8: Support for Islamist political parties (%) and number of İstanbul Chamber of Industry top 500 companies in Anatolian Tiger regions

identity markers together with piety, which is counterpoised against 'secular' capital. In turn, this has been closely associated with the ascent of Islamists (see Figure 8) and assumed moderation – until recently (further discussed in Chapter 6) (Balkan et al. 2015; European Stability Initiative 2005; Gümüşçü 2008; Şen 2010: 71; Yankaya 2014; Yavuz 2003, 2006). Broadly, there are three main approaches to explaining the rise of Muslim business organisations. as Cengiz (2013) has pithily summarised and critiqued, the first articulates their emergence within the metanarrative of the Muslim majority's triumph over the authoritarian secular elite. It is claimed that Muslim entrepreneurs were stifled by the secular Kemalist state until the liberalisation policies of the post-1980 era (Demir et al. 2004; Gümüşçü 2008: 961; Yavuz 2003, 2004a, 2006) and that neoliberal restructuring implemented by the ANAP government 'helped the crystallisation and expansion of a countercultural bourgeoisie class with Anatolian roots [...] Özal replaced the statist and corporatist Kemalist development strategy with a new vision of free-market policies that supported his neo-populist coalition' (Yavuz 2004a: 277). This largely echoes claims made by conservative business associations such as MÜSİAD, which was established in 1990. MÜSİAD stresses that the M stands for *müstakil* (independent) rather than Muslim, because they claim that it has not been supported by the state. Özal's policies in the 1980s and the economic liberalisation agenda are described as 'revolutionary', and much of MÜSİAD's members' success and opportunities are attributed to this neo-liberal turn (MÜSİAD 2005, 2010). By extension, this also involves ideological justification for neo-liberal economic policies that are presented as democratisation, but which they see as involving the channelling of state resources to the majority – Muslim businesses – and away from what is categorised as the minority, secular and Kemalist traditional centres. Accordingly, this narrative naturalises the claims of identity politics, depicting conservative business organisations as the authentic representatives of a Muslim society and their monopolisation of economic resources as a natural and democratic right. Cengiz (2013) has equally shown in his work on Kayseri that narratives of victimhood and exclusion are without basis.

The second view is more functionalist in arguing that the emphasis on Islamic identity and the narrative of historical exclusion have provided useful rhetorical resources for conservative business organisations to gain greater access to political and economic resources through, for example, the channelling of state funds to Anatolia or the incorporation into the clientelistic networks enjoyed by big business (Buğra and Savaşkan 2012; Yankaya 2014). For instance, in its initial years, MÜSİAD had more limited access to clientelist networks with political parties, which at the time were dominated by established business associations: the Turkish Industry and Business Association (Türk Sanayicileri ve İşadamları Derneği, TÜSİAD) was close to ANAP, while the Union of Chambers and Commodity Exchanges of Turkey (Türkiye Odalar ve Borsalar Birliği, TOBB) had links with the DYP (Yankaya 2014: 105–109).[1] Instead, relations with the Islamist RP, with which MÜSİAD enjoyed common networks, had begun to deepen as the party ascended to government and began to provide opportunities to gain easier access to state resources, such as state incentive schemes and important public tenders in privatisations and the domestic defence industry (Yankaya 2014: 105–109). These clientelist links continued under the AKP, as MÜSİAD members played a role in the party's founding and have undertaken positions within it. The AKP has adopted various policies to benefit small and medium-sized enterprises (SMEs), including a tax amnesty law in 2005 and banking reform in 2004 to increase the availability of credit

---

[1] Since its establishment, MÜSİAD has grown into one of the largest business associations in Turkey, with around 7,000 members and 35,000 affiliated companies employing around 1.5 million workers (MÜSİAD website). It differs from TÜSİAD in terms of size, membership, sector and regional basis (see also Demiralp 2009).

for SMEs (Demiralp 2009: 328–329). Accordingly, Muslim identity is considered to have served a partly functional and partly symbolic purpose and is utilised

as a resource to bind the businessmen whom it represents into a coherent community and to represent their economic interests as an integral component of an ideological mission; as a basis for cooperation and solidarity between producers; as a device to create secure market niches or sources of investment finance; and as a means of containing social unrest and labour militancy. (Buğra 1998: 522)

Buğra and Savaşkan (2012: 52) argue that rather than a Muslim bourgeoisie empowered by neoliberalism, it marks the 'emergence of a new vintage of state-created bourgeoisie that enjoys central government favours, as defined by new legislative and administrative mechanisms and used within networks drawing on cultural resources informed by religious identity'.

As an alternative, accounts that have drawn on the Marxist tradition (e.g. Balkan et al. 2015) have underlined the contradictions (e.g. between big and small business) and fractionalisation of capital in the Turkish case, resulting in the 'struggle for hegemony [...] over different strategic and tactical priorities' (Tanyılmaz 2015: 113). Yet beyond the insights into how these business associations utilise religious identity to pursue their interests, there remains the question of why these strategies have proved more attractive and plausible for actors to adopt. There is sometimes an implicit assumption that the choice of religious markers in political and economic competition is somehow natural because of a Muslim majority context. This would, therefore, mean an underlying essentialism that is also inherent in the first approach. For instance, in a different, non-Muslim majority setting, like the UK, business organisations do not distinguish themselves through religious markers. There is no reference to a 'Christian bourgeoisie' or 'Christian majority', even if the population may be nominally categorised as majority Christian. In this case, such strategies are not attractive or plausible because religious group boundaries are not, or have ceased to be, salient within political and economic competition. Buğra (1998: 529) has argued that the use of religion by MÜSİAD reflects a 'minority psychology, manifested in the expression of a feeling of being excluded from economic life controlled by a big-business community supported by the secularist state ... [that has] a significant place in the organizing rhetoric of this association'. However, such an explanation leaves unanswered why this sense of exclusion involved the deployment of religious markers rather than class, for instance, when there was no exclusion of Muslims from economic life.

The proposition here is that the usefulness of employing religious markers in economic and political struggles relates to *longue durée* processes of boundary building. In particular, this refers to the religiously coded ways in which class formation and nation building have unfolded since the late Ottoman Empire and how these have influenced the forms of social closure in the Republic. Following the establishment of the Republic, state elites continued to pursue the elimination of non-Muslims from the economy and the privileging and establishing of a national bourgeoisie, which in practice, meant Muslim Turkish domination as a fundamental aspect of nation building policies. This effectively ended the conditions of class bifurcation of the bourgeoisie into non-Muslims and Muslims (Göçek 1996) that had emerged in the late Ottoman Empire. Together with the state's homogenising drive, an outcome of these practices was that the non-Muslim population had fallen to below 1 per cent by the 1950s. Yet, religious markers have continued to pervade the discourses utilised in economic competition. In other words, while the material conditions of bifurcation disappeared, a symbolic bifurcation has persisted and become more prominent over time, typified by the emergence of conservative business associations like MÜSİAD in the 1990s.

This was because, on the one hand, these religious markers maintained their political salience owing to path-dependent effects generated by the religious majoritarian nature of nation-state building that was mirrored in economic policy and structure. This included citizenship policies, the advantaging of a Muslim Turkish bourgeoisie in the early Republic and the absorption of the Ottoman *ulema* (outlined in Chapters 1–3), which were later reinforced with the expansion of the religious field. On the other hand, as the balance of power within the state and wider institutional framework became more favourable, the utilisation of these markers in economic and political competition became more advantageous and was thereby transposed upon new distributional conflicts.

More specifically, the bifurcation experienced between the non-Muslim and Muslim tradesmen in the later Empire was supplanted in the Republic by regional economic segmentation. This, in turn, was a product of the differentiated effect of European imperial economic penetration during the Ottoman Empire and late capitalist development. Traditional industry was decimated during the late Ottoman Empire following increasing external imperial penetration, especially after the 1838 Anglo-Ottoman Treaty (Keyder 1987: 29–32). Integration into the world capitalist economy had resulted in the growth of harbour cities in western Anatolia (İstanbul and İzmir) that enjoyed trade with Europe and better transport links, while exacerbating the decline of the inner Anatolian regions (Dinler 1994: 181–182; Keyder 1987: 29–33). The

Table 1: *Industrial activity according to type of economic activity and regional distribution (from the 1915 Industrial Survey)*

Industry	Istanbul	Izmir	Other areas	Total
Food industry	45	23	10	78
Land industry	20	1	–	21
Leather industry	11	2	–	13
Tree industry	15	9	–	24
Textile industry	15	8	55	78
Paper and publishing industry	44	11	–	55
Chemicals industry	5	8	–	13
Total	155	62	65	282
% of Total	55	22	23	100

Source: (Dinler 1994: 186).

results of a 1915 industrial survey (see Table 1) demonstrate the sharp regional economic divergence, with İstanbul and İzmir accounting for 76 per cent of workplaces (İstanbul, 57 per cent; İzmir, 19 per cent) (Dinler 1994: 186–187) and minimal industrial activity occurring outside these regions. As Keyder argues, the effects of this integration of the Ottoman economy with the European capitalist order reflects the 'common experience of capitalist integration in the periphery. What was specific to Turkey was the overdetermination of the class conflict accompanying this restructuration with religious and ethnic differences' (Keyder 1987: 32–33).Against this backdrop and with a drive to establish a national bourgeoisie, Republican elites adopted a strategy of state-led industrialisation (see Figure 9), or statism (*etatism*), following the outbreak of economic crisis in 1929, which marked the start of the Great Depression (Boratav 2003: 27; Dinler 1994: 193). However, despite efforts to incorporate the peripheral regions through state investments, by the end of the one-party era, industry remained concentrated in the traditional centres such as İstanbul, İzmir, Adana and Bursa (Dinler 1994: 194; Tekeli and Soral 1976: 100). It was partly owing to concerns about the impact of regional equality on national unity and ethnic unrest in the eastern provinces that, in 1960, the junta regime subsequently established the DPT (Koçak 2010b: 556). Accordingly, starting in the mid-1960s, governments sought to further industrialisation in Anatolia first by channelling the savings of Turkish immigrants in Europe and later through targeted regional industrialisation programmes, such as the 1968 strategy of demarcating 'priority development areas' (Kalkınma Öncelikli Yöreler) (Hosgör 2011: 344).

At the same time, regional disparities had been sharpened by the import substitution industrialisation (ISI) regime owing to the concentration of economic power in the hands of a small number of business conglomerates largely based in the traditional industrial centres. The distribution of state funds remained concentrated in the traditional centres: the five-year development plans in the period 1963–1983 envisaged that only around a third of the total planned public investments would be destined for the forty least developed provinces, where just less than half of the population resided (Barkey 1990: 132–133). As Jacoby (2006: 55) argues, 'Industrial development in Turkey tended to perpetuate and, in some cases, reinforce the types of pre-modern centre/periphery divide which industrialisation in Europe gradually diminished'. It was onto this struggle for resources that older religiously delineated majority and minority boundaries were transposed. In other words, business sector fragmentation, or fractionalisation, of the social classes exacerbated by the ISI regime became articulated along religious majority and minority delineations as a result of the dynamics of nation building. Consequently, in their struggle for the resources of the state, conservative and Islamist actors, in particular, seized upon these delineations to assert their claims, for two main reasons. First, it was a plausible strategy to follow because it resonated with the religious majoritarian logic of the nation-state, whereby the legitimate owners had been defined as the (constructed) Sunni Muslim Turkish majority bloc. Second, it became an attractive strategy because political liberalisation in the 1940s had heralded a shift towards more conservative and Islamist actors within the state, as demonstrated by both successive rightist conservative governments and expansion of state actors such as the Diyanet (outlined in Chapters 3 and 4).

Exemplifying this politics was a key Islamist figure, Necmettin Erbakan, a former member of the centre-right Justice Party (Adalet Partisi, AP) and founder of the Islamist National Outlook movement in 1969 and the MNP in 1970, which resurfaced as the MSP in 1971. His fame had followed his controversial election in 1969 to the leadership of the TOBB, a corporatist private-sector body established by the state in 1952 as the representative of small and medium-sized businesses. This was a manifestation of the increasing dissatisfaction with the effects of the ISI regime outlined earlier; Erbakan accused the TOBB of becoming an instrument of a 'comprador-masonic minority' (Sarıbay 1985: 98–99), arguing that the İstanbul and İzmir groups were blocking the development of Anatolian business (Barkey 1990: 132).[2] This was in essence a

---

[2] Erbakan was eventually ousted from the TOBB following political manoeuvrings by the governing AP.

reference to the economically privileged position of non-Muslim minorities in the Ottoman Empire who had benefitted from links to European imperial powers under the capitulations regime. Except that with those non-Muslims eliminated from the economy, Erbakan was minoritising the first generation of 'state-created bourgeoisie' (Buğra 1998: 526) by inferring they were non-Muslims, even though they were, categorically speaking, Muslims. The MSP articulated itself through Islamic references, but it had emerged as the representative of the Anatolian petty bourgeoisie, seeking to increase its share of the economic pie: its party programme in 1973 was as much concerned with regional inequalities as the Islamic cause.[3] This was epitomised by Erbakan's question, 'Why shouldn't the Anatolian person own a factory?' and his arguments that the Anatolian bourgeoisie, with the help of the state, had to be strengthened against the İstanbul bourgeoisie, which he characterised as 'the happy minority' (Tekeli and Soral 1976: 99–100).

The focus on a Muslim or national bourgeoisie was not exclusive to conservative and Islamist actors but permeated the wider public discourse. In the 1970s, the CHP's People's Sector programme that was outlined in the party's manifestos also promised social justice between regions, involving greater investment in Anatolia by generating a just and balanced development model in a bottom-up manner (CHP 1973: 16, 44). The 1973 CHP election manifesto, 'Ak Günlere' ('Towards Bright Days'), argues in this vein that the state's incentive schemes were being channelled to 'monopoly capital' – business elites in the traditional economic centres – rather than Anatolian businesses, described as being more national and 'at one with the people' and not embroiled with foreign capital, as compared to established business elites (CHP 1973: 82).

The subsequent breakdown of the ISI regime and the adoption of economic liberalisation measures following the 1980 military coup marked a critical juncture that saw a significant restructuring of political and economic life, which further reinforced the symbolic bifurcation. The transition to an export-oriented economy and liberalisation involved a move away from the monopolistic competition and capital concentration under the ISI regime, facilitating a degree of economic redistribution and the ongoing process of industrial diffusion into the Anatolian heartlands. This was driven by the shift of state incentives towards export-oriented industries, which, in conjunction with privatisation policies, opened up new opportunity spaces for SMEs, especially in labour-intensive sectors

---

[3] The party programme also contained an emphasis on the importance of religious education. For more detail on the programme, see Sarıbay (1985) and Tekeli and Soral (1976).

such as textiles, leather, clothing and the food industry, all of which were also the rising sectors of the post-1980 era (Şen 2010: 71). Hosgör (2011: 345) also notes the importance of Saudi Arabia's investments, especially through the establishment of Islamic finance organisations, which supported capital accumulation and expanded access to credit alongside the channelling of the savings of Turkish guest workers from Europe. Consequently, this spurred on the transformation of the Anatolian provincial petty bourgeoisie into a group of entrepreneurs fronting medium-sized and large companies (Şen 2010: 71–72), essentially giving rise to a 'second generation of the bourgeoisie' (Bozkurt 2013: 380; Çokgezen 2000: 532). One can, therefore, view this growth in Anatolian capital as a product of economic diffusion, as shown by the historical breakdown of the top 500 companies (based on turnover) published by the İstanbul Chamber of Industry (İstanbul Sanayi Odası, İSO) since 1970 (Figure 10),[4] as also shown by Buğra and Savaşkan (2014), rather than the triumph of Muslim capital against the minority secularist state. Indeed, as scholars have shown, much of this growth in Anatolian capital, while articulated as part of a narrative of Muslim self-made entrepreneurs despite the Kemalist state, was based largely in the very sites where the state had been investing in expanding industrial infrastructure since the one-party period, such as Kayseri and Eskişehir, while other tigers, such as Gaziantep and Denizli, were already identified as development priority areas in 1968 and 1973, respectively (Bedirhanoğlu and Yalman 2009: 246; Cengiz 2013: 70). In particular, as compared to the ISI period, in the post-1980 period, and particularly since the 1990s and under the AKP, there was a shift towards the channelling of state incentives and rents towards SMEs. It was in this context that Turkey saw the rise of what have been described as Islamist or pious business associations, such as MÜSİAD, in the 1990s.[5] Depicted as representing the rise of an Anatolian capital, and also dubbed Anatolian Tigers,[6] the distinctive

---

[4] The data starts in 1968, listing the top 100 companies. Between 1977 and 1979, 300 companies were published, and around 1980, İSO began to publish the top 500 companies.

[5] Rival business associations include Gülenist Turkish Confederation of Businessmen and Industrialists (Türkiye İşadamları ve Sanayiciler Konfederasyonu, TUSKON) which has been closed since the attempted coup in July 2016, and the Association of Anatolian Businessmen (Anadolu Aslanları İşadamları Derneği, ASKON).

[6] This term is widely used in the literature and within business associations such as MÜSİAD. These particular areas were determined on the basis of both academic literature and MÜSİAD publications, and they are Ayvalık, Bafra, Balıkesir, Bilecik, Çarşamba, Çorum, Denizli, Eskişehir, Gaziantep, Gediz, Kahramanmaraş, Karaman, Kayseri, Konya, Kütahya, Malatya, Niğde, Ordu, Samsun, Trabzon and Ünye. For further discussion of the term 'Anatolian Tigers' see Buğra (1998: 524–525) and Bedirhanoğlu and Yalman (2009: 247, 263).

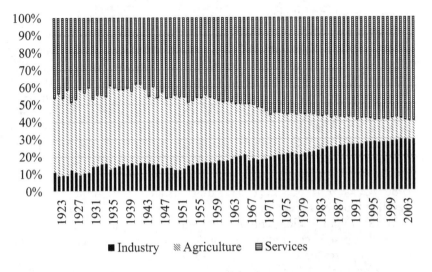

■ Industry   ⧄ Agriculture   ▤ Services

Sources: Statistical Indicators, 1923-2013' from the Türkiye İstatistik Kurumu [Turkish Statistical Institute, TUIK].

Figure 9: Sectoral growth: percentage of total real gross domestic product

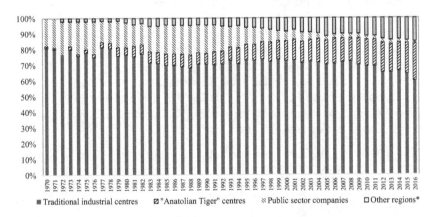

■ Traditional industrial centres   ▨ "Anatolian Tiger" centres   ⧄ Public sector companies   ▢ Other regions*

Sources: İstanbul Sanayi Odası [İstanbul Chamber of Industry, İSO]; İstanbul Sanayi Odası Dergisi [İstanbul Chamber of Industry Magazine] 1968-2016. Calculations and categorisations author's own
*Other regions include all areas that are outside of the i) traditional centres and ii) 'Anatolian' Tiger' areas.

Figure 10: İstanbul Chamber of Industry top companies by region (percentage of total)

aspect of these associations has been their emphasis on their identity as Muslims and as a distinct social group compared with the traditional business establishment represented by TÜSİAD, which is typically characterised by Islamists as representing İstanbul-based secular and minority capital.[7] While TÜSİAD was the representative of the first generation of state-created bourgeoisie, MÜSİAD represented the second generation (Buğra 1998: 526; Hosgör 2011; Buğra and Savaşkan 2014). Reflecting this, MÜSİAD comprises largely young and family-owned SME-scale enterprises, with around half of them established during the 1980 to 1990 period and a third of them after 1990 (Şen 2010: 71). Around half of MÜSİAD's members are located in Anatolia, in particular in politically conservative Anatolian cities such as Konya and Kayseri (Buğra and Savaşkan 2010: 42–43), with the rest in industrial centres. In comparison, TÜSİAD was established in 1971 and is strictly restricted to large business enterprises, with 70 per cent of member firms established before 1980 (Çokgezen 2000: 531) and most located in İstanbul and other traditional business centres.

MÜSİAD publications commonly describe the organisation's members as Muslim people committed to Islamic lifestyles and morality and raised on 'Turkey's traditional and religious values' in which 'economic development is not [an] end but a means to an end' (MÜSİAD 1991, 1994b, 1998, 2005, 2010; Yarar 1997). In this vein, MÜSİAD (alongside conservative-Islamist actors) has typically asserted that it represents Anatolian national capital, a bottom-up social (Muslim) movement in a Muslim society that it claims has been deprived of access to resources previously dominated by minority, monopolistic İstanbul rentier capital that comprises an elitist group of secularist Kemalist bureaucrats and big business and that are dependent on state patronage. Narratives of victimhood pervade the body's discourse, with MÜSİAD's journey being described as a 'painful walk from periphery to the centre' while facing discrimination and being impeded by the Kemalist elite and centre (MÜSİAD 2010). Reflecting this very logic, a special report published in 2005 marking the fifteenth anniversary of the organisation declares proudly that

The history of MÜSİAD is a story of one walking uphill. As 'indigenous' entrepreneurs that first emerged towards the end of 1829, and were protected and developed since the Hayriye Tüccarları [Muslim tradesmen], they were for the first time stalled by fabricated events [*yapay dalga*] after the 28 February process. (MÜSİAD 2005)[8]

---

[7] It is not argued here that all MÜSİAD members are Islamist or religious/pious. Çokgezen (2000), however, notes that MÜSİAD members have always brought their Islamic identity to the forefront.

[8] During the 28 February process initiated by the 1997 post-modern coup, a number of MÜSİAD companies were targeted by the military authorities as 'green capital' and blacklisted for allegedly having links with 'reactionary forces'. The claims that the 1997 coup targeted Islamists/conservatives and the Anatolian Tigers to prevent their rise has been a prevalent discourse among Islamist actors, including the AKP.

This narrative of continuity with the *hayriye tüccarları* of the Ottoman Empire is particularly pertinent. During the reign of Sultan Selim III (1789–1809), the Ottoman state established its own system of privileges for its non-Muslim tradesmen subjects as a countermeasure against the expansion of the capitulations system of privileges for foreign tradesmen (Masters 1992: 579–580). Following disquiet among Muslim tradesmen about these measures for non-Muslim tradesmen, the status of the *hayriye tüccarları* was established and Muslims were granted the same privileges and protection enjoyed by the non-Muslims (Ulutaş 2012: 503). In this sense, these policies marked the first efforts in the Empire to support Muslim subjects in the economic sphere, which had hitherto been dominated by non-Muslims.

This effort to construct a narrative of historical oppression of the Muslim majority has, in turn, become a common practice utilised by Islamist and conservative actors in their populist politics of *ressentiment* (Kandiyoti 2014). Certainly, as Buğra and Savaşkan (2014: 138) argue, such narratives of disadvantage and exclusion imposed by secularists have been useful in masking favourable relations between Islamic business associations and the government. Indeed, following the ascent of the AKP in 2002, conservative or Islamist businesses have significantly expanded in terms of their significance within the Turkish economy while increasing their share of the distribution of state rents. Crucially, writes Hosgör (2011: 354–355), the AKP 'not only articulated the economic demands of the petty-bourgeoisie to the interests of the newly arisen medium-sized business groups from Anatolia, but also forced big-business circles from İstanbul to adopt a selective strategy that included strategic compromises to the newly growing medium-sized firms'. Conversely, the multifaceted competition and dynamics within the business community alone cannot be reduced to a simple classification that pits Islamic Anatolian bourgeoisie against secular businesses based in the traditional industrial centres (Buğra and Savaşkan 2014: 151; Hosgör 2011: 357).

The question however, is why, even though such categorisations are not necessarily meaningful in reality, actors have adopted religious delineations in the competition for resources. The argument here is that the fragmentation of business groups has resulted from the particular forms of social closure at the point of nation building, which in the Turkish case meant that class formation did not evolve through an eradication of ethnic and religious distinction but rather was imbued by these markers of identity. This, in turn, generated path-dependent effects. Even though there was no longer a material bifurcation or segmentation between a Muslim majority and non-Muslim minority, as in the late Ottoman

Empire, such boundaries were reproduced owing to the elevation of Sunni Muslim identity by the nation-state project and by an expanding religious infrastructure since the late 1940s, and they came to be extrapolated onto new distributional conflicts. A key point in the emergence of this struggle in the Republic was therefore the Erbakan event in 1969, when he ran for the presidency of the TOBB, which was symptomatic of the emerging competition between 'monopolistic big business' and 'smaller capitals and sections of the commercial bourgeoisie', which buoyed Islamist mobilisation (Öztürk 2015: 124). As Schumpeter (2007: 111) has written, social groups or classes 'coexisting at any given time bear the marks of different centuries on their brow [...] Classes, once they have come into being, harden in their mould and perpetuate themselves, even when the social conditions that created them have disappeared'.

The Growth of Religious Education

A further aspect of why religious markers maintained and increased their salience over time related to the expansion of the religious field. In particular, the relationship between religious education and Islamism has been an area of focus and contention not just in Turkey but also in other Muslim majority contexts. This is because of the critical role played by the educational system in nation building, the shaping of collective identities and the socialisation of citizens (Bourdieu 1979; Giroux 1981). The link between Islamist mobilisation and religious education has also been corroborated in recent studies of the wider Middle East. For instance, Ketchley and Biggs (2017) found that, in Egypt, a disproportionate number of Islamist students came from al-Azhar University and have received formal religious education. The growing literature on education policies under the AKP have underlined the transformation of mainstream education driven by the regime's goal of creating an 'Islamized version of national identity and [...] a pious generation' (Lüküslü 2016: 645), 'a new generation of Islamist intellectuals' and a new 'Islamic civil morality' (Türkmen 2009). Likewise, Kandiyoti and Emanet (2017: 869) pithily summarise these developments as the 'capture of minds', relating how education has emerged 'as a site of hegemonic struggles and overt forms of social engineering, culminating in a totalizing vision [under the AKP] for a "New Turkey" project that aims to fashion pliant citizen/subjects'. Aside from the general trend of Islamisation of the educational system, the expansion of state-administered religious education (under the MEB) in the form of *imam-hatip* (prayer leader and preacher) schools is a particularly important facet of the

Islamisation of the educational system. They have not only become a key channel for social group reproduction of pious conservatives but are also a means by which the ranks of the Islamist movements have reproduced and grown. Indeed, stratified and differentiated systems of education, from a Bourdieusian perspective, will endow actors with differentiated types of cultural capital or internalised dispositions. Based on her ethnographic study of *imam-hatip* schools, Özgür (2012: 24) argues that these institutions essentially 'impart a habitus' in that they

re-enforce students' attachment to religious values and traditions and further their process of religious socialisation [...] Schools formally inculcate Islamic knowledge [...] They also informally expose their students to an Islamic lifestyle through manners of speech, dress, and conduct [...] When they graduate, *imam-hatip* school students seek to mold their environments according to their beliefs.

This is further corroborated by Coşkun and Şentürk's (2012: 165) account that religious schools have become the grass roots of Islamist parties: 'the function of IHSs [*imam-hatip* schools] was redesigned as an instrument to create new modern, conservative intellectuals by articulating the AKP's discourse and contributing to the dispersion of its ideology, and that IHS students are inspired by the AKP's political discourse'. This section contributes to this body of work by tracing how the expansion of religious education has been enabled by rightist conservative and Islamist actors operating within and outside the state, particularly since the emergence of the Cold War.

Religious Education in the Early Republic

Compared to other Muslim majority contexts, Turkey's experience of religious education has significantly differed owing to a far-reaching *étatization* of education that took place during the early years of the Republic (Hefner and Zaman 2007: 15). Following the adoption of the Law on Unification of Education (Tevhid-i Tedrisat) in 1924, education was brought largely under the control of the MEB. Although the 1924 law did not specifically mention the *medreses*, religious schools focused on Islamic learning, these establishments were also shut down and religious education was brought more firmly under state auspices. This also resulted in a major diminution of the *ulema*'s power and role, as detailed in Chapter 2. The introductory statement for the law stated

Since the beginning of the Tanzimat period following the 1839 Imperial Edict of the Rose House, the Ottoman sultanate, which is no longer in existence, attempted to unify education but was unsuccessful, which led to the development of a duality. The members of a nation can only have one education. Two types of education result in the raising of two types of people. This in turn contravenes the unity of feeling and mind and the aim of solidarity. (ZC 3 March 1340[1924]: 25)

This very much echoed leading nationalist ideologue Ziya Gökalp's vision and his writings in and after 1923, in which he similarly argued that the unification of education was necessary for the unity of minds and for Turkey to be a 'homogenous nation – intellectually and spiritually' (Bayar 2009: 366). Early nation-state builders in the Republic were particularly cognisant of the experiences and effects of the modernisation of education under the late Ottoman Empire. In response to growing European encroachment, the Ottoman state had developed Western-style education to counter growing imperialist penetration, resulting in a parallel system alongside the traditional *medreses*. This duality in the educational system has been regarded as catalysing the divisions between elites in the late Ottoman Empire. For Hasan Ali Yücel, education minister between 1938 and 1946, 'The decision for Unification of Education was the most important event in our history in terms of ending the cultural duality that has existed since the 1839 Tanzimat movement' (Ayhan 1999: 21). Still, as Fortna (2002) has shown, the extent of a secular/religious split resulting in a cultural bifurcation can be overstated, since not only did Islam remain central to the message of the Westernised schools but the *ulema* played a pivotal role in their development. A key area of contention, however, was the reform of the *medrese* system, considered to be outdated by some who advocated for their abolition. Reforms of the *medrese* system picked up pace in the second constitutional period as the reformist *ulema* gained prominence with the ITC. It was these reforms undertaken after 1913 that, according to Dinçer (1974: 10), constituted the origins of the *imam-hatip* schools that were established in the Republic.

By the 1920s, however, for some republican elites, the establishment of a centralised and standardised national education system was regarded as necessary for the fostering and development of national consciousness and as a means to counter social fragmentation and differentiation as well as curb the power of the *ulema*. In fact, while, in 1924, both the *ulema* and the military lost control over education, a 1925 law had reassigned military academies back to the Ministry of National Defence, indicating the military's growing prominence within the ruling coalition. The *ulema*, in turn, were only able to maintain control of Qur'an schools, which in fact served as a de facto mechanism for bringing *tariqa* orders under the umbrella of the Diyanet. With the establishment of a centralised educational system in 1924, the 479 *medreses* were closed, and in their place, 29 *imam-hatip* schools were opened as vocational schools for training religious personnel.[9] However, these schools were also closed by 1930 owing to overall restrictions on religious activity and interference by state actors, the loss of the profession's prestige, the lack of state incentivisation, the worsening of employee personal rights and resistance by the Diyanet, which saw these schools as insufficient, resulting in a lack of career opportunities and reduced student interest (Çakır et al. 2004; Dinçer 1974: 11; Karaman 2015c: 381; Ünsür 2000: 140–142). As a result, alongside the Diyanet's Qur'an courses, the now illegal parallel *medrese* system remained the main source of religious education until the reopening of *imam-hatip* schools in 1951.[10] In sum, in the one-party years of the Republic, there was a shrinking of religious education connected to the power struggle between different factions of the ruling coalition and attempts to instil and disseminate Turkish national consciousness.

The expansion of religious teaching in all segments of education was to begin in the late 1940s. Driving this growth was the increasing focus of the CHP regime on the fight against communism, with the emerging Cold War, alongside the push by the Diyanet, which used this window of opportunity to urge for the reopening of religious schools.[11] Starting in 1948, this meant the increasing incorporation of religious teaching in mainstream public education as religious lessons were reintroduced into primary schools. Yet, as Bayar (2009: 364, 2016a: 91) argues, while there has been a tendency to view education policies in the one-party era as simply an extension of a drive towards Westernisation and secularisation, in fact, the role of Islam in defining nationhood was never dismissed. There was not necessarily a secularisation of education even during the one-party era. Instead, educational policies evolved over time from more religious conceptualisations of nationhood to more ethnic understandings, but rather than a separation, there was a unification of religious and secular teachings together with the state's involvement in both of these

---

[9] There were 479 *medreses* with around 18,000 students (see Dinçer 1974; Özgür 2012: 33).

[10] There is a dispute as to whether Qur'an courses were ever closed down, as well as about their overall numbers. One plausible view is that with the efforts of the Diyanet chief, they remained in operation to raise religious personnel, albeit in smaller numbers (see Öcal 2015: 472–475).

[11] As with the Diyanet, religious education has involved the inculcation of Sunni (Hanefi) Islam and, while non-Muslims have been given the choice of opting out, for Alevis, it has been compulsory despite opposition from Alevi organisations who have taken the matter to the European Court of Human Rights (ECHR). The ECHR has since ruled that the mandatory religious education introduced by the 1982 Constitution is discriminatory. See Massicard (2013: 158–159) and Karakaya-Stump (2018: 58–59).

aspects of education (Bayar 2009: 364).[12] Despite the institution of secular education, and far from a purely secular and positivist educational policy, the state continued to promote 'Islam as a social morality system that is, along with nationalism, also functional in providing the social cement to bind the community together' (Parla and Davison 2004: 70).

The Cold War Opening: The Diyanet and Religious Education as an Antidote to Communism

Following the period of curtailment of religious education in the early Republic, from the late 1940s onwards, a multitude of actors, including the Diyanet and Islamist and conservative governments, driven by different visions and interests, pushed to expand religious education, sometimes in cooperation and other times against other elements of the state, including actors within the military. Together with the reintroduction of religious lessons, the establishment of new religious schools was crucially related to the widening role of the Diyanet. Debates about religious education began in the early 1940s, in part catalysed by international developments, and they gathered momentum with the decision to transition to multi-party politics. Yet, as Kara (2016: 214, 295) notes, there was not a sufficient mass push for the reintroduction of religious education in this period, despite the fact that the authorities presented their decision to do so as a response to such demands. Instead, for the CHP government, widening of the Diyanet's role was perceived as crucial in the fight against communism, as well as a means to strengthen national unity and raise 'enlightened' functionaries to teach 'true' Islam. A crucial turning point was the CHP's seventh congress, held in 1947, during which the regime formulated its policies for the expansion of the Diyanet and religious education, as well as the relaxation of restrictions on religion. During the meeting, the prominent nationalist lawmaker and writer Hamdullah Suphi Tanrıöver (who later joined the DP) emphasised the importance of religion, arguing for the need to ensure that there was a mosque in every village (of which he noted there were 40,000) (CHP

---

[12] Conversely, both Bayar (2009) and Copeaux (2000) drew attention to the emphasis on Turkish race and ethnicity during the 1920s and 1930s and the attempts of the one-party regime to stress pre-Islamic and pre-Ottoman history. This reflected not only nation building but also the influence of racist and fascist ideas that were prevalent and on the ascent globally at the time. Copeaux argues that the shift from the focus on Turkish ethnicity and race occurred after Atatürk's death in 1938, which saw the gradual increase in emphasis on Islam and became prevalent following the 1980 coup and the adoption of the TIS programme.

1948: 457). Indeed, Tanrıöver had been a long-time proponent of religious education to support the *ulema*'s ability to pass on Islamic learning, as evidenced by his passionate defence of these institutions during the 1920 parliamentary debates on the educational system. Such an expansion clearly necessitated more training of religious personnel, yet, various lawmakers noted later in parliament that there were not enough religious functionaries to conduct basic services such as funerals (CHP 1948: 50, 558).[13]

It was following such debates that the decision was made to open *imam-hatip* courses and hire theology faculties to train 'enlightened men of religion' for an expanded Diyanet and teachers to teach religious education within the regular school system. A 1948 report on religious education prepared by CHP lawmakers for the party group had recommended that *imam-hatip* schools should be established on the grounds of religious freedom of the 98 per cent Muslim Turkish society and due to the need to raise religious personnel for the Diyanet (Dinçer 1974: 53–60). However, when it came to how they would be administered, all but two members of the seventeen-member commission recommended that these schools should be established and regulated by the Diyanet, but they opposed giving full control to the body, arguing that it would result in the revival of a scholastic *medrese* mentality (Dinçer 1974: 53–60). Owing to resistance by this oppositional faction within the CHP, religious education was expanded under the body of the MEB, beginning in 1949 with the introduction of ten-month *imam-hatip* courses (later raised to two years), then optional religious lessons in primary schools and a theology faculty in Ankara. Following these developments, in 1950, Akseki proudly declared in a press statement reported by the conservative/Islamist *Sebilürreşad* (1950: 163–165) magazine that the government had finally accepted policies that had been pursued by the Diyanet for a long time. As Gökaçtı (2005: 186) also notes, a key demand of Akseki was for the Diyanet to be the responsible body for religious education. Akseki had been lobbying for the expansion of religious education by arguing that the Diyanet lacked qualified religious personnel to carry out basic functions, such as funerals and guiding the public in 'true' Islam and against superstition. This move was necessary, according to Akseki, so that the population did not come under the influence of divisive fake *tariqa* orders, external religions and communism, as he outlined in his 1950 report (also discussed in Chapter 2). According to Akseki (1997: 362–379), for this to be achieved and for the

---

[13] For further elaboration of these debates and the reforms introduced, see also Gökaçtı (2005: 167–178) and Toprak (1981: 76–79).

Diyanet to act as a bulwark against communism, *imam-hatip* schools should be opened and religious education should be introduced at all levels of the mainstream educational system under the body's authority and control.

Expanding Religious Education with the Transition to Multi-Partism

The emergence of the *imam-hatip* schools as a parallel educational system, together with the expansion of religious teaching within the mainstream educational system, was reflective of the changing balance of power within the state with the transition to multi-partism. Following its 1950 electoral victory, the DP took major strides in the expansion of religious education. Restrictions on Qur'an schools were eased, which led to their numbers more than doubling from 144 in 1950 to 326 in 1960. Religious lessons became part of the regular primary schools' curriculum in 1950 (with parents having the right only to opt out rather than opt in), following which they were incorporated into secondary education in 1956. Two important avenues for Islamist mobilisation, however, were the reopened *imam-hatip* schools and the High Islamic Institutes (Yüksek İslam Enstitüsü, YİE) established in 1959, which were incorporated as theology faculties in 1982, after the 1980 military coup.

Led by the efforts of the education minister, Tevfik İleri, the DP government established four-year *imam-hatip* middle schools (known as *orta okul*, or secondary schools) in 1951; then, in 1953 to 1954, they extended this to seven years by introducing three-year senior schools, or *imam-hatip* high schools (Gökaçtı 2005: 189).[14] There were some levels of continuity between the (re)established *imam-hatip* schools and the *medreses*, which were officially closed in 1924, as some had continued to operate underground (Aktay 2003: 140). As Kara (2016: 297) relates, many of the teachers in the *imam-hatip* schools were in fact the *mudarris*

---

[14] İleri was the former president of the nationalist National Turkish Students Union (Milli Türk Talebe Birliği, MTTB), established in 1916 with the aim of spreading nationalism among students and which became the largest student association in Turkey until its closure (alongside all other associations) by the junta regime in 1980. It reopened in 2008 as the Talebe Birliği Federasyonu. The MTTB started life largely as a rightist Turkish nationalist and pan-Turkist organisation, enjoying support from key figures in the one-party regime, such as the interior minister Şükrü Kaya (1927–1938). After the 1940s, the MTTB was increasingly influenced by anti-communism. Then, beginning in the mid-1960s, it became decisively Islamist. During the 1960s and 1970s, its members included many prominent rightist, conservative and Islamist actors, including Abdullah Gül (AKP), Recep Tayyip Erdoğan (AKP), Bülent Arınç (AKP), Devlet Bahçeli (MHP) and Mustafa Ok (MHP). The evolution of the ideological stance of this organisation is an indicator of the shifting balances within the state.

and *dersiam* (religious teachers) of the *medreses*. The expansion of *imam-hatip* schools met resistance from different factions within the state. Their continuity with the *medreses* was noted in a report presented to the MEB in 1959 by the Turkey Education National Commission (Türkiye Eğitim Milli Komisyonu), established in 1958, which also underlined the dangers of raising 'two types of Turkish intellectuals that were at odds with each other' (Dinçer 1974: 68–69). It was noted that the re-emergence of such a polarity, given 'painful experiences of our 100 years of history of a struggle between two mentalities at odds with each other', should be prevented. The recommendations of the commission came to nothing, with Tevfik İleri pushing through the establishment of YİEs despite the resistance. One factor in the drive to open YİEs was the provision of a path to higher education for *imam-hatip* graduates in their field, given that they were blocked from entering the Ankara Theology Faculty. The İYC was an active supporter of the establishment of YİEs for *imam-hatip* graduates. Other drivers included the need for qualified religious teachers necessitated by the growing number of *imam-hatip* schools and the aim of raising personnel for the Diyanet.

Following the 1960 coup, a drive for the overhaul of the *imam-hatip* schools and religious education was initiated as part of a wider reform of the educational system following the launch of the National Education Planning Council (Milli Eğitim Planlama Komisyonu) in 1961. The outcome of this was a 1961 report on religious education containing a series of recommendations that were prepared together with the MEB and a Diyanet official, the vice-president Sadettin Evrin, a theologian and a retired general appointed during the junta regime.[15] The report, which was criticised from within the Diyanet and by Islamist circles as narrowing the function of the *imam-hatip* schools, had suggested either closure or reform of fifteen of the nineteen schools in existence, such as for training religious personnel for villages. This recommendation was driven by two considerations in particular. First, the report noted that the overall quality of the schools' infrastructure and teaching were insufficient and poor. Second, and more important, there was a concern that these schools should maintain their vocational character and not become a parallel system of education whereby conservative parents were increasingly sending their children to get more extensive religious education free of charge thanks to support from various civil associations. While the necessity of religious education for training personnel for an expanded Diyanet was underscored, it was noted that the

---

[15] Evrin is referred to fondly by Hayrettin Karaman (2015a: 257–259), who helped him secure a job as a preacher in Istanbul in the 1960s.

graduates of these schools had not filled the 500 cadres allocated within the Diyanet but were instead choosing non-theology courses at universities (MEB 1961: 9–13).

Meanwhile, despite the depiction of the 1960 junta regime as highly secularist, key pedagogical recommendations included the importance of instilling a love of Islam rather than imposing it through fear, as well as showing that theology faculties should work to improve the image of Islam abroad, particularly through the establishment of a religious affairs envoy in foreign embassies located in Muslim countries (MEB 1961: 7). However, the recommendations of the report were dropped or ignored, as a result of which, no *imam-hatip* schools were subsequently closed. Instead, the 1960 junta regime displayed its favourable approach by opening seven more such schools (Özgür 2012: 41). In 1962, the legality of *imam-hatips* was confirmed by a decision taken by the seventh National Education Council that 'The primary goal of religious education and teaching by the MEB is to provide vocational training for religious functionaries that will be employed by the Presidency of Religious Affairs, and those they will teach in the field of religion to become qualified in their role' (Öztürk 2010: 194). In fact, one prominent supporter of *imam-hatip* schools and the YİE was one of the prominent leaders of the 1960 coup, Mehmet Özgüneş, who had called for the establishment of an Islamic academy as well as the entry of *imam-hatip* graduates into the theology faculty (Karaman 2015a: 422).

The first successful pushback against *imam-hatip* schools came in the early 1970s. Prior to the 1971 intervention, the eighth National Education Council meeting held in 1970 recommended the move towards uniform secondary education that would involve the closure of *imam-hatip* middle schools. A key motivation behind these decisions, plus debates about extending compulsory basic education (in regular schools) to eight years (introduced after the 1998 military intervention and lifted by the AKP), was the aim of maintaining the vocational character of these schools and preventing their growth as a parallel educational system. Despite vocal criticisms from the Diyanet and *imam-hatip* circles, these recommendations were largely approved following the 21 March 1971 military intervention (Dinçer 1971: 53–58, 1974: 81; Öztürk 2010: 197). Following a decision in August 1971, *imam-hatip* middle schools were closed and their options for university placements restricted. Yet this was short-lived. In 1973, the decision was largely reversed thanks to the votes of the conservative rightist AP, which was the leading bloc in the technocratic transition government between 1973 and 1974.

After 1973, *imam-hatip* schools were transformed from vocational into mainstream schools and categorised as *imam-hatip lycée* (*imam-hatip lisesi*), and the restrictions on their graduates from entering certain university programmes were lifted (Yavuz 2003: 125). In 1974, the middle sections of these *imam-hatip* schools were reopened, meaning *imam-hatip* education was again extended to seven years. In addition, female students gained the right to enter *imam-hatip* schools following the Council of State's ruling in 1966 on equal access to education – they had been previously excluded since these schools had originally been envisaged for training male religious personnel, as women were traditionally excluded from becoming preachers and prayers leaders (Öcal 2015: 227).[16] This meant that, no longer just vocational schools for training religious functionaries, *imam-hatip* schools emerged as a parallel educational system for pious or conservative families. Equally, the fact that they often provided free boarding for students made them preferable, particularly for the poorer sections of society (Öcal 2015: 234–235). The 1973 decision was, therefore, a turning point in the development of a parallel religious educational system in Turkey. In a report prepared for the ninth National Education Council (Milli Eğitim Şûrası) held in 1974, the Diyanet sought further expansion of religious education on the basis that it was the state's duty to raise citizens loyal to Turkish national and religious customs and traditions. In this vein, it proposed that history and literature classes in primary and secondary education should not be without Islamic sentiments, that the number of hours of religious teaching should be increased, that the syllabus for psychology, sociology and philosophy classes in high schools be changed to include Turkish Islamic thinkers rather than 'materialist thinkers' and that music teaching should focus on national anthems and national music (Erdil 1974).

The 1970s, therefore, effectively saw a flourishing of religious education. In 1974, the CHP–MSP coalition government made religious courses called 'moral education' (*ahlak bilgisi*) compulsory in regular schools. Subsequently, under the conservative-Islamist right-wing coalition National Front (Milli Cephe) government in the 1970s, *imam-hatip* schools proliferated, increasing by 313 per cent from 129 schools in the 1970–1971 academic year to 716 by 1980–1981, compared with an expansion of 187 per cent between the 1960–1961 and 1970–1971 academic years, as can be seen in Figures 11, 12 and 13. Meanwhile, the number of *imam-hatip* school students rose from 48,895 in 1974–1975 to 200,300 by 1980–1981. Qur'an schools also increased by more than 230 per cent in this period, rising from 786 schools in 1970 to 2,385 by 1980, as shown in Figure 14. As Tuğal (2009b: 453) points out,

---

[16] This has changed in recent years with the emergence of female preachers (*vaize*) employed by the Diyanet. See Hassan (2011).

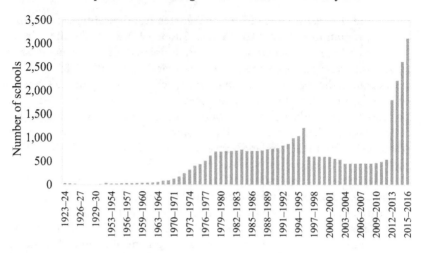

Sources: (Öcal 2008: 267-270; Milli Eğitim Bakanlığı [Ministry Of National Education, MoE])
*Data includes both middle level and senior level high schools

Figure 11: The number of *imam-hatip* schools

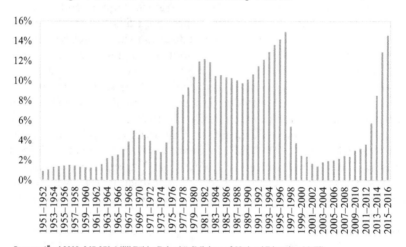

Sources: (Öcal 2008: 267-270; Milli Eğitim Bakanlığı [Ministry of National Education, MoE])
*Data include middle and senior levels of high schools. In 1996–1997 8-year compulsory education resulted in closure of middle level sections of imam-hatip schools. In 2012–2013 there was a shift to a 4+4+4 system which saw the re-opening of these schools.

Figure 12: The number of *imam-hatip* school students as a percentage of the total secondary and lycée student population

the goal of the Islamist movement had been the 'production of subjects who will have different daily conducts, different rituals, and therefore different "internalized political programs" [...] than the secularist officials', and it is the nurturing of this distinct habitus that underpins the

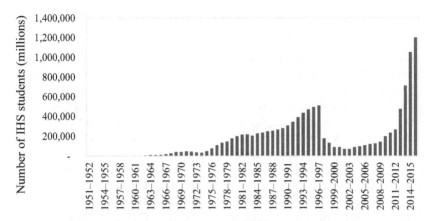

Sources: (Öcal 2008: 267-270; Milli Eğitim Bakanlığı [Ministry of National Education, MoE])
*Data includes middle and senior high schools

Figure 13: The number of students attending *imam-hatip* schools

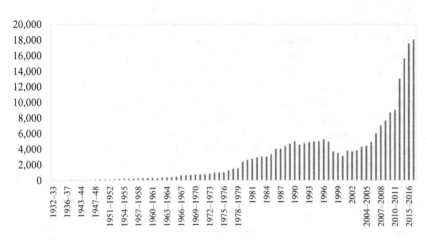

Sources: DİB.

Figure 14: The number of Qur'an courses

reproduction and persistence of religious delineations that shape political and economic competition and thereby provide the basis of Islamist mobilisation. Still, not all Islamist and Islamic actors were happy with the expansion of state-administered religious education, as demonstrated by the campaign of the Süleymancılar against *imam-hatip* schools (see Chapter 2).

The Post-1980 Era: The TIS Programme to the 1997
Clampdown on Imam-Hatip Schools

Generally championed by the Islamist and conservative parties together with the Diyanet, religious education, including *imam-hatip* schools, also found support among the 1980 junta leaders. Reflecting the adoption of the TIS programme, the junta regime made compulsory religious teaching a constitutional principle, in line with the TIS programme, while the subsequent ANAP government carried out an Islamisation of the curriculum.[17] At the same time, all restrictions barring *imam-hatip* graduates from entering a university course of their choice were lifted. Yet there were elements within the military that questioned the expanding *imam-hatip* schools, and the MEB under Hasan Sağlam were considering plans to close 174 of the 374 *imam-hatip* schools. According to the acting Diyanet chief at the time, Tayyar Altıkulaç (2011b: 546–550), such plans were largely thwarted, apparently as a result of his efforts to explain that if these schools were closed, then it would be harder to raise qualified personnel for the Diyanet, thereby making the organisation more vulnerable to political forces.

At the same time, the parallel rapid expansion of Gülenist schools since the 1980s (reportedly with the support during the junta regime of the vice-general secretary of the MGK, Hasan Sağlam, see Chapter 5) has been interpreted by some Islamist circles as an effort by the state to create an alternative to *imam-hatip* schools and is allegedly the reason for Gülen's relative silence on the clampdown on *imam-hatip* schools in 1997 (Kara 2016: 286). In this period, the number of *imam-hatip* students had risen by more than 50 per cent, from 200,300 in 1980–1981 to 309,553 by 1990, while the number of Qur'an courses more than doubled. While the first generation of *imam-hatip* school graduates (1951–1973) were chiefly from similar socio-economic backgrounds, such as poor or lower middle-class families, typically those who had migrated from Anatolia to the cities, by the 1980s (with the lifting of restrictions on university entry), the schools had gained wider appeal for conservative citizens (Kara 2016: 297; Özgür 2012: 42–43, 46, 50). At the same time, reflecting the 12 September regime's view of religion as a social cement, *imam-hatip* schools were also utilised as a mechanism of assimilation. The only *imam-hatip* school during military rule had been opened in (Alevi majority) Tunceli province, and the junta regime had

---

[17] Yavuz (2003: 75) notes that the education minister, Vehbi Dinçerler, was a Naqshbandi disciple.

made thousands of Alevi children from there, among other areas, attend *imam-hatip* schools (Kenanoğlu 11 April 2013).

However, this symbiotic relationship between these various factions within the military, the Diyanet and conservative and Islamist actors appeared to break down during the late 1990s. In 1995, the Islamist RP gained 21.4 per cent of the general vote, the largest percentage for such a party in republican history, marking the rise of Islamist parties. The increasing struggle within the state erupted in 1997, when the military issued a memorandum on 28 February and effectively worked from then on to force the resignation of the Islamist-led coalition government. Many of the RP's members, including deputies and mayors, had *imam-hatip* roots (Coşkun and Şentürk 2012: 169). In this period, *imam-hatip* schools, which became branded as centres of reaction, experienced the biggest setback since they had been re-established in 1951: the expansion of regular compulsory education to eight years (5+3) resulting in the closure of the middle school level of *imam-hatip* schools, as in the early 1970s; a ban on *imam-hatip* school graduates entering employment in certain arms of the state, such as the police and the army; and the introduction of the coefficient factor (an automatic reduction in the entrance exam scores of *imam-hatip* school graduates), which limited entry into non-theology programmes at universities. This resulted in significantly weakening the demand for *imam-hatip* schools, leading to a decline in student numbers from a peak of 511,502 in 1996–1997 to 64,534 by 2002. Kara (2016: 296–297) has argued that one result of these restrictions was the switch to Gülenist schools, which did not face a clampdown like the *imam-hatip* schools. While Gülen had remained largely silent and, in fact, supported the 28 February intervention by blaming the RP, the Diyanet had continued to actively voice its opposition to restrictions on religious education. Such a stance was reflected in the action plan agreed to at the November 1998 religious council (Din Şûrası) meeting (held every five years since 1993), in which it was decided that the Diyanet would work towards lifting the university entrance exam coefficient for *imam-hatip* schools, including by lobbying the MEB.

The AKP Era: Islamisation and Unprecedented Expansion of Religious Education

Since the Islamist AKP's ascent to power in 2002, a religious educational renaissance has taken place. Having often stated its goal of creating a so-called pious generation, the AKP has undertaken an Islamisation of the curriculum within the mainstream educational system, which has included the purportedly 'optional' (but often compulsory in practice) religious classes, such as on the Qur'an and the life of the prophet. Türkmen (2009: 391) argued that this augmented the Sunnite-centric focus of religious training in Turkish high schools. Other efforts at the Islamisation of education have involved the observance of Islamic celebrations, allowing pupils to veil, encouragement of religious observance and banning republican celebrations like the 19 May youth and sports day (Kandiyoti and Emanet 2017: 872). Most important for the AKP, ending the restrictions on *imam-hatip* students in the university entrance exam had been one of the two main priorities during its 2002 election campaign, alongside the lifting of the headscarf ban (Kaya 2015: 55). Accordingly, restrictions on Qur'an courses were lifted in 2003, resulting in an exponential increase in the number of courses (see Figure 14), and the university entrance coefficient that had put *imam-hatip* schools at a disadvantage was abolished in 2009, once again allowing *imam-hatip* students to enter non-theology university courses. This has entrenched the attractiveness of these schools as a more religious parallel educational system rather than as vocational training. Based on a survey of *imam-hatip* students, Coşkun and Şentürk (2012: 169) found that more than 60 per cent of them prefer non-religious professions.

A further boost to *imam-hatip* schools was a major overhaul of the educational system in 2012 which replaced the eight-year compulsory primary educational system adopted after 1997 and resulted in the closure of *imam-hatip* middle schools. In March 2012, the AKP introduced the so-called 4+4+4 law, which purportedly increased compulsory education to twelve years but also defined primary, elementary and high school education as four blocks of four years. This meant that, in fact, the law enabled parents to send their children to vocational, or rather, *imam-hatip*, schools after completing their four-year primary education, and therefore at a much earlier age than under the eight-year compulsory system. In the 2012–2013 academic year, there was a 236 per cent increase in the number of *imam-hatip* schools owing to the 4+4+4 reform, which led to the reopening of the middle sections of *imam-hatip* schools. Overall, *imam-hatip* schools have grown by 588 per cent between 2003 to 2004 and 2015 to 2016, from 452 to 3,110 schools, the largest number on record (see Figure 11). *Imam-hatip* student numbers have also increased, from 90,606 to 1,201,500 over the same period, a 1,226 per cent increase from 2 per cent of total students enrolled in middle schools and *lycée* to 15 per cent, which compares with 1 per cent in 1960, 12 per cent in 1980 and 15 per cent in 1996, just before the secondary level *imam-hatip* schools were shut in 1997 (see Figures 11, 12 and 13).

Not only has the AKP reversed the decline of *imam-hatip* schools but many regular high schools are effectively being transformed into *imam-hatip* schools. According to statistics produced by leftist trade union Eğitim-Sen, 1,477 regular high schools were converted into *imam-hatip* schools between the 2010–2011 school year and the 2013–2014 school year. Pithily summarising the AKP's policy on this transformation is the declaration by AKP parliamentarian Ali Boğa in 2012 that 'we are here as Imam Hatip graduates or as allies. We will increase the number of these schools in records. We have the chance to turn all schools into Imam Hatip schools' (*Voice of America* 25 September 2012). *Imam-hatip* schools are also receiving an increasing share of the state budget under the AKP. According to the MEB's investment strategy announced in 2014, around 37 per cent of its investment budget (TRY 1.75 billion) was allocated to *imam-hatip* high schools, and this included the establishment of 109 new schools in 56 provinces.

A further step by the AKP in solidifying the nexus between *imam-hatip* schools and Islamist mobilisation was the move in September 2014 to enable the cooperation of these schools with various Islamist foundations, such as the Foundation of Youth and Education in Turkey (Türkiye Gençlik ve Eğitime Hizmet Vakfı, TÜRGEV), Ensar Foundation (Ensar Vakfı), the Humanitarian Relief Foundation (İnsani Yardım Vakfı, İHH), Unity Foundation (Birlik Vakfı, which is regarded as a continuation of the National Turkish Students Union, Milli Türk Talebe Birliği, MTTB [see note 14]), Hayrat Foundation (Hayrat Vakfı) and Hizmet Foundation (Hizmet Vakfı). As a result, these organisations have gained access to the student population and a means to influence their education and syllabus, including by providing other services such as boarding and career opportunities. Equally, there has been closer cooperation between the MEB and the Diyanet, which has expanded the latter's reach in the provision of religious education. One case has been the launch of free Qur'anic education for four- to six-year-olds. Increasingly, the Diyanet has pushed for religious education to come under its patronage and guidance, which was also a key goal outlined in the fifth religious council meeting held in 2014 (*Anadolu Agency* 13 December 2014). Since 2012, the Diyanet has been active in providing religious education for foreign students – around 64,000 as of 2017 – as part of a joint project with the Diyanet Foundation (Türkiye Diyanet Vakfı) (DİB 2017b). Likewise, it called for an overhaul of religious education following an Emergency Religious Council Meeting (Olağanüstü Din Şurası Toplantısı) held following the 15 July 2016 coup attempt, presenting an opportunity for the institution to expand its control over religious education (*Habertürk* 14 November 2016). The Diyanet has since proposed that closed

Gülenist schools should be handed to the Diyanet *waqf* to be converted into *imam-hatip* schools; the Qur'an schools administered by the Diyanet for four- to six-year-olds should be treated as nursery education; private *imam-hatip* science schools should be set up; and Diyanet-run religious education should be established within the General Staff of the Republic of Turkey (Genel Kurmay Başkanlığı).

The Religious Education–Islamist Nexus: The Case of the Generation Movement

One particular example of how the expanding infrastructure behind religious education supported Islamist mobilisation is revealed by the activities of what came to be known as the Generation Movement (Nesil Hareketi), founded by influential Islamists who also produced the *Generation Magazine* (*Nesil Dergisi*) between 1976 and 1980.[18] This was a leading group of Islamists, led chiefly by the first generation of graduates from the YİE, with *imam-hatip* roots, including the three who came to be the highly influential triumvirate, Hayrettin Karaman, Tayyar Altıkulaç and Bekir Topaloğlu, who were at its centre (Kara April 2016; İnal and Alagöz 2016: 31, 34). In the 1960s, these individuals came together while studying at the YİE and worked out a plan of action to organise for their aim of building an Islamic society and civilisation (Karaman 2015a: 306). Focusing on a strategy of 'bottom-up' Islamisation, they regarded *imam-hatip* schools as the vehicle for raising a 'service generation' (*hizmet nesli*) who would work towards the unity of Muslims and develop a common programme of actions and goals to serve their mission. In one sense, therefore, the Nesil group's goal for the state-administered *imam-hatip* schools paralleled the Gülenist movement's aim of raising a Golden Generation (Altın Nesil) through its own private educational network (see Chapter 5 on the Gülenists). Accordingly, the Nesil group focused on religious education through both the formal school infrastructure and the Diyanet, which was to be utilised to teach the public about Islam. In this vein, it worked to shape the syllabuses and content of religious education, including by writing and producing the key textbooks used in these schools while also trying to expand the opportunities available to

---

[18] Karaman (2015b: 92) also describes it as an 'unnamed' organisation. A foundation called Nesil Vakfı was subsequently established by the holder of the magazine's concession (İnal and Alagöz 2016: 34). The account of the Generation Movement given here is based on the memoirs of Hayrettin Karaman (2015a, 2015b) and works by Kara (2016: 566, April 2016), who describe it as a highly influential movement within the *imam-hatip* generation and Islamist circles. Accounts of this group are limited. For one example, see İnal and Alagöz (2016).

graduates. Each member of the organisation would choose a number of students to give special attention to, training them as leading guides or cadres and orienting them towards becoming teachers and *imam-hatip*s in villages, with the aim of kick-starting a new İrşad [guidance/showing the true path] movement in which they would work towards the Islamisation of the masses and 'revival of the Muslim Turkish nation' (Karaman 2015b: 35–36, 42–43).

At the same time, some of the fiercest opposition to the Nesil group's activities came from within the ranks of the Islamist movement. The MSP and National Outlook movement, as well as various more conservative or traditionalist *tariqa* orders (such as the Süleymancılar and Işıkçılar as well as the İsmailağa community), led a vociferous campaign against the Nesil group, who were attacked for being reformists or modernists influenced by the earlier Islamist reformists like Jamāl al-Dīn al-Afghānī, Muḥammad Abduh and Rashīd Riḍā (İnal and Alagöz 2016: 31). The Nesil group members were accused of 'subverting religion' (*din tahripçileri*) and being heretical, masons, and without sect (*mezhepsizlik*), in addition to being anti-Sunni Islam (anti-Ahl al-Sunna) and 'divisive and fake scholars raised by laicism' (Karaman 2015c: 24–107; Kara 2016: 542; İnal and Alagöz 2016: 40–47). İnal and Alagöz (2016: 42) argue that one underlying reason for the attack by the Süleymancılar was related to the competition between the Süleymancı Qu'ran schools and *imam-hatip* schools (see the earlier discussion in the section 'Expanding Religious Education with the Transition to Multi-Partism'). Likewise, the prominence of the Nesil group within the Diyanet was another bone of contention with the more traditionalist groups that characterise themselves as protectors of Ahl al-Sunna (Sunni Islam).

The Nesil group built a network and worked in close relation with their '*da'wah*[19] friends' in *imam-hatip* schools, the YİE, theology faculties, the MEB and the Diyanet, and while centred in İstanbul, its members operated across the country in close cooperation and consultation with the centre. Indeed, according to Karaman (2015a: 291), the Diyanet was largely taken over by the *imam-hatip* and YİE graduates, and their 'souls' had become allied. Indeed, in his account, there were many members of the movement within the Diyanet, resulting in a close working relationship involving collaboration on projects which became stronger with the appointment of Altıkulaç as deputy head of the organisation in 1971 and president in 1978. Although denied by Altıkulaç, who insists that it was his own decision, Karaman (2015c: 91) notes that it was the Nesil group

---

[19] This relates to activities involving the propagation of Islam or Islamic missionary activity.

that decided to send Altıkulaç to the Diyanet in order to 'strengthen the Ankara leg of the movement'. Likewise, the movement worked closely with the MEB, which was again strengthened when Altıkulaç was appointed as chief of the Religious Education General Directorate (Din Öğretimi Genel Müdürlüğü) (1976–1977). During this period, Altıkulaç was able to provide important resources and support the movement's mobilisation efforts, including creating 100 job openings in the YİE, which were used to train a generation of theologians who would become the core of the new theology faculties.

Again, this underlines not only the fluid relationship between state and social actors but also the ways in which the expansion of religious education was facilitated in cooperation with different factions within the state. And, just as the Diyanet is not merely a passive instrument of control, rather than serve the interests and goals of the so-called oppressive laicists to divide Muslims, these schools, helped by the efforts of their graduates who formed the Generation Movement, instead helped to raise a moral army with a separate identity (Aktay in Karaman 2015c: 383). In the words of the prominent Islamist academic and vice-chair of the AKP Yasin Aktay (2015: 378), Hayrettin Karaman played a leading role in the transformation of *imam-hatip* schools into a means for the reproduction of a new Islamist generation. Exemplifying the organic nexus between the *imam-hatip* system in Turkey and Islamist mobilisation is the prominent place of *imam-hatip* school graduates within the Islamist movement, including the AKP.[20] As a student of Bekir Topaloğlu, one of the members of the Nesil group's leading triumvirate, President Erdoğan, stated, 'I owe everything to the Imam Hatip School I attended. My life was predestined in that school' (Heper and Toktaş 2003: 163).

The Neo-Liberal Restructuring and Expansion of Faith-Based Organisations and Islamic Finance since the 1980s

The Spread of Islamic and Islamist Associations and Foundations

Alongside religious education, the expansion of Islamic and Islamist faith-based organisations[21] has been an important facet of Islamist mobilisation. Through their welfare activities, in particular, faith-based

---

[20] For example, seventy-three out of 341 AKP deputies in the 2002 elections spoke Arabic, indicating a background in *imam-hatip* schools (Sayari and Hasanov 2008: 355).

[21] This refers to associations that include a reference to an Islamic religious ethos or principle. According to Challand (2008: 231), one can distinguish between those who have a political project, described as 'Islamist', and those who do not, who are known as 'Islamic', although drawing a distinction may be difficult in practice.

organisations advanced Islamisation and Islamist mobilisation through vertical operations that provide services for and recruit poorer, disadvantaged classes, while at the same time fostering horizontal middle-class Islamist networks (Clark 2004b: 845; Pierret and Selvik 2009: 596–597; White 2002; Zubaida 1992: 10). There are, broadly, two approaches to the spread of faith-based organisations in the Middle East since the late 1970s. For some, the expansion of these organisations represented a counter-hegemonic force in expanding the space of the civil sector vis-à-vis the (authoritarian and secular) state (Challand 2008: 241–242). Zubaida (1992: 9) has challenged this positive reading by noting that while such organisations may be outside the state, they are not necessarily against it. This is because they often enjoy special privileges and favours and have cosy relations with state actors. From this perspective, therefore, they should be regarded as an important mechanism of social control. Conversely, other critical works have considered Islamic charities within the context of neo-liberal practices or redeployment of the state. In particular, this refers to the retreat of the state from public welfare provision to deal with fiscal crises, while maintaining overall control of the economy through delegating the provision of those services to civil actors (Pierret and Selvik 2009, 596–597; Pioppi 2004).

In Turkey, faith-based organisations include both foundations (*waqf*, *vakıf*) – a type of charitable organisation – and associations (*dernek*). Associations that are directly involved in religious activities, including the building of places of worship and the running of Qur'an courses, comprise some 17 per cent of the 100,312 active organisations in Turkey (Figure 15), which have just less than 9 million members, comprising around 12 per cent of the population (as of 2014), according to the Department of Associations (Dernekler Dairesi Başkanlığı, DoA). The total number of faith-based associations is likely to be much larger, however, since the DoA classification does not capture Islamic/Islamist organisations that are focused on other activities, such as welfare provision. Alongside these are 5,192 *waqfs*, managed and audited by the Directorate General of Foundations (Vakıflar Genel Müdürlüğü, DoF). Their roots are in Islamic principles, and in the Ottoman Empire, they functioned to help the poor and to provide public services or assistance to various groups and individuals (Göçmen 2014: 98). They differ from associations in that they do not have members and are 'legal corporations founded on the basis of continual use of proceeds from a reserved form of property', and they can be established for the purpose of making a profit (White 2002: 200). Particularly since the 1980 military intervention and the subsequent neo-liberal restructuring of the economy, these associations and foundations have emerged as alternative avenues of social

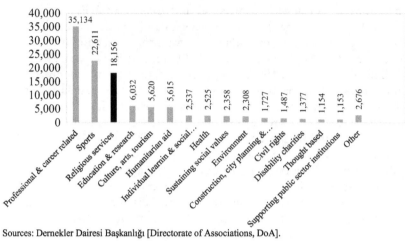

Sources: Dernekler Dairesi Başkanlığı [Directorate of Associations, DoA].

Figure 15: A breakdown of associations by area of activity

welfare provision and have come to form a major component of Turkey's associational environment. The significant increase in the number of new *waqf*s since the late 1980s was catalysed by the establishment of the Fund for Social Cooperation and Solidarity (Sosyal Yardımlaşma ve Dayanışma Vakfı) by the ANAP government in 1986 (Law 3294), which was envisaged as an umbrella organisation and mechanism for the provision of means-tested social assistance to the poor through the establishment of local foundations, to be managed and funded by the government (Buğra and Candaş 2011: 519). The preamble to the law emphasised the Islamic character and continuation of Ottoman tradition (Buğra and Candaş 2011: 520), and the aims were that, like the Ottoman foundations, the fund 'could be used in order to mobilize private donations with the initiative and under the guidance of the state and alleviate the burden of welfare provision on the budget' (Buğra and Keyder 2006: 222). Consequently, reflecting the neo-liberal redeployment policies of the state in delegating social welfare provision to civil society, the number of *waqf*s increased from fewer than 1,000 in the early 1980s to just less than 2,000 by the early 1990s, following a 92 per cent increase in 1986. Then, by the mid-1990s, they had climbed to 4,500, with an increase to 5,192 by 2014. A key piece of legislation that further extended the privileged position of faith-based organisations was adopted by the Islamist AKP in 2004, easing restrictions on matters such as foreign funding and partnerships.

The spread of Islamist and Islamic faith-based foundations and associations in turn played a crucial role in widening Islamist organisational networks and capital through their vertical and horizontal activities that target and link rich and poor. For Göçmen (2014: 92, 99), however, the growing presence of faith-based organisations is not just the state's response to a greater demand for social assistance but also an outcome of the rise of political Islam and particularly the availability of economic capital following the emergence of Islamist/conservative 'networks of reciprocity'. Similarly, for J. White (2011: 178–179), with the military having suppressed the left in the 1980s, the field was left open for Islamic charities to take up the cause of social justice. Yet, beyond the support received by Islamist governments since the 1980s, faith-based organisations, in fact, enjoyed support from within the state prior to the 1980 coup and the emergence of a successful Islamist movement.

One means of gauging the level of state support for Islamic and Islamist organisations is to consider the increase in the number of faith-based associations the state has granted an exemption from paying taxes and the status of Association for Public Interest (Kamu Yararına Çalışan Dernek). The award of these is tied to ministerial decisions and made through government decrees. Crucially, they are a means to provide foundations and associations with significant financial privileges, including greater freedom with regard to funding activities that are normally subject to various restrictions by and permissions from the Ministry of the Interior. The importance of such privileges is shown by the AKP's move to adopt a new law on foundations in 2004 (Law 5253), after its decrees to award public benefit status to one of the largest Islamist organisations, the Association of Lighthouse (Deniz Feneri), was overturned twice by the Council of State (Danıştay).

Tracing the level of state support over time, as Figure 16[22] shows, there has been a steady increase in the granting of public benefit status and tax exemptions to (Sunni Muslim[23]) faith-based organisations (Figure 17), which has accelerated under the AKP. Crucially, it is notable that among the foundations and associations accorded privileges by the state, Islamic (Sunni) organisations feature prominently in the field of social welfare provision. Some 597 associations have been granted public benefit status between the establishment of the Republic and 2015. Fewer than 10 per cent of these were established prior to 1950 and approximately 50 per cent between 1950 and 1980. Of these

---

[22] The DoA refused to provide this data upon my request for information under the freedom of information act. Since historical statistics on public benefit status and tax-exempt associations and foundations are not readily available, data was compiled from the DoA, the DoF and the Council of Ministers decrees in the *Official Gazette*.

[23] The 1998–2002 period is an exception, when certain Alevi organisations also received funds (see Chapter 3).

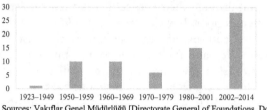

Sources: Vakıflar Genel Müdürlüğü [Directorate General of Foundations, DoF];
Dernekler Dairesi Başkanlığı [Directorate of Associations, DoA]; T.C. Resmi Gazete
[Official Gazette, RG].

Figure 16: Religious associations and foundations granted state
privileges

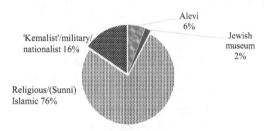

Sources: Vakıflar Genel Müdürlüğü [Directorate General of Foundations, DoF];
Dernekler Dairesi Başkanlığı [Directorate of Associations, DoA]; T.C. Resmi Gazete
[Official Gazette, RG]. Data as of December 2014.

Figure 17: Tax-exempt foundations: percentage breakdown by
ideological/religious orientation

bodies, around 47 per cent were related to health, 8 per cent to education
and 7 per cent to professional bodies, while around 6 per cent can be
categorised as faith-based organisations acting in either cultural and
educational fields or social welfare. At least half of the associations acting
in the area of social welfare provision were faith-based organisations. In
terms of foundations, out of a total of 281 enjoying tax-exempt status,
forty-four (16 per cent) can be categorised as faith-based organisations,
of which forty were (Sunni) Islamic, one was Jewish and three Alevi. In
addition to their tax-exempt status, as of the end of 2013, there were
twenty foundations that had the status of 'legal personalities having the
status to collect charity without permission'. Of these, 30 per cent were
religious organisations, including the Diyanet-associated DV. As a comparison, the historical data suggests that religious associations and foundations (including those close to the AKP) enjoying tax exemptions and
public benefit status numbered around thirty-six and forty-three,
respectively, while those that could be classified as military associations

and foundations, Kemalist or nationalist, numbered nineteen and eight, respectively (Figure 17).[24] The award of these privileges to faith-based organisations also reveals the dimensions of continuity with respect to state support. For instance, the İYC, which played an important role in lobbying and working for the expansion of religious education, has enjoyed public benefit status since 1953 (Decision No. 4/169, *Resmi Gazete* 6 March 1953, No: 8352). Aside from the spread of *imam-hatip* schools, it also supported the establishment of the YİE. According to Hayrettin Karaman's (2015a: 249) account, the head of the İYC, Vehbi Bilimer, played a role in convincing his former schoolmate, Cemal Gürsel, the chief of the 1960 junta regime, to not close the YİE. Crucially, acting as a key mechanism of horizontal mobilisation, the İYC enabled the development of networks between rightist, Islamist and conservative actors, academics and politicians, with its members including figures such as the former prime minister, Turgut Özal, the AKP mayor of İstanbul, Mustafa Topbaş and Prof Ali Fuat Başgil. The founders of the İYC were also involved in the establishment of the Associations for Fighting Communism, the state-supported Islamist and nationalist mobilisation against communism since 1948 and the emergence of the Cold War; closely associated with the Hearth of the Enlightened, formed in the 1960s against left/communist currents; and pioneered the TIS programme promoted by the 1980 junta regime (see Chapter 5). On the other hand, the İYC engaged in horizontal mobilisation, with its goal of raising a generation who embrace national and religious moral and cultural values. This involved advocating and expanding the religious educational infrastructure through building *imam-hatip* schools, as well as cooperation with the MEB and the Diyanet. For example, the Diyanet requested help from the İYC for facilities to train Diyanet *muftis* (İYC 1964). The case of the İYC, therefore, highlights the deeper roots of the TIS project adopted in 1980, which is commonly regarded as constituting a break with the republican tradition.

In the AKP era, the manner in which Islamic/Islamist organisations have enabled both vertical and horizontal mobilisation, together with the generation of economic resources, were highlighted by the eruption on 17 December 2013 of a corruption probe against the Islamist government. At the centre of the allegations was TÜRGEV, which was established in 1996 (with public benefit status granted in 2011) and includes on its executive board President Erdoğan's son and daughter as well as

---

[24] These have included the Turkish Armed Forces Foundation (Türk Silahlı Kuvvetlerini Güçlendirme Vakfı) and the Atatürkist Thought Association (Atatürkçü Düşünce Derneği).

various AKP politicians. According to the allegations made during the corruption probe, TÜRGEV collected bribes (e.g. in monetary form or land) from businessmen, including a large Saudi-sourced donation, in return for support from the government for prime real estate land and construction permits. This kind of case is not uncommon: various actors within the Islamist movement have written about such mechanisms (referred to as *havuz*). For instance, Mümtaz'er Türköne, a prominent nationalist–Islamist academic, author and former columnist for the Gülenist daily newspaper, *Zaman Gazatesi*, alleged that in the 1990s, Hayrettin Karaman, an influential Islamic theologian close to the AKP, had issued a *fatwa* to facilitate 'donations' from businessmen to Islamic and Islamist organisations in return for favours and benefits, while funds raised for the associations and *waqfs* would, in turn, support the mobilisation of political support for the Islamist movement (Türköne 16 January 2014).[25] Such patterns of mobilisation have also been noted by a number of studies on Islamist mobilisation in the 1990s, which reported the important role played by Islamic charities in municipalities run by Islamist parties in which businessmen submitting proposals for tenders (i.e. for construction or property development) were encouraged to make 'mandatory contributions' to Islamic charities or to the party. In turn, these funds would be channelled through the party, or Islamic charities close to the party, to those in need of welfare support (Akinci 1999: 89; J. White 2002). According to Demir et al., such faith-based organisations, 'while building mosques, Qur'an courses, schools and student dormitories with money collected from members or friends who give to charity out of religious duty, also prepared a customer and capital base for the schools, businesses and enterprises of their members' (2004: 171). Equally important was the support of these organisations in developing an Islamist media sector, which is exemplified by the founding in 1994 of the influential Islamist daily, *Yeni Şafak* (*New Dawn*) (also with the efforts of Karaman) by the Ensar Foundation (Ensar Vakfi), a foundation established in 1979 to promote 'religious and moral education'.

In sum, faith-based organisations generated important organisational networks between social groups, acting as multilevel intermediaries in terms of the horizontal mobilisation of business and the vertical mobilisation of the poor and, in turn, providing a pool of capital for the governing AKP. At the same time, Islamist social group mobilisation and networks were privileged from within the state even prior to the 1980 military intervention and adoption of the TIS, thereby crucially supporting the

---

[25] Türköne was imprisoned following the 15 July 2016 coup attempt, on the allegation that he belongs to what AKP has designated the Gülenist Terrorist Organisation (FETÖ).

reproduction of religious social group boundaries in economic and political competition. In the AKP period, this support for Islamist and Islamic organisations has increased significantly and has included tax exemptions and granting of association for public benefit status to chiefly Islamist and pro-AKP foundations and associations.[26] Direct transfers to religious associations also take place at the municipality level, but there is less transparency with these, making them harder to trace historically.[27] One example is the 2012 grant of TRY 542,530 by an AKP-run municipality in İstanbul for the repair of student halls of residence run by the İYC.

The Development of Islamic Banking in the 1980s

Similar to faith-based foundations and associations, Islamic banking in Turkey has provided a key mechanism of accumulating capital that supported the growth of Anatolian industry. In this sense, the development of Islamic banking, which comprises financial activities that conform to *shari'a*,[28] has provided an important source of 'structural power' (Smith 2004: 176) for Islamist movements. Emerging in the 1970s, the spread of Islamic banking was catalysed by differing aims. In 1971, the Egyptian state established the first Islamic bank, partly owing to a desire to increase the poorer classes' participation in banking. Together with this, the rise of Islamic banking in this period also crucially comprised an extension of the Saudi-supported pan-Islamism during the Cold War against socialism and Arab nationalism (Warde 2004: 37).

---

[26] Examples include the Association of Lighthouse, the İHH, the Ensar Foundation, the Albayrak Foundation, the Nakşibendi Es-Seyyid Osman Hulusi Efendi Foundation, the Suffa Foundation (linked to the Nur movement), the Journalists and Writers Foundation [Gazeteciler ve Yazarlar Vakfı]) and the Is Anybody There Association (Kimse Yok Mu Dayanışma ve Kalkınma Derneği) linked to the Gülen movement. Islamic business organisations Müstakil Sanayici ve İş Adamları Derneği (Independent Industrialists' and Businessmen's Association), MÜSİAD) and the Gülenist Türkiye İşadamları ve Sanayiciler Konfederasyonu (Turkish Confederation of Businessmen and Industrialists, TUSKON) also enjoyed or enjoy public benefit status, as does the leading secular association Türk Sanayicileri ve İşadamları Derneği (Turkish Industry and Business Association, TÜSİAD). Many Gülenist associations and foundations, including Is Anybody There Association and TUSKON, have been closed by decree since the July 2016 coup attempt. Business associations were discussed earlier in this chapter.

[27] The transfer of budgetary funds to faith-based organisations began in 1996 under the CHP–DYP government (Cangöz 2010: 138). However, the detailed breakdown of budget allocations to foundations and associations was halted in 2003 under the AKP government, making it difficult to analyse how these dynamics have shifted since then.

[28] This includes the prohibition of interest. See www.worldbank.org/en/topic/financial sector/brief/islamic-finance.

The emergence of Islamic banking in Turkey was spearheaded by the ANAP government in the 1980s. On the one hand, the governing ANAP party, which was effectively a rightist coalition of conservative and Islamist political actors, wanted to further augment its strength and clientelistic networks by incorporating wider conservative-Islamist actors (Yankaya 2014: 84–91). On the other hand, the move reflected a search for new sources of capital, particularly from the oil-rich Gulf states and by attracting savings deposits of conservative citizens following neo-liberal economic restructuring (Başkan 2004: 225). Furthermore, as a net oil importer, Turkey's need for oil in the 1970s, particularly following the oil crisis in 1973, had resulted in a reorientation of its foreign policy towards developing closer relations with the Gulf oil exporters, particularly Saudi Arabia.

Consequently, through a prime ministerial decree issued in 1983, just days after it came to power, the ANAP government opened up the establishment of Islamic banking in Turkey under the banner of Special Finance Organisations and granted them a number of privileges compared with conventional banks. For one, Islamic banks were exempted from the conventional banking regulatory framework and accorded significant advantages in terms of lower reserve requirements (funds required to be held at the central bank) (Moore 1990: 247–249). Being exempt from complying with legal ratios set by the central bank also meant that Islamic banks were able to raise cheaper funds and pay their customers a higher return.[29] Consequently, they offered a potential new channel for SMEs struggling to access credit from conventional banks that deemed them too risky (so-called Anatolian capital). From this perspective, therefore, these banks offered a means of advancing Islamist capital accumulation, and over time, they developed a close relationship with a number of the conservative business organisations like MÜSİAD (discussed earlier in the section 'The Rise of the "Muslim Bourgeoisie"').

The establishment of Islamic banking also played a crucial role in building a cross-class and transnational coalition of conservative and Islamist actors and thereby contributed to group-making along religious delineations. Turkey's first two Islamic banks were established in 1985 with the help of Gulf capital (Eligür 2010: 130; Başkan 2004: 224–227). Faisal Finance was founded with Saudi capital, and its shareholders comprised various prominent Islamists, including former MSP lawmakers and ministers, some of whom were active members of the

---

[29] These were scrapped by the central bank in 1994 but were restored by Bülent Ecevit following pressure.

Saudi World Muslim League, such as Salih Özcan. Al-Baraka Turk was also founded with Saudi capital, together with prominent Islamist actors associated with the Naqshbandi *tariqa*, the İskenderpaşa community and the İYC (Köni 2012: 103–104), including Korkut Özal, who was a former MSP parliamentarian and minister and the brother of the then prime minister, alongside Eymen Topbaş, chairman of the ANAP and brother of Musa Topbaş, a Naqshbandi sheikh (Başkan 2004: 218). Similarly, Kuveyt Turk was established in 1989 with Kuwaiti funds, with Kuwait Finance House having 62 per cent ownership, Kuwait Social Security Institution 9 per cent, Islamic Development Bank 9 per cent and the DoF of Turkey 18 per cent. Other examples include Enver Ören, owner of İhlas Finance House, affiliated with the Işıkçılar (an offshoot of the Naqshbandi order) and the Gülen movement's Asya Finans (Başkan 2004: 219).[30]

Together with the institutionalisation of horizontal social networks and pooling resources, Islamic banking has also served as a means of vertical mobilisation by building alliances with less wealthy, pious and conservative sectors of society that eschew interest-based commercial banking. Indeed, these Islamic banks then went on to establish Islamic and Islamist associations and foundations such as the Bereket Foundation, the Özbağ Foundation and the Aköz Foundation, providing scholarships for students and social welfare services for the poor, while also supporting many other faith-based organisations, including the İYC (Eligür 2010: 130; Köni 2012: 103–104). Investigative journalist Uğur Mumcu also claimed that these Islamic banks provided funds for many Islamist media companies and publications (Mumcu 1993: 142–144, 148; Köni 2012: 104).

Islamic banking has continued to receive support under the Islamist AKP. The 2007 to 2013 five-year economic development plan, for instance, outlined strategies to boost interest-free banking with the aim of raising the sector share in total banking from around 5 per cent in 2017 to 15 per cent by 2023 (Thomson Reuters Zawya 2013: 113). Additionally, the sector was supported by regulatory changes following the 2000–2001 financial crisis, when Islamic banks were integrated into the banking regulatory framework and gained equal status with conventional banks, which meant that customers' deposits in these banks would from then on be guaranteed under the Savings Deposit Insurance Fund.

---

[30] Asya Finans, later renamed Bank Asya, was established in 1996. Following the intensified struggle between the AKP and Gülenists, the bank was closed after the state took over its management in 2015 and declared it bankrupt in 2017. Many of its shareholders have also been arrested.

Nevertheless, the Islamic finance sector remains small compared with conventional banking, accounting for around 5.5 per cent of total banking sector assets in 2013. In January 2014, Islamic banks accounted for 6.6 per cent of total banking sector deposits (up from 2.2 per cent in 2002) and just less than 7 per cent of credit. The Islamic banking sector in Turkey, at around 5 per cent of the total banking sector in 2015, is also small compared with other countries, such as Saudi Arabia, where Islamic bank assets comprise around 51 per cent of the total banking sector, the United Arab Emirates with 22 per cent, Malaysia with 21 per cent, Bahrain with 29 per cent, Kuwait with 45 per cent and Qatar with 26 per cent (EY 2015: 12).

In sum, from the start, the establishment and spread of Islamic banking in Turkey has been supported by the state. Alongside facilitating Islamist mobilisation, a further outcome of its expansion is Islamisation, as well as opening new opportunities for the *ulema*. The existence of Islamic banks has resulted in increasing research on *shari'a* and deepening the reach of Islam over finance and economics while also creating new sources of income and associations for the *ulema* (Kahf 2004: 26–27). For example, the influential and prominent theologian, Hayrettin Karaman, who is also close to the AKP, sits on the *shari'a* boards of all five Islamic banks in Turkey, while another prominent member of these boards is Hamdi Döndüren, who has stirred controversy over his propagation of *shari'a*.

Conclusion

The salience of Islamic markers in economic and political struggles in Turkey are neither a product of instrumentalist practices of actors nor the natural reflexes of a nominally (in the sense of being categorised) majority Muslim society reacting to authoritarian secularism. While instrumentalist approaches cannot explain why religion was chosen over other markers, the second approach is inherently essentialist and tends to conflate a nominal or social category (majority Muslim) with a politicised group identity (Islamism). A core argument of this book is that these choices and the salience of religious markers are rooted in the path-dependent effects generated during nation-state building. This does not refer to an unchanging essence but rather a Barthian understanding of identity boundaries (elaborated in the Introduction) as persisting despite change in its content. It is in this sense that the particular phenomenon of a Muslim bourgeoisie, manifesting in the rise of conservative business associations such as MÜSİAD, and thereby the salience of religious markers, should be situated within the *longue durée* processes of boundary making. As Chapter 1 traced how the legacy of the Ottoman Empire shaped the construction of citizenship and design of institutions during the early phases of nation-state building, this chapter has elaborated its implications for the economic structure. In particular, the distinction underpinning the notion of a Muslim bourgeoisie is related to the bifurcation of the bourgeoisie into Muslims and non-Muslims in the late Ottoman Empire (Göçek 1996) and the efforts since 1908 to build a national bourgeoisie (Toprak 1995), which continued in the Republic and, in practice, involved the privileging of Muslim and Turkish elements in economic life. Within this context, the assertion of Islamist or conservative business organisations of their Muslim identity can be read as not just a claim of authenticity but their assertion of an assumed right to a monopoly of state resources. In this claim, they simply mirror the religious majoritarian logic of nation-state building.

At the same time, the salience of boundaries and level of social closure is not constant but shifts over time. In the Turkish case, salience of religious markers over others has increased with time. This, in turn, is related to the expansion of the religious field since the 1940s, in parallel and connected to the expansion of the Diyanet's role as outlined in Chapters 2 and 3. While not disregarding Islamist mobilisation from below, this expansion, including the infrastructure behind religious education, Islamic and Islamist organisations and Islamic finance, is understood within the context of the struggle within the state which was affected by both endogenous factors, including the multiple strategies adopted by the Diyanet, and exogenous factors, which were Cold War related anti-communism policies and neo-liberal economic restructuring in the 1980s. The outcome of these was an augmentation of the religious majoritarianism of the state, which essentially involved a more favourable institutional framework that increased the attractiveness and plausibility of mobilisation and politics based on the utilisation of religious identity, thereby underpinning both its persistence and increasing salience over time.

The reintroduction of religious lessons in mainstream schools and religious education was motivated by the anti-communism drive beginning in the 1940s. It was encouraged by the Diyanet, as these schools not only produced a pool of human capital to join the body's ranks but were also a critical tool in the pursuit of Islamisation through the inculcation of religious values. The re-establishment in 1951 of state-provided religious education, the *imam-hatip* schools, and its emergence as a parallel educational system alongside mainstream education, was important in imparting a distinct habitus (Özgür 2012: 24). The example of the Generation Movement reveals how leading Islamists, including and with the cooperation of senior actors in the Diyanet, saw these schools as a field to pursue Islamisation by engaging in *da'wah* activities and Islamist mobilisation. In Turkey, and more globally, the neo-liberal restructuring of the economy that accompanied the crushing of the left was important in the spread of religious associations and organisations alongside Islamic finance since the 1980s. They were particularly incentivised by a more favourable institutional environment and legal framework with the ascendance of more conservative factions within the state under the Özal government. Together with religious education, these organisations expanded the Islamist movement's capacity to engage in horizontal and vertical mobilisation, networking rich and poor, and thereby also growing its pool of economic resources and capital.

This expansion of the religious field – including the Diyanet (discussed in Chapters 2 and 3), religious education, Islamist organisations and Islamic finance – therefore both facilitated Islamist mobilisation from within the state and was also the product of Islamist mobilisation. Reflecting the elusive and mobile boundary between state and society (Mitchell 1991), this fluid relationship and webs of reciprocity between the Islamist movement, the *ulema* of the Diyanet (some of whom were Islamists) and other state factions is further elaborated in Chapter 5 on the history of Turkey's Islamist movement. Equally, this infrastructure also underpinned not only the persistence of boundaries over time but also the basis of social stratification or distinction through the development and (re) production of a distinct habitus. This has manifested over time in increasing physical distinction and differentiation in the socio-political life of the Muslim pious, conservative and Islamist sectors of society, including in fashion and dress and the restructuring of social space with the establishment of venues without alcohol, as well as Islamic holiday destinations with venues offering segregated spaces for men and women. This stratification or distinction can, therefore, be understood as the outcome of what Bourdieu would characterise as a 'symbolic struggle' by 'different classes and class fractions', or actors both within and outside the state, 'to impose the definition of the social world most in conformity with their interests' in order to obtain 'the monopoly of legitimate symbolic violence, i.e. the power to impose (and even inculcate) instruments of knowledge and expression (taxonomies) of social reality' (Bourdieu 1979: 80). Chapters 5 and 6 will examine both the rise of Islamism and how Islamist politics has become more dominant over other factions of the state through path-dependent path-shaping strategies.

5 The Islamist Movement in Turkey and the Emergence of the AKP

The preceding chapters have so far demonstrated the ways in which mobilisation on the basis of religious identity in Turkey was facilitated from within the state as opposed to a purely bottom-up driven reaction to a secular state. This did not mean that a monolithic secular state actor was utilising or trying to control religion in a top-down manner. Rather, the case of the Diyanet shows not only the differentiated character of the state itself but the fluid boundaries between the state and society, underlining the nature of the state as an arena of struggle between different actors with varying political visions. The terms and nature of this struggle between the dominant factions within the state were determined by the particular institutional framework – the extent to which the state was religious majoritarian – established during nation building, since institutions such as the Diyanet provided the ability of social actors, including the *ulema* and Islamists, to reproduce themselves over time, resulting in persistence. What tipped the balance of power within the state towards more conservative projects, thereby providing a more favourable environment for the mobilisation and success of religio-politics, was the role of contingent events that provided windows of opportunities for these actors to expand their social base and obtain access to resources of the state, as elaborated in Chapter 4.

Within this context, this chapter shifts the focus onto the Islamist movement itself and the AKP, with an emphasis on the expanding power of the coalitions of Islamist, conservative and nationalist currents and factions both within and outside the state that has underpinned successful mobilisation over time. The first section situates the AKP ideologically and politically, placed within both the intellectual accumulation and the experience of the Islamist movement and, more broadly, within the political tradition of the right in Turkey. Accordingly, a historical background of the development of the Islamist movement traces both different intellectual traditions and how these elements have evolved and developed new and contrasting strategies through engagement with the Turkish nation-state project. In particular, the establishment of the nation-state, and the 1980 and 1997 interventions, have crucially shaped the trajectory of the Islamist movement, facilitating first its integration with Turkish nationalism, and second, its rearticulation within a pro-capitalist neo-liberal framework. The second section considers in particular the case of the Gülenists as one of the most powerful elements of the Islamist movement that played a consequential role not only in the AKP's consolidation of power but also in the transformation of the state. The third section traces Islamist party political mobilisation. Prior to the AKP, Islamist political parties had enjoyed limited success and the Islamist movement has been far from uniform, instead being highly fragmented and riven by power struggles despite the common pursuit of the wider goal of Islamisation. On the other hand, the AKP, at least until the split with the Gülenists, had been the most successful Islamist party in Turkish history in its ability to bring together and emerge as the primary political umbrella under which diverse and heterogeneous Islamist, conservative and nationalist actors, with different strategies, visions and traditions, gathered. This, in turn, has been facilitated by a confluence of political learning with contingent events, together with the increasing capacity of the party to deliver through rent distribution the benefits of incumbency, which will be charted in Chapter 6. The final section concludes by reflecting on the fluid boundaries between the *ulema* and Islamist movement, state and society, and the weakness of the binary perspectives that position Islamism as a movement from below against the secular state. Equally, it also questions the Turkish Islamist narrative of victimhood as a type of 'dissident but hegemonic discourse' (Yalman 2002).

The Evolution of the Islamist Movement in Turkey

While the rise of Islamism, as a type of religio-politics that is analogous to nationalist or identity movements, is associated with the emergence and establishment of nation-states, its intellectual roots can be traced to developments within Islamic thought, particularly from the late eighteenth century. This first phase was based essentially on a revitalisation of Islam, emerging largely in reaction to European imperial encroachments and the perceived decline of Muslim power vis-à-vis the Western world (Keddie 1966: 48, 1994: 463; Lapidus 1997: 444; Mandaville 2014: 58–63; Price 1999: 18; Tibi 2001: 120; Tunaya 2007: 13–15; Zubaida 1993: 43–45) and processes of social closure heightened by war and major demographic change. It was the Young Ottomanists, such as the poet Namık Kemal (1840–1888), who developed ideas of pan-Islamism in the 1870s, popularising the Islamic term for unity of the Muslims (*ittihad-i Islam*) in reaction to Russian expansion over Muslim lands as both 'pan-Islamism and pan-Turkism', stating they 'were born in nineteenth-century Russia as part of the process of nation formation and the rise of nationalism among the Muslims there' (Karpat 2001: 18, 68; Keddie 1966: 48). Scholars have broadly distinguished between the earlier revivalist or renewalist currents and the later reformist or modernist Islamic intellectuals. Despite encapsulating a diverse set of Islamic intellectual trends, a revivalist or renewalist trend has most notably been associated with the Wahhābīyah, followers of Ibn ʿAbd al-Wahhāb (1703–1792) from the Arabian Peninsula, concerned with *bida'* (innovations), including Sufi mysticism and practices declared un-Islamic and corrupting of the faith (Mandaville 2014: 56–63), and seeking its revival (*ihya*) or renewal (*tajdīd*) through a return to a pure Islam accompanied by a highly literalist reading of the texts. The revivalist current also included a more militant orthodox neo-Sufi movement influenced by the Naqshbandism that mobilised to achieve the re-Islamisation of the social order as well as protect against imperial encroachments (Karpat 2001: 44).

The so-called reformist or modernist currents of the nineteenth century arose more directly as a reaction to external imperial interventions. Together with other intellectual trends at the time, such as Ottomanism and Turkism, they were both a product (reaction to) and a part of the modernisation and reform movement, concerned with addressing the legitimacy crisis of the state and ensuring its continuity and survival, which were regarded as fundamental for the protection of Islam and the *umma*. The modernisation drive under the Tanzimat reforms (1939–1976) was criticised as moving the state away from Islamic principles and embodying an imitation of the enemy, Western civilisation, which needed to be fought. Instead, Islamists sought to counter Westernisation and imperialism, on the defence and at pains to emphasise that Islam did not impede progress (Tunaya 2007: 15), arguing instead that the remedy for reversing the decline of Muslim power was an Islamic revival and a return to what they perceived as the fundamentals, including the religious texts (the Qur'an and Sunnah), and an imagined golden age (Asr-ı Saadet). Led by key figures such as Jamāl al-Dīn al-Afghānī, Muḥammad ʿAbduh and Rashīd Riḍā, as well as Young Ottomans such as Namık Kemal, these reformists or modernists rejected so-called imitative Westernisation and tried at the same time to reinterpret Islamic principles to naturalise modern concepts, such as constitutionalism and parliamentary representation, as Islamic. In this manner, they sought modernisation through a 'restoration of Islam's rationalist and scientific spirit and the interpretation of its basic tenets in ways more suited to

Muslims' current conditions and needs' (Hunter 2014: 14; Keddie 1994: 484). Thus, as Tibi (2001: 120) notes, this first phase of Islamism had both '*modernist* components, that is, Islamic reform (the borrowing of modern science and technology for enriching Islam), as well as *millenarian-nativist* components' that had been promoted first by the Wahhabis.

Catalysed by the loss of lands and the rise of nation-states, which had brought to the fore questions of authority and legitimacy, Islamic responses to the decline in Muslim power evolved from the emphasis on a renewed focus on religious identity, to Islamism essentially a '"religionised politics" that includes the promotion of an order based on religious tenets' (Tibi 2012: 1). Overall, however, the boundaries between the two currents, revivalist and reformist, were in essence fluid, with both sharing common visions despite sharp differences in means and methods. As Karpat (1959: 18) elaborates, both talked about a restoration of a golden age and the survival of Islamic identity and civilisations, which in fact was 'a form of nationalism in Islamic garb'. Likewise, despite the plethora of approaches under the umbrella of contemporary Islamism that have been influenced by and evolved from these currents, Islamists share a common view of the necessity of the Islamisation of government and the public space based on their reconstruction (or practice of 'invention of tradition' [Tibi 2012: 44; Zubaida 1993: 1–3]) of Islam as comprising a distinct political order.[1]

Alongside advocating a return to Islam, rather than Westernisation, to save the Ottoman state, a matter that crucially underpinned nascent Islamist reaction in this first phase of Islamism, was the granting of equality to non-Muslims as part of the modernisation drive under the Ottoman Reform Edict of 1856 (see Chapter 1). Criticisms of the introduction of equality can be observed in the efforts in 1868 of Ziya Pasha, an Ottoman bureaucrat, intellectual and member of the Young Ottomans, to distinguish between legal equality (*müsavat fi'l-hukuk*) and the equality of moral values or honour (*müsavat fi'ş şeref*), which reflected such tensions and resistance to the principle of equality for Muslim and non-Muslim subjects (Kara 2007; Taştan 2012: 35). Indeed, it was in this period of a perceived erosion of the privileged status of Muslim subjects under modernisation reforms that Islamist ideas gained strength and expanded, together with the emergence of the idea of pan-Islamism in the 1870s that was subsequently adopted by

---

[1] The precise nature of this common goal of Islamisation significantly varies for different Islamist groups and can indeed clash, yet it remains an overarching means to differentiate Islamism from other ideological movements.

Abdülhamid II, faced with the Muslimisation of the Ottoman lands following major military losses.

Gaining increasing currency during the second constitutional period after 1908 with the liberalisation of politics, Turkish Islamism, in particular, as an intellectual current, was certainly overlapping and in a close relationship with the other prevalent currents, Ottomanism and Turkism, with many of its prominent intellectual leaders involved with the ITC and the movement to restore the constitution in 1908. As Çetinsaya (1999: 353–354, 356) notes, Turkists and Islamists readily accepted a synthesis between religion and nationalism, albeit differing on their priorities. Between 1908 and the Balkan Wars in 1912 to 1913, this contributed to a de facto alliance between modernist Islamists and Turkish nationalists. A group characterising themselves as Turkish Islamists had arisen during this period within the circles that produced the Islamist *Sebilürreşad* and nationalist *Türk Yurdu* journals, which had subsequently sealed this synthesis by publishing the journal *İslam Mecmuası*.[2] Writers in this journal, 'brimful [with an] earnest desire for the reform of Islam' and to free it from superstition (Arai 1992: 86–88), included reformist *ulema* and Islamists such as Musa Kazım Efendi (Sheikh ul-Islam, 1910–1911 and 1916–1918), Mehmed Şerafeddin Yaltkaya (Diyanet chief 1942–1947) and Şemsettin Günaltay (prime minister 1949–1950), together with Turkish nationalists and ideologues such as Ziya Gökalp, Tekin Alp and historian Fuat Köprülü. Based on an analyses of these journals, Arai argues that the *İslam Mecmuası* writers, particularly those who were members of the *ulema*, saw the ITC policies that are typically associated with secularisation – from the reform of the *medreses* to the transfer of the religious courts to the domain of the Ministry of Justice – as a means of revitalising Islam, 'substituting superstition with the true religion' and, as such, 'the policy was not that of secularisation but that of Islamisation'. Reflecting its Islamic reformism, *İslam Mecmuası* also undertook the translation of the Qur'an into Turkish 'as a way to regain the truth of Islam' (Arai 1992: 90), which was to continue as a concern in the Republic. Indeed, Dressler (2015: 522) notes that the ideas of Ziya Gökalp, the Republic's and Turkish nationalism's foremost ideologue, rather than a prelude to the republican secularisation policies, had parallels with Islamic modernists such as Rashīd Rida, which is testament to the mutual interaction and overlapping between different ideological currents which persisted in the Republic.

---

[2] This journal was founded by the ITC and was keen to demonstrate that nationalism was not contrary to Islam (Arai 1992: 83).

Particularly during the Turkish War of Independence, the synthesis and ideological intertwining between the Turkists and Islamists deepened as 'Islamists wholeheartedly supported and even served the Ankara government' (Çetinsaya 1999: 361). From the viewpoint of the Islamists, the Turkish War of Independence was won together with the Islamists, *ulema* and sheikhs, driven by a pan-Islamism and the goal of saving the caliphate. This was why, they argued, these actors had constituted one of the largest groups in the first parliament in 1921. For Kara (2013: 27), a prominent theologian and scholar of Islamism, together with other Islamists, it was this heritage that was betrayed in 1924 because of three key laws relating to the unification of education, the abolition of the caliphate and the Ministry of Shari'a and Religious Foundations, which, he argues, resulted in a break in state–religion–society relations. Yet, at this point, religious actors, Islamists and *ulema* from within various Islamic currents adopted different strategies in their engagement with the nation-state project. While some went into active or passive opposition or exile, others remained within the system, comprising part of the nascent state and cooperating with other factions, thereby gaining an opportunity to pursue its political vision over time.

Consequently, rather than an exclusion of these actors, nation building, given its territorially bound logic, in a sense attempted to sideline pan-Islamist (*ümmetçi*) traditionalist *ulema* or Islamic revivalist currents that rejected Turkish nationalism, such as the last Sheikh ul-Islam, Mustafa Sabri Efendi, who went into self-exile in Egypt and remained a critic of the Republic until his death.[3] Others who reconciled, or were willing to cooperate, with the nationalist project for the sake of religion and/or were in the Islamic reformist camp were absorbed by the republican state. Just as during the ITC period, therefore, the cooperation with reformist *ulema* and the Islamic reformist camp continued in the Republic. As Bein (2011: 108–109) relates, following the establishment of the Republic, the reformist circles associated with the *İslam Mecmuası* were some of the most enthusiastic supporters of the government, since some of the religion-related reforms had already been debated and justified in Islamic terms among them during the ITC era, while other *ulema* and Islamists also supported the regime by providing Islamic legitimation for the reforms (Bein 2011: 108–109). Key figures included Şemsettin Günaltay, Ahmed Hamdi Akseki (Diyanet chief 1947–1951), Mehmed Şerafeddin Yaltkaya, Mehmet Ali Ayni, İsmail Hakkı İzmirli and Fenni Ertuğrul. Crucially, such figures were involved in the reform of religious

---

[3] Said Nursi, for instance, had also supported the pan-Islamist Mohammedean Union (Ittihad-i Muhammadiyya) (Kuru and Kuru 2008: 101).

institutions, including the Diyanet, and the nationalisation of religion by narrating the leadership role of Turks in the Islamic world while endeavouring to maintain Islam as a fundamental marker of public morality (see Chapter 2). The efforts by constitutional framers during different periods of constitution making to emphasise the constitutive role of Islam for Turkish national identity while distinguishing it from pan-Islamism alongside Turanism underlines the concern of state elites to instil loyalty into the nation-state (see Chapter 1). In this manner, the Diyanet's Consultative Committee (Hey'et-i müşavere)[4] of this period contained figures who included Ahmed Hamdi Akseki (appointed in 1924), Halim Sabit Şibay (1883–1946, publisher of *İslam Mecmuası*), Kamil Miras (1875–1957, involved in the *medrese* reforms under Musa Kazım Efendi (1858–1920), a reformist 'alim who became Sheikh ul-Islam under the ITC), theologian Yusuf Ziya Yörükân (1887–1954) and Arvasîzade Seyyid Taha Efendi (1864–1928). Alongside them were other members of the *ulema* who rose to prominence during the Turkish War of Independence, such as Mehmet Bahaeddin Efendi (*mufti* of Ulukışla and supporter of the independence movement Kuva-yi Milliye) and Hacı Mustafa Tevfik Efendi (*mufti* of Amasya).

At the same time, Islamists and *ulema* who were critical of the government were increasingly being dismissed and targeted as reactionaries. According to İrem (2002: 100), Republican conservatives became actively involved in a struggle against opposition Islamists in the 1930s, perceiving this as a clash between a 'nationalist–modernist current represented by themselves and an anti-modernist universalist one represented by Islamic reactionism that viewed national culture and institutions as harmful to the universal Muslim community, or umma'. In 1921, the nascent state was faced with the Alevi–Kurdish Koçgiri rebellion, and in 1925, a rebellion by the Naqshbandi Sheikh Said was regarded by the one-party regime as involving both a Kurdish nationalist and Islamic challenge to the nation-state project, triggered by the abolition of the caliphate.[5] It was following the 1925 rebellion in particular that Islamists and *ulema*, together with all other political currents, were faced with a widespread clampdown. The subsequent emergency 1925 Law for the Maintenance of Order closed off political life and drove political opposition underground. Consequently, both reflecting its

---

[4] This combined the Committee for Islamic Research and Writing (Tetkikat ve telifat-ı İslamiye Heyeti) and the Fatwa office (Şûrayı İfta). Members of the former included reformist Islamists such as Abdülaziz Çaviş and İsmail Hakkı İzmirli.

[5] The Sheikh Said rebellion has been regarded as an Islamic and Kurdish nationalist rebellion (Gunter 2007: 121; Olson 1989; Yeğen 1996: 221).

intertwining with nationalist and conservative currents in the late Ottoman period and owing to constitutional restrictions, particularly from the 1940s, Islamism as an ideological current increasingly became articulated within the discourse of the Turkish right and conservatism, which were characterised by a staunch anti-communism and heavily statist orientation (Bora 2013: 518–519; Duran 2004: 135–139; Kara 2013: 27–28; Mert 2004: 414).[6] Within the Republic, therefore, as Bora (2003b: 519, 2017: 437) argues, Islamism together with nationalism and conservatism came to constitute the three pillars nested harmoniously in the body of the politics of the right. Reflecting this, many prominent intellectuals of the right, such as Nurettin Topçu, Necip Fazıl Kısakürek and Hayrettin Karaman, have comfortably straddled these three currents.

By the 1940s, new opportunities for religio-political mobilisation were provided by the emergence of the Cold War, as anti-communism[7] emerged as an area of overlapping consensus between different factions within and outside the state that catalysed or strengthened new coalitions within the right, strengthening its weight within the state. As earlier chapters have suggested, these windows of opportunity were important for rightist Islamist and conservative factions within the state such as the Diyanet, which used them to expand its role and religious infrastructure, thereby ultimately tipping the power balance in its favour and facilitating a more favourable environment for Islamist politics by increasing the access to and share of the state's political and economic resources. The extent to which the anti-communism drive catalysed and solidified networks within the right, Islamist, nationalist and conservative factions within and outside the state is revealed by the KMD. This association dates to the late 1940s and became operational after 1950. By the 1960s, there were 110 branches across Turkey (Poulton 1997: 139; Seufert 2014: 7). In 1950, the DP government had established a Fighting with Communism Commission (Komünizmle Mücadele Komisyonu)

---

[6] I am not suggesting here that the CHP/SHP/DSP can easily be positioned on the left of the political spectrum, and in fact, it has been widely argued that the CHP's politics sit more to the right on various issues such as Kurdish rights and basic freedoms. Historically, however, and within public discourse, it has been articulated within the centre-left bloc, and in the 1970s, at least, it adopted a social democratic discourse that differed from that of the traditional right parties.

[7] Meşe (2017: 53–116) argues that this anti-communist stance was influenced by US anti-communist propaganda, Turkic intellectuals originally from Russia, the foreign policy stance of Stalin towards Turkey and demands for territory and control over shipping in the Turkish straits.

together with the education minister, former chief of the MTTB (see note 14 in Chapter 4 about another anti-communist nationalist formation with close links to the state) and active proponent of religious education, Tevfik Ileri, a keen cooperator with the commission (Meşe 2017: 108–109).[8]

In particular, the Nurcu movement emerged as critical actors within the anti-communism coalition and campaign in this period. The Nurcus were followers of Bediüzzaman Said Nursi (1877–1960), a prominent Islamist of Kurdish origin who was at one point a member of the ITC and who straddled the worlds of both Kurdish nationalist and Islamist movements. Nursi has been characterised in divergent ways as an Islamic reformer (Özdalga 2000: 85) with positive attitudes towards ideas of constitutionalism (Mardin 1989: 213; Seufert 2014: 12), a Turkish revivalist rooted in traditional Sufi networks,[9] a scriptualist influenced by Ibn Taymiyyah (1263–1328) and an Islamist.[10] Nursi initially supported the 1908 Young Turk revolution but later became a critic of the ITC and was arrested following the 1909 counter-revolution. Despite backing the Ankara government during the independence struggle, he was disappointed that the new republican regime had not subsequently embraced an Islamic political order and went into reclusion beginning in 1926 with a mission to preserve the faith (Bora 2017: 424). During this period, he built his network of followers into a sizeable community called the Nurcus, which became increasingly engaged in political life with the transition to multi-partism in the 1940s, developing strong links with the DP and its successors.

Like other political currents within the rightist tradition, the Nurcus also developed a highly anti-communist stance with the emergence of the Cold War, with Nursi actively calling on the state authorities and offering his cooperation in fighting communists. A prominent Nurcu and Said

---

[8] In 1952, a unit within the army, particularly those trained in unconventional warfare practices in the United States in the late 1940s, established the Tactical Mobilisation Group (Seferberlik Tetkik Kurulu), which in 1965 became the Special Warfare Department (Özel Harp Dairesi). This organisation, allegedly closed in 2013, has been claimed to be part of Operation Gladio, a Cold War policy of NATO, or deep state, and associated with Turkey's history of military coups (Meşe 2017: 108–109).

[9] Çakır (2002: 89–90) argues that one cannot describe the Nurcu as a *tariqa* order because Nursi was against Sufi practices and instead suggests the designation 'belief movement'. Kuru and Kuru (2008: 108–109) similarly differentiate the Nurcus from Islamism and Sufism, arguing that it should be seen as a form of faith-based activism.

[10] His association with Naqshbandism remains an area of dispute. On the basis that he never described himself in these terms and was critical of Sufism, Kuru and Kuru (2008) argue that Mardin, among others, misrepresented Nursi. They thereby suggest that it is distinguished from sufism and is, instead, a new type of faith-based movement.

Nursi's lawyer, Bekir Berk became a leading actor in the fight against communism in this period, spearheading the 1963 establishment of, and his election to, a parliamentary Fighting with Communism Commission backed by all-party support (Meşe 2017: 126–135). Berk was also the former head of the Nationalists Federation, established in 1950 as an umbrella group to bring together various nationalist associations in the fight against communism, and published the *Fighting Against Communism* (*Komünizme Karşı Mücadele*) magazine (Meşe 2017: 110, 126, 136). In the 1960s, he also cooperated with Fethullah Gülen (see next section), who led the opening of the KMD branch in Erzurum. The extent of involvement and support in these efforts from different elements of the state is demonstrated by the placement of Cemal Gürsel, head of the 1960 to 1961 junta regime and subsequent president, to a brief position as honorary president of the KMD.

As Meşe (2017) underlines, after the 1950s, the anti-communism drive contributed to assembling a wide rightist front comprising the different factions within the state, including the government, alongside the KMD and other parties such as the AP, the CKMP/MHP, the New Turkey Party (Yeni Türkiye Partisi), the Nation Party (Millet Partisi, MP), the MSP, rightist trade unions Türk-İş and Ülkü-Sen, the Nationalist Teacher's Trade Union (Milliyetçi Öğretmenler Sendikası), student organisation the MTTB, other student associations such as the MHP's youth organisation the Idealist Hearths (Ülkü Ocakları) and the İYC (Meşe 2017: 170, 279).[11] This rightist social network structure of Islamist, conservative and nationalist actors and intellectuals has been categorised as a nationalist conservative (*milliyetçi muhafazakar*) or nationalist sacredist (*milliyetçi-mukaddesatçı*) bloc. While Islam was an important element in the conceptualisation of Turkish nationalism and society for these circles, in common with the synthesis that developed in the late Ottoman Empire, Çetinsaya (1999: 369) notes that one, and the only, difference was that now 'Islam, in the formula of Turkish nationalism, was no longer required to be modernist Islam'.

The integration between these circles was also facilitated by the expansion of religious education after the 1950s. For instance, *imam-hatip* students were taught the prominent works of both Islamist and conservative Turkish nationalist writers such as Mehmet Akif, Yahya Kemal, Necip Fāzıl Kısakürek and Peyami Safa alongside the usual religious texts (Çetinsaya 1999: 369). As Çetinsaya (1999: 370) also notes, in

---

[11] The fascist/nationalist CKMP/MHP was also closely associated with elements of the military. The founder, in 1969, of the MHP was Colonel Alparslan Türkeş, who was involved in the 1960 coup.

the 1960s and 1970s, especially, graduates of these schools were as close to the nationalist right as the Islamist MSP. In 1970, these circles of actors and intellectuals established the Hearth of the Enlightened, whose members included influential Islamists such as Hayrettin Karaman, again, to further the cooperation and integration between the conservative nationalists and Islamists in the fight against communism. It was the Hearth of the Enlightened's TIS programme, envisaging systematic Islamisation, together with the inculcation of Turkish nationalism, that was subsequently adopted as the official programme of the 1980 junta regime and propagated as state policy, as evidenced in the 1983 National Culture Report (see Chapters 1 and 2).

The Gülenist Movement

A prominent element of the Islamist movement that has flourished, particularly since the 1980s, is the Gülenists.[12] One of the most powerful and influential movements in the Republic's history, they deserve a section in their own right given the role they played not only in the AKP's rise to power but also in the ways in which they facilitated the transformation of the state. The subsequent competition and struggle between Erdoğan and Gülen, particularly since 2011, is examined in Chapter 6.

Led by Fethullah Gülen, who was officially born in 1941, the Gülen Movement emerged after the 1970s as the most prominent offshoot of the Nurcu community, the followers of the teachings of Said Nursi, who died in 1960.[13] Up until the struggle with the AKP, both scholarly and non-scholarly assessments of the Gülenists, although highly polarised, were dominated by generally positive or benign evaluations of their nature and aims. Various journalistic accounts and former insiders have detailed Gülenist infiltration of the state bureaucracy and alleged a secret agenda of Islamisation of the state and society.[14] Two such journalists, Ahmet Şık and Nedim Şener, were in fact imprisoned following their exposés of the Gülenists under an initiative of the Gülenist bureaucracy

---

[12] Defining the Gülenists as an organisation is a highly contested matter. The Gülenists have themselves shunned the word *cemaat* (community), presenting themselves either as a civil society movement or, more recently, as a Hizmet (service) to emphasise their stated goal of serving the nation (Seufert 2014: 15). Consequently, studies have typically adopted various designations, including civil society movement, religious community and non-governmental organisation network, depending on the extent of their sympathies, albeit with some exceptions. Here, the Gülenists are considered to be a religio-political or Islamist movement.

[13] Gülen himself claims to have been born in 1938, the year of Atatürk's death.

[14] Prominent examples include Ahmet Şık (2012). There are also former Gülenist confessors such as Nurettin Veren.

in 2011, as had been a former Gülenist and chief of police, Hanefi Avcı, in 2010. Meanwhile, the prevalent tendency within scholarly documents, both in insider accounts and in those that are at least indirectly affiliated, is to present a benign picture of the Islamist community. The plethora of positive insider accounts or those with an affinity with the community characterised the Gülenists as chiefly an Islamist Enlightenment, representing a liberal, 'renewalist and modernist approach to Islam' (Yavuz 2003: 184) with a 'tolerant normative framework' (Kuru 2005: 257), aiming to create a 'modern Muslim' (Yavuz and Esposito 2003: 52–53) or 'modernity without Westernization, that is, it seeks to create a non-Western modernity in contrast to Kemalist non-modern Westernization' (Bilici 2006: 17). Gülen was thereby portrayed as a 'moderate Islamic spiritual leader whose views on Islam are surprisingly liberal' (Aras 1998), which 'illustrates the ability of religious traditions to absorb global discourses of democracy, human rights and the market economy' (Yavuz 2013: 134) that 'no doubt [. . .] deepens the project of democracy and modernity in Turkey' (Bilici 2006: 17).

On the other hand, scholars who are at least not directly affiliated with the Gülenists curiously either took for granted the claims of the insider accounts or, because they remain wedded to the metanarrative of Turkish secularism (see Chapter 1), presented the movement as a liberal Islamism distinguished from radical Islamism and/or as a force of democratisation against the authoritarian secular Kemalist state (Gözaydın 2009b; Özdalga 2000; Tittensor 2014; Turam 2007). In this vein, Tittensor's portrayal of the Gülenists published in 2014 largely mirrors the insider accounts with the argument that

Contrary to the picture painted by the secularists in the Turkish academe and media, the nature of Islam within the Movement is a softer reflexive brand that is indigenous to Turkey [. . .] Rather than reject modernity and globalization, he and his movement have embraced the current age and sought to incorporate it into an Islamic frame of reference. (Tittensor 2014: 174)

This was despite noting the Gülenists' missionary intent and its 'degree of conservatism'. Many other accounts have similarly been underpinned by the framework of moderation and democratisation that also infuses insider accounts. For Turam (2007), while Gülen shares the wider goal of other Nurcus in terms of revitalising the faith, the movement has accidentally facilitated democratisation (25) despite its homogenising Islamic agenda by constructively engaging with the authoritarian secular state: 'Gülen genuinely despises confrontation and conflict and admires moderation and harmony' (52). Özdalga (2000: 87–88) likewise concludes that 'Gülen's views have little to do with seeking political power or even traditional Islam but rather have more in common with Max Weber's ideas about "worldly asceticism", which has facilitated democ-ratisation of Turkey'. In a similar but more nuanced moderation approach, Hendrick (2013: 84) builds on Tuğal's analysis of the absorp-tion of Islamic radicalism by Islamist parties to argue that the goals of Gülenists, which rely on the market for their continued expansion and have 'internalised the notion of third way political pluralism', are less concerned with 'seizing the state and implement[ing] Islamic law, and more [about] capturing the imagination of Turkish society by becoming a market leader in the production of a new "post-Kemalist," "post-Islamist" national identity'. Conversely, a rare critical scholarly review of Gülen's publications and speeches is Çobanoğlu's (2012: 237, 251) account, which underlines the Gülen movement's highly statist and nationalist ideological underpinnings together with its ambition to seek power by replacing the state bureaucracy with its own cadres infused with Islamic morals.

In any case, Gülen played a critical role in the rise and form of religio-political mobilisation that has occurred in Turkey in two ways. First, his rise illustrates the ways in which religio-political mobilisation has been facilitated from within the state as much as through grass-roots mobilisa-tion. It was while working as a Diyanet-appointed *imam* between 1959 and 1981, which included preaching in İstanbul's two most prom-inent mosques, that Gülen had the opportunity to disseminate his ideas, building and expanding his own network of followers. Taking advantage of the opportunities to build networks within the right, and cooperation and collaboration with different factions of the state, as with other Nurcus, in this period, Gülen was also heavily involved in anti-communist activities and, by his own account, led the opening of the KMD in Erzurum in the early 1960s. It was, in a sense, through these actions that he became equipped with new strategies of survival and adaptation to pursue his goals while growing his networks by engaging with different state factions and political actors across the party divide, as evidenced, for example, by his close relationship with Kasım Gülek, a prominent CHP member who served as party general secretary from 1950 to 1959. It is also likely that as a member of the Diyanet *ulema*, during these activities, he learnt how to negotiate and position himself with different actors within the state, such as by supporting military crackdowns on radical Islamist groups and presenting himself as a mod-erate force, thereby potentially creating new opportunities for cooper-ation and avoiding any restrictions on the community. Yet, in substance, there was nothing moderate or that different, ideologically, between the convictions and aims of Gülen and other Islamist actors, such as the RP

(Seufert 2014: 8–9), and even positive accounts note his conservatism on matters such as gender roles (Tittensor 2014).

While still employed by the Diyanet, Gülen began to establish a network of educational institutions, including student dormitories and university preparation courses. This focus on education is a largely unique and defining feature of the Gülenists, setting them apart from other Islamist movements, and together with the community's non-confrontational strategy towards the state, it has led many analysts to consider the organisation as apolitical. Yet education was a key aspect of Gülen's strategy of raising a so-called Golden Generation (Altın Nesil) – the title of his first known book, based on his speeches delivered at a conference in 1976 – of pious and nationalist Muslim elites committed to the cause of Islam in Turkey and, over time, a network of friendly elites outside the country (Çobanoğlu 2012: 403).

Indeed, since the 1980s, Gülen had been advising his followers to join the ranks of the judiciary and security forces in order to effect a transformation of the bureaucracy and state by replacing its cadres with his Altın Nesil (Çobanoğlu 2012: 411). By 1986, there was clear evidence of the success of this strategy, as journalist Ruşen Çakır, a prominent expert on Islamist movements in Turkey, broke a story about Gülenist infiltration within the military (Çakır 23 July 2016). According to Air Force Command Military Prosecutor (Hava Kuvvetleri Savcısı) Judge Ahmet Zeki Üçok, who conducted the only official investigation into the Gülen movement's activities within the military, it was discovered at the time that around 250 students had cheated on the military school exams (Bozan 20 July 2016). The movement's strategy of placing its cadres in state institutions by stealing public service examination questions was to become widespread in the 2000s (Şık 2014: 280–302). Following the 15 July coup attempt, the national security minister, Fikri Işık, stated that the answers to the entrance examinations for military high schools had been stolen throughout the period from 2000 to 2014 (Bozan 21 July 2016).

Yet, thanks to the TIS programme and the support provided by elements within the military, such as Hasan Sağlam and Prime Minister Turgut Özal, Gülen's prominence rose further following the 1980 military coup. Not only did he continue to expand his educational institutions but, according to Yavuz (2003: 183), Özal's move to lift the military's ban on Gülen's religious lectures (*vaaz*) in 1986 marked a 'turning point in terms of his utilization of the national religious networks to carve a space for himself'. In 1989, the Diyanet not only reinstated his licence to resume preaching but granted him the status of emeritus preacher, allowing him to preach in any mosque in Turkey (Çetin 2010: 460). Between 1989 and 1991, Gülen was thus able to preach in the largest mosques in İstanbul and İzmir, thereby further expanding his influence. He had good relations with key political figures, including Bülent Ecevit (former leader of the DSP and prime minister in 1974, 1977, 1978–1979 and 1999–2002), Tansu Çiller (former leader of the DYP and prime minister from 1993 to 1996) and Alpaslan Türkeş (former leader of the MHP). With the fall of the Soviet Union, new avenues of cooperation opened up with different factions of the state, as Gülen effectively became a foreign policy arm of the state in establishing schools across Central Asia throughout the 1990s.[15] In 1999, he went into self-enforced exile in the United States following the 1997 military intervention against the Islamist RP-led coalition government, despite the fact that he had sided with the military, which reflected his gradualist non-confrontational strategy. Yet he continued to expand his reach in education, business and other sectors, including the establishment of Bank Asya in 1996, the Turkish Confederation of Businessmen and Industrialists (Türkiye İşadamları ve Sanayiciler Konfederasyonu, TUS-KON) in 2005, and some 1,000 Gülenist schools in more than 120 countries as well as several think tank-like outfits promoting his teachings and agenda by the 2000s (Hendrick 2013: 4).

Gülen's rise is revealing of the fluid and complex relationship and engagement between the *ulema* and Islamists, state and society, and levels of cooperation that belie simplistic accounts of Islamist mobilisation as a reaction to the secular state. It underlines the key role of the Diyanet *ulema* in driving Islamisation and facilitating religio-political mobilisation, encouraged by the shift in balance of power within the state with the development of the anti-communism drive in the late 1940s. Gülen, as part of the Diyanet *ulema*, was able to channel state resources into not only Islamisation but also mobilisation, constructing a constituency on the ground that would seek to transform the state according to its vision by pursuing a replacement of its cadres with a new generation of Islamists.

The second aspect of Gülen's rise relates to the relationship between Islamism in Turkey and Turkish nationalism. His staunchly Turkish nationalist orientation is widely recognised (Bilici 2006: 11–12; Bora 2017: 434; Turam 2007: 35; Yavuz 2013: 595), although some 'insiders' argue that he is a proponent of Turkish Islam or Turkish Muslimhood (Türkiye Müslümanlığı) comprising a pluralistic approach to national identity rather than an ethnic Turkish one (Bulaç 2008: 318) 'between

[15] The schools were established with the support of the General Directorate for Services for Education Abroad, part of the Ministry of National Education (Milli Eğitim Bakanlığı) (Seufert 2014: 10).

religion and nationalism' (Bilici 2006 17–18).[16] As Aras (1998) has also argued that Gülen has sought both the 'Islamization of Turkish nationalist ideology and the Turkification of Islam'. In this manner, he has steered the Nurcus significantly away from Said Nursi's Kurdish nationalist leanings, replacing the terms 'Kurds' and 'Kurdistan' in Nursi's writings with 'Easterners' and adopting a highly hostile attitude to Kurds, particularly Kurdish-speaking Alevis (Bora 2017: 428; Seufert 2014: 13). Yavuz (2003: 202) notes that some radical Islamist groups have been suspicious of Gülen's closeness with the state, viewing his efforts as the nationalisation of Nursi's works. In this, he shared an overlapping consensus with the military, for whom the relationship between the Islamists and, particularly, elements of the Naqshbandi *tariqa* order with Kurdish identity has been a concern, alongside communism and Alevis.[17] For one, Islamist parties from the MSP to the RP and the AKP have enjoyed strong support in the south-eastern predominantly Kurdish areas (Yavuz 2003: 54, 210; Gündoğan 2012: 126–129).[18] The accusation of having links with Kurdish nationalist elements was also an aspect of the indictment against the DP government following its overthrow in the 1960 coup. As Aktürk (2015: 793) notes, Kurdish demands were

[16] The notion of a Turkish Islam is not peculiar to Gülen and is another articulation of the Turkish–Islamic Synthesis. According to Özdalga (2006: 552, 560–562), Hearth of the Enlightened and Gülenists are the most articulate defenders of the notion of a Turkish Islam that 'is unique and superior in its adherence to liberal values and practices', in contrast to fundamentalist groups. The notion of a Turkish Islam has also been associated with or seen as underpinning the Turkish model or Muslim democracy, see Yavuz (2004b: 226). Gülen's efforts to differentiate between Turkish Islam and Arabised Islam also parallel efforts by different factions within the state, including the military (*Sabah* 23 January 1997).

[17] Islam has acted as a carrier of Kurdish identity similar to that of Turkish identity (Cizre 2001: 238; Kutlay 2015; Yeğen 2007). In particular, there was a strong relationship between Naqshbandism and Kurdish identity because the founder of the influential Khalidiye branch of the Naqshbandi order, Mevlana Hadid, was Kurdish (Kutlay 2015: 109). The most formidable challenge to the early Republic came from the Kurdish Naqshbandis during the Sheikh Said Rebellion in 1925, and Said Nursi, too, had been involved in Kurdish nationalism (Zürcher 2004: 169–172). Çağatay (2006: 102) argues that Kurdish nationalism was the biggest challenge to the Turkish nation-state project given that it is the only sizeable ethnically non-Turkish community in Turkey, comprising 15–20% of the population. Exemplifying this perception of the link between Islamist and Kurdish nationalism are the works of historian of Islam Neşet Çağatay (1972: 46) (1917–2000), former assistant of nationalist historian M. Fuad Köprülü and appointed member of YÖK by 1980 junta leader Kenan Evren. According to Çağatay, Said Nursi's real agenda was to destroy Turkish nationalism and establish a Kurdish state by creating Kurdish nationalism instead.

[18] Gündoğan (2012: 126–129) notes that the historical roots of this go back to the DP period in the 1950s and the co-optation of *medrese* leaders, sheikhs and tribal leaders in the south-east, which the JP and MSP continued with following the closure of DP. Such linkages also constituted part of the accusations of the 1960 junta regime against the DP.

channelled through Islamist and socialist parties from the 1960s to the late 1980s. Likewise, the 1960 junta regime was so concerned with Said Nursi's Kurdish roots that when he died in 1960 and was buried in the south-eastern city of Urfa, which had a large Kurdish population, the head of the MBK, Cemal Gürsel, out of fear Urfa would become a centre of Kurdish nationalism, ordered that his grave be relocated to Isparta under the pretence that Nursi had seen this in a dream (Koçak 2010a: 68, 194). Thereby, what has been commonly perceived as the most secular, the 1960 junta regime, was so concerned about thwarting Kurdish nationalism around Nursi that it preferred to elevate his Islamic credentials and aura. Similar lines of thinking were observable behind the 1997 military intervention, with the MGK being concerned that the 'separationist terror organisation', the PKK, was using radical Islamists to carry out its mission against Turkey (DMAK1 2 November 2012: 1068). In other words, construing Kurdish unrest as Islamist reaction marked a strategy of denial of Kurdish identity and agency, which was regarded as a bigger threat than an Islamically imbued opposition. Accordingly, similar to the interventions of different state actors against Alevism to rearticulate it within a Turkish–Islamic framework, Gülen's moves can arguably be viewed as a strategy of Turkification of the Nurcu movement that was shaped by its engagement with the nation-state project and an institutional structure that elevates both Turkish and Muslim identity.

Islamist Party Politics and the AKP's Road to Electoral Success

The MNP and the MSP: Islamist Party Mobilisation in the 1970s

A critical point in the political mobilisation of Islamist actors was the creation in 1970 of an Islamist political party, of which the AKP is a successor.[19] The MNP was spearheaded by conservative and Islamist politicians and actors, including a faction within the AP and the chair of the Hearth of the Enlightened. It was established in 1970 under the leadership of Necmettin Erbakan, who also founded the National Outlook (Millî Görüş) movement (Eligür 2010: 66). As outlined in Chapter 4, Erbakan had emerged as a voice of the provincial petty bourgeois, small provincial businessmen and traders who were

---

[19] Of the twenty-four parties founded in 1946, eight had Islamic themes in their programmes, with the MP gaining a seat in parliament (see Toprak 2005).

concerned with, and accused the AP of favouring, so-called monopoly capitalists, big business in İstanbul and İzmir, and campaigned for the reorientation of state resources towards Anatolia as well as pushing for greater ties with Muslim majority countries. In the words of Yavuz (2003: 210), the MSP campaigned for industrialisation rather than Islamisation. As a result, newspapers at the time characterised the party as the 'voice of the "oppressed Muslim masses"' (Yavuz 2003: 209). The MSP's discourse in this sense echoed the religious majoritarian logic of the state in that it sought a privileged position for the Muslim majority against a laic or Masonic minority based in İstanbul (see Chapter 4).

At the same time, the MNP's emergence was also the product of increasing political mobilisation by Turkey's various religious groups and Naqshbandi *tariqa* orders that had become organised with the anti-communism drive. A key actor behind the MNP project was Mehmet Zahid Kotku, the leader of the İskenderpaşa community, belonging to the Khalidi branch of the Naqshbandi *tariqa* order, with which Necmettin Erbakan and other prominent leaders, such as Turgut Özal (prime minister 1983–1989, president 1989–1993) and president Tayyip Erdoğan, have been affiliated. According to Yavuz (2003: 141), Kotku played an important role in spearheading the transformation of the

mosque-based community into a semipolitical movement. The mosque, in this case the İskenderpaşa Camii [mosque], was no longer a place for elders to sit and pray. It became a center for shaping young people, and many of his students, as noted, came to occupy critical positions in the higher echelons of the bureaucracy.

Kotku celebrated the establishment of the MNP by declaring that 'in the aftermath of the deposition of the Sultan Abdülhamid II, the country's governance has been taken over by Masons,[20] who are imitating the

---

[20] The roots of these conspiracy theories about Freemasons that comprise ideas about an international plot go back to at least the Ottoman Empire. Often a linkage with Jews is made, which Landau (1996: 200) notes started as part of anti-Semitic propaganda in Europe in the eighteenth century, as well as with communism (regarded as an anti-religious ideology). Within these conspiracies, Freemasons are blamed 'in conjunction with the others, of undermining religion (particularly Islam), being responsible for the French and Russian revolutions, as well as for the Young Turk coup d'etat and others', and as such, they also comprise anti-modernist or anti-Westernist reaction (Landau 1996: 194; Özman and Dede 2016: 183–184). Indeed, a prevalent theme of Islamist conspiracy theories is that the Masons and Jews within İTC undermined the rule of Abdülhamid II and caused his downfall, thereby harming the *ummah* and religion. Feeding into the narrative of victimhood of the Islamists, therefore, the Freemasons and Jews have been targeted as scapegoats for plots against Muslims and Turks within right-wing ideology (Özman and Dede 2016: 169, 183–184; Yılmaz 2017: 488, 504).

West. They are a minority. They cannot represent our nation. It is a historical duty to give the governance of the country to the real representatives of our nation by establishing [a] political party' (Eligür 2010: 86). As Yılmaz (2017: 487) has argued, 'Victimhood in relation to the rising secularist Western world and Kemalist elites is a constitutive element of the hegemonic imaginary of Turkish–Islamist ideology in Turkey. [. . .] This claim has been raised also against the Western forces, Jews, Masonic networks and their internal collaborators, particularly Kemalist elites, who have been accused of being part of a historical ploy to erode Islam's power and Islamist spirit in Turkey'. While other prominent Islamic communities, including the Qadiriyya and some arms of the Nurcus, had also backed the MNP, they subsequently withdrew support from the MSP in 1977, following a power struggle. The İskenderpaşa community, on the other hand, remained a loyal supporter of the MNP's successors until 1990, when they had a falling out with Erbakan. The Islamist MNP and its successors also enjoyed support from key factions within the state, including the Diyanet. Several Diyanet chiefs, including Lütfi Doğan (1968–1971) and Süleyman Ateş (1976–1978), were supported by and associated with the MSP, while Mustafa Sait Yazıcıoğlu (1987–1997) and the longest serving, Tayyar Altıkulaç (1978–1986), joined the AKP. On the other hand, various other *tariqa* orders, such as the Süleymancılar (see Chapter 2) and the Işıkçılar (followers of Hüseyin Hilmi Işık), as well as some Nurcu groups, continued to support the AP.

In 1971, the MNP was closed following the coup on the basis that it sought to undermine the secular state. However, generals such as Refet Ülgenalp, the general secretary of the MGK, were against the party's closure, and the Islamist leader Erbakan was allowed to return from self-enforced exile in Switzerland to reopen the party (despite it being against the constitution for the leader of a banned party to become the chairman of a new one) (Yavuz 2003: 209). Such elements of the military apparently considered the Islamist party to be a useful counterweight against not only the dominance of the AP but also, and more importantly, communism, an area of overlapping consensus between the two sides. By 1970, the leftist movement had gathered momentum, which included the spread of massive workers' strikes and stirrings among radical elements within the military. Such cooperation and collaboration between elements of the military and Islamist actors should not be considered simply an effort by a secular state to utilise and control religion to widen its hegemony. Indeed, the military, prior to 2016 and with the exception of the 1980 junta regime, has typically been portrayed as the biggest foe of Islamists, which has mirrored the official discourse of the junta leaders regarding protecting the Republic against reactionism (*irtica*).[21] As earlier chapters have revealed, even when the (also not monolithic) military may have held such objectives, it did not mean that the other side was composed simply of passive actors; rather, they possessed the agency and goals to make use of such opportunities to pursue their own agendas. Crucially, from this period of time onwards, the balance within the military also shifted towards the right, particularly following the discovery of a coup plot – the so-called Madanoğlu Junta – in early 1971 by a leftist faction within the military, including Cemal Madanoğlu, who had been a prominent member of the 1960 intervention. Concerns about the association between some officers and the radical left are considered to have played a key role in triggering the 12 March 1971 coup d'etat with the support of the Central Intelligence Agency (CIA) (Jacoby 2003: 675). Subsequent measures to purge left-leaning officers (Koelle 2000: 48–49, 56; Ulus 2010: 51–52, 59–62) from within its ranks heralded the more rightist and conservative 1980 junta, together with greater cooperation with Islamist and religious groups. Bulut (2016: 366) has claimed that under the vice-general secretary of the MGK, Hasan Sağlam, who was responsible for education under the 1980 junta regime, Islamist Fethullah Gülen continued to open colleges despite officially being on the police search list. From 1986 to 2002, Sağlam was the president of the Islamist association the İYC, which has played an important role in the expansion of religious education (see Chapter 5).

However, despite the backing provided by the military for the MSP, the party's electoral support remained relatively limited. By 1973, it had gained 11.8 per cent of the national vote, but by 1977, its support had fallen to 8.56 per cent, partly reflecting the fracturing of alliances between the different religious groups, such as the creation of the rival Islamist Order Party (Nizam Partisi, NP) by the Nurcus after they withdrew their support from the party. Neither had alliance with the Gülenists lasted, owing to a developing power struggle. Şık (2014: 52–57) has argued that not only had the MSP grown uncomfortable with the Gülenists' efforts to monopolise its supporters and infrastructure, but Gülen was critical of Erbakan's confrontational stance against the state, insisting on a more gradualist approach. Nevertheless, the MSP's influence stretched beyond its size as the party formed a coalition with the CHP in 1974 and subsequently took a key place within the right-wing National Front coalition together with the AP and the MHP from

---

[21] For example, it has been argued by scholars that, with the exception of the 1980 coup, military interventions were not legitimated or supported by religion and that, in this sense, the TIS was a break from this tradition (see Can and Bora 2004: 148).

1973 to 1980. It was during this time that it expanded its ranks within the bureaucracy and achieved key policies in the pursuit of Islamisation, including lifting of the restrictions on *imam-hatip* schools and appointing its preferred candidate, Süleyman Ateş, as the head of the Diyanet (1976–1978).

Yet, as the case of the MSP highlighted, in reality, the Islamist movement was highly fragmented and, to some extent, divided. According to Hayrettin Karaman (2015b: 242–243), before the 12 September 1980 coup, the Islamist movement, much like the left, was busy with infighting owing to internal struggles. On one level, the disputes related to strategic, and to some extent theological, differences. For instance, Islamists such as Hayrettin Karaman and Tayyar Altıkulaç of the Generation Movement (see Chapter 4), described as 'neo-Salafis', had stood at a distance from Sufi movements as well as the MSP (Kara April 2016: 55). The Generation Movement had been growing since the late 1960s and had gathered momentum with the appointment of Altıkulaç to the Diyanet in 1971 (Kara 2016: 566). Relations with the MSP and Erbakan had been difficult and tense owing to differing strategies as well as efforts to influence and incorporate *imam-hatip* graduates into their own cadres. In 1974, the Diyanet's publication of Hayrettin Karaman's updated version of a 1914 translation by Ahmet Hamdi Akseki of the works of Rashīd Rida (1865–1935), a prominent early Islamist reformist, drew the ire of various orthodox *tariqa* orders and Islamist actors. The members of the Generation Movement, including those within the Diyanet, were accused by traditionalists such as the Süleymancılar and prominent Islamists like Necip Fazıl Kısakürek of being deviants, followers of the reformist Islamists of the late Ottoman Empire such as Muhammad Abduh and Jamal al-Din al-Afghani, and of harming Islam and undermining *ahl as-sunnah* (the Sunni community) by calling for unity. Equally for the traditionalists, it was the reformist *ulema* who had engaged with political authorities in the late Ottoman Empire and helped to end the caliphate (Albayrak 1977: 366). At the same time, there was an economic dimension to the struggles related to the breaking of the monopoly of religious education of the Süleymancılar following the establishment of *imam-hatip* schools and the YİE (see Chapter 4). Karaman (2015a: 296) says that he was shocked that, despite attempts to end the divisions, the Süleymancılar went to great lengths, such as inciting the authorities, including the military, against *imam-hatip* schools and the YİE by accusing them of being against the Republic and pursuing *shari'a*. The Diyanet has also written counter-reports against the Süleymancılar (Altıkulaç 2011b: 744–746; Kara 2012: 114; Karaman 2015a: 296). Despite the fact that such reports have typically been presented as evidence of the secular state's control over the institution, in fact, they were often a product of the internal struggles within the Islamist movement. Yet, while these power struggles were at times very violent, relations were to improve significantly in the aftermath of the 1980 military intervention, possibly as the access of Islamists to the state spoils and rents grew much larger with the TIS programme.

The RP, the SP and the FP: The Rise of Islamist Parties as Mass Parties

Following the 1980 coup, the MSP faced closure yet again as political parties were shut down by the junta regime. However, together with the shifting balance of power within the state towards the nationalist conservative and Islamist coalition, the capacity of these actors to steer public policy also increased, as epitomised by the Hearth of the Enlightened's TIS programme. Crucially, while this not only provided a benign environment supporting Islamist mobilisation, it also involved an intervention to shape the contours of the Islamist movement, just as the Turkish nation-state building project had involved an attempt to sideline more traditionalist and pan-Islamist currents in favour of reformists and those who were reconciled with nationalism. Starting in the late 1960s, some Islamist currents had begun to come under the influence of pan-Islamist, and potentially anti-systemic revolutionary, discourse influenced by the Iranian Ali Shariati and the Arab Egyptian Sayyid Qutb, and they were galvanised in 1979 by the Iranian Revolution. The Turkish Islamist movement in general had shown caution towards more radical currents, largely owing to its Turkish nationalist conservative core, with mainstream Islamist circles dismissing radical Islamists as foreign elements, a delineation typically reserved for communists (Bora 2013: 527). Likewise, influential elements within the Islamist movement, including sections within the MSP, as well as some of the more traditionalist *tariqa* orders, led a vociferous campaign against modernist or reformist Islamist and Muslim Brotherhood currents such as the Nesil group (discussed in Chapter 4) (İnal and Alagöz 2016; Kara 2016: 542; Karaman 2015c). In particular, the concern about the more radical currents, which were regarded as a danger to the Turkish nation-state project, can be seen in the 1982 debates on the constitution, which took place under military auspices (Chapter 1).

Within this context, while the TIS project had been envisaged as an antidote to communism, it was also a means to solidify and entrench the long-standing cooperation between and integration of Islamists and conservative nationalists and to keep pan-Islamist or any anti-systemic currents in check. In other words, there was an effort to maintain and solidify the link between Islamism and Turkish nationalism. Yet, while both nationalism and mainstream Islamist parties such as the MSP and its successors arguably performed an absorptive function of more radical Islamist formations (Kara 2013: 33; Tuğal 2009a: 95–96), the boundaries between them were in fact fluid, and they also provided these groups with a platform and ability to pursue their agendas. Much as the Diyanet positioned itself as enlightened Islam, keeping in check superstition and *tariqa* orders (Chapter 2), Islamist actors (e.g. Gülen) and parties strategically saw fit to position themselves as moderates, offering cooperation in return for more space and resources to pursue their own agendas.

The MSP was subsequently reborn as the RP in 1983, founded by the MSP leader Erbakan and two lawyers. It was only in the late 1990s that the party began to garner widespread electoral support in transitioning towards a mass party. In the 1987 elections, it failed to cross the 10 per cent threshold, garnering only 7.2 per cent of the national vote. In 1991, it fought the parliamentary elections together with the rightist nationalist National Work Party (Milliyetçi Çalışma Partisi, MÇP, the heirs of the MHP) and received 16.9 per cent of the national vote. Şen (2010: 64) notes that, significantly, it was the leading members of the Hearth of the Enlightened who had played a key role in forging this alliance. The MSP's electoral fortunes began to change, first with success in municipal elections in 1994, when it gained 19 per cent of the vote and control of the key cities of İstanbul and Ankara, and then later, in the 1995 general election, when it emerged as the leading party, with 21.4 per cent of the national vote.

Compared with the petty bourgeois roots of the MSP, the RP attracted both the expanding Anatolian capital comprising the medium-sized and large companies that had benefited from the economic liberalisation of the 1980s and the urban poor, thanks in large part to the annihilation of the left after the 1980 coup (Şen 2010: 66). Indeed, as previous chapters have outlined, the religious field was greatly privileged and endowed with significant organisational and material resources and networks that were not afforded to alternative currents and formations. Duran and Yıldırım (2005: 233) show likewise that the membership of the Islamist trade union Hak-İş had only attracted mass membership after the military regime suspended all other labour unions, such as the leftist Confederation of Progressive Trade Unions (Devrimci İşçi Sendikaları Konfederasyonu), and allowed only the statist and right-wing Türk-İş and Islamist

Hak-İş to operate. This had also ensured the latter's support of the junta leaders.[22] Many of the themes espoused by the MSP were incorporated into the RP's programme, including the criticism of secularism, the championing of the interests of Anatolian capital, anti-Westernism, and anti-Zionism, which were packaged under the concept of the Just Order (Adil Düzen). The Just Order programme was presented as a third way between capitalism and socialism and has been described by scholars as utopian, socialistic, third worldist and populist fiction in that it comprised an economic model 'supplemented by a leftist discourse of capitalist exploitation, without using a Marxist vocabulary, combined with anti-Zionist proclamations that verged on anti-Semitism' (Toprak 2005: 182; see also Çakır 1994: 131–149; Gülalp 2001: 442; Tuğal 2002: 105–106, 2009a: 137–140; Yavuz 2003: 221–222). Tuğal (2009a: 249) notes that 'the Just Order program was not radical enough for the radicals and too radical and unrealistic for the emergent capitalist sectors within the [Islamist] movement. Therefore [. . .] the Welfare Party (RP) slowly moved away from it'.

Cognisant of constitutional restrictions, the RP had remained elusive with respect to its Islamist agenda, and the Just Order was a similarly ambiguous programme which was beset by contradictions in its emphasis on redistribution for the poor while championing private enterprise directed by the state. As an Islamist party, similar to the MSP, the predominant concern of the RP was the restructuring and Islamisation of state, society and economic relations in ways that privileged the Muslim majority. Neither was the RP's emphasis on legal pluralism, which would have consisted of different laws for different religious communities in a manner similar to the Ottoman *millet* system, reflective of a liberal democratic agenda. Influenced by the works of Islamist intellectuals such as Ali Bulaç on the so-called Medina Contract (Medina Vesikası), such a system would have involved a subdivision of communities on the basis of religion, together with the institution of an Islamic state (Toprak 2005: 182). Yet, as Tuğal (2007: 12) notes, the Just Order programme was also approached with suspicion among Islamists, who had doubts about its feasibility as well as its anti-capitalist dimensions. Indeed, the prominent Islamist and theologian Hayrettin Karaman, who is close to the AKP, was one of the organisers, alongside other prominent Islamists, of a private report that was written by a well-known Islamist economist and founding member of the İYC, Sabahattin Zaim. While

---

[22] Hak-İş did not take root among the working class when it was first established by the Islamist MSP in 1976. The military's measures in the post-1980 period therefore gave the organisation a significant boost (Duran and Yıldırım 2005: 232–233).

underlining that what these groups of Islamists regarded as the positive aspect of the Just Order programme was, in fact, a vision of an Islamic state which was not explicitly stated for fear of legal repercussions, a key criticism was that it moved away from a market economy, which was considered to be a necessary element in the Islamic economic model (Karaman 2015b: 325–333).[23] In any case, it was following the 28 February 1997 military intervention that the comparatively more pro-capitalist Islamists would come to dominate the movement and drop the Just Order programme.

Splintering in the Islamist Party and the Rise of the AKP

By the late 1990s, the Islamist movement and particularly its political party forms, mainly the RP, had come to a crossroads. Previously, the Naqshbandi, Qadiriyya and Nurcu alliance, which had given birth to the MSP, had not proved lasting. The Nurcus had abandoned the MSP in the 1970s; the Nurcu Yeni Asya offshoot maintained strong clientelist links with the AP and its successors, such as the ANAP; while the İskenderpaşa community broke with the RP in 1990 owing to a clash with Erbakan (Çakır 2002: 39). Essentially, however, divisions were related to personalities and political strategies rather than the ideological vision. Similarly, by the 1990s, the RP was again faced with the question about the direction of the party – between different strategies rather than ideological goals (Çakır 1994: 76).

The 1997 military intervention (see Chapter 1) proved to be a consequential moment for the Islamist movement in shaping the direction of future strategies. Two currents had emerged among the former members of the RP. The so-called traditionalists (Gelenekçiler) had wanted to maintain the party as an ideological cadre party, while the reformists (Yenilikçiler), comprising a newer generation of Islamists backed particularly by newly expanding Anatolian capital, had sought to convert it into a mass party capable of seizing power. The reformists, in particular, were cognisant of the experience of the 1997 military intervention, which had catalysed a process that can be described as pragmatic adaptation among the Islamists, precipitating a split in which the reformists founded the AKP and the traditionalists established the Felicity Party (Saadet Partisi, SP). The reformists thereby led the shift in the Islamist public

---

[23] Scholars such as Atasoy (2009: 6) and Hoşgör (2011: 351), on the other hand, argue that the Just Order in reality saw no contradiction between Islam and capitalism and that it was an 'articulation of the capitalist economy, technology, culture, and Islam within a state-led national economic developmentalism'.

discourse, adopting moderate language and realism, relatively speaking, to avoid confrontations with the military (Cizre and Çınar 2003: 326–327).

Crucially, the 1997 intervention, rather than purely an anti-Islamist measure by the military, furthered the rearticulation of Islamism within a neo-liberal framework and toned down its anti-Westernism. One indicator revealing the more complex nature of this so-called anti-Islamist military intervention is the continued budgetary support for Islamist organisations and foundations during the 28 February process. These included the Ahmet Yesevi Foundation, associated with the influential Naqshbandi İsmailağa community alongside the Turkish Religious Education Foundation (Türkiye Din Eğitimi Vakfı, TÜDEV), established by the MEB in 1996 but which was subsequently accused of engaging in anti-secular and anti-Atatürk activities (*Hürriyet* 4 January 2001; *Hürriyet* 6 May 2001). In particular, a key aspect of the intervention was the perceptions of the large capital groups such as TÜSİAD that saw the expansion of Islamist capital, with their vision of an Islamic union, pro-Asian and anti-Western stance and economic populism as a challenge that needed to be, in effect, put in its place (Buğra 1998: 534; Doğan 2009: 296–303). During the Refah-Yol government, state rents and major privatisation tenders were channelled towards the rival MÜSİAD members, which threatened the military traditional business rent-seeking coalitions that had formed during the ISI era and persisted despite neo-liberal restructuring. In 1997, a number of these companies were planning to enter defence industry tenders that were expected to generate a USD 100 billion market, and for the first time, Turkish firms were going to be given priority (Yankaya 2012: 33–34). Following the 28 February intervention, however, companies blacklisted as Islamist capital were excluded from military contracts, which was a stance supported by TÜSİAD. In this sense, one could see 28 February as a struggle among the different factions within the bourgeoisie (Doğan 2009: 294–305; Yankaya 2012: 33–34).

While the 28 February process thereby undercut the challenge to TÜSİAD for the time being, it also catalysed the abandonment by the RP's successors of the pseudo-socialist Just Order discourse that had comprised a critique of capitalism and its fervent anti-Western and anti-EU stance.[24] Even before the AKP, this dynamic was evident in the

---

[24] Erbakan was a proponent of an Islamic Union instead of the EU. See also interviews in *Birikim* (Birelma September 2013) with the Anti-Capitalist Muslims, a movement that gained public prominence following the Gezi Park protests in which it took part, who also argued that the 28 February intervention ended the intense debates around

adoption by the Virtue Party (Fazilet Partisi, FP) (which had won 15.4 per cent of the national vote in the 1999 general elections) of a more liberal economic programme compared with that of the RP, having abandoned the Just Order and adopting a pro-EU and human rights stance (which was nevertheless focused primarily on religious freedom).

Reflecting this pragmatism, in its early years, the AKP downplayed its Islamist roots by characterising itself as a 'conservative democratic' party adopting a pro-market, pro-Western and pro-EU stance (AK Parti 2002; Akdoğan 2003). Unlike the RP, which had sided against the US-led campaign in the 1991 Gulf War,[25] the AKP adopted a pro-US stance in 2003 by supporting the US invasion of Iraq. This contrasted with the SP, which had continued to emphasise its commitment to the National Outlook agenda (SP 3 November 2002). The AKP's strategy and adoption of a conservative democrat identity also played a crucial role in the party's ability to attract a wider base of votes, including those of centre-right parties such as the DYP and ANAP, alongside the nationalist vote (Özbudun 2006: 546; Şen 2010: 64–65). This also involved leading members of the Hearth of the Enlightened who joined the AKP, becoming ministers and parliamentarians, which reveals continuity between the National Front governments of the 1970s, ANAP and the AKP, according to Şen (2010: 65). Thanks in part to the downfall of the traditional centre-right parties, since its emergence in 2001, climb to power in 2002, and falling out with the Islamist Gülenist movement in 2013, the AKP also emerged as the primary address for Islamist actors. This involved support by the various *tariqa* orders and religious communities, including the Naqshbandi and Qadiriyya, alongside the various arms of the Nurcu movement, a feat that the MSP struggled with. In contrast, the (traditionalist) SP received just 2.49 per cent of the total vote in the general elections in 2002, 2.34 per cent in 2007 and 1.27 per cent in 2011, compared with the AKP's 34.3 per cent, 46.6 per cent and 49.8 per cent, respectively. Yet this so-called absorption of Turkish Islamism – which had never become anti-systemic or anti-capitalist – into a secular neo-liberalism did not necessarily mark a process of moderation or passive revolution,[26] as has been argued, as demonstrated by

---

capitalism among Islamist and *imam-hatip* youth, who were influenced by and reading Islamists such as Ali Shariati, as well as the abandonment of the Just Order discourse of the Islamist movement.

[25] The US-led campaign was supported by the ANAP government and also by Gülen.

[26] According to Tuğal (2007), Islamism had lost its revolutionary fervour, and radical groups were absorbed into the Welfare Party in the 1990s, becoming naturalised as part of daily life and reconciling with nationalism, traditional religion and modernity.

the AKP's Islamisation drive, including the expansion of the Diyanet's role, religious education and authoritarian politics.

This pragmatism was useful as part of the AKP's ability to become the primary, and effectively only, party of the right that supported its ascent to power following the 2002 general elections in a context of deep political and economic crisis (see Chapter 1). The 1990s were marked by party fragmentation and unstable coalition governments with a life-span of just over a year, resulting in the formation of nine cabinets between 1999 and 2002. A lack of stable government combined with populist measures, corruption and rent-seeking behaviour had precipitated four economic crises during the 1990s and catalysed one of the worst financial crises in Turkish history in 2000 to 2001. The sense of political crisis was further heightened by the conflict in the south-east of the country with the Kurdish nationalist movement, the outbreaks of sectarian violence against the Alevis, political assassinations, the unravelling of the 'deep state' with the Susurluk incident in 1996 and the state's apparent inability to cope with a major earthquake in 1999 that left thousands dead. Undoubtedly, a further element supportive of the rise of Islamist politics in this period was the global context, particularly after the 11 September 2001 attacks in the United States, and the promotion of a so-called moderate Islam against radical Islamism. The ways in which this shaped the AKP's presentation of itself internationally opened up opportunity spaces and a more receptive Western audience, and the engagement of these Islamists with various Western policy circles has been alleged by prominent Islamist actors who were involved in the establishment of the AKP.[27] Broadly, it was in this environment of changing global dynamics, domestic crisis and voter disillusionment with the traditional parties that the AKP managed to secure the first one-party majority in Parliament since 1987, appealing to and building coalitions between conservatives, nationalists and Islamists, as the major traditional parties of the right, such as the ANAP and the DYP, were effectively wiped out when they fell below the electoral threshold of 10 per cent for the first time since their establishment. The AKP has continued to successfully absorb politicians from the centre-right such as Süleyman Soylu, former head of the DP and DYP politician, and Islamist challengers such as Numan Kurtulmuş, former leader of the People's Voice Party (Halkın Sesi Partisi), who joined the governing party in 2015 and 2012, respectively.

---

[27] For example, see articles by prominent Gülenist and Islamist Ali Bulaç (22 December 2014) and actors within the National Outlook movement (*Milli Çözüm* 29 January 2015).

The growing authoritarianism of the AKP and discrediting of the Gülenist project (discussed further in Chapter 6), both strategically marketed as a moderate Islam, will prove consequential for the future direction of the face of Islamism in Turkey. Changing regime structures and conflict since the outbreak of the Arab uprisings in 2011 have opened up new avenues and spaces for violent radical and Salafist Islamists across the Middle East. Turkey's greater engagement with the Middle East under the AKP, its involvement in the Syrian conflict and its support for various Islamist opposition factions has meant an increasing spillover of these dynamics of radicalisation. Particularly since 2011, when Turkey began to host Syrian opposition groups on its soil and then closed its embassy in Damascus in March 2012, the country has come to be described as a 'jihadi highway' where fighters from across the world have taken advantage of its porous border with Syria, which is also precipitating Islamist network building domestically (Scott and Christie-Miller 2 December 2014). This has involved the growth of ISIS (the Islamic State of Iraq and Syria) on Turkish soil and the increasing recruitment of Turkish citizens, supported by a more radical-friendly environment created under the AKP (Tezcür and Çiftçi 2014). While Turkish Islamists' engagement with Salafism is not new, dating in particular to the late 1970s and the cooperation between the Diyanet and Saudi-based Rabita (Hammond 2015), there has been growing criticism, including by former members of the AKP's power circle, that Salafi extremism has been normalised with Turkey's involvement in Syria.[28]

Conclusion

While Chapter 1 elaborated why religious markers mattered in boundary building and institutional design during nation-state building, Chapters 2, 3 and 4 underlined how the persistence of these boundaries was achieved over time. The growing salience of religious markers in political and economic struggles was traced to not only this but also contingent events that shifted the balance of power within the state and facilitated the expansion of the religious field. This chapter has looked more closely at the Islamist movement, comprising a diverse coalition of factions and projects but which all unite on the common goal of Islamisation of state and society, regardless how much the content might change. In an influential article, Sakallıoğlu (1996: 231) argued that 'it is the Turkish

---

[28] An example is an article by Yusuf Müftüoğlu, who was an advisor to the former president, Abdullah Gül. www.huffingtonpost.com/yusuf-muftuoglu/salafi-extremism-turkey_b_10814254.html.

state, not the initiative and self-sustenance of grass-roots Islam, that has been the most important determinant of the political role of Islam and its relevance in politics throughout the republic'. This is correct; yet, for her, the state was ultimately a secular one, and its engagement with Islamists was intended to control and utilise religious politics for its own purposes. Instead, the proposition in this chapter is that, far from being outside the state, Islamists, conservatives or pious citizens were an organic part of the state from its inception. Far from being a periphery force and excluded from the centre or the Kemalist state, there was a symbiotic relationship between the state and Islamists, or webs of cooperation between these currents and factions within and outside the state. The very strategies of Islamist or religious factions within the state that have been there since its birth have, over time, supported Islamist mobilisation, such as through the expansion of the Diyanet and religious education.

The webs of cooperation in the Republic between rightist Islamist and conservative factions within and outside the state since the late 1940s involved their mobilisation against communism, crystallising in the Fighting Against Communism associations. This, in turn, played an important role in building and solidifying networks between different factions of the right – nationalist, Islamist, conservative – resulting in the assembling of a wide rightist front. It was these networks, factions and coalitions which became increasingly influential within the state over time, revealed by the adoption of the TIS programme by the 1980 junta regime. Equally crucial for the development of the Turkish Islamism was the engagement within the nation-state framework and military interventions which shapes an integration with Turkish nationalism and also neo-liberal capitalism.

So what explains the commonly utilised narrative of victimhood against the so-called Kemalist secularist state by the Islamist movement, which is also mirrored in the master narrative of Turkish secularism? One way of interpreting and situating this discourse is through Galip Yalman's (2002) conceptualisation of a 'dissident but hegemonic discourse'. His usage relates particularly to the neo-liberal agenda propagated following the 1980 military intervention, which he describes as (i) dissident or oppositional because it presents itself as being against a state conceived of as governing since the Ottoman era and that is cut off from society, a power in itself, and (ii) hegemonic because it presents this picture of the state as if it is reality. In the same vein, the Islamist discourse situates itself as (i) oppositional to a so-called secularist authoritarian minority Kemalist state, which is presented as being cut off from society (conceptualised as majority Muslim) and is an autonomous power in itself and (ii) a hegemonic discourse, since it has successfully presented the above point as if it is reality.

In this manner, the Islamist narrative has mirrored and subverted the official historiography of Turkish modernisation to project itself as the authentic victim and as outside of and excluded by the state, a view that has been taken on board and widely accepted by Turkish scholarship. This is reflected in the mantra of the Islamist conservatives and the AKP that the 'era of minority domination of majority is over' (AK Parti 16 June 2013; AK Parti 22 April 2014; Metiner 5 September 2013), referring to the narrative that the Kemalist, laicist civil and military bureaucracy, the 'minority-elitist tyranny regime', has oppressed the excluded (Sunni) Muslim pious majority. These practices and discourses have, therefore, involved a process of minoritisation in the sense of elites, who are ostensibly representatives of a majority, stigmatising or trying to isolate groups as inferior by depicting them as a minority (Burity 2016: 139). Within the Turkish context, 'minority' has been not just a numerical category but also negatively associated in the public psyche with an imperial intervention in the Ottoman Empire that undermined sovereignty and resulted in its breakup. Chapter 6 discusses how these narratives have been utilised in undermining anti-majoritarian checks and balances on executive power.

At the same time, these strategies of emphasising the Muslim majority reflect the embedding and reproduction of the religious majoritarianism of the nation-state project, whether through the operations of the Diyanet or through the construction of national identity. This provides a vast lexis that is readily available for Islamists to appropriate, thereby enabling parties such as the AKP to occupy the ideological centre. The AKP and Islamist utilisation of this discourse can therefore be distinguished and characterised as reflecting a type of populism that is based on a 'politics of *ressentiment* that encourages the projection of hatred onto groups or classes seen as privileged and exclusionary and as oppressors of the national "underdog"' (Kandiyoti 2014). Yılmaz (2017: 487) has argued that 'Turkish Islamist identity is deeply structured around the claim of victimhood [. . .]Turkish Islamist intellectuals have constantly promoted the idea that devout Sunni Turks from Anatolia were the real victims of the elitist top-down modernization process and modern state building', and this 'discourse of social suffering culminates in the writings of Necip Fazıl Kısakürek, which are greatly admired by President Erdoğan'. This articulation of the conservative or pious masses as an oppressed underdog can be described as the most important denominator of the Turkish right and as reflective of its quest and struggle for power (Açıkel 1996).[29] Accordingly, in much the same way as the neo-liberal agenda was portrayed as being against the state when, in fact, it was both derived from within the state and a hegemonic strategy, Islamist actors and the AKP presented Islamism as against the state. This meant that increasing Islamisation and emphasis on Muslim identity could be marketed as democratisation when, in fact, it constituted a hegemonic strategy of the right in their struggle for power within the state. As traced earlier in this chapter and in earlier chapters, the growth and success of Islamist parties should be situated within these symbiotic webs of cooperation on areas of overlapping consensus and struggle over the rest among dominant actors within the state who have different visions of the ideal polity (more Islamist vs. more Turkist, etc.).

---

[29] How Islamists use this narrative of victimhood and articulate and differentiate themselves along religious lines is evident from, for example, an influential article by Yahya Kemal (1884–1958), a leading poet, politician and diplomat of the early Republican period, which remains an important reference point for Islamists/conservatives. The article, written in 1922 and titled 'Neighbourhoods without the ezan [call to prayer]', has been reprinted in various formats since, and in 2013, the Ministry of National Education under the AKP government took the decision to include the article as part of its approved reading material for use in primary schools. The article distinguishes between Muslim neighbourhoods and ones that are regarded as being insufficiently Muslim or too Westernised: 'I say to myself, do the Turkish children that are born, grow and play in neighbourhoods such as Şişli, Kadıköy, Moda share in nationhood to the full extent? In those neighbourhoods minarets cannot be seen, the ezan cannot be heard, the Ramadan and Kandil days are not felt. How do the children see the children's dream of being a Muslim? [...] Today the majority of children are again born and grow in Muslim neighbourhoods [...] But the children of the top stratum that have civilised too much, are raised in the new neighbourhoods without the ezan and according to alafranga [European style] education and do not see the most beautiful dream of Turkish children [...] We grew up by hearing the sound of ezan amongst the trees and minarets [...] However, Turkish children raised in neighbourhoods without the minarets, ezan, and according to frenk [European] education will not remember where to return!' (Kemal 1963).

6   The Rise of the AKP and the Struggle within and for the State since 2002

The preceding chapters have shown that the rise of religio-politics in Turkey has not been a break with an authoritarian secular pattern of nation-state building. Instead, Islamist mobilisation has been the product of a dynamic struggle and competition within the state, the terms of which have been shaped by path-dependent processes occurring within the longer-term dynamics of nation-state building and contingent events. The course of the rise and increasing monopolisation of power under the AKP together with the personalisation of the regime under President Erdoğan therefore exemplifies the processes by which rightist Islamist conservative nationalist factions with state and non-state actors have come to constitute and transform one another. This chapter sets out the ways in which the AKP has engaged in 'path-dependent path-shaping' (Hausner et al. 1995) – exercising strategic choice in a structure where constraints are path-dependent, highlighting how actors are both shaped by and are shaping institutional structures and, in this case, the system of government – not only to augment religious majoritarianism of the state as outlined in previous chapters but also to affect regime transformation.

   The first section elaborates the highly majoritarian system of government (using Arend Lijphart's typology) that the AKP inherited as an element of the path-dependency of the Turkish system. On the one hand, this majoritarian system has shaped party competition and strategies by adopting a winner-takes-all logic. This has resulted in both a disdain for power-sharing and a focus on capturing the median voter to gain at least a plurality, if not the majority, of votes which has underpinned the adoption of an electorally successful political discourse that has fetishised the 'national will' and the notion of 'Muslim majority', particularly by parties of the right, including the AKP. Yet, it is because of the religious majoritarianism of the state involving the elevation of Sunni Muslim Turks as the base of the nation-state that such a political discourse can occupy the ideological centre. On the other hand, once captured by a single party, the majoritarian political framework has facilitated executive dominance, concentration and centralisation of power, owing to its unitary and centralised institutional character, its weak separation of powers and the disproportional effect of an electoral system that favours large parties. Since the AKP's ascent to power in 2002, there has been an intensification of the majoritarian framework of government that is on a par with the 1924 Constitution. Once the AKP was in power, successive electoral victories that prolonged its tenure in government also expanded the benefits accruing from incumbency, enabling the party to extend its hold and capture both formal and informal institutions. Crucially, this has, in turn, supported its ability to engage in preference-shaping strategies involving the forming of a favourable electoral base. The second section elaborates the intensification of the struggle within the state and the AKP's and President Erdoğan's push to monopolise power, focusing on the confrontation with the Gülenists and the military as the two key challengers in its path. In this sense, the 15 July 2016 coup attempt constituted a monumental event or rupture in which the struggle between different factions within the state to monopolise its resources evolved into a violent form. The third section considers the 16 April 2017 referendum and the nature of regime transformation. The final section concludes by reflecting on how the AKP's path-dependent path-shaping has resulted in a path-breaking transformation of the regime.

Turkey's Majoritarian System and the AKP's Path-Dependent Path-Shaping

The AKP's ascent to power in 2002 was widely heralded as a point of democratisation of Turkish politics. This was largely based, as elaborated above, on the master narrative of Turkish politics that 'counterpoises republican authoritarianism against democracy where democratization is, for all practical purposes, treated as coterminous with the ascent of previously marginalized Islamic actors to positions of cultural, economic and political prominence' (Kandiyoti 2012: 515). Connected to this, the party quickly arose as the poster child of the thesis of Islamist moderation, proof of the ability of Islamist parties to become democrats.[1] This was in no small part related to the series of reforms undertaken in the early years of AKP government, including measures for the civilianisation of the military; engagement with minorities, particularly the Kurds;

---

[1] Schwedler (2011: 347–350) notes that, while arguments about Islamist moderation have been made explicitly and implicitly since the 1980s and 1990s, they took centre stage in the 2000s, which also reflects the move away from 'abstract debates about the compatibility of Islam and democracy and toward empirical studies of the practices and commitments of Islamist groups' (2011: 347).

expansion of Sunni Muslim institutions and education; commitment to and continuation of liberal market policies; and the start of EU accession negotiations in 2004.[2] Particularly given the politics of the AKP's Islamist predecessors, which involved a fervent anti-EU stance and a somewhat ambiguous approach to a market economy, these policies were described as 'path-breaking' for both the Islamist movement and in relation to Turkish democratisation (Somer 2007: 1272). Likewise, the AKP's Alevi and Kurdish openings and engagements were considered equally groundbreaking for an Islamist party, especially in the case of the Alevis.[3] Based on this context, analysts declared the rise of a 'Muslim democracy' (Kuru and Stepan 2012; Nasr 2005; Yavuz 2006;)[4] or a 'conservative democracy' (Hale and Özbudun 2009), echoing the AKP's self-representation as a conservative democratic party.

Various accounts have, therefore, sought to explain the dynamics of this transformation of Islamist politics, adopting viewpoints from political economy to institutionalist perspectives and pointing to reformist leadership and external factors such as Europeanisation (Somer 2014: 247). The political economy perspectives, in particular, have emphasised the rise of a 'Muslim bourgeoisie' (Gümüşçü 2010; Kuru and Stepan 2012; Nasr 2005; Yavuz 2006), essentially borrowing from modernisation and historical sociology theoretical frameworks of democratisation in explicitly or implicitly linking capitalist development, democratisation and bourgeoisification with democratic politics. Yet, there is little explanation within these analyses of the problematic nature elaborated within the wider democratisation literature of the assumption that bourgeoisification results in a commitment to liberal democracy or that capitalist development results in democractisation.[5]

---

[2] By according to the AKP a central role in these reforms, some of these accounts have underplayed the importance of the accumulation of decades of democratic struggles by civil society actors, such as the feminist movement, in pushing some of these policies through in the early years of the AKP, which was facilitated by the context of the EU negotiations at the time. See, for instance, Arat (2010) on the civil and penal code amendments.

[3] See Chapter 3 for a critique of the Alevi openings and Çiçek (2011) for the limits of the AKP's Kurdish initiative.

[4] Kuru (December 2017) has since written, 'Contrary to the expectations of myself and many other observers, the leader of the AKP, formerly Prime Minister and currently President Tayyip Erdoğan made an authoritarian turn [...] The great expectation about Turkey becoming a model "Muslim democracy" has entirely failed. All major Turkish groups, the AKP, the Gülen movement, and the Kemalists have shared responsibility in this failure'.

[5] For examples, see Rueschemeyer et al. (1992) for the argument that the bourgeoisie are, at best, contingent democrats and Przeworski et al. (2000) for a critique of the thesis that economic development leads to democratisation.

Institutionalist perspectives instead emphasise how the behaviour of Islamists are shaped by institutional constraints and opportunities (Schwedler 2006: 11–12) and argue that moderation occurs as a result of political learning from inclusion in the political system, exclusion and/or repression, or changes in the beliefs of the leadership.[6] Accordingly, reference is made to the participation of Islamist parties in Turkish elections since the 1970s alongside military interventions, namely the 28 February 1997 post-modern coup. This, in turn, has resulted in two levels of analysis focusing on: (i) behavioural moderation, involving the party's or group's operation within a competitive institutional framework and (ii) ideological moderation, which includes reducing 'the political emphasis of religious goals' and the embracing of 'democratic norms and values' (Berland 2017: 132; Tepe 2012: 468–469).[7] The basic assumption is that behavioural moderation results in ideological moderation (Tezcür 2010: 72).

Until at least the late 2000s, much of this literature emphasised the moderation of the Islamist movement both behaviourally and ideologically. Thus, even when the authoritarian characteristics of the party were recognised, it was argued that there would be democratisation without democrats under the AKP (İnsel 2003). Particularly in the earlier scholarship, one major problem with various accounts of the AKP's transformation was that the elaboration of the causal link between inclusion, repression and exclusion of Islamist parties and ideological moderation

---

[6] These are based on a conceptualisation of moderation originally developed within the democratisation literature, particularly with reference to the experiences of moderation of Christian and socialist organisations and their political parties (Schwedler 2011: 353). For a selection of the classic texts, see Huntington (1991), Kalyvas (1996), Przeworski and Sprague (1986) and Schumpeter (1950). The theoretical problems with these iterations of the moderation thesis – inclusion, exclusion and repression – are well established within the literature. For an overview of these critiques and ways it may be addressed, see Schwedler (2006, 2011).

[7] Scholars have noted problems with definition and the slippery nature of the concept of moderation (Schwedler 2006: 2, 2011: 351; Somer 2014: 245), which has also spurred efforts to distinguish it from pragmatism, strategic action and non-confrontation (Hamid 2014: 45; Yenigün 2016: 2308). The definition of democracy is not always given, but the literature suggests a commitment to more substantial definitions of democracy that, for example, include acceptance of minority rights and protection, rather than proceduralist or minimalist definitions of democracy that require only the existence of competitive elections (for a summary of these debates, see Grugel and Bishop 2013: 20–51). Equally problematic is the moderate–radical distinction, as Schwedler (2011: 351–351) notes, given that groups may be radical on some issues and moderate on others. In addition, as Tezcür (2010: 72) points out, radical parties may have reformist or democratic agendas, but moderated radical parties may turn to collaboration with authoritarian regimes and thereby stifle democratisation.

remained limited and empirically weak.[8] Cornell pithily summarises this in his answer to the question of whether the AKP's transformation was tactical, opportunistic or sincere: 'In hindsight, arguments can be made both ways' (Cornell 2017: 25–26).[9] A further issue relates to the assumptions of inclusion or exclusion of Islamist groups in Turkey. Not only have Islamist parties been included and participating in elections since the 1970s, but the analysis above has demonstrated that they were not necessarily excluded from the state. In fact, not only is the AKP now seen as an example of an Islamist party that has 'demonstrated less moderation over time' (Berland 2017: 137) but it is also seen as overseeing radicalisation by allowing free rein for radical Islamist groups (Tezcür and Çiftçi 2014).

Further, if Islamists in Turkey were behavioural moderates, why did they not moderate ideologically as predicted and initially widely assumed? Or, in other words, what accounts for growing authoritarianism? As many have already pointed out, neither democratisation nor moderation is a 'linear and inexorable process automatically resulting from participation or socio-economic development' (Somer 2011: 511). More recently, with the AKP's increasingly authoritarian turn, focus has shifted to ideological red lines (Somer 2017) and the lack of moderation or illiberal nature of the leadership (Berland 2017: 138; Çağaptay 2017). Tezcür (2010: 82) has also pointed out the limits of ideological moderation given the hierarchical and oligarchic nature of political parties in Turkey. Equally, Tepe (2012: 482) has argued that moderation should not be considered in binary terms and that the Turkish case 'reveals that being a loyal player in the game of democracy does not necessarily translate to recognition of the rights and claims of other groups and ultimately a principled commitment to liberal democracy'. Both a (re)emphasis on ideology and the nature of political organisations are well placed. Yet, what these accounts are missing is that behavioural moderation – participation of Islamist parties in elections – has taken place in an institutional environment that is not conducive to ideological moderation

---

[8] Important exceptions include Cihan Tuğal's (2009a) work, which provides a nuanced and empirically rich analysis that employs a Gramscian framework to explain how a combination of both the rise of 'Muslim capital' and political learning from the military interventions resulted in the Islamist movement's absorption into 'secular neoliberalism' (2009a: 36–58). Tuğal (2016) has since refined this framework following the AKP's growing authoritarianism to argue that the marriage of Islamic liberalism and democracy was contingent on the external context and was challenged by the Arab uprisings from 2011.

[9] There are a plethora of examples here, but one can note the AKP's move to criminalise adultery in 2004, around the same time as it was conducting talks with the EU to begin accession negotiations.

or liberal or consensual politics.[10] To move beyond the question of whether the AKP has gone through (now several) ideological transformations or was merely acting strategically or pragmatically to achieve its goals, an examination of the political structure is important for understanding what types of opportunities and constraints shaped the practices of these agents when in power. Hence, the notion of path-dependent path-shaping offers a means to understanding not only how political structures shaped the AKP but also how the AKP has strategically acted to reshape the political structure.

The operating logic of the Turkish regime can be traced through the use of Arend Lijphart's typology of democracies. Lijphart distinguishes between majoritarian political systems, underpinned by the principle of majority rule and involving the concentration of power, and consensus democracy, where power is dispersed and decisions are made based on the widest possible consensus (Bulsara and Kissane 2009; Lijphart 1999). The application of this typology of democratic regimes to the Turkish case is not without problems given that Turkey has hardly met the criteria of a liberal democracy, as demonstrated with one such measure by the US-based and government-funded organisation Freedom House.[11] The evolution of the Freedom House index scores since its launch in 1972, displayed in Figure 18, shows that Turkey has been classified for the majority of the multi-party period as a hybrid regime, and was for the first time classified as 'Not Free' – a closed regime – in 2018. The Turkish regime type in this vein can be considered to have been a hybrid one since the transition to multi-party politics in 1950 up until the constitutional referendum in 2017, with the exception of praetorian interruptions.[12]

---

[10] Various studies, such as Wickham (2004), have argued that ideological moderation can occur in the absence of democratisation. However, these studies typically examine Islamist parties and groups in opposition and in more authoritarian settings (at least until recently) than Turkey, focusing on how they respond to political openings, as there are limited comparable cases of an Islamist party like the AKP taking and maintaining power.

[11] For further details of the methodology used to calculate scores, see the Freedom House website: https://freedomhouse.org/report/freedom-world-2015/methodology#.UuEq87 Qo71I.

[12] There have been frequent violations of the basic criteria of liberal democracy, such as freedom of speech, information, media, association and assembly, coupled with praetorian interventions and the military's tutelary role. Despite the military's recent pacification under the AKP, it has historically acted as a key veto player over the political system. Equally, the Lijphart framework cannot capture the effects of informal institutions and executive discretion over implementation in a hybrid regime such as in Turkey, where the gap between the letter of the law and what happens in reality can be wide.

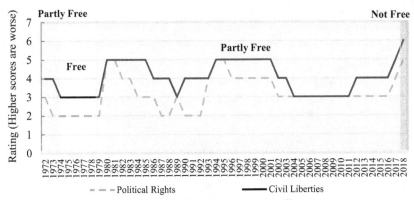

Source: Freedom House, https://freedomhouse.org/); *Political Rights and Civil Liberties are measured on a one-to-seven scale, with one representing the highest degree of Freedom and seven the lowest; Free (1.0 to 2.5), Partly Free (3.0 to 5.0), Not Free (5.5 to 7.0).

Figure 18: Political cyclicality of non-democracy in Turkey (Freedom House Democracy Index)

Nevertheless, since hybrid regimes possess both democratic and authoritarian features, the Lijphart typology offers a means of assessing long-term patterns of institutional evolution and the operating logic of the governing framework, at least until 2017. The characteristics of the two models of government are outlined in Figure 19, where the variables along the executive parties dimension focus on the nature of executive power, while the federal–unitary dimension relates to the extent to which power is devolved or fragmented within the political system as a whole.

The evolution of the Turkish political system over time, based on Lijphart's typology, is shown in Table 2 and Figure 20.[13] The foundations of Turkey's highly majoritarian system were laid by the 1924 Constitution (the longest surviving one at thirty-six years), which comprised a centralised unitary government with no checks and balances in the form of a separation of powers constraining the sovereignty of the parliamentary majority, resulting in a concentration of power in the executive that left little room for pluralism and consensual politics. Reflecting the nationalising concerns of nation-state builders, and

---

[13] For a detailed overview of this evolution and discussion of Lijphart's variables, see Lord (2012). Excluding central bank independence and referendums from the typology, Turkey's evolution under the AKP would be closer to, if not worse than, the 1950–1960 period.

Two dimensions of majoritarian vs. consensus democracy

Executive–Parties Dimension

1. Concentration of executive power in single-party majority cabinets versus executive power-sharing in broad multi-party coalitions.

2. Executive legislative relationships in which the executive is dominant versus executive–legislative balance of power.

3. Two-party versus multi-party systems.

4. Majoritarian and disproportional electoral systems versus proportional representation.

5. Pluralist interest group systems with free-for-all competition among groups versus coordinated and 'corporatist' interest group systems aimed at compromise and concertation.

Federal–Unitary Dimension

1. Unitary and centralized government versus federal and decentralized government.

2. Concentration of legislative power in a unicameral legislature versus division of legislative power between two equally strong but differently constituted houses.

3. Flexible constitutions that can be amended by simple majorities versus rigid constitutions that can be changed only by extraordinary majorities.

4. Systems in which legislatures have the final word on the constitutionality of their own legislation versus systems in which laws are subject to a judicial review of their constitutionality by supreme or constitutional courts. constitutional courts.

5. Exclusively representative democracy versus systems where there is direct involvement of citizens in decision making. decision making.

6. Central banks that are dependent on the executive versus independent central banks.

Source: Lijphart 1999; Bulsara and Kissane 2009.

Figure 19: Two dimensions of majoritarian vs. consensus democracy

lacking a liberal legacy, the majoritarian system established in 1924 subsequently bound the evolution of the framework and nature of political competition in the Republic and thereby constituted a key element of path-dependency within the Turkish political system. Since the transition to multi-partism in 1946 was achieved with only minimal legal changes, the 1950–1960 period shown in Figure 20 reflects the highly majoritarian system established in 1924 which underpinned the growing authoritarianism experienced under the DP government.

Turkey has adopted a new constitution twice since 1924 – in 1961 and 1982 – and both of these were initiated and adopted under military rule. However, the latter has been amended substantially, most recently in a manner that has transformed the entire regime, in April 2017. The 1961 Constitution was an exception to the extent that it saw the introduction of a number of anti-majoritarian checks and balances, including greater separation of powers, together with the establishment of a

Table 2: *Summary of institutional change in Turkey, 1950–2016*

Variable	Majoritarian	Consensus	1950–1960	1961–1980	1983–2001	2002–2016	Shift to majoritarianism
Executive-party dimension							
1. Party system	Two-party system	Multi-party system	1.4	2.8	3.5	2.4	Yes (distorted by electoral 10% threshold)
2. Cabinets	Single-party majority cabinets system	Power-sharing multi-party coalitions	100%	50%	59%	100%	Yes (since 1961)
3. Executive–legislative	Dominant executive	Executive–legislative balance of power	3.4	1.0	1.4	3.0	Yes (since 1961)
4. Electoral system	Disproportional first-past-the-post system	Proportional representation	26.0	5.4	11.9	11.6	Yes (since 1961)
5. Interest groups	Informal pluralist interest group interaction	Coordination and corporatist interest group interaction	Low-1	Low-1	Low-1	Low-1	Always majoritarian/ no change
Federal–unitary dimension							
6. Federal–unitary	Unitary and centralised government	Federal and decentralised government	Unitary-1	Unitary-1	Unitary-1	Unitary-1	Always majoritarian/ no change
7. Unicameralism–bicameralism	Concentration of power in a unicameral legislature	Division of power between two equally strong but differently constituted houses	Unicameral-1	Bicameral-2	Unicameral-1	Unicameral-1	Always majoritarian except for 1961–1980 interlude

Table 2: (*cont.*)

Variable	Majoritarian	Consensus	1950–1960	1961–1980	1983–2001	2002–2016	Shift to majoritarianism
8. Constitutional amendment[a]	Flexible constitution	Rigid constitution	Flexible-1	Rigid-3	Medium-2	Medium-2	Yes
9. Direct democracy (number of referendums)	Low level of public involvement in decision-making	High level of public involvement in decision-making	0	1	3	2	No
10. Legislative supremacy	Legislature has the final word on the constitutionality of legislation	Legislation subject to judicial review of constraint by a supreme or constitutional court	Low-1	High-3	Medium-2	Medium-Low-1.5	Yes
11. Central bank independence[b]	Dependent on the executive	Independent central bank	Low-1	Low-1	Low-1	Medium-2	No

[a] Turkey's 1924 Constitution was rigid in the sense that it specified the need for a two-thirds majority for constitutional changes, but the lack of a constitutional court meant there was nobody to check the parliament and the constitutionality of laws until a high court was established by the 1961 Constitution.

[b] Central bank independence granted in April 2001.

Note: Calculations are my own.

Sources: Bulsara and Kissane (2009); Constitutional Court of Turkey (Anayasa Mahkemesi); Flinders (2005); Gallagher and Mitchell (2008); Kalaycioğlu (2005); Laakso and Taagepera (1979); Lijphart (1999); Özbudun (2009); Taagepera (2002; Turkish Grand National Assembly of Turkey (Tükiye Büyük Millet Meclisi); Turkish Statistical Institute (İstatistik Kurumu)

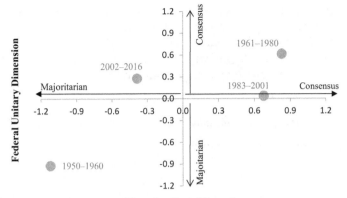

Executive Party Dimension

References: Lijphart 1999; Flinders 2005; Bulsara and Kissane 2009; Taagepera 2002; Özbudun 2009; Kalaycıoğlu 2005; Laakso and Taagepera 1979; Gallagher and Mitchell 2008.
Data sources from Anayasa Mahkemesi [Constitutional Court of Turkey]; TUIK; TBMM. Calculations are my own.

Figure 20: Majoritarian vs. consensus democracy (composite z-scores)

Constitutional Court, a bicameral legislature and a PR electoral system.[14] These changes played an important role in shifting the political system closer to a consensual model, as highlighted in Figure 20. Yet, since the 1961 changes were not themselves underpinned by a more pluralistic or consensus-driven vision (see Chapter 1), they were easily chipped away at and undermined. Figure 20 shows how majoritarianism has been augmented since the military interventions of 1971 and 1980 as well as under the AKP. The 1982 Constitution moved Turkey closer to semi-presidentialism by establishing a stronger role for the president, introducing a 10 per cent electoral threshold and restricting the role of the Constitutional Court. Despite the introduction of countervailing institutions in 1961, therefore, the governing system remained majoritarian at heart, reflecting the persistence of a centralised and unitary administration, the concentration of power in the executive branch and a weak parliament. Such a political framework has been consequential in influencing the nature of political competition, and thereby AKP party

---

[14] Characterising the Constitutional Court, for example, as typifying a consensual institution within the Turkish context is therefore problematic given its constitutive ideological underpinnings. Indeed, the court has acted in a manner antithetical to deepening consensus democracy in being 'selectively activist, protecting social and political members of a particular coalition but not other political groups' and adopting a narrow take on civil liberties, which has entailed blocking the increased representation of excluded groups (Belge 2006: 656).

strategies, and also in enabling the accumulation of power once the party was able to form a single-party government in 2002. How the AKP has shifted the political system closer to the 1924 Constitution over the period 2002 to 2016 (shown in Table 2) in a manner that is not fully captured by this typology is traced later in this section.

Party Competition and Strategies in Majoritarian Systems

Turkey's majoritarian system has framed the nature of political competition by influencing how political parties and actors shape their strategies in two ways. On the one hand, the system has given rise to a disdain for power-sharing (as highlighted by Figure 21), which is reflected in the predominance of minimal winning coalitions that resulted in short-lived and unstable governments during periods of voter volatility and party system fragmentation in the 1960s, 1970s and 1990s. This is because the winner-takes-all dynamic of the system means that once a majority party is able to capture power, it is empowered to dominate both formal as well as informal institutions through the control of clientelistic networks. Political competition, therefore, is dominated by zero-sum logic as political actors remain focused on capturing the state, which remains the centre of rent distribution. On the other hand, the majoritarian system also influences the types of appeal that parties make in order to maximise their votes. According to Hechter (2004: 427–428), a characteristic of governments in

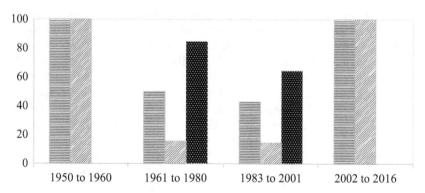

≣ Average of minimal winning, minority and one-party cabinets, %

▨ One party government only, %

✿ Coalition government only, %

Sources: (Taagepera 2002; 'Election of Representatives Statistics' from the Turkish Statistical Institute [Türkiye İstatistik Kurumu, TUIK]   ; Kalaycıoğlu 2005). Calculations are my own.

Figure 21: A disdain for power-sharing

majoritarian systems is that they 'tend to produce collective goods that are earmarked for the electorally dominant cultural group' since 'the median voter belongs to the cultural majority: he speaks the dominant language, attends the dominant church, and lives in a core rather than a peripheral region'. In contrast, within consensus democracies which adopt PR electoral systems, party systems are more likely to incorporate and reflect differences rather than a focus on and concern with a dominant majority (Hechter 2004: 427–428). This is because, within PR systems, all votes count, which provides opportunities for smaller constituencies to share power, unlike in majoritarian systems where a plurality of the vote is sufficient for a party to form a single-party government.

Reflecting the majoritarianism of the system, in the multi-party era, the dominant and mainstream political parties, particularly on the right, including the AKP, have generally shaped their political strategies and campaigns based on an appeal to the Muslim Turkish majority, omitting the actual heterogeneity of the community differentiated by various factors including language, class, sect and religion. More specifically, this has involved the utilisation of a populist discourse appealing to and emphasising the prominence of the national will, which has been a staple of the Turkish right, comprising the traditional centre-right, nationalists, Islamists and conservatives since the DP government in the 1950s (Bora 2013: 532). As Yavuz (2003: 208) notes, the preference for the term *milli* (national) by the right reflects the fact that it 'connotes [a] religious ethnos [...] [it] easily could be used interchangeably with "religiously defined community"'. The national will therefore stipulates a monolithic and homogenous idea of the nation, defined largely as a Sunni (Hanefi) Muslim majority (Taşkın 2008: 66), and at the same time is underpinned by the vision of this constructed bloc's uninhibited sovereignty in a manner that resonates with the religious majoritarian logic of the nation-state. Taşkın argues that it was this 'tendency of silencing the real plurality of the people in favour of a fictitious notion of a unified nation [that] was also the underlying reason of Menderes' increasing authoritarianism in the late 1950s' (2008: 66). Likewise, the AKP has dismissed any checks on the national will as anti-democratic, elitist or secularist Kemalist and as being against the (Sunni) Muslim masses.

In continuity with this tradition, the AKP has extensively utilised the national will discourse and the notion of the Muslim majority in its professed struggle against military-bureaucratic tutelage to silence the opposition (Akman 2010; Bora 2013: 532). Its 2023 vision (AK Parti 30 September 2012) declaration also underlines the party's predominant concern with restructuring the state and society, characterised as predominantly Muslim, in a way that is essentially more favourable for the Muslim majority. The push for the centralisation of power in the office of the executive, whether by undermining the independence of the judiciary or by changing the governing system to an executive presidency, has been legitimised by the AKP by reference to the national will, together with their (essentially majoritarian) fetishisation of the ballot box as reflecting this will. Equally, the AKP has sought to discredit any opposition to its rule, such as during the Gezi Park protests in 2013, by characterising it as an attack on the national will and as an effort by the minority to tyrannise the majority (AK Parti 16 June 2013). Particularly since the emergence of mass opposition to the AKP in 2013, this has involved repressive minoritisation and securitisation of various communities and individuals, including Alevis, atheists and leftists, or anyone depicted as having a so-called Kemalist–CHP mentality, who are stigmatised and portrayed as a national security threat. Such practices have, in turn, catalysed a hardening of group boundaries, precipitating an ethnicisation of politics along sectarian lines, which has seen increasing reports of discrimination and hate crimes against the Alevi community under AKP rule.

Capturing Formal Institutions

The success of this electoral strategy of targeting the median voter has been an important aspect of the AKP's emergence as a dominant party, as conservatism (*muhafazakarlık*) has translated into large successes at the polls (Kalaycıoğlu 2007: 233), winning between 34.3 and 49.8 per cent of the vote in the general elections held between 2002 and November 2015. Indeed, parties of the right – including the centre-right DP, AP, ANAP, and DYP, which comprised both liberal and conservative tendencies; the Islamist AKP and its predecessors, the MSP and RP; and the far-right CKMP and MHP – have been electorally hegemonic ever since the transition to multi-partism, holding governmental power 84 per cent of the time between 1950 and 2017. This has included forming single-party cabinets (60 per cent of the time), rightist coalitions (8 per cent) or participating in coalition cabinets with the (purportedly) centre-left CHP, SHP and DSP (22 per cent). The centre-left parties have been able to form single-party governments less than 0.01 per cent of the time, while there was both direct and indirect (through technocratic government) military rule over 11 per cent of this period. This has meant that parties on the right of the ideological spectrum have enjoyed the benefits of incumbency and state power to engage in preference-shaping of the electorate, bringing the median voters' position 'closer to the party's fixed policy stance, for longer than any other political party or group with differing ideological visions' (Dunleavy 1992: 135). Majoritarian systems, according to Dunleavy (1992: 128–141), are in particular more amenable to preference-shaping strategies as compared to preference-accommodating strategies (in which parties reflect public opinion) adopted by political parties because governments are empowered by the unitary and centralised state, weak separation of powers, majoritarian electoral system, weak enforcement of codified constraints and strong ideological commitments.

Within this context, the AKP emerged as what can be described as a 'dominant party' (Dunleavy 2010; Gümüşçü 2013; Sartori 2005: 193; D. White 2011: 658–659) between 2002 and 2017, which is reflected not just in its ability to win consecutive electoral majorities and its long tenure in government, but also because it has a core bloc of highly loyal voters and is widely recognised as having greater effectiveness and appeal than parties in the opposition (Gümüşçü 2013; Müftüler-Baç and Keyman 2012; Musil 2015). A crucial factor that helps the AKP to transform its electoral appeal into a majority in Parliament is Turkey's mixed plurality PR electoral system. At least until the widely rigged April 2017 constitutional referendum, the AKP's dominance resembled other cases of dominant party regimes, such as the Institutional Revolutionary Party (Partido Revolucionario Institucional, IRP) in Mexico (until 2000). The party's ability to form long-lasting and durable majority one-party governments was helped not only by a degree of electoral manipulation but also by a combination of both popular support and a disproportional electoral system that favours large parties (Domínguez and Poiré 2013).

The electoral system, despite being a PR framework, tends to produce a majoritarian outcome owing to the 10 per cent threshold that discriminates against smaller parties and those who are geographically concentrated. The majoritarian outcome of the framework was most clearly observed in the 2002 general election, when the AKP's 34 per cent of the national vote translated into a 66 per cent seat share, leaving 45 per cent of the national vote unrepresented in Parliament (see Figure 22). Without a 10 per cent threshold, the AKP's vote share in the 2002 and 2007 elections would have garnered 35 per cent and 47 per cent of the total seats, compared with the respective 66 per cent and 62 per cent received under the current system. The current electoral framework, adopted in 1982, has therefore had a significantly disproportionate effect in favouring the largest party, as Tables 3 and 4 demonstrate. This is indicated by the high values for the AKP in terms of all three calculated disproportionality indicators, which measure the divergence between the vote share and the final allocation of seats.[15] A closer look at variations in the disproportionality with regard to individual parties (Table 3) shows

---

[15] The Loosemore–Hanby Index measures the disproportionality for a particular election. The Rae Index is a measure of disproportionality for a particular party. Gallagher describes the least squares index as a 'happy medium' between the two (1991).

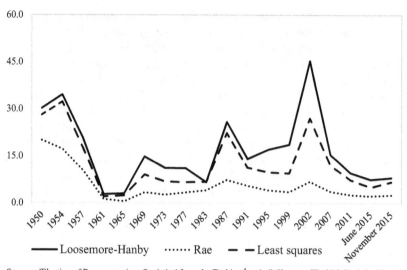

Sources: 'Election of Representatives Statistics' from the Türkiye İstatistik Kurumu [Turkish Statistical Institute, TUIK]. Calculations are mine.

Figure 22: Disproportionality in Turkish parliamentary elections

that the current electoral system clearly favours larger parties, allocating a larger boost to the incumbent party than others. For example, the score for the Loosemore–Hanby Index, which measures the difference between votes cast and seats gained for a particular election (with larger numbers indicating greater disproportionality), was 31.7 for the AKP in 2002, 15.4 in 2007, 9.6 in 2011, 6 in June 2015 and 8.1 in November 2015, compared with 13.0 for the CHP in 2002, 0.5 in 2007, 1.4 in 2011, 1.0 in June 2015 and 1.0 in November 2015. Yet, at the same time, the declining levels of disproportionality suggest that the AKP's electoral dominance was not simply a product of the majoritarian electoral system. For instance, the Loosemore–Hanby Index has declined from a high of 45.3 in 2002, indicating a high level of disproportionality, to 8.1 in the November 2015 election (Table 4). Similarly, the Rae Index (Gallagher 1991: 38–41), which measures disproportionality for a particular party rather than for a particular election, has declined from 6.8 in 2002, indicating higher levels of disproportionality, to 2.5 in November 2015 (Table 4). How the monopolisation of rent distribution channels has enhanced the AKP's preference-shaping capacities, and thereby its elect-oral appeal, will be discussed later in the chapter.

These electoral successes for the AKP in turn resulted in the augmen-tation of majoritarianism of the political system on a par with the

Table 3: *Electoral disproportionality in Turkish parliamentary elections across parties, 2002–2015*

	Votes %	Seats %	Loosemore–Hanby	Rae	Least squares
2002 General Elections					
AKP	34.3	66.0	31.7	31.7	1006.1
CHP	19.4	32.4	13.0	13.0	168.3
MHP	8.4	0.0	8.4	8.4	69.9
Independents	1.0	1.6	0.6		0.4
Total			90.7	88.5	1465.1
Value of Index			**45.3**	**6.8**	**27.1**
2007 General Elections					
AKP	46.6	62.0	15.4	15.4	237.7
CHP	20.9	20.4	0.5	0.5	0.3
MHP	14.3	12.9	1.4	1.4	1.9
Independents	5.2	4.7	0.2		0.3
Total			30.8	29.1	1465.1
Value of Index			**15.4**	**3.6**	**11.9**
2011 General Elections					
AKP	49.8	59.5	9.6	9.6	92.6
CHP	26.0	24.5	1.4	1.4	2.1
MHP	13.0	9.6	3.4	3.4	11.4
Independents	6.6	6.4	0.2		0.0
Total			19.2	17.9	109.4
Value of Index			**9.6**	**2.6**	**7.4**
June 2015 General Elections					
AKP	40.9	46.9	6.0	6.0	36.5
CHP	25.0	24.0	1.0	1.0	0.9
MHP	25.0	14.5	1.7	1.7	3.0
HDP	13.1	14.5	1.4	1.4	2.0
Total			14.9	13.3	49.7
Value of Index			**7.5**	**2.2**	**5.0**
November 2015 General Elections					
AKP	49.5	57.6	8.1	8.1	66.2
CHP	25.3	24.4	1.0	1.0	0.9
MHP	11.9	7.3	4.6	4.6	21.4
HDP	10.8	10.7	0.0	0.0	0.0
Total			16.1	15.0	90.5
Value of Index			**8.1**	**2.5**	**6.7**

Higher levels indicate higher disproportionality on the Loosemore–Hanby Index.
Note: Calculations are mine.
Source: 'Election of Representatives Statistics' from the Turkish Statistical Institute (Türkiye İstatistik Kurumu, TUIK).

Table 4: *Electoral disproportionality in Turkish parliamentary elections, 2002–2015*

	Loosemore–Hanby	Rae	Least squares
1950	30.2	20.0	28.1
1954	34.6	17.2	32.2
1957	20.9	10.4	17.7
1961	2.8	1.2	2.0
1965	3.0	0.5	2.3
1969	14.8	3.4	9.0
1973	11.1	2.6	6.8
1977	11.1	3.3	6.6
1983	6.6	4.0	6.7
1987	25.8	7.3	22.3
1991	14.1	5.5	11.3
1995	17.1	4.0	9.8
1999	18.6	3.5	9.5
2002	45.3	6.8	27.1
2007	15.4	3.6	11.9
2011	9.6	2.6	7.4
June 2015	7.5	2.2	5.0
November 2015	8.1	2.5	6.7

Higher levels indicate higher disproportionality on the Loosemore–Hanby Index.
Note: Calculations are mine.
Source: 'Election of Representatives Statistics' from the Turkish Statistical Institute (Türkiye İstatistik Kurumu, TUIK).

1924 Constitution on both the executive-party and federal–unitary dimensions that comprise Lijphart's typology (see Figure 19). On the executive-party dimension, the move towards greater majoritarianism reflected executive dominance, which resulted from the AKP's ability to form long-lasting, durable cabinets thanks to the disproportionate electoral system. On the other hand, while there was no change in the overall unitary and unicameral state structure, the shift in the federal–unitary dimension of the Lijphart framework, as observed in Figure 18 and Table 2, was still an underrepresentation of the extent of the majoritarian turn during the AKP period. This was chiefly the result of the erosion of judicial review and the separation of powers that have effectively curbed any checks on executive power and, eventually, an undermining of the constitutional and legal order.[16] A critical point marking

---

[16] Examples include the unlawful arrest of opposition actors and the illegal and unconstitutional decision by the Supreme Election Board (Yüksek Seçim Kurulu, YSK) to accept unstamped ballots on 16 April 2017.

the beginning of significant encroachments on the judiciary was the 2010 constitutional referendum that garnered a 58 per cent yes vote and that was pushed by the AKP in alliance with the Gülenists.[17] The referendum was a highly polarising moment in which what have been described as liberal intellectual circles and academics, together with the AKP, defended the reforms as deepening democratisation and pluralism within the judiciary by undermining what was described as the Kemalist orientation of the judiciary. Instead, the reforms not only expanded Gülenist cadres within the judiciary but also augmented parliamentary and presidential control over the appointment process by increasing the number of appointed seats at the Constitutional Court and the Supreme Board of Judges and Prosecutors (Hâkimler ve Savcılar Yüksek Kurulu, HSYK), which effectively allowed the AKP government to make its own appointees. Consequently, the so-called democratic control over the judiciary in fact resonated more closely with the majoritarianism of the 1924 to 1960 period in augmenting the power of the parliamentary majority.

However, a further erosion of the separation of powers occurred following the launch of the corruption probe into the AKP in December 2013 by Gülenist elements (see Monopolising Informal Institutions) within the judiciary. In order to undermine the Gülenists within the judiciary and thwart the corruption investigation, the AKP not only moved to reverse some of the reforms adopted in 2010 but also increased its own control over judicial appointments.[18] Under the February 2014 law passed by the AKP, the powers of the HSYK were largely transferred to the justice minister, thereby further undermining independence from the executive. For example, the justice minister, who was already the head of the HSYK council, was granted more direct control over the organisation and its decision-making and over the judicial academy (involving the training of judges) and was given powers to authorise investigations into misconduct and disciplinary matters concerning council members. The law was also designed to remove various levels of personnel within the HSYK, thereby opening the way for restaffing with

---

[17] The constitutional amendments included (i) increasing the number of Constitutional Court judges from eleven permanent and four substitute to seventeen, with Parliament selecting three members and the president choosing the rest from a list of candidates put forward by various bodies; (ii) expanding the members of the Supreme Board of Judges and Prosecutors (Hâkimler ve Savcılar Yüksek Kurulu, HSYK) from seven to twenty-two members and (iii) restricting the ability of the courts to review administrative matters by stating that judicial power cannot be used as a review of expediency. For further details see SGEU (2010).

[18] The law was criticised internationally by human rights organisations and the EU. See, for instance, Human Rights Watch 21 February 2014. For reporting of the purge and government allegations, see *Sabah* (5 February 2014) and Yetkin (3 May 2014).

pro-government appointees. In addition, the authority to launch investigations against council members raised the possibility of politically motivated decisions and increased pressure on the council. This law was later partially annulled by the Constitutional Court, which ruled as unconstitutional the transfer of powers, such as the justice minister's control over HSYK's inspection and control board and sweeping powers over personnel and appointments to HSYK departments, but maintained the executive's new control over the Turkish Justice Academy (Türkiye Adalet Akademisi). However, the decision had no retroactive effect: the AKP justice minister simply declared that he disagreed with the decision and did not overturn the removal of around 600 personnel replaced by new appointees of the government. Subsequently, the HSYK launched disciplinary and criminal investigations into a number of the prosecutors involved in the December 2013 corruption investigations, which were duly closed by late 2014.[19] The political authority's control over the judiciary was further expanded following the 16 April 2017 constitutional referendum (see Monopolising Informal Institutions).[20]

This centralisation of power in the executive branch was also revealed by the undermining of the autonomy of regulatory agencies during the later years of AKP rule. Alongside ongoing questions about central bank independence,[21] a statutory decree introduced in 2011 (KHK/649 No: 28028) granted ministries greater executive oversight of regulatory bodies such as the Banking Regulation and Supervision Agency (Bankacilik Düzenleme ve Denetleme Kurulu, BDDK), the Capital Markets Board of Turkey (Sermaye Piyasası Kurulu, SPK), the Radio and Television Supreme Council (Radyo ve Televizyon Üst Kurulu, RTÜK) and the Competition Authority (Rekabet Kurumu), thereby undermining their autonomy, which for some had been granted following the 2000–2001 crisis.[22] In addition, the curbing of the powers of public

---

[19] Leaked corruption tapes (confirmed by the government) have also shown direct intervention in judicial matters by the executive, including in appointments and decisions against government adversaries (*Evrensel* 5 March 2014).

[20] One example of this is the refusal by the lower courts to act on the Constitutional Court ruling to release two prominent writers, Ahmet Altan and Mehmet Altan, who were jailed in 2016 on allegations of links to the Gülenists and involvement in the 15 July coup attempt (PEN 24 January 2018).

[21] Gradual personalisation and centralisation of power during the AKP period have led to the erosion of the autonomy of the central bank. This is evidenced by the (widely recognised) political pressure on interest rate setting and the government's purges of the central bank's (and other agencies') personnel since December 2013 as a result of the allegation that they are Gülenists.

[22] For example, the AKP's deputy chairman has stated that the regulatory bodies have to be in line with the AKP's 2023 Vision and the political will, which are 'responsible to the people' (*Radikal* 14 May 2014).

professional organisations in 2013 was driven by efforts to undermine the Chamber of Turkish Architects and Engineers (Türk Mühendis ve Mimar Odaları Birliği, TMMOB), which, owing to its ability to grant final approval for urban planning projects, was a constraint on executive action. The bounds of executive action were further expanded by the declaration of the state of emergency (SoE) in July 2016, which enabled the AKP regime to engage in dramatic restructuring of the bureaucracy through executive decrees. As of the start of 2018, 110,778 civil servants had been dismissed, according to AKP's Deputy Prime Minister Bekir Bozdağ (*Deutsche Welle* 31 January 2018).

Monopolising Informal Institutions

This capture of formal institutions of government by the AKP (as outlined earlier) has, in turn, enabled the party to monopolise informal institutions, including clientelistic networks and mechanisms of rent distribution.[23] The privileged access to state resources, control over patronage distribution and overall ability of regimes to politicise public resources and prop up their rule by sharing the spoils of power which accrue from and are the benefits of incumbency are crucial in explaining the longevity of dominant parties within both democratic and authoritarian settings (Gandhi and Lust-Okar 2009; Geddes 1999; Levitsky and Way 2012: 869; Magaloni 2008; Reuter and Turovsky 2014; Smith 2005: 422). Through the use of patronage, therefore, the AKP has been able to influence expectations and, hence, political behaviour, with those on the receiving end being cautious about losing their benefits if they withdraw support. The AKP's ability to engage in 'partisan social engineering', involving privileging of pro-government constituencies, as a facet of its 'preference-shaping strategies' (Dunleavy 1992) has been better buttressed the longer it has been able to stay in power. Table 5 contains a summary – albeit not an exhaustive one – of key legislative changes adopted during the AKP period (2002–2014) that have augmented the centralisation and the regime's patronage powers and, in turn, facilitated strategic action or path-shaping to reconfigure the institutional environment. Frequent adjustments to public procurement laws, the expansion of the role of the Mass Housing Association (Toplu Konut İdaresi, TOKI) and the particularistic and partisan nature of the distribution of social welfare services (outlined later in this chapter) are some of the key

---

[23] Patronage politics has been a persistent feature of the Turkish political system, with political parties seeking to enhance their voter base through rent distribution (Sayari 2011).

Table 5: *Key legislation expanding the monopoly over rent distribution, 2002–2014*

Year	Law	Summary of law and changes introduced	Impact
2002–2014	Public Procurement Law (No. 4734) amendments.	The law established rules with regards to participation and awarding of public tenders and has been changed twenty-nine times between 2000 and 2013 and amended over 100 times (Buğra and Savaşkan 2014: 79). Some of the key amendments have included the extension of exemptions. For example, changes include a domestic price advantage clause to privilege domestic tenders over foreign ones; the exemption of purchases of the state-owned Turkish Coal and Mine Management Company; exemptions of purchases of goods and services for research and development projects; exemption of certain contract award procedures by the Turkish Petroleum Corporation; and exemption of acquisition of goods and services of the agencies under the Law Establishing the Regional Development Agencies and Investment Support and Promotion Agency.	• Expanding and monopolising patronage channels; influence over private sector and rent distribution. • Centralisation of rent distribution channels.

2004	In 2004, TOKI, which had previously been under the Ministry of Public Works, was tied to the Prime Ministry (Law No. 5162/2).	TOKI was established in 1984 (Law 2985) for the purpose of constructing social housing, but its powers and role were expanded under the AKP to provide not just housing for middle- and low-income individuals but also to offer luxury housing and services. The new expanded remit of the company includes engaging in profit-oriented projects with the private sector, transformation of squatter areas and undertaking urban planning. In addition, the responsibilities and power, as well as a land bank of 64.5 million square metres of the Urban Land Office, were transferred to it (Gündoğdu and Gough 2013).	• Expanding and monopolising patronage channels; TOKI is an important rent distribution mechanism. • Centralisation of rent distribution channels.
2010, 2014	Laws related to the Constitutional Court and the HSYK (Law No. 6087, adopted 2010; Law No. 6524, passed in 2014).	The constitutional changes adopted with the 12 September 2010 referendum include those related to the composition of the Constitutional Court and the HSYK. The 2014 amendments to the law granted more direct control over the HSYK and decision-making within the body to the Ministry of Justice. This law was partially overturned by a ruling of the Constitutional Court, although the Ministry of Justice retains control over the Turkish Justice Academy, which is tasked with the training of judges.	• Centralisation and undermining of separation of powers by expanding executive intervention in judicial processes.

Table 5: (*cont.*)

Year	Law	Summary of law and changes introduced	Impact
2011	Decree with the Force of Law (Statutory Decree) No. 28028 on reorganisation of public bodies.	The decree grants ministries the power of supervision over regulatory bodies such as the Banking Regulation and Supervision Agency, the Capital Markets Board of Turkey, the Radio and Television Supreme Council and the Competition Authority, thereby ending their autonomy, which had been supported in the aftermath of the 2001–2002 crisis by international organisations such as the International Monetary Fund.	• Undermining autonomy of regulatory agencies; increasing majoritarianism and centralisation of power in executive branch.
2012	Metropolitan City Law (No. 6360).	The new law involves redistricting whereby provincial cities with a population of more than 750,000 will be turned into metropolitan cities with borders extended to the province border, thereby absorbing formerly separate villages.	• Further centralisation by reducing local government in villages and involves redistricting to bolster the party's electoral strength by, for example, adding conservative municipalities to opposition-run districts to dilute and weaken their voter strength.
2012	Circular 2012/15, No. 28325, stipulating that the Prime Ministry has to give permission regarding usage and allocation of immovables of public sector organisations.	This circular gives the Prime Ministry authority to grant mining licences.	• Expanding monopoly over patronage channels and centralisation of power: The power to decide on granting of licences and revoking them is another means of intervening in the private sector and supporting or punishing businesses.

mechanisms that have supported AKP partisan social engineering, thereby bolstering and solidifying the party's electoral support and executive power. These changes have facilitated the emergence of new rent-seeking coalitions consisting of construction companies, which contrasts with the big business–bureaucracy–military coalitions (Demir 2005) of former periods. An example of a businessman who has gained prominence under the AKP is the owner of Kalyon Group, Hasan Kalyoncu, who has been closely associated with the Islamist movement, playing a role in the establishment of the AKP and launching a Naqshbandi foundation. The Kalyon Group has been a key beneficiary of public tenders under the AKP, having been awarded major infrastructure projects worth an estimated TRY 100 billion (*Hürriyet* 20 December 2013), including the construction of a third airport, TOKI projects, metro construction and the Taksim pedestrianisation project (*Radikal* 28 September 2012). In turn, the Kalyon Group has supported the government through the purchase of the *Sabah* and ATV media groups, which have adopted a strongly pro-government line. Equally, these relationships have been facilitated, as Buğra and Savaşkan (2014: 79) note, by the frequent alterations to the Public Procurement Law, which had been changed twenty-nine times between 2000 and 2013 and amended over 100 times. Increasing the number of exemptions enabled the AKP to intervene to advantage favoured capital groups and businessmen.[24] According to Public Procurement Agency statistics, around 32 per cent of procurement contracts were exempted from the Public Procurement Law in 2013, with 36 per cent exempted in 2012. This rose from 23 per cent in 2005, with an upward trend observable since 2008. Exemptions account for around 10 per cent of the value of total public procurement. In addition, just less than half of state-owned enterprise tenders have been exempted. Gürakar (2016: v) has provided systematic evidence of favouritism in public procurement in Turkey by analysing contracts awarded between 2004 and 2011 and contends that it is 'one of the most influential tools [...] to touch upon the very lives of the voters through for instance social housing projects and municipal services, and [...] to create a business elite through procuring these construction work projects and municipal services from the "politically connected" private sector firms' (2016: v).

Another key mechanism of the patronage politics utilised by the AKP is TOKI, which was transferred to the Prime Ministry from the Ministry of Public Works in 2004. TOKI was established in 1984 for the

---

[24] For an extensive and detailed discussion of the new business links and groups, see Buğra and Savaşkan (2012: 53–58) and (Gürakar 2016).

construction of social housing, but its powers and role were expanded under the AKP to include the provision of not just housing for middle- and low-income earners but also of luxury housing and services, which has involved engaging in profit-oriented projects with the private sector as well as undertaking urban planning through the transformation of squatter neighbourhoods (Gündoğdu and Gough 2013: 18–19). TOKI's expansive urban planning powers and access to public land means that partnerships are highly profitable for the private sector, thereby making it a major source of rent distribution. For example, together with a local authority, TOKI can simply mark out an area as requiring 'urban regeneration', often leaving tenants with little say about vacating their property, and 'in this way, the inner city squatter areas are cleared and redeveloped for luxury housing, with the MHA [TOKI] as well as developers reaping the profit' (Gündoğdu and Gough 2013: 20).

Other legislation and government decisions that have expanded the mechanisms of rent distribution under the AKP include the 2B Forest Law in 2012, the 2013 law allowing the exemption of major infrastructure projects from environmental impact assessments (EIAs) and the granting to the Prime Ministry the sole authority to provide mining licences. The power to decide on the granting and revoking of licences is another means of intervening in the private sector and supporting or punishing businesses, and it has been deployed by the AKP against rivals. Aside from the utilisation of state mechanisms to intervene in the private sector to privilege pro-government business groups, social welfare provision forms another leg of rent distribution mechanisms. In the AKP era, the established social security regime for the formal sector has been eroded by neoliberal policies, while clientelistic and arbitrary distributions to the informal sectors have been emphasised (Buğra and Candaş 2011: 525–526; Buğra and Keyder 2006: 221–227; Köse and Bahçe 2009). The expansion of this clientelistic social welfare regime in areas such as the health sector, the distribution of free school books and cash payments to the poor have also translated into political benefits for the AKP in terms of increasing the party's voter base.[25] An example of this is the rapid growth in coal distribution to poor families since it was initiated by the AKP in 2003, from 1.09 million to 2.1 million families by 2016 (Figure 23).

The particularistic and partisan nature of this type of distribution of social welfare services was underlined during the 2014 local elections when the AKP mayor of Ankara pledged to give priority in the provision

---

[25] For further discussion and a description of the mechanics of the AKP's social policies, see Köse and Bahçe (2009: 492–508), Buğra (2013: 233–255) and Topak (2012: 280–281).

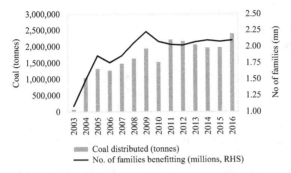

Sources: Türkiye Kömür İşletmeleri Kurumu [General Directorate of Turkish Coal, TKİ].

Figure 23: Distribution of coal to families as social welfare provision

of services to the areas that voted for him (*Bugün* 5 April 2014) as well as frequent reports of withdrawal of public services from anti-government or Alevi neighbourhoods. Partisan social engineering and the ways in which the AKP has intervened in changing social and economic positions are also suggested by the differentiation of perceptions of economic well being among voters, which was highlighted by a survey conducted by KONDA (16 April 2014), a Turkish public opinion research and consultancy company, following the 30 March 2014 local elections. According to the survey, while 52 per cent of AKP voters stated that they expected their economic position to improve over the next year, this compared with 19 per cent for CHP voters, 20 per cent for BDP voters and 20 per cent for MHP voters, and while 36 per cent of CHP, 32 per cent of MHP and 31 per cent of BDP voters said they expected a deterioration, this was just 7 per cent for AKP voters. Similarly, in terms of the improvement in economic position experienced over the past year, 36 per cent of AKP voters said they saw an improvement, compared with just 8 per cent for CHP, 12 per cent for MHP and 11 per cent for BDP voters. In turn, only 12 per cent of AKP voters said that their situation had worsened, compared with 42 per cent of CHP, 32 per cent of MHP and 38 per cent of BDP voters.

The Intensification of the Struggle within the State

The AKP and the Military

Not captured by the Lijphart typology was the struggle with the military and its changing institutional role within the Turkish political system that defined the period between 2002 and 2011. The military, as self-designated guardians of the state and Republic, has played a central role in Turkish political life as a type of veto player or tutelary power. It has staged multiple coups since 1960, when it established and formalised its role as guardian with the creation of the MGK as a mechanism through which to communicate views to the civilian authorities and formulate national security policy. The remit of the MGK was expanded following subsequent interventions in 1971 and 1980, resulting in the formalisation of a 'dual system of executive decision making' (Sakallıoğlu 1997: 158). By 1997, the military did not have to declare a coup with tanks but instead issued a memorandum that eventually forced the resignation of the Islamist-led coalition government. Yet, since 2001, a series of legal structural changes that effected a shift in the balance of power in civil–military relations were a result of Turkey's EU accession process and the reforms undertaken since the decision to extend candidate status to Turkey at the 1999 EU Helsinki Summit. The series of conditionalities for accession, as summarised in the Copenhagen Criteria, involved the requirement for Turkey to end the military's involvement in politics. Following this, a series of reforms were enacted, including the redefinition of the MGK's role back to more of an advisory capacity rather than an executive decision maker; the adjustment of the composition of the MGK to include greater numbers of civilians; the introduction of increased civilian supervision of military expenditures; the ending of its involvement in various civilian agencies such as the RTÜK and the YÖK; and the abolition of various powers and departments within the general secretariat, which curbed the military's ability to conduct 'psychological operations' (Cizre 2008: 138; Gürsoy 2011: 295–296; Michaud-Emin 2007).

However, despite the significance of these reforms, a 2007 e-memorandum appeared to kick-start a new struggle between the military and the Islamist AKP and also showed that legal structural change alone was not sufficient to contain the military's power.[26] Yet, as outlined in Chapter 5, to see the ensuing struggle as one between two ideologically opposed and clearly defined unitary actors, or more plainly, as a secular–Islamist confrontation, would be a misleading and narrow perspective. The symbiotic webs of cooperation and collaboration between the military and Islamist political parties and actors, together with the changing composition of the military since 1971 and Gülenist inroads into its cadres since the 1980s, which were exposed by the 2016 coup attempt

---

[26] Gürsoy (2011: 296–297) argues that the reduced role of the MGK as an instrument of intervention was a crucial reason for the attempt failing.

(see Erdoğan vs. Gülen), are evidence not only that the military is not a monolithic entity but also that it comprised elements and factions that had common cause with the AKP. In the struggle for power within the state, the AKP, together with its Gülenist allies, successfully hit back at factions within the military after 2007, as senior military members, as well as journalists and politicians, were accused of conspiring against the government and were arrested and put on trial under what has been called the Ergenekon investigations. These concerted efforts against the military were characterised as marking the civilianisation of the institution (Bardakçı 2013: 425; Gürsoy 2011: 297), although the 2016 coup attempt suggests that rather than an end to the military tutelage over civilian politics, this process resulted in the expansion of Gülenist cadres within the military. These increasing inroads of the Gülenist cadres thereby had effectively sidelined a key veto player within the political system, providing the AKP with room to manoeuvre and power that its predecessors in the multi-party period, with the exception of the toppled DP in the 1950s, never had.

Since the July 2016 coup attempt, there has been a major overhaul of the legal framework for civil–military relations. This has included significant changes to military education, such as the closing of military high schools and the establishment of a National Defence University, the rector of which will be chosen by the president.[27] Crucially, the commanders of the navy, land and air forces have been tied directly to the Ministry of National Defence, which will be able to issue orders outside the chain of command. Finally, a further key change has been introduced into the composition of the Higher Military Council (Yüksek Askeri Şura, YAŞ), which has seen its number of civilian members increase to ten and its military members fall from twelve to four. It remains to be seen whether these extensive institutional purges of the military personnel will contribute to significant pacification of the military or at least the expansion of President Erdoğan's influence over it.

Erdoğan vs. Gülen

As much as the AKP's standoff with the military defined the early years of AKP rule, particularly between 2002 and 2010, the period since 2011 has been characterised by the escalating struggle with its former partner, the Gülenists. The Gülen movement, together with its leader, Fethullah Gülen, who has been in self-imposed exile in the state of Pennsylvania

---

[27] In October 2016, President Recep Tayyip Erdoğan appointed a pro-government columnist, Professor Erhan Afyoncu, to head this institution.

in the United States since 1999, was named the key culprit of the 15 July 2016 attempted coup, which is an accusation that remains contested. In any case, this event has revealed the most violent fracturing within the Islamist movement in modern Turkish history.

The AKP and Gülenists' Fruitful Alliance in Its Early Years

Despite their common and overlapping goals, the AKP–Gülen coalition was initially tentative and cautious. Gülen had typically maintained some distance from Islamist parties, reflecting not necessarily ideological differences but, rather, strategic ones (see Chapter 5). At the same time, the RP cadres, along with other groups in the Islamist movement, had been critical of Gülen for support of the 1997 military intervention and also accused him of working with the military and CIA against the Islamist movement under the guise of promoting moderate Islam against radicalism (Çakır 2002: 113–116; Şık 2014: 125–130). Yet, the AKP and Gülen built a powerful alliance in 2002 that lasted until it began to crack around 2011 and publicly fell apart in December 2013. A confluence of factors underpinned this alliance. For one, thanks to its extensive domestic and international network of schools, business operations and missionary and lobbying activities, the Gülenists had built a carefully managed reputation as a moderate Muslim force. This proved highly valuable for the AKP in the initial years of the alliance. Seufert (2014: 17) argues that the alliance offered a means for the AKP to, in effect, appear as moderates and also have access to Gülenist networks in the bureaucracy that had been established over the years.[28] Indeed, these cadres proved immensely useful in the battles with the military and against the AKP's opponents. As Ali Bayramoğlu, a columnist in the pro-AKP daily *Yeni Şafak*, comments,

---

[28] One of the most important accounts of the establishment of Gülenist cadres within the bureaucracy is provided by award-winning investigative journalist Ahmet Şık (2012). He was first imprisoned by prosecutors in 2011 for his work about the Gülenists, and copies of his book were seized by the authorities and banned. Another writer-journalist, Nedim Şener, who was investigating what he alleged were the links between the police officers responsible for the Ergenekon investigation (believed to be Gülenists) and the murder of the Armenian journalist Hrant Dink in 2007, was also arrested at the same time. It is widely believed that the arrests were the work of Gülenist bureaucrats. Against a backdrop of the continued alliance between the AKP and Gülenists at that time, Recep Tayyip Erdoğan, who was the then prime minister, appeared to approve of the arrest by likening Şık's book to a 'bomb' (*T24* 10 June 2011). Despite the subsequent fallout between the two allies, Şık – who had published another work tracing the alliance between the AKP and Gülenists – was again arrested following the 15 July coup attempt over his social media posts and articles and has been accused of 'helping and being a member of terrorist groups' (*Hürriyet Daily News* 13 December 2017).

In its dispute with the military, the judiciary and the universities, the AKP had recourse to no other instrument than to this network created by the [Gülen] movement within the police force, which had been formed by the latter for the purpose of undermining the power of the military [within the State] in order to protect itself. (Bayramoğlu 21 February 2012; translation from Seufert 2014: 17)

Since the 1970s, Gülen had enjoyed support from different factions within the state and from prominent political actors (see Chapter 5), but his efforts to place his own cadres within the military had faced resistance, too. Between 1983 and 2014, some 400 people were dismissed from the Turkish Armed Forces (Türk Silahlı Kuvvetleri, TSK) (Bozan 20 July 2016). The importance of the AKP alliance is revealed by the fact that, from 2003 onwards, there were no further dismissals from the military based on Gülenist affiliation (Bozan 20 July 2016). Crucially, according to the former chief of staff, İlker Başbuğ (2008–2010), during this process of expansion, the Gülenists also pushed out other religious communities within the military, such as a prominent Nurcu offshoot known as the Mehmet Kurdoğlu group (Başbuğ 2016: 30). Still, the alliance was to step up following the AKP's first confrontation with the military in 2007 over the presidential office, of particular importance given the president's veto powers and his role in bureaucratic appointments. The party's successful manoeuvring of the crisis and eventual capture of the presidency to which it elected its own candidate, Abdullah Gül, meant that it had effectively removed both a key veto power within the system and further obstructions to the systematic formation of both AKP and Gülenist cadres within the bureaucracy.[29] Between 2008 and 2014, the AKP, together with the Gülenists within the judiciary and security forces, cooperated in a campaign against the military in which hundreds of senior military officials, including Başbuğ, journalists and opposition politicians, were imprisoned under the Ergenekon and Balyoz (Sledgehammer) trials, alleging the existence of a deep state clandestine

---

[29] The Constitutional Court had effectively machinated a block of the AKP's attempts to elect its own candidate, Abdullah Gül, to the presidential office following the end of tenure of Ahmet Necdet Sezer (2000–2007), the former head of the Constitutional Court, who had been a highly activist president in using his power of veto against the AKP government. Sezer holds the record for the most number of vetoes, totalling seventy-three laws. Conversely, the AKP-affiliated former president, Abdullah Gül, vetoed only four out of 836 laws between 2007 and 2014. On 27 April 2007, the military released a so-called e-memorandum that was regarded as a clear move against the AKP. Yet the challenge was met by the party through the calling of snap parliamentary elections, which were held on 22 July, following which the AKP was able to elect Gül as president, while a constitutional referendum on electoral reform on 21 October 2007 introduced a directly elected president, moving the country towards a presidential system.

organisation that was plotting a coup against the AKP government. Many of the verdicts were reversed in the course of 2014, after the falling out between the two allies, and all 236 suspects in the Sledgehammer case were released that June following a Constitutional Court ruling that the evidence presented by the prosecution had been fabricated.[30] Consequently, the AKP was able to emerge as the dominant actor within the system by eroding the tutelary power and role of the generals, while the Gülenists were able to free up cadres to fill with their own members (Cizre 10 August 2016). Many of the top-ranking generals who were accused of participating in the 15 July coup attempt were the same ones who came to the fore following the Balyoz and Ergenekon trials (*Cumhuriyet* 10 December 2016; Ergin 22 July 2016).

Alongside the struggle with the military, significant inroads were made into capturing the judiciary, which for a long time had been an ideological battleground with the Constitutional Court, described as a 'bastion of secularism'. In July 2008, the AKP had narrowly escaped, by one vote, a closure case against the party that was being considered by the Constitutional Court, while the higher court had struck down a legal amendment on the headscarf ban in July 2008 on the basis that it contravened the fundamental principles of the Republic.[31] Marking the apogee of the alliance with the AKP, Gülen publicly endorsed the constitutional referendum in September 2010, which passed with 58 per cent of the vote and was to effectively further facilitate Gülenist and AKP control over the judiciary.

The Emerging Power Struggle and Faltering of the Alliance from 2010 to 2013

Signs of a fracture in the alliance were evident from around 2010, and one can discern two interlinked areas of antagonism, differing political strategies and, crucially, a power struggle, rather than a fundamental ideological divergence. These are illuminated by three developments over this period: (i) disagreement over foreign policy strategies, (ii) competition over the spoils of power with the AKP's 2011 election win and (iii) Gülenist attacks against the AKP over their handling of the Kurdish matter.

First, foreign policy and the nature and depth of the relationship with the United States were revealed as an area of contention with the unfolding of the Gaza flotilla incident in 2010. A diplomatic crisis broke out after a flotilla arranged for by a number of organisations, including

---

[30] The last defendants of the Ergenekon case were acquitted in 2017 (*Al-Monitor* 12 April 2017).

[31] See Note 37.

the pro-government İHH, headed to Gaza to break the blockade were stopped and raided by Israeli forces, which resulted in the killing of ten Turkish citizens. What was significant in terms of Gülen's reaction was his public criticism of the AKP government's support for the flotilla – which was quite unprecedented at the time. Gülen's pro-US (and pro-Israel) positioning has been cited from different quarters and by the AKP regime as evidence of his close relations with the American state and intelligence, particularly given the fact that former CIA officers had supported his green card application in the United States. Dani Rodrik (30 July 2016), a Harvard professor of economics whose father-in-law, retired general Çetin Doğan, was imprisoned and subsequently acquitted under the Ergenekon investigations, states in this vein that

It is not farfetched to think that there are some groups in the [US] administration – perhaps in the intelligence branches – who have been protecting Gülen because they think he is useful to US foreign policy interests. This could be because Gülen's brand/mask of moderate Islam is a rare thing in that part of the world.

Either way, Gülen's links with the US administration and perceptions that the United States backed the coup attempt on 15 July 2016 remain a rare matter of agreement among the highly polarised Turkish public, and it has been used by the AKP regime to feed conspiracy theories about an international plot against it.

The subsequent intensification of the competition between the two sides became increasingly evident following the June 2011 general election, which gave the AKP its third successive win with 47 per cent of the vote. The disquiet from the Gülenist camp was most evident from the flurry of articles in the movement's media by affiliated columnists, as well as those by Gülen himself, implicitly accusing the AKP government and Erdoğan of the dangers of 'hubris' (Ünal 11 September 2011). Opposition journalists have claimed that a key reason for the upset was that, given his electoral popularity, Erdoğan no longer felt he needed the alliance and refused to bow to the demands by Gülenists for more lawmakers to be elected under the AKP ticket.

However, by September 2011, the fracturing between the two allies appeared to have deepened, as revealed by the leaking of secret negotiations that were conducted in 2005 between the National Intelligence Organisation (Milli İstihbarat Teşkilatı, MİT) and the Union of Communities in Kurdistan (Koma Civakên Kurdistan, KCK), an umbrella group founded by and comprising the PKK. In particular, the move by the allegedly Gülenist state prosecutors to subpoena Hakan Fidan on his engagement with the KCK in February 2012 was viewed by Erdoğan as a direct threat to himself as the then prime minister who had ordered the negotiations (Gürsel 18 November 2013). Erdoğan subsequently blocked the subpoena through a change in the law (No. 6778) that required investigations by MİT personnel to have the permission of the prime minister. The Fidan crisis has been regarded and portrayed by the AKP as evidence of Gülen's highly anti-Kurdish stance, given his staunch Turkish nationalism (see Chapter 5). However, beyond the Kurdish matter, the move against Fidan also coincided with criticism of the spy chief from elements of the US establishment and media in relation to Turkey's role in busting the Iranian sanctions regime. In any case, it marked an intensification of the struggle over the capture of the country's security and intelligence institutions.

Following the MİT crisis in February 2012, Erdoğan hit back by targeting Gülen's vast education empire, a key source of income for the movement. News emerged in November 2013 that the government was preparing a bill to target Gülenist university preparation schools, and this was passed in March 2014. By late 2013, the struggle had escalated to the extent that seasoned observers were describing it as 'open war' (Gürsel 18 November 2013). One arena of the conflict was the newspaper columns of the media outfits close to, or owned by, each side, in which Gülenists and AKP supporters were fundamentally focused not on scriptures or ideology but rather on the nature of the Turkish state and who its rightful owners were, revealing the struggle between them over the state's mechanisms of power and rent distribution.

From Allies to Parallel State to FETÖ

The date 17 December 2013 marks a major point in the struggle when allegedly Gülenist prosecutors launched a corruption investigation into senior members of the government and a closely associated businessman accused of money laundering to circumvent the Iranian sanctions regime.[32] Coupled with a stream of recordings which were anonymously disseminated on social media and websites, the prime minister and his

---

[32] The corruption investigations and the subsequent leaking of evidence of arms shipments to Syrian opposition fighters in January 2014 (Tastekin 20 January 2014) followed allegations from US media sources that Turkey was helping to break Iranian sanctions and charting an overly independent foreign policy in Syria (Ignatius 16 October 2013; *Wall Street Journal* 10 October 2013). One of the prime suspects, the Iranian-born businessman Reza Zarrab, was arrested during a trip to the United States in March 2016. During his testimony, he implicated Erdoğan in money laundering and Iran sanctions busting (*New York Times* 3 January 2018). Connected to this case, in January 2018, Mehmet Hakan Atilla, a Turkish banker and executive of Turkey's majority state-owned Halkbank, was convicted in US courts for taking part in a scheme to evade US sanctions against Iran.

immediate family were directly implicated in the corruption allegations. Although four ministers were effectively forced to resign owing to public outrage, Erdoğan was able to successfully manoeuvre this challenge partly by presenting it as an externally orchestrated coup against Turkey, and he managed to receive 43 per cent of the popular vote in the March 2014 local elections and 52 per cent of the vote in the presidential election on 10 August 2014. From that point, Erdoğan stepped up his purge of the bureaucracy and extended his reach over the judiciary while attacking the financial power of the Gülenists, as the fight against what came to be designated as a 'parallel state'[33] took centre stage. In a telling moment, Erdoğan vented his frustration in a public speech when he directed this question to his former allies: 'What did you ask that you didn't get?' He also warned that they would 'enter their [the Gülenists'] caves and [. . .] they will pay the price' (BBC 31 March 2014). This was followed in December 2014 by a warrant issued for Gülen under the Parallel State Operation investigation (Paralel Devlet Operasyonu) for founding of an armed terror group, while a new operation against him and the movement's members, now designated as Fethullah Gülen Terrorist Organisation (Fethullahçı Terör Örgütü, FETÖ), was kick-started in December 2015 by the Ankara Public Prosecutor's Office.

The 15 July Coup Attempt: Purges and Opposition Crackdown

The precise flow of events and reasons for the coup attempt on 15 July 2016, which resulted in 241 casualties and 2,196 wounded, remain a mystery. In part thanks to the government's propagation of its own narrative, a widespread consensus has emerged among the population in Turkey over the AKP's claim that the mastermind of the plot was Gülen. However, together with the AKP's lack of cooperation in the parliamentary committee for the investigation of the coup attempt, and the fact that senior Gülenists in various positions have been left untouched, many questions remain unanswered. There are several theories about what happened that night. One is that the Gülenists were expecting a widespread crackdown on their affiliates within the military following the 30 August Supreme Military Council (Yüksek Askeri Şura) meeting and believed they had little to lose if they pushed for absolute power. Another claim is that the coup attempt was initially within the chain of command, and the plotters comprised Gülenists, so-called Kemalists and others

---

[33] Similar to references to the existence of a so-called deep state in Turkey, the notion of a parallel state refers to allegations of groups operating within the state outside the control of and unaccountable to elected bodies.

opposed to the AKP, but that this alliance faltered owing to the stance of the chief of the land forces, who commands more than 100,000 soldiers.[34] Indeed, in the end, the military high command remained loyal to the government, which was critical to the coup's failure, while the civil resistance, galvanised by the Diyanet, also worked against the putschists. On the other hand, some, including the head of the main opposition party, the CHP, argue that 15 July was a controlled coup and that the government knew in advance that it would take place, subsequently using it to expand its control over the state and purge all opposition.[35]

Either way, the coup attempt, described as a 'gift from God' by President Erdoğan, offered the government carte blanche to not only carry out a widespread purge and crackdown on all opposition but, at the same time, to transform the regime, expanding its hold over the state. On 20 July, the AKP regime declared an SoE for three months, which has continued to be renewed with no clear end in sight. Crucially, the president has been empowered by the SoE to preside over the cabinet, issuing decrees that bypass Parliament and cannot go to appeal at the Constitutional Court. The decrees have been heavily criticised by international human rights organisations for conflicting with basic human rights, including provisions that enable dismissals from public service without investigation, confiscation of property without judicial review, incommunicado detentions and police custody of up to 30 days (Human Rights Watch 2017). There has also been a crackdown on freedom of information, assembly and association, with many leftist, Kurdish, Alevi and non-Gülenist opposition organisations, plus media and politicians, being targeted.[36]

The extensive purges have not only pointed precisely to the question of the nature of the state but also revealed that the Gülenists formed a major power bloc within it. As of January 2018, based on thirteen SoE decrees since July 2016, approximately 114,674 public sector workers had been

---

[34] For examples of these types of arguments and an overview of some of the unanswered questions, see Şık (17 August 2016; 13 December 2016) and parts of a report by the European Union's Intelligence and Situation Centre (EU INTCEN) leaked to the media (*The Times* 17 January 2017).

[35] Şık (10 November 2016) has pointed to articles by pro-government columnists about the possibility of a Gülenist coup plot several months before 15 July 2016.

[36] These include the jailing of pro-Kurdish HDP politicians, the replacement of elected heads of municipalities in the south-east with appointed trustees, the closure of Alevi media channels and the detention of Alevi community leaders. The second decree, for instance, closed down forty-five papers, sixteen television stations, fifteen journals and magazines, three news agencies, twenty-three radio stations and twenty-nine publishing companies, including the Human Rights Foundation of Turkey. For a useful roundup of events, see the Council of Europe Monitoring Committee reports on Turkey (12 December 2016).

dismissed (around 4 per cent of total public personnel, excluding military, as of December 2016), under 4,000 of whom were subsequently returned to their jobs. Of these, 29 per cent were from the MEB, 20 per cent from the General Directorate of Security, 7 per cent from the Ministry of Health, 5 per cent from universities, 5 per cent from the Ministry of Justice, 3 per cent from the gendarmerie, 3 per cent from the Diyanet, 4 per cent from the HSYK and Constitutional Court and 4 per cent from municipalities. According to a statement by the interior minister, Süleyman Soylu, in April 2017, some 113,260 individuals were taken into custody on allegations of having links with FETÖ, of which 47,155 were arrested, and of those, 23 per cent were police, 16 per cent were soldiers, 0.4 per cent were military generals, 5 per cent were judges and prosecutors and 56 per cent were civilians (*Anadolu Agency* 2 April 2017). Crucially, based on December 2016 total public personnel numbers, this amounts to the imprisonment of 17 per cent of all judges and prosecutors. Investigative journalist Ahmet Şık suggests that Gülenists comprised around 40 per cent of the judiciary, based on the 2014 HSYK elections, when pro-Gülenist candidates received more than 5,000 votes (Şık 17 August 2016). These figures do not reflect the many thousands who have been suspended (estimated at 76,000 in October 2016) or are under investigation (European Commission Progress Reports 2016: 16). Personnel figures from the TSK also show that, as of October 2016, a third of the total military personnel had been dismissed, resulting in a drop from 518,166 to 355,212. Around half of the 358 generals and admirals were detained. Former military members who were imprisoned during the Ergenekon trials estimate that up to 80 per cent of soldiers who became army officers in the last nine or ten years may be Gülenists (Bozan 21 July 2016). In the indictment prepared by the Ankara public prosecutor, a former Gülenist, Kemalettin Özdemir, is said to have claimed that some 60 per cent to 80 per cent of the TSK may be Gülenists (Bozan 21 July 2016).

The ongoing purges also raise the question of what will replace the Gülenist cadres. The AKP's so-called drive to 'clean' the Gülenists also marks the most systematic and extensive transformation of the bureaucracy since the establishment of the Republic, which absorbed many Ottoman bureaucrats and civil servants within the new state. Alongside the personalisation of the regime under Erdoğan, there is evidence of what Kandiyoti (2016: 38–39) has described as the increasing 'transmutation of the state' in which various religious orders are establishing their own fiefdoms of patronage, competing for power, not unlike failed states such as Iraq. Just such a warning about various *tariqa* orders seeking to replace the Gülenists within the bureaucracy was made by a member of the Diyanet's DİYK, Prof Mustafa Öztürk. For instance, the Naqshbandi Menzil *tariqa* order has allegedly been growing within the Ministry of Health and Department for Social Welfare, while an orthodox Nurcu group called the Kurdoğlus are reportedly targeting military posts (*Birgün* 29 October 2016). Together with their common agendas, expectations of such new opportunities also underpin the continued support if the AKP by *tariqa* orders, revealed by their backing of the constitutional referendum in April 2017 (*Duvar* 12 April 2017).

Regime Change and the 16 April 2017 Constitutional Referendum

In the AKP's push for the monopolisation of power, its alliance with Gülen and the subsequent falling out proved to be decisive milestones. The AKP's initial collaboration with the Gülenists to undercut factions within the military (through the Ergenekon investigations), and its subsequent fallout and campaign against Gülenists involving the deployment of the narrative of fighting against the 'parallel state', or 'FETÖ' threat, has contributed to the suspension and undermining of the constitutional order. The results from these dynamics, together with a stepping up of a violent campaign against Kurds in the south-east of the country, paved the way for President Erdoğan to push regime change towards a so-called Turkish-style presidential system on 16 April 2017. Conducted under the SoE, which meant a further curtailment of basic freedoms, including the freedom of association, as well as the ongoing clampdown on free speech and the media[37] meant that, even more so when compared with previous polls, the referendum was not conducted on a level playing field and was not free and fair. The referendum stands as the most disputed poll since the transition to multi-partism in 1946, rejected as illegitimate by mainstream opposition parties owing to indications of extensive vote-rigging identified by a number of independent domestic and international election monitors.[38] The last-minute and illegal decision by the Supreme Election Board (Yüksek Seçim Kurulu, YSK) to accept unstamped ballot papers, thereby opening the doors to ballot stuffing, on the AKP's demand, by the body's own admission (BBC 16 April 2017), was testament to the suspension of constitutional order. The AKP's

---

[37] For example, Turkey ranks 149th out of 180 countries in the Reporters without Borders World Press Freedom Index (http://en.rsf.org/).

[38] See the Organization for Security and Co-operation in Europe (OSCE) 17 April 2017 report for an overview and assessment of the election. It concludes that 'fundamental freedoms essential to a genuinely democratic process were curtailed' and notes that the YSK decision to change the ballot validity criteria undermined an 'important safeguard'.

ability to ride roughshod over such institutions likely contributed to a 51.4 per cent yes vote. The constitutional changes introduced by the referendum were essentially a means to put a legal veneer on the increasing undermining of the rule of law or, in other words, 'de jure formality to a de facto situation' (Cizre 2017) of regime change into a form of highly authoritarian and personalised rule under President Erdoğan.

The 16 April referendum thereby marked a decisive moment in modern Turkish history, ending the country's parliamentary tradition, which dates to the first Ottoman constitution adopted in 1876. The push for a presidential system was a common demand of parties on the political right, reflecting their majoritarian politics, but it gained further currency following the 1982 Constitution and especially the 2007 constitutional referendum. Turkey began its move away from parliamentarism with the 1982 Constitution imposed by the junta regime, which introduced both a strong presidency and various changes to inhibit autonomous legislative action and encourage autonomous executive action through various mechanisms, including:

- the use of executive decrees to bypass Parliament (although later, they did need to be approved by Parliament);
- restrictions on the use of parliamentary investigations and interpellations used largely by opposition parties to delay or prevent bills in the pre-1980 period (Gençkaya 1999: 2–21); and
- the introduction of extra-budgetary funds giving the executive branch considerable fiscal power outside parliamentary supervision, which acted as a major channel of rent distribution (Demir 2005: 676) and thus augmented the prize and power of office.

The 1980 junta regime had envisaged the presidential office as (its) guardian of the state, in keeping with the designation of the president as national chief during the later years of the single-party era. Accordingly, the president was granted significant powers, chiefly of veto and of appointment (Article 104), despite having minimal legal accountability (Article 105) (Kalaycıoğlu 2005: 128). How the system operationalised depended heavily on the personalities in office, with the partisan presidencies of Özal and Demirel using the presidential office as an alternative locus of decision-making and Sezer's presidency from 2000 to 2007 seeing the return to a more parliamentary system. Nonetheless, the importance of capturing presidential office was particularly underscored during the active presidency of Ahmet Necdet Sezer (2000–2007), a former head of the Constitutional Court who vetoed a record seventy-three laws by the AKP (compared with four by the AKP's presidential nominee and former party member, Abdullah Gül). Sezer also referred twenty-six laws to the Constitutional Court (Gül referred none) and blocked a number of AKP nominations to crucial bureaucratic posts. It was the AKP's bid to nominate its own candidate to the presidency in 2007 that saw the escalation of the struggle with elements of the military (see The AKP and Gülenists' Fruitful Alliance in its Early Years) and the Constitutional Court, to which the AKP responded with a constitutional referendum moving the country closer to presidentialism. The 2007 constitutional referendum introduced a hybrid parliamentary–presidential system comprising a popularly elected president (previously elected indirectly by a two-thirds majority in Parliament) alongside a government drawn from the parliament, resulting in a dual executive structure.

Erdoğan's subsequent push for the adoption of a type of executive presidency to further bolster his power was an important factor in the breakdown of the all-party commission working on a new constitution between 2011 and 2013 (see Chapter 1) and accelerated following his ascent to the post in 2014 with 51.8 per cent of the vote. Yet it was clear from his statements that what he envisaged was not a pure presidential system typified by the US case, defined by a strict separation of powers and, thereby, strong checks and balances against accumulation of power within one branch of government. Rather, he advocated a 'Turkish-style' presidency, a type of delegative hyper-presidentialism (Boyunsuz 2016) involving a weak separation of powers and minimal constraints on executive power, which was also revealed by his continued reference to the one-party era and the efficiency of the 'unity of powers'. Reflecting this vision, the 16 April constitutional amendments, which will come into force following the June 2018 elections, will result in the following:

- A stronger president and, effectively, a rubber-stamp parliament, especially when both the executive and majority group in Parliament belong to the same party:
  - The president will become both head of state and executive, per presidential systems (Article 104). Presidential neutrality will no longer be required, as previously, with candidates being nominated by either a party that has garnered 5 per cent of the general vote or 100,000 citizens. Presidential candidates will need to gain an absolute majority of the vote (51 per cent) and will be able to serve up to two 5-year terms. If no candidate receives a simple majority, a second round of elections will be conducted with the top two candidates of the first round, and the candidate who gains the majority of votes will be elected (Article 101). Accordingly, President Erdoğan will theoretically be able to remain in power until 2029.

o The president alone will have greater scope to declare an SoE. Previously, the cabinet, under the chairmanship of the president, was empowered to declare an SoE for three months in the event of 'natural disaster, dangerous epidemic diseases or a serious economic crisis'. The new constitution allows the president to declare an SoE for up to six months at a time in the case of more extensive, ambiguously defined triggers, including uprisings that threaten the 'indivisibility' of the nation (Article 119).

o The cabinet will be appointed directly by the president (Article 104) without the requirement of a vote of confidence by Parliament, as was previously the case (Article 110). A crucial source of presidential power will be the ability to dissolve the parliament at will – albeit only by triggering a presidential election together with a parliamentary election (they are required to be held at the same time) – while Parliament will require a three-fifths majority to call elections (Article 116). In this manner, the president will be more likely to ensure a friendly parliament controlled by his own party, effectively turning it into a rubber stamp. Significantly, the granting of such power to the presidency was successfully resisted and denied when it was pushed by Atatürk in 1924 during one-party rule.

o The president will have extensive legislative authority, including the ability to issue decrees that carry the force of law (Article 104) and, significantly, will be responsible for the budget (Article 161). Parliament will require an absolute majority (301 votes out of 600) to overturn presidential vetoes, whereas previously, it could bypass them with a simple majority of a quorum.

• Severe curtailment of Parliament's ability to scrutinise and check executive power by abolition of parliamentary mechanisms such as censure motions to probe ministers, which previously empowered it to force the resignation of the government (Article 98):

o The barriers to holding the president accountable will become very robust. Previously, presidents could be impeached on the proposal of at least one-third of the total members of Parliament and on the decision of least three-quarters of the TBMM (Article 105). After the new changes, an absolute majority (51 per cent) of Parliament is required to request an investigation, and a decision by at least three-fifths of lawmakers is necessary to open it. On completion of the investigation, Parliament will require two-thirds of members to refer the matter to the Constitutional Court, where 80 per cent of members are appointed directly by the president.

• Greater control over the judiciary will further undermine the separation of powers.

- ○ The president will appoint thirteen of the fifteen (80 per cent) Constitutional Court members, compared with fourteen out of seventeen (82 per cent) previously, with the remaining members being elected by Parliament (Article 146). The HSYK will be composed of thirteen members (compared with twenty-two previously), with four appointed by the president and seven by Parliament, while the justice minister and his deputy will also sit as the head of the council and as a natural member of the body, respectively. This means a reversal of the 2010 constitutional amendments whereby the president appointed four; the Court of Cassation, three; the Turkish Academy of Justice, one; and the judges and prosecutors, four members. Moreover, since the president will appoint the justice minister, this means that he will effectively directly control at least six members of the HSYK. In effect, the president will directly appoint nineteen out of the twenty-eight high-ranking judges, and assuming he commands a parliamentary majority, his party will elect the rest, thereby significantly undermining judicial independence (Article 159).

The 16 April constitutional amendments have, therefore, involved transformation of the Turkish system of government into a highly personalistic type of regime defined by an extreme level of concentration of power in the presidential office that dominates the legislative and judicial organs and is thus faced with very weak or minimal checks and balances. Following the relative mollification of the military since 2007 to 2008, it was mistakenly assumed that Turkey had taken an inevitable step towards democratisation with the end of the tutelary role exercised by the military. Yet there was no democratic transition since transitions do not have a predefined path towards liberal democracy. Since hybrid regimes are characterised by a wide gap between codified law and rule enforcement (Levitsky and Murillo 2013), the Turkish system facilitated cycles of enhanced authoritarianism and contestation, creating a sense of democratic politics while supporting path-dependent path-shaping and, eventually, path-breaking to effect transformation. For instance, the very institutional structures that facilitated enhanced majoritarianism under the ANAP government in the 1980s and under the AKP since 2002 also produced weak coalition governments throughout the 1990s. The AKP was able to shape the path, therefore, and thereby catalyse the transition to another hybrid regime type which has been described as competitive authoritarianism (Esen and Gümüşçü 2016; Kalaycıoğlu 2015; Özbudun 2014), delegative or hyper-presidentialism (Boyunsuz 2016) and patronal presidentialism

(Hale 2005; Lord 2017), all with the common characteristic of an extremely powerful and unchecked president, as found in many authoritarian Latin American and post-Soviet states.[39] Yet the regime's willingness to engage in massive electoral fraud in April 2017 suggests that the minimal democratic features of the regime – that is, competitive elections – are also being undermined, suggesting that rather than a hybrid system, Turkey is transitioning towards autocratic rule.

Conclusion

Having traced the factors behind the salience of religious markers in political and economic struggles, together with the drivers and infrastructure behind Islamist mobilisation, this chapter examined the Islamist AKP's politics since its ascent to power in 2002. The success of the AKP, and expansion of the religious field under it, was long equated with the narrative of democratisation in Turkey, reflecting the master narrative of Turkish politics or a secular state pitted against the religious masses. The party had become the poster child of the notion of Islamist moderation.

Besides an illiberal ideological agenda, a key aspect of why the AKP government evolved into an authoritarian regime lies in the path-dependency effects generated by the highly majoritarian system of government the party inherited. The ability of the AKP to form a one-party government was particularly significant owing to this majoritarian system, which made it very amenable to the centralisation of power and, eventually, system capture. This has involved the erosion of separation of powers, including the undermining of the judiciary as well as the dominance of clientelistic networks and mechanisms of rent distribution. With each electoral success, the AKP expanded its benefits of incumbency, enabling the further monopolisation of both formal and informal institutions of the state, augmenting its ability to engage in path-dependent path-shaping for path-breaking transformation of the regime.

---

[39] Based on his analyses of Russia and post-Soviet states, Henry Hale (2005) defines patronal presidentialism as comprising two key components: a directly elected president with significant powers relative to the other arms of the state and extensive informal power based on patron–client relationships. It is the control of, and ability to selectively distribute, state resources (i.e. wealth, jobs, etc.) that makes this regime type self-reproducing, given the mutual dependence between the president and the elites: 'the president depends on elites for implementing decisions and delivering votes while elites depend on the president for resources and/or continuation in their posts – patronal president has a decided advantage' (Hale 2005: 138).

In its bid for the monopolisation of power, the AKP has been facing two major challengers, the military and its former allies, the Gülenists, neither of which are unitary actors themselves. In fact, Gülenist infiltration of the military underlines how interlinked these two challengers are. Equally, the extent of Gülenist influence within the AKP and Islamist movement remains an important question as, so far, the AKP has refrained from purges from its own ranks. To date, this struggle within and over the state has facilitated only a suspension of the rule of law and constitutional order, which was effectively routinised and subsequently legalised by the rigged April 2017 constitutional referendum. That poll sealed the country's transition towards a personalised autocratic rule.

Conclusion

What accounts for the rise and success of the AKP and its ability to transform the regime? Why has the Turkish context proved so conducive to the religio-political mobilisation or politicisation of religious identities? This concluding chapter first elaborates religious majoritarianism as an alternative prism for situating the AKP's rise. Drawing on lessons from the Turkish case, it then compares it with India, Malaysia and Ireland to demonstrate the applicability of this analytical framework in tracing a more complex and intertwined relationship between state, religion and society over time and identifying contexts which prove more amenable to religio-politics. Most countries, while they differ in terms of religion, legal framework, region and regime type, demonstrate relatively high degrees of religious majoritarianism of the state at the foundational stages. While religio-politics found space in Turkey, Malaysia and India, where states became increasingly religious majoritarian over time, in the Irish case, the state has become less majoritarian, and religious articulations have not shaped political and economic competition in the same manner as in the other cases in question. Such a variation in outcome was the result, crucially, of independent variables, the particular forms and levels of social closure and types of institutions that arose, which will be underlined by a comparative selective historical account of each case.

Situating the AKP's Rise in the Context of the Unfolding of Religious Majoritarianism

Until the 2013 Gezi Park protests, which were forcefully crushed by the AKP regime, it was common to depict the AKP period as one of moderation, democratisation and Europeanisation. Such a reading was chiefly based on the metanarrative that has dominated Turkish studies holding that the trend of rising religious politics demonstrated democratisation involving the empowerment of the previously marginalised Muslim majority against the authoritarian secular state. Subsequently, the narrative shifted to emphasising the illiberal and majoritarian nature of the

AKP regime, but such explanations remained largely focused on the agents themselves, pointing to factors such as President Erdoğan's personality, reform fatigue, the effects of power itself or on geopolitical developments. Such studies have also mirrored the wider literature, which has conceived of religio-political movements typically as purely grass-roots phenomena and a reaction to a confluence of secularism, modernity, Westernisation and capitalism. Cases where the role of state institutions has been recognised as providing opportunity spaces for Islamist actors, such as studies drawing on social movement theory, have continued to regard the state in monolithic terms as a secular actor. Consequently, any state-led Islamisation or engagement with Islamist actors is regarded as either a malfunction or an opportunistic effort by secular elites to utilise religion.

Certainly, these analyses have provided extensive insight into the motivations of Islamist actors and their mobilisation. However, they do not alone explain why religio-political mobilisation became prominent in Turkey and some other Muslim and non-Muslim contexts in the world since the 1970s, but not in others. The limitations of such a binary framework, drawing a sharp distinction between a secular state and religious society, were underlined again by the 15 July 2016 coup attempt. Not only was the state exposed as an arena of struggle, but the ensuing purges in the aftermath raised the question of the extent to which treating the state as a monolithic, secular actor was a reasonable assumption in analysing Turkish politics if the Gülenists had so thoroughly infiltrated it for nearly three decades. Equally important was the critical role played by the Diyanet, previously largely ignored as a passive and marginalised apparatus of the Kemalist state, in mobilising opposition to the coup.

The dominant approaches thus have a number of implications for the study of religio-politics. First, they have a homogenising impact on the variables in question. The state is taken as a secular unit, monolithic and sharply demarcated from society. Religion, in turn, is taken as a uniform, independent and transhistorical unit, while the assumption of 'religious society' presumes a level of groupness. Second, the role that institutional structures or the state play in facilitating and constraining certain types of strategy and politics is neglected. Third, a more general point is that these assumptions distort the nature of change and overall political evolution while overlooking important dimensions of continuity. This book thus addresses the disjuncture between the theory and reality on the ground, drawing on the insights of historical institutionalism in treating institutions and the state as independent variables in exploring political outcomes rather than as dependent variables and integrating structure and agency.

The Prism of Religious Majoritarianism

As an alternative to the binary analytical approaches, the prism of religious majoritarianism refers to a political structure in which a religiously denominated group constituting a numerical majority is elevated as the owner of the state and its resources. The extent to which a state becomes religious majoritarian is underpinned by

- the levels (high, low) and forms (religious, ethnic, tribal, etc.) of social closure; and
- the particular configuration of institutional structures that arise during nation-state building which comprise the antecedent conditions at a critical juncture.

High levels of social closure based on religion therefore influence the extent to which religion becomes a marker of citizenship and the degree to which it is incorporated into the nation-state project. The degree of social closure at the point of nation-state building can trigger strong path-dependency effects through their institutionalisation. The stronger the social closure, the greater the influence on the types of institutions that are established and incorporated within the nation-state. The types of institutions that are adopted during the foundational stages of nation building are relevant because: (i) institutions determine the structure of political competition by shaping and being shaped by the strategies of actors in terms of what boundaries are created and thereby become salient; and (ii) they underlie the ability of social actors to perpetuate themselves through time, acting as a mechanism of social reproduction. This is why institutions generate path-dependent effects which produce persistence of group boundaries over time even if their content changes significantly. Institutions thus crucially determine whether the types of boundaries that are created matter for political and economic competition and, therefore, tell us about what contexts prove to be more conducive to the rise and success of religio-political mobilisation.

How this analytical prism can be used to overcome the problems in the dominant literature has been demonstrated in its operationalisation to explain the Turkish case. A key proposition of this book in this vein has been that, far from marking democratisation or a break with secular state building, the rise of the AKP and the phenomenon of religio-politics more broadly should be situated in the context of path-dependent processes occurring within the longer-term dynamics of nation-state building. As a form of identity politics, Islamism, or religio-politics, should therefore not be seen as the natural outcome or reaction of a Muslim society, which at root is an essentialising approach to the nature of (nominally) Muslim populations. Rather, what facilitates this type of politics and makes mobilisation on the basis of religious identity both an attractive and plausible option in political and economic competition is the structural environment that is mutually constituted through socio-political struggles, which are thus reflective of power and power relations.

Since groupness is not a natural but rather a contingent political project, before a particular identity can be utilised by political actors, group consciousness needs to be raised through the construction of boundaries. The question of why religious delineations of group boundaries acquired political salience that has persisted over time and has underpinned Islamist mobilisation is answered by the high levels of social closure and the institutional framework that arose during nation-state building in the 1920s. At the point of nation-state building, which marked a critical juncture, elites were faced with two antecedent conditions in the form of two legacies of the Ottoman Empire. These were the incorporation of religious institutions within the state and the emergence of religion as an ethnic marker. On the one hand, the Turkish Republic emerged through the efforts of a diverse coalition, within which ideological boundaries were fluid and overlapping. While the particular faction led by Mustafa Kemal gained prominence during the consolidation of one-party rule, Islamist and other conservative or religious actors were hardly eliminated from the state. Generally speaking, Islamist currents and actors, together with and including the *ulema* who had reconciled with the nation-state, tended to be absorbed into the republican state, while the pan-Islamist, or traditionalist, *ulema* and Islamists decided to go underground or into direct confrontation with the nascent state. On the other hand, reflecting the predominant forms of social closure at the end of the empire, one common denominator among the new and diverse power-holders in the nascent state was their Muslim identity.

Both dynamics had been influenced by the institutional framework of the Ottoman state, but they also ensured important dimensions of continuity within the Republic in terms of the elevation of Sunni Muslim identity and religious institutions, albeit in a significantly reconfigured manner. This intertwined nature of religion and nation, together with the continuity in religious institutions, albeit significantly reconfigured, meant that the Turkish nation-state building project has been significantly religious majoritarian in nature despite its ostensibly secular designation. Secularisation marked the ascendancy of one faction within the nationalist coalition, but it did not involve a neutrality or separation from Islam; in fact, it incorporated the elevation and privileging of Sunni Muslim identity, as revealed by the role of the Diyanet. In turn, by enabling the reproduction of Islamist or conservative social groups, it was these particular institutions that underpinned path-dependency and thereby the persistence of the political salience of religious delineations of identity.

Together with this structural environment, the agency of Islamist or conservative actors combined with contingent events, facilitating Islamist mobilisation. Over time, the balance of power within the state between the different factions, with their varying visions of society and politics, shifted. These shifts were driven by both the endogenous strategies of actors within the state and by exogenous factors, including the Cold War anti-communism drive, neo-liberal restructuring and political liberalisation, which provided windows of opportunity for different actors to reshape the institutional milieu, shift the balance of power in their favour and thereby establish new paths (Hausner et al. 1995). The Diyanet is at the heart of the struggle within the state in two ways. First, having absorbed the Ottoman *ulema*, the guardians of Sunni orthodoxy in the Ottoman state, it played an important role in negotiating the boundaries of national identity, delineating the parameters of inclusion and exclusion, articulating and reproducing it as Sunni (Hanefi) Muslim Turkish to the exclusion of Alevis. Second, the evolution of the Diyanet reveals how the *ulema* were able to successfully exploit opportunities such as the anti-communism drive in pushing for an expansion of their role and the infrastructure behind religion, thereby providing a favourable environment for Islamist mobilisation with which they share a common goal: the Islamisation of public and private space and morality. Likewise, the expansion of the infrastructure behind religious education, associations and Islamic finance, catalysed by the shifting balance of power within the state, together with the agency of actors, particularly on the political right, was crucial in imparting a distinct habitus and its social reproduction over time. The Turkish case reveals the misleading nature of making a sharp distinction between a secular state and religious society, and in the same vein, the rise of the Islamist movement and, subsequently, the AKP cannot be treated purely as a reaction of religious society or as marking democratisation. The instrumentalisation of religion by political actors, grass-roots mobilisation, role of contingent events such as economic crises, ideological or emotional commitment of actors, or actors' resistance to phenomena such as modernity were all important factors. Yet the state institutional milieu that emerged as a result of the particular dynamics of nation building and how it has had a bearing on the politicisation of religious identity, given the crucial role of these institutions in the construction, reproduction and persistence of group boundaries, has been a critical neglected angle.

Within this context, a confluence of factors, such as the annihilation of the left by the 1980 junta regime, political and economic crises in the

1990s and the discrediting of traditional mainstream parties, paved the way for the AKP's 2002 electoral success. The ability of the AKP to form a one-party government was crucial because the highly majoritarian system of government that it inherited made it amenable to the central-isation and monopolisation of power. With each electoral success, the AKP expanded its benefits of incumbency, enabling it to further monop-olise both formal and informal institutions of the state, augmenting its ability to engage in path-dependent path-shaping for path-breaking transformation of the regime. On the one hand, it has been able to further augment the religious majoritarian nature of the state through its expan-sion of religious infrastructure as well as its increasingly sectarian politics against Alevis, but it has also gone further with its wider Islamist agenda of the Islamisation of society and a state based on Islamic doctrine. On the other hand, in its bid for the monopolisation of power within the state, the AKP has faced two major challengers, the military and the Gülenists, which are by no means unitary actors themselves nor neces-sarily ideologically opposed to the AKP project. However, this struggle within and over the state has, to date, facilitated a suspension of the rule of law and constitutional order, which was effectively routinised and subsequently legalised by the rigged April 2017 constitutional referen-dum, thereby sealing Turkey's transition towards a new and more auto-cratic regime type.

Religious Majoritarianism from a Comparative Perspective

More widely, the prism of religious majoritarianism can also be used to situate the growth of religio-politics in other contexts, both Muslim and non-Muslim. How the level of religious majoritarianism, determined by the particular forms and levels of social closure and types of institutions adopted during nation-state building, has influenced the possibility of religio-politics will be highlighted by a comparative selective historical account of each case.

India

India, as a post-colonial, non-Muslim majority, weakly federal and vastly heterogeneous (from language to religion) polity, is significantly different from the Turkish case. Yet it, too, has experienced the rise of religio-politics since the 1970s, as evidenced by the increasing prominence of the Hindutva movement followed by the widening appeal and electoral success of the Hindu majoritarian Indian People's Party (Bharatiya

Janata Party, BJP). Similar to the Turkish case, various studies of religio-politics in the Indian case have juxtaposed a secular nationalism and state associated with the Indian National Congress (INC) – the leading umbrella organisation of the nationalist movement pre-independence and the dominant party of government following independence in 1947 to 1977 – with a religious society, the Hindutva or Hindu majority, and the so-called communalism of the Muslim community, which is a legally recognised minority (Bose 2009: 9). Adopting such a line of reasoning, Madan (1987: 748–750), for instance, argues that, in India, 'secularism is the dream of a minority which wants to shape the majority in its own image', while 'society seethes with [. . .] expressions of a vibrant religiosity'. From the standpoint of these approaches, the ascent of religio-politics is a natural reaction to the secularism project of the modernist and secular state elites. In contrast, as Bose points out, 'to explain the rise of Hindutva, we must critically dissect and challenge widely unquestioned dichotomies: such as the presumed antimony, whether in theory or practice, between categories such as "secularism" and "communalism"' (Bose 1997: 105). Indeed, these binary analytical approaches, or the depiction of the Hindutva as merely an ideology of manipulative elites neglect structure, context and, more importantly, the role of the ostensibly secular state in the rise of religio-politics.

Religion was an important dimension along which social closure took place in the lead-up to Indian independence from the UK in 1947, but with some crucial differences from the Turkish case. The evolution of Indian nationalism can be traced to the decline of the Mughal Empire and British imperial penetration. Within this context, partly spurred by British colonialists and Christian missionaries, upper-caste (Brahman) Hindus began to construct Hindu identity in the 1890s with the reimagining of a Hindu past resisting Muslim domination, which was blamed for the decline of the Hindu nation. This was a narrative that was later blended with the emerging anti-colonial critique of British imperialism (Vanaik 1992: 45). Subsequently, in a bid to construct and establish a core nation that involved the elevation and construction of a dominant majority ethnicity, Indian nationalists set about trying to reconcile the anti-colonial nationalist movement with the existence of the caste system and religious diversity. For Bal Gangadhar Tilak, the first leader of the independence movement, Hinduism was conceived as the spiritual essence of Indian civilisation or *dharma* (religion), which was characterised as 'inextricable' (Tejani 2008: 96). Through this logic, the different religious communities, such as Muslims and Christians, could be absorbed into Hindu nationalism by positing that they were, at their core, Hindus. Such an approach to non-Hindus also has parallels with the Turkish nationalist project with regard to Alevism in the way that Alevis were initially rearticulated as 'real' Turks so as to absorb them. The alignment of Hinduism with Indian identity under 'dharmic universalism' was, therefore, presented as being compatible with the ostensible secularism of the INC, and Hinduism was propagated as an 'all-encompassing social system subsuming diverse peoples and cultures' (Jalal 1995: 26). Consequently, just as Sunni Muslim identity was intertwined with Turkish nationalism, underlying the seemingly inclusionary or even secular Indian nationalism were Hindu ideals and myths, with those contesting this articulation or manifesting different identity claims, such as Muslims, being branded as communal or un-national in a manner similar to the branding of difference in Turkey as separatism. The notion of a Hindu majority totalling 80 per cent of the population (against a Muslim minority of around 13 per cent) was, therefore, just as imaginary as the Muslim majority is in the Turkish case: as Bose (2013: 42) notes, it is no more than a census majority, given the highly heterogeneous make-up of society in terms of class, caste, and linguistic and regional differences.

These processes of social closure and the sharpening of communal boundaries were precipitated in crucial ways by the British colonial administration, which had shaped 'new ways of imagining Hinduism and Islam as communities' (Corbridge 2000: 180; see also Hibbard 2010; Tejani 2008). Actors were forced to articulate themselves through the language of religious tradition, following various colonial measures, such as the population censuses initiated in 1872, the declaration of a policy of non-interference in religious conflict in 1858, the Morley–Minto Reforms of 1909 involving the institution of separate electorates for different communities and the division of Bengal into a Muslim east and Hindu west, while Muslim personal law had been codified by the colonial government from the 1920s to the 1940s. As a result of these dynamics, the idea of Indian nationalism as meaning the Hindu majority had been broadly established by the 1930s (Tejani 2008: 23). Religiously defined boundaries became hardened, precipitating social closure and being further reinforced following the experience of Partition: the split and establishment of Muslim majority Pakistan in 1947. Consequently, drawing hard-and-fast distinctions between INC nationalism and the Hindutva is misleading, since such an opposition comprises an 'ideological edifice . . . [upon which] the post-colonial Indian nation-state has rested' (Jalal 1998: 2183).

These dynamics of social closure and colonial era institutions were important antecedent conditions during nation-state building, marking a critical juncture at which there were both significant elements of continuity with the colonial legacy and sharp breaks (Brass 1990: 2) reflecting the concerns and motivations of the nation-state builders. On the one hand, the nation builders faced the challenge of establishing an 'integrative national narrative ... in a post-colonial society divided by religious and caste cleavages' (Kandiyoti 2009: 3) and where the dominant tendencies were 'towards pluralism, regionalism and decentralisation' (Bose 1997: 112). The concerns about eradicating religious or communal violence in the context of caste and religious differences institutionalised under the colonial government, as well as about the preservation of unity following the anti-colonial struggle and Partition, therefore resulted in the interpretation of secularism as comprising the ideal of a 'neutral' state. Consequently, state builders adopted temporary compromise positions on religious legislation and postponed the secularisation of personal law for all citizens regardless of religion in order to ensure unity (Lerner 2014: 406, 409) within an open political system of the diverse nationalist coalition, which also incorporated different factions with varied and sometimes overlapping political visions. Thus, while the project of secularism, rather than just as a matter of marking a line between public and private religion, was part and parcel of nation building efforts to build unity, in India, as in Turkey, the different contexts resulted in a variation in its interpretation and institutionalisation.

Nevertheless, the particular nature of state and religion relations in India has remained a heavily contested matter. Critics have described and dismissed secularism in India as reflecting the positivistic and anti-religious modernisation drive of the INC and, particularly, the worldview of Prime Minister Jawaharlal Nehru (1947–1964). Conversely, approaches that are more positive have presented the Indian case as an alternative variety of secularism, underpinned by the principle of 'equal respect of all religions' (*sarva dharma sambhava*) (Pantham 1997: 526) or a 'principled distance' (Bhargava 2011: 105–108) as opposed to a wall of separation between religion and state. Based on Kuru's (2009) popular typology, the Indian case can be characterised as 'passive secularism', in contrast with the common depictions of Turkey (before the AKP) as epitomising a case of 'assertive secularism', in which the secular state sought to remove religion from the public sphere.

Yet as critics of these two approaches to Indian secularism have pointed out, both underplay or neglect the deeply enmeshed nature of the state and the majority religion in India. In reality, the INC's drive to reform Hinduism through the adoption of various Hindu reform bills following independence, such as the 1955 Hindu Code Bill pertaining to Hindu personal law, meant that 'by associating the Indian state with the reform of the social practices of people belonging to a particular religious tradition, it placed the state in a unique position in relation to that tradition' (Chiriyankandath 2000: 16). Despite the lack of a state religion and no officially enforced education of a single religion in state schools, there was state funding for religious educational institutions, reservations for seats in government institutions for the 'scheduled classes and castes', who were retained as a body of the Hindu community, and significantly, the Madras Hindu Religious and Charitable Endowments Act of 1951 'created an entire department of government devoted to the administration of Hindu religious endowments' (Chatterjee 1994: 1770). At the same time, a pluralistic legal structure, maintained by the preservation of Muslim personal laws in the name of religious freedom, particularly following Partition, served in practice to reproduce the boundaries between groups whereby citizenship rights were linked to communal identities, furthering the process of social closure along religious delineations. In sum, the institutionalisation of majority–minority dynamics at the foundational stages, and the issue of reservations and separate Hindu and Muslim personal laws, had essentially served to reaffirm the outsider minority status of Muslims and their marginal status with respect to national identity, while the pluralistic legal structure, initially considered to be a temporary compromise, had instead 'shaped religious regulations in ways that turned out to be difficult to change' (Lerner 2014: 409).

Highlighting the role that institutions play in reinforcing group boundaries in a path-dependent manner and underpinning their salience over time, this institutional structural context was important for the expansion of the Hindutva movement from the 1970s. This period had been marked by an increasingly authoritarian turn under Prime Minister Indira Ghandi, who declared an SoE in 1975 as she was faced with the declining popularity of the INC, which had been governing India since 1947, in a context of increasing societal contestation owing to the economic crisis and frustration with corruption. Ghandi's centralisation of power had also involved greater emphasis on religious communalism and appeal to the Hindu majority against what was declared the threat of Muslim minority separatism (Hibbard 2010: 140–144). In an environment where the predominantly Muslim Jammu and Kashmir National Conference party was depicted as 'anti-national' and 'pro-Pakistani', such policies served to normalise the discourse of the Hindutva movement. In turn, group boundaries became sharpened, as evidenced by the subsequent increase in communal violence in which the state was implicated as acting on the side of Hindu actors (Hibbard 2010: 142–144). Both the Shah Bano case in the 1980s, which reignited debate about the pluralist legal structure, and the Ram Janmabhoomi campaign to convert the Babri Masjid mosque into a temple reinforced these trends.

However, as Gupta (1991: 573–575) argues, INC's communalist policies did not reflect a bid to outdo the Hindutva movement or to contain a threat from it. Indeed, Hindutva organisations in the 1960s and 1970s enjoyed weak electoral performance and limited popular support, as evidenced by the electoral defeats of the Shiv Sena, which was another Hindutva party. Not dissimilar to the military's view of the MSP as a bulwark against communism in Turkey, in the late 1960s to early 1970s, Shiv Sena had been an important ally, rather than an adversary, of INC, helping to curb the growing labour movement. The Hindutva movement began to grow and strengthen particularly after Indira Gandhi's reign, as religio-political mobilisation was facilitated by a shifting balance of power within the government and the state more widely, with the Hindu majoritarian BJP emerging as a mass party only in the 1990s. Against the broader dynamics of the nation-state project, it would be misleading to situate the rise of the BJP or religio-politics purely in terms of a reaction to the secularism–modernity project of INC or as the secular state elite's manipulation of religion in response to such a reaction. As Bose argues, the Hindutva 'is no chance, arbitrary phenomenon. It is deeply rooted in the historical development of India's post-colonial political and social structures' (Bose 1997: 162).

Yet the religious majoritarianism of the state has obviously been much weaker in India than in Turkey, reflecting the variation in social closure and the institutional milieu. Prevalent forms of social closure in India developed not solely on the basis of religious delineations but also around other boundaries of caste, class, region and language, as is evidenced by the regionalisation of Indian political life since 1989 and caste-related protests and violence in the early 1990s. Caste and class dimensions were also important in terms of the Hindutva movement's traditional base, which largely comprised the urban lower middle class and traditional upper-caste landed elites who had been threatened by changing economic policies that had benefited the 'intermediate caste', or 'agrarian bourgeoisie' (Bose 2013: 60). Overall, the Indian nation-state project was, in a sense, forced to accept diversity, which moderated the degree of religious majoritarianism of the state involving the elevation of Hindu identity. Crucial to this has been a loose federal structure, instituted as a result of popular resistance to centralisation in the founding years, which has incorporated a trend towards regionalisation together with broad-based coalitions. This contrasts sharply with the highly centralised and majoritarian political system in Turkey, which has facilitated the augmentation of religious majoritarianism by imparting a majoritarian dynamic into political competition, contributing to the success of Islamist and conservative parties. Equally, these dynamics arguably limit the

BJP's ability to dominate or monopolise the state in the same way as the AKP has been able to in Turkey.

Malaysia

The salience of religio-politics in the Malaysian case has been explained with reference to the *dakwah* movement, in part inspired by external Islamist movements and in part a reaction against modernisation. Despite the embeddedness of Islam within the constitution (rather than laicism or secularism), since the establishment of the Malaysian nation-state, Islamist actors such as the Pan-Malaysian Islamic Party (Parti Islam Se-Malaysia) have accused the governing ruling party, the United Malays National Organisation (Pertubuhan Kebangsaan Melayu Bersatu, UMNO), of not safeguarding the interests of the majority Muslim Malay community and Islam against the Chinese and Indian minorities (Peletz 2002: 247). Consequently, it has been argued that the 1980s Islamisation policies of Prime Minister Mahathir bin Mohamad (1981–2003) marked an instrumental reaction of the secular UMNO to the rise of Islamism designed to reinforce the party's declining authority. The Islamisation policies included the introduction of Islamic finance institutions, the official declaration of the state's role as 'instilling Islamic values into the government machinery', the expansion of various religious institutions and education, the upgrading of the status of *shari'a* courts, the increase in construction of mosques and the greater utilisation of Islamic language and symbols in the media and in public life (Barr and Govindasamy 2010: 296–299; Hamid 2007: 457–461; Lee 1990: 495). However, rather than a break, Mahathir's Islamisation policies marked continuity with a highly religious majoritarian nation-state project compared with the Indian and Turkish cases, whereby Muslims enjoy a privileged position within the legal hierarchy.

Malaysia's highly religious majoritarian state reflects the elevated levels of social closure along religious lines and a legal framework that institutionalised these boundaries at the point of independence in 1957. Malaysia, which has a nominally Muslim majority population alongside significant Chinese and Indian communities with overlapping ethnic and religious markers, has developed a pluralistic legal system in which, aside from the federal statutory laws, Islamic law (chiefly pertaining to personal law) is adopted at the state level and applied only to Muslims. With parallels to the late Ottoman period, British colonial economic penetration catalysed the rise and bifurcation of the bourgeoisie, with the emergence of 'comprador capitalists', composed chiefly of Chinese merchants who acted as middlemen (Brennan 2008: 197). This bifurcation, coupled with war and a stratified educational system in which Christian missionaries offered better educational opportunities that were utilised by non-Muslims further reinforced group boundaries in the lead-up to independence. Identities were thereby transformed under British colonial rule, which resulted in the institutionalisation of the privileges and rights of Malays over Chinese and Indians, considered non-permanent settlers, regarding the three main areas of land law, recruitment and public services, and education (Lee 1990: 484–485; Means 1978: 393). These rights and privileges were expanded and given constitutional status in the post-colonial period. Religious identity, or Islam, became constitutive of Malay national identity alongside the Malay language and customs in the post-colonial nation-state, as defined in the constitution. In this vein, Malay identity has been intertwined with Muslim identity: 'Malays viewed Islam not only as defining community boundaries, but also distinguishing between those who were believed to have legitimate domicile rights and those who should properly be excluded from participation in the political system because they were deemed to be "aliens"' (Means 1978: 386). Following the introduction of elections in 1955, the protection of these systems of privileges and status gained prominence, translating into pressure for greater government support for Islam.

Consequently, while prior to independence, the role of religion pertained only to state law under the Federation Agreement of 1948, following independence in 1957, the new constitution adopted (Sunni) Islam as the official religion of the federation and declared that 'other religions may be practiced in peace and harmony in any part of the federation' (Article 3). Indeed, 'a special status for Islam was but one way that constitutional guarantees could be given to the Malays to provide both material benefits and psychological assurances that the country was still theirs' (Means 1978: 389). Accordingly, Malaysia can be said to display high levels of social closure along religious lines in that a clearly ethnicised bureaucracy which is dominated by Muslim Malays has meant that competition over resources has also been ethnicised. This is in the sense that 'resources and services dispensed by an ethnicised bureaucracy do not appear to be public benefits available to all, but rather collective goods attainable only by those who belong to the "proper" ethnic group' (Wimmer 1997: 643–651). In such an ethnicised state, religious majoritarianism pervades all aspects of state institutional configurations, their authority and the distribution of state resources. Indeed, the status of Islam and Muslim identity is directly tied to an elaborate system of special privileges, meaning that 'religious issues intrude directly or indirectly into the whole area of inter-ethnic relations and become entangled in nearly all government social, economic, and educational policies' (Means 1978: 393), and this, in turn, underpins the salience of religious delineations in shaping political and economic competition. Indeed, political parties have largely been divided along ethnoreligious lines. At the same time, the policy of Bumiputraism and the New Economic Policy (1971–1990) programmes adopted in the aftermath of the 1969 race riots with the aim of improving the economic position of (predominantly Muslim) Malays compared with Chinese and Indians have involved important economic privileges for Muslims, such as easier access to universities and public-sector jobs. The so-called new Muslim bourgeoisie, a Malay-Muslim middle class fostered by the NEP, has in turn also seen its growing wealth and privileged position tied to the strengthening of the status and role of religion which has underpinned support for Islamist parties (Hamid and Fauzi 2009). This is a self-reinforcing process:

Malay religious elites quickly developed a vested interest in the expansion of government support for Islam and helped to stimulate increased demands that the government more actively defend and promote Islam. The Departments of Religious Affairs cultivated active advocates in various Islamic associations and among Malay politicians who wished to exploit Muslim sentiments for partisan political purposes (Means 1978: 388–389).

In this vein, with some parallels to Turkey and India, it is possible to argue that the growth of religio-politics, particularly in the 1980s, was facilitated by the high degree of religious majoritarianism of the state as institutionalised in the foundational years.

Ireland

Ireland presents a case in which different types of religious institutions may affect the persistence of religious delineations in shaping political competition and the possibility of religio-politics. Ireland, a small and majority Catholic (91 per cent [Dillon 2002: 47]) country, offers a contrasting case to those of Turkey, India and Malaysia. Despite the religious majoritarianism of the state, involving its association with and elevation of a Catholic majority at the outset, religio-political movements have not emerged in the same way, and religious group boundaries have comparatively less or no salience within the party system or in political behaviour.

With some parallels to the Islamic revival catalysed by imperial penetration in the Ottoman state, religion became a dominant marker of ethnic identity in pre-independence Ireland, in part owing to the experience of being colonised by an empire with a different religion. British colonisation crucially influenced the construction of community boundaries, which became reinforced through the systematic persecution, and economic and political dispossession, of Catholics. Policies such as the plantations during the sixteenth and seventeenth centuries, which involved confiscation and reoccupation of lands by settlers from the UK, and the Penal Laws (1695–1829) effectively meant that Catholics were excluded from access to authority and influence as well as economic resources, serving as a means to bolster and allow Protestant elites to restrict access to its privileges (Dillon 2002: 48). This resulted in high levels of social closure along religious lines, as Catholicism became a symbol of resistance and a carrier of national identity against foreign domination by Protestant Britain (Breen and Reynolds 2011; Dillon 2002: 47–48), comparable to the case of Poland under the impact of Russian rule. A further legacy affecting Irish nation-state building was an institutional framework in which the Catholic Church was significantly empowered by the British colonial power which had accorded it extensive control and responsibility over public life, including education and health provision (Garvin 2004: 3).

It was the confluence of these legacies that had a bearing on the nature of nation-state building and the institutional framework established following the declaration of the Irish Free State in 1922 as an independent state and the adoption in 1937 of the Valera Constitution. In particular, despite the official separation of church and state, the 1937 constitution codified the close association of the state with the majority religion, as 'nationalists defended the prominent role accorded the church in areas of public policy', including Catholic Church control over primary and secondary education, while laws around marriage, contraception and freedom of expression were harmonised with Catholic teachings (Kissane 2003: 75). Consequently, Catholicism has been 'well inscribed both institutionally (in law, education, social policy, etc.) and in the Irish collective memory, and in its symbols and meanings' (Dillon 2002: 47). Together with the elevation of the Catholic majority, the religious majoritarian nature of the state was indicated by the curtailed rights of non-believers as well as the lack of state neutrality towards other religions (Kissane 2003: 79). However, despite an institutional milieu that was amenable to mobilisation on the basis of religious identity, processes of political and economic modernisation in the 1960s and 1970s did not catalyse religio-politics as in the cases considered above. Instead, these contingent events, including membership in the EU in

1973, produced a moderation of the religious majoritarianism of the state, resulting in a shift away from 'Catholic, nationalist, and patriarchal values' (Bulsara and Kissane 2009: 186), together with the decline of church power marked by, for instance, the removal of Article 44 of the constitution, the granting of the special position of Catholicism in 1972 following a referendum, the legalisation of contraception in 1979 and the lifting of the prohibition on divorce in 1995.

Given relatively high levels of social closure and the close association and cooperation of the state with the majority religion, what, then, explains the absence of religio-political movements? For one, the Irish state was comparably less religious majoritarian than the other cases considered. The constitutional framework had an important liberal thrust in that other religions were recognised, and the state was prohibited from subsidising a particular religion and from discriminating on the basis of religious belief (Kissane 2003: 77). Equally, the democratic system of government, while rooted in the majoritarian Westminster model, became more consensual over time and comprises a PR electoral system which facilitates more pluralistic politics. This contrast with the aversion to power-sharing and the zero-sum logic of party political competition set it apart from the (hybrid) majoritarian system in Turkey, which has reinforced the politics of referring to a cultural majority. In addition, contingent events, from EU integration to economic development, which reduced the influence of the church have also meant declining levels of social closure, reducing the salience of religious boundaries in determining access to political and economic resources. As Inglis notes, there has been a 'decline in the value and importance of religious capital in obtaining other forms of capital [...] With the important exception of education, it is no longer necessary to be a "good" Catholic to be employed in fields such as health and social welfare' (Inglis 2007: 206). Consequently, one might come to the conclusion based on the Irish case that despite the importance of structure in shaping political action, contingency must also be taken seriously. Contingent events played an important role in shifting the balance of power within the state and between the state and the church, which acts as an autonomous or independent hierarchical force in the political sphere – in a sense, as a state within a state (Garvin 2004: 2–3). Compared with the Irish integration into the EU in the 1970s, which supported the moderation of religious majoritarianism, an important dynamic in the Turkish case was Cold War anti-communism, which catalysed the expansion of the religious infrastructure that led to the reproduction and persistence of religious delineations and their role in structuring mass politics.

Beyond Religio-Politics as Reaction: Bringing Back Institutions

What the above cases underline is the ways in which the prism of religious majoritarianism, determined by the level and forms of social closure and institutional configurations that arise during nation building, can help us to trace contexts which prove more amenable to religio-political mobilisation while avoiding essentialising approaches. At the same time, a further utility of the prism is that it is useful for tracing continuity with earlier phases of nation building. Religion served as an ethnic marker in each of the cases, although to varying degrees, with social closure occurring based on religious identity. Consequently, religio-ethnic boundaries mattered during the process of national identity construction. In the Turkish and Indian cases, the project of secularism was tied to nation-state building and ultimately involved a distinction being made between the majority and minority religions, which resulted in the elevation of the former. Subsequently, as group boundaries became hardened, they were reproduced through accommodative institutional structures, facilitating their persistence in shaping political competition. In Malaysia, the high degree of social closure and institutional legacies during the critical phase of nation building meant that the state was highly religious majoritarian and resulted in the establishment of ethnicised institutions, including a system of religio-ethnic based privileges for Muslims and a pluralistic legal system. Since access to state resources is determined by religious identity, political competition has, therefore, also been ethnicised and reduced to religio-ethnic categories. In all three cases, the state's role was crucial in shaping the context in which religious delineations of groups mattered for access to and competition for political and economic resources to varying degrees, underpinning their salience over time. Conversely, the Irish example is an important counter-case of a state that began to some extent as religious majoritarian but moderated over time, with religious delineations ceasing to be politically relevant.

The findings and the comparative analysis also raise various questions for further research. It has been argued that social closure matters in conjunction with the particular configuration of institutions that entrench majority–minority relations within the structure of the state. Consequently, this raises questions about the impact that different institutional configurations (e.g. decentralised or consensual) have on the persistence of politically salient religious group delineations. Such questions are raised by the Irish case, where social closure was strong but, unlike in the Muslim contexts, the church was a hierarchical and autonomous religious authority. In the Turkish case, the majoritarian political system facilitated the augmentation of religious majoritarianism over time. In India, the loosely federal structure moderates religious majoritarianism in addition to the BJP's efforts to augment it. This is related, in turn, to the question of how the politics of Hindutva or Islamists are influenced by the fact that India is a highly diverse and post-colonial entity, while Turkey is a non-colonial case where there was already a sizeable nominally Muslim majority by independence. Hence, in explaining different outcomes, a further issue to take into account is the extent to which the imperial institutional legacies were conditioned by the demographic and social realities before independence. Explaining which came first in the Turkish case would be impossible: the important point is that they have been mutually constituted for long periods of time.

My findings are, therefore, of relevance not just to the Turkish case in understanding the rise of the AKP but also to the broader study of religio-politics. This book demonstrates that the conceptual prism of secularism and the binary approaches to state, society and religion hinder our understanding of the phenomenon of religio-politics in crucial ways. Moving beyond these approaches, religio-politics is situated within the longer historical context of nation-state building rather than being considered as a purely primordial or contingent reaction to modernisation, secularism and secularisation. Religious majoritarianism offers an alternative framework for examining state–religion relations in order to stress how path-dependent this example of religious resurgence has been and how this prism is better suited to analysing the dynamics of continuity and change in the Turkish state. Ultimately, this is not a deterministic argument but a probabilistic one, which takes contingency seriously while integrating structure and agency in positing that the degree of religious majoritarianism can facilitate the possibility of religio-politics.

Appendix: Presidents of the Diyanet

Presidents	Appointment	Departure
Mehmet Rıfat Börekçi	1 April 1924	5 March 1941
Ord Prof Dr Mehmet Şerafettin Yaltkaya	14 January 1942	23 April 1947
Ahmet Hamdi Akseki	29 April 1947	9 January 1951
Eyyüp Sabri Hayırlıoğlu	17 April 1951	10 June 1960
Ömer Nasuhi Bilmen	30 June 1960	06 April 1961
Hasan Hüsnü Erdem	6 April 1961	13 October 1964
Mehmet Tevfik Gerçeker	15 October 1964	16 December 1965
İbrahim Bedrettin Elmalı	17 December 1965	25 October 1966
Ali Rıza Hakses	25 October 1966	15 January 1968
Lütfi Doğan	15 January 1968	25 August 1972
Dr Lütfi Doğan	26 August 1972	26 July 1976
Doç Dr Süleyman Ateş	28 July 1976	7 February 1978
Dr Tayyar Altıkulaç	9 February 1978	10 November 1986
Prof Dr Mustafa Said Yazıcıoğlu	17 June 1987	2 January 1992
Mehmet Nuri Yılmaz	3 January 1992	19 March 2003
Prof Dr Ali Bardakoğlu	28 May 2003	11 November 2010
Prof Dr Mehmet Görmez	11 November 2010	1 August 2017
Prof Dr Ali Erbaş	17 September 2017	–

Source: Diyanet İşleri Başkanlığı – Presidency of Religious Affairs, Diyanet; www.diyanet
.gov.tr/tr-TR/Kisi/Baskanlar/3

Bibliography

Archives and Other Primary Sources

Akakuş, Recep. (2003). 'Toplumu Din Konusunda Aydınlatma Açısından Cami ve Mescidlerin Önemi' in *1. Din Hizmetleri Sempozyumu*. Ankara: Diyanet İşleri Başkanlığı Yayınları, pp. 379–394.

Akçura, Yusuf. (1976). *Üç Tarz-ı Siyaset*. Ankara: Türk Tarih Kurumu Basımevi.

Akdoğan, Yalçın. (2003). *Muhafazakâr Demokrasi*. Ankara: AK Parti.

(2010). *İnsanı Yaşat ki Devlet Yaşasın*. İstanbul: Meydan Yayıncılık.

Akekmekçi, Tuba and Pervan, Muzaffer. (2010). *Doğu Sorunu – Necmeddin Sahir Sılan Raporları (1939–1953)*. İstanbul: Tarih Vakfı Yurt Yayınları/Necmeddin Sahir Sılan Arşivi [Necmeddin Sahir Sılan Archives].

(2011a). *Dersim Harekatı Ve Cumhuriyet Bürokrasisi (1936–1950)*. İstanbul: Tarih Vakfı Yurt Yayınları/Necmeddin Sahir Sılan Arşivi.

(2011b). *Doğu Anadolu ve Bürokrasisi (1939–1951)*. İstanbul: Tarih Vakfı Yurt Yayınları/Necmeddin Sahir Sılan Arşivi.

(2012). *Dersimlilerden Mektuplar (1941–1953)*. İstanbul: Tarih Vakfı Yurt Yayınları/Necmeddin Sahir Sılan Arşivi.

AKP (AK Parti). www.akparti.org.tr

(2002). *Ak Parti Kalkınma ve Demokratikleşme Programı*.

(30 September 2012). *2023 Political Vision*. AK Parti.

(16 June 2013). *Biz Yüzde Yüzün Hükümetiyiz*. AK Parti. www.akparti.org.tr/mobil/haberler/biz-yuzde-yuzun-hukumetiyiz/46043

(22 April 2014). *Milletten Yetki Alan C.Başkanı Olacak*. AK Parti. www.akparti karabuk.org.tr/tr/haber/genel-baskandan/milletten-yetki-alan-cumhurbaskani-olacak/62472

Akseki, Ahmed Hamdi. (1997). 'Dinî Müesseseler Ve Din Eğitiminin Meselelerine Dair Rapor' in İsmail Kara (ed.), *Türkiye'de İslamcılık Düşüncesi 2*. İstanbul: Kitabevi.

Alevi Bektashi Federation (Alevi Bektaşi Federasyonu, ABF). www.alevifederasyonu .org.tr/abfhakkindadetay.php?id=5

Alevi Opening Report (Alevi İnanç Rehberleri Çalışma Yemeği) [Alevi Faith Leaders Working Dinner]. (14 January 2010). Ankara: TC Başbakanlık, Ankara.

Altıkulaç, Tayyar. (2011a). *Zorlukları Aşarken I*. Ankara: Ufuk Yayınları.

(2011b). *Zorlukları Aşarken II*. Ankara: Ufuk Yayınları.

(November 2013). '13. Diyanet İşleri Başkanı Dr. Tayyar Altıkulaç'ın Görüşleri ... "Daha Yürekli Bir Diyanet"'. *Altınoluk*. dergi.altinoluk.com/ index.php?sayfa=yillarandMakaleNo=d093s020m1

Anayasa Mahkemesi [Constitutional Court of Turkey]. http://www.anayasa.gov .tr/icsayfalar/kararlar/kbb.html

Artam, Nurettin. (1953). *Müslüman Türkler, Ayrılıktan Kaçının!* Ankara: Ulus Basımevi.

Atatürk, Mustafa Kemal. (1997). *Nutuk*. İstanbul: Ege Yayınları.

AUK (Anayasa Uzlaşma Komisyonu) [Constitutional Reconciliation Commission]. (2012–2013a). 1 Nolu Yazım Komisyonu Tutanakları. Anayasa Portalı. TBMM. Yenianayasa.Tbmm.Gov.Tr/Default.Aspx

[Constitutional Reconciliation Commission]. (2012–2013b). 2 Nolu Yazım Komisyonu Tutanakları. Anayasa Portalı. TBMM. Yenianayasa.Tbmm.Gov .Tr/Default.Aspx

Bali, Rıfat N. (2011). *Revival of Islam in Turkey in the 1950s through the Reports of American Diplomats*. Libra: Kitap.

Balkan, Sadık, Uysal, Ahmet E. and Karpat, Kemal H. (Trans.) (1962). 'Constitution of the Turkish Republic'. *Middle East Journal*, 16: 15–38.

Bardakoğlu, Ali. (2004). 'The Evasive Crescent: The Role of Religion in Politics'. *Turkish Policy Quarterly*. İstanbul: ARI Movement.

(2006). *Religion and Society: New Perspectives from Turkey*. Ankara: Publications of Presidency of Religious Affairs.

(2008). 'The Structure, Mission and Social Function of the Presidency of Religious Affairs'. *The Muslim World*, 98(2–3): 173–181.

(2009). *Religion and Society*. Ankara: Diyanet İşleri Başkanlığı.

(2010a). *21. Yüzyıl Türkiye'sinde Din Ve Diyanet, 1*. Ankara: Diyanet İşleri Başkanlığı.

(2010b). *21. Yüzyıl Türkiye'sinde Din Ve Diyanet, 2*. Ankara: Diyanet İşleri Başkanlığı.

Başar, Serap. (2008). 'Diyanet İşleri Başkanlığı'nın Yürüttüğü Cami Dışı Din Hizmetleri Kapsamında Hastanelerde Din Hizmeti ihtiyacı' in *1. Din Hizmetleri Sempozyumu*. Ankara: Diyanet İşleri Başkanlığı Yayınları, pp. 620–646.

Basın Yayın ve Enformasyon Genel Müdürlüğü [Turkish Directorate General of Press and Information]. www.byegm.gov.tr

BCA (Başbakanlık Cumhuriyet Arşivi) [Prime Ministry's Republic Archives].

[Prime Ministry's Republic Archives]. (22 May 1923). Code: 30.10.0.0; Place No: 26.149.5.

[Prime Ministry's Republic Archives]. (7 March 1924). Code: 51.0.0.0, Place No: 2.1.30.

[Prime Ministry's Republic Archives]. (10 April 1926). File No: 906, Code: 30.10.0.0, Place No: 102.667.7.

[Prime Ministry's Republic Archives]. (21 February 1929). Code: 30.10.0.0; Place No: 102.668.8.

[Prime Ministry's Republic Archives]. (7 March 1929a). Code: 30.10.0.0, Place No: 102.668.13.

[Prime Ministry's Republic Archives]. (7 March 1929b). Code: 30.10.0.0, Place No: 102.668.13.

[Prime Ministry's Republic Archives]. (6 January 1930). Code: 30.10.0.0; Place No: 26.150.12.

[Prime Ministry's Republic Archives]. (24 January 1936). Code: 490.1.0.0; Place No: 589.38.1.

[Prime Ministry's Republic Archives]. (8 February 1938). Code: 51.0.0.0; Place No: 12.102.10.

[Prime Ministry's Republic Archives]. (20 February 1939). Code: 51.0.0.0, Place No: 4.36.9.

[Prime Ministry's Republic Archives]. (4 April 1942). Code: 30.10.0.0; Place No: 26.151.16.

[Prime Ministry's Republic Archives]. (16 February 1944). Code: 51.0.0.0, Place No: 4.30.7.

[Prime Ministry's Republic Archives]. (19 August 1944). Code: 30.10.0.0; Place No: 86.571.10.

[Prime Ministry's Republic Archives]. (5 September 1944). Code: 30.10.0.0; Place No: 86.571.8.

[Prime Ministry's Republic Archives]. (15 April 1946). Code: 51.0.0.0; Place No: 4.30.14.

[Prime Ministry's Republic Archives]. (8 August 1957). Code: 30.1.0.0; Place No: 105.657.8.

[Prime Ministry's Republic Archives]. (28 September 1960). Code: 51.0.0.0; Place No: 4.33.29.

[Prime Ministry's Republic Archives]. (1 April 1964). File No: F14, Code: 30.1.0.0, Place No: 105.657.10.

Bilimer, Vehbi. (1963). *Diyanet İşleri Başkanlığı Kuruluş ve Görevleri Kanun Tasarısı Hakkında Mütalaa*. İstanbul: Sönmez Neşriyat ve Matbaacılık.

Bolay, Süleyman Hayri. (1996). *Türk Eğitim Sistemi: Alternatif Perspektif*. Ankara: Türkiye Diyanet Vakfı.

Çalışlar, İzzeddin. (2010). *Dersim Raporu*. İstanbul: İletişim.

Cangöz, M. Coşkun. (2010). *Redistribution of Power and Status through Public Finance: The Case of Turkey (1980–2003)*. Ankara: Republic Of Turkey Ministry of Finance Strategy Development Unit.

CHP (Cumhuriyet Halk Partisi). (1948). *CHP Yedinci Kurultay Tutanağı* [CHP 1947 Congress Minutes]. Ankara: Cumhuriyet Halk Partisi.

(1973). *Ak Günlere, 1973 Seçim Bildirgesi* [CHP Party Programme]. Cumhuriyet Halk Partisi.

Çolak, Yaşar and Özdemirci, Harun. (2001). *Din-Devlet Din-Siyaset İlişkisi*. Ankara: Diyanet İşleri Başkanlığı.

Constitution Portal, Turkish Grand National Assembly of Turkey (Anayasa Portalı, TBMM). Yenianayasa.Tbmm.Gov.Tr/Default.Aspx

CSAK (Cumhuriyet Senatosu Araştırma Komisyonu) [Republic's Senate Investigation Committee]. (17 Febraury 1975). *Diyanet İşleri Başkanlığında Görevli Yaşar Tunagür'ün Faaliyetleri Konusunda Kurulan Cumhuriyet Senatosu Araştırma Komisyonunun Üçüncü Raporu (10/44)*.

Dernekler Dairesi Başkanlığı [Directorate of Associations, DoA]. www.dernekler .gov.tr/

DİB (Diyanet İşleri Başkanlığı) [Presidency of Religious Affairs]. www.diyanet .gov.tr/

(1961). *Müftü Ve Vaizlerin İrşad Vazifelerini İfa Ederken Göz Önünde Tutmaları Gereken Hususlar Hakkında Açıklama.* Ankara: Diyanet İşleri Başkanlığı Yayınları.

(1962). *Aydın Din Adamları.* Diyanet İşleri Başkanlığı.

(1964a). *Nurculuk Hakkında.* Diyanet İşleri Reisliği.

(1964b). *Komünizm Hakkında İslami Görüşler.* Diyanet İşleri Başkanlığı.

(1985). Diyanet İşleri Başkanlığı Merkez Ve Taşra *Teşkilatı* Görev ve Çalışma Yönergeleri. Diyanet İşleri Başkanlığı.

(1988). *Din Öğretimi ve Din Hizmetleri Semineri.* Ankara; Diyanet İşleri Başkanlığı.

(2002). *2000 İnanç Ve Hoşgörü Çağında Dinler Toplantısı.* Diyanet İşleri Başkanlığı.

(30 June 2005). *İl Müftüleri Semineri Sonuç Bildirgesi.* Abant – Bolu.

(12 February 2006). *Basın Açıklaması.*

(28 February 2006). *İl Müftüleri Semineri Sonuç Bildirgesi.* Antalya.

(13 September 2006). *İl Müftüleri Semineri Sonuç Bildirgesi.* Kızılcahamam-Ankara.

(21 March 2007). *İl Müftüleri Semineri Sonuç Bildirgesi.* İzmir.

(13 November 2007). *İl Müftüleri Semineri Sonuç Bildirgesi.* Antalya.

(30 May 2008). *İl Müftüleri Semineri Sonuç Bildirgesi.* Van.

(2008). *TC Diyanet İşleri Başkanlığı Stratejik Plan (2009 – 2013)* [Presidency of Religious Affairs 2009–2013 Strategy Report]. Ankara: Türkiye Diyanet Vakfı.

(2014). *Türkiye'de Dini Hayat Araştırması.* Ankara: Diyanet İşleri Başkanlığı.

(22 January 2014). *İl Müftüleri Semineri Sonuç Bildirgesi.* Ankara.

(25 March 2014). *Diyanet İşleri Başkanlığı Basın Açıklaması. İstismarı.* Ankara: Diyanet İşleri Başkanlığı.

(2017b). 'Diyanetten Binlerce Yabancı Öğrenciye Din Eğitimi'. http://kocaeli .diyanet.gov.tr/basiskele/Sayfalar/contentdetail.aspx?MenuCategory=Kurumsal& contentid=114

(12 June 2017). 'Suriye'de Terörden Temizlenen Bölgeye Koordinatör Müftüler'. www.diyanet.gov.tr/tr-TR/Kurumsal/Detay/10176/suriyede-teror den-temizlenen-bolgeye-koordinator-muftuler

(July 2017). *Diyanet İşleri Başkanlığı 2017 Yılı Kurumsal Mali Durum ve Beklentiler Raporu.* Ankara: Strateji Geliştirme Başkanlığı.

Diyanet Aylık Dergisi [Diyanet Monthly Magazine]. Ankara: Diyanet İşleri Başkanlığı.

Diyanet İşleri Başkanlığı Yayınları [Presidency of Religious Affairs Publications].

Diyanet-Sen. (26 July 2017). 'Diyanet-Sen'in Teklifi Mecliste Müftüler de Nikah Kıyabilecek'. www.diyanet-sen.org.tr/diyanet-senin-teklifi-mecliste-muftu lerde-nikah-kiyabilecek

DM (Danışma Meclisi Tutanak Dergisi) [The Journal of the Consultative Assembly Records]. (29 June 1981–1 December 1983.)

(1 September 1982.) Vol. 9, Assembly 1, Session 140.

DMAK1 (TBMM Darbe Ve Muhtıraları Araştırma Komisyonu) [Parliamentary Commission Investigating Military Coups]. (2 November 2012). *Ülkemizde Demokrasiye Müdahale Eden Tüm Darbe Ve Muhtıralar Ile Demokrasiyi İşlevsiz Kılan Diğer Bütün Girişim Ve Süreçlerin Tüm Boyutları Ile Araştırılarak Alınması Gereken Önlemlerin Belirlenmesi Amacıyla Kurulan Meclis Araştırması Komisyonu, Cilt 1.* No: 376, Period: 24, Year: 3. www.Tbmm.Gov.Tr/Ara stirma_Komisyonlari/Darbe_Muhtira/

DMAK2 (TBMM Darbe Ve Muhtıraları Araştırma Komisyonu). [Parliamentary Commission Investigating Military Coups]. (November 2012). *Ülkemizde Demokrasiye Müdahale Eden Tüm Darbe Ve Muhtıralar Ile Demokrasiyi İşlevsiz Kılan Diğer Bütün Girişim Ve Süreçlerin Tüm Boyutları Ile Araştırılarak Alınması Gereken Önlemlerin Belirlenmesi Amacıyla Kurulan Meclis Araştırması Komisyonu, Cilt 2.* No: 376, Period: 24, Year: 3. www.Tbmm.Gov.Tr/Ara stirma_Komisyonlari/Darbe_Muhtira

DoF (Vakıflar Genel Müdürlüğü) [Directorate General of Foundations]. www.vgm.gov.tr/

Doğan, Bilal. (January 2009). *TC Diyanet İşleri Başkanlığının Görevleri Bakimindan Yapılması Gereken Hususlar İle İlgili Güncelleştirilmiş Bir Rapor.* Diyanet İşleri Başkanlığı.

DPT (Devlet Planlama Teşkilatı) [State Planning Organisation]. (1983). *Milli Kültür Özel İhtisas Komisyonu Raporu.* Ankara: Devlet Planlama Teşkilatı.

Earle, Edward Mead. (1925). 'The New Constitution of Turkey'. *Political Science Quarterly,* 40(1): 73–100.

Erdil, Kemal. 1974. *İmam Hatip Okulları ve Diyanet İşleri Başkanlığı'nın İstihdam-İhtiyaç Sorunu.* Ankara: Diyanet İşleri Başkanlığı; Ayyıldız Matbaası.

Erdoğan, İsmail. (1996). XX. 'Yüzyıl Amasya Tarihi ve İnanç Coğrafyası'. Unpublished master's thesis.

Erol, Ayten V. (2008). 'Bayanlara Yönelik Din Hizmetleri'. *1. Din Hizmetleri Sempozyumu.* Ankara: Diyanet Işleri Başkanlığı Yayınları, pp. 650–662.

European Commission Progress Reports. (2016). https://ec.europa.eu/neighbour hood-enlargement/countries/detailed-country-information/turkey_en

Gökalp, Ziya. (2011). *Kürt Aşiretleri Hakkında Sosyolojik Tetkikler.* İstanbul: Kaynak Yayınları.

Görmez, Mehmet. (2008). 'The Status of the Presidency of Religious Affairs in the Turkish Constitution and its Execution'. *The Muslim World,* 98(2–3): 242–248.

Hammadi, Muhammad Ibn Malik. (1948). *Batiniler Ve Karmatilerin İç Yüzü.* Ankara: Diyanet İşleri Başkanlığı Yayınları.

(2004). *Batiniler Ve Karmatilerin İç Yüzü.* İstanbul: Sebil Yayınevi.

İskurt, Mustafa. (1995). 'Diyanet Televizyonu'. *I.Din Şurası Tebliğ ve Müzakereleri.* Ankara: Diyanet Işleri Başkanlığı Yayınları.

İstanbul Sanayi Odası (İSO) [İstanbul Chamber of Industry].

İstanbul Vaizleri. (1963). *Diyanet İşleri Başkanlığı Kuruluş ve Görevleri Kanun Tasarısı Hakkında İstanbul Vaizlerinin Görüş ve Tenkidleri.* İstanbul: Ahmed Said Matbaası.

Kafesoğlu, İbrahim. (1999). *Türk İslam Sentezi*. İstanbul: Ötüken Yayınları.

Kalafat, Yaşar Kaya. (1995). 'İrşad Hizmetlerinde İnanç Tabakalaşması ve Konunun Haritalanmasının Önemi'. *I.Din Şurası Tebliğ ve Müzakereleri*. Ankara: Diyanet İşleri Başkanlığı Yayınları, pp. 127–130.

Karabekir, Kazım. (1994 [1948]). *Kürt Meselesi*. İstanbul: Emre Yayınları.

Karaman, Hayrettin. (2015a). *Bir Varmış Bir Yokmuş – Hayatım ve Hatıralarım 1*. İstanbul: İz Yayıncılık.

(2015b). *Bir Varmış Bir Yokmuş – Hayatım ve Hatıralarım 2*. İstanbul: İz Yayıncılık.

(2015c). *Bir Varmış Bir Yokmuş – Hayatım ve Hatıralarım 3*. İstanbul: İz Yayıncılık.

Koçak, Cemil. (2003 [1936]). *Umumi Müfettişler Toplantı Tutanakları*. Ankara: Dipnot/Tarih Dizisi.

(2010a). *27 Mayıs Bakanlar Kurulu Tutanakları*. Ankara: Yapı Kredi Yayınları/ Tarih.

(2010b). *Umumi Müfettişlerliler*. İstanbul: İletişim.

Kültür ve Turizm Bakanlığı [Ministry of Culture and Tourism].

Kürkçüoğlu, Kemal Edib. (1956). *Din Ve Milliyet*. Ankara: Diyanet İşleri Reisliği Yayınları.

Kutlu, İbrahim. (1976). *Ziya Gökalp, Türkleşmek, İslamlaşmak, Muasırlaşmak*. Ankara: Ankara Kültür Bakanlığı Yayını.

Kuzgun, Şaban. (2000). 'Türkiye'nin İnanç Coğrafyası-Araştırma Projesi'. *Fırat Üniversitesi İlahiyat Fakültesi Dergisi*, 5: 5–11.

Maliye Bakanlığı Bütçe ve Mali Kontrol Genel Müdürlüğü [Ministry of Finance General Directorate of Budget and Fiscal Control].

MEB (Milli Eğitim Bakanlığı) [Ministry of National Education]. www.meb .gov.tr/

(1961). *Din ile İlgili Eğitim ve Öğretim Komitesi Raporu*. Ankara: Milli Eğitim Basımevi.

Milli Güvenlik Konseyi Tutanak Dergisi (MGK TD) [The Journal of the National Security Council]. (19 September 1980–6 June 1983).

MÜSİAD (Müstakil Sanayici ve İşadamları Derneği). www.musiad.org.tr

(1991). *Çerçeve Dergisi*. İstanbul: MÜSİAD Yayınları.

(1992). *Orta Büyüklükteki İşletmeler ve Bürokrasi*. İstanbul: MÜSİAD Yayınları.

(1994a). *Türkiye Ekonomisi*. İstanbul: MÜSİAD Yayınları.

(1994b). *İş Hayatında İslam İnsanı (Homo Islamicus)*. İstanbul: MÜSİAD Yayınları.

(1998). *Çerçeve Dergisi*. İstanbul: MÜSİAD Yayınları, No. 8.

(2005). *15. Yılında MÜSİAD*. İstanbul: MÜSİAD Yayınları, No. 1.

(2008). *Yeni Bir Anayasa İçin Görüş ve Öneriler*. İstanbul: MÜSİAD Yayınları.

(2010). *20. Yıl. MÜSİAD*. İstanbul: MÜSİAD Yayınları.

(2011). *TC Anayasa Önerisi*. İstanbul: MÜSİAD Yayınları.

Mustafa, Ülger. (1997). XX. 'Yüzyil Eskişehir İli Tarihi Ve İnanç Coğrafyası'. Master's thesis.

Nihai Rapor (Alevi Çalıştayları Nihai Rapor) [Alevi Workshops Final Report].
(2010). Ankara: T.C. Başbakanlık.

Nomer, Kemaleddin. (1964). *Diyanet İşleri Başkanlığı Kuruluş Ve Görevleri Hakkındaki Kanun Tasarısına Dair Düşüceler.* İstanbul: Çeltüt Matbaacılık.

Ottoman Constitution of 1876. www.Anayasa.Gen.Tr/Kanunuesasi.Htm

Özdemir, Şuayip. (2007). 'Cezaevi Din Hizmetlerinin Temel Problemleri'. *1. Din Hizmetleri Sempozyumu.* Ankara: Diyanet İşleri Başkanlığı Yayınları, pp. 163–175.

Öztürk, Kazım. (1966a). *Türkiye Cumhuriyeti Anayasası,* Vol. 1 [Constitution of the Turkish Republic, Minutes and Proposals of the 1961 Constitutional Debates]. Ankara: Türkiye İş Bankası Kültür Yayınları.

(1966b). *Türkiye Cumhuriyeti Anayasası,* Vol. 2. Ankara: Türkiye İş Bankası Kültür Yayınları.

Republic of Turkey Ministry of Finance Strategy Development Unit. *Resmi Gazete [Official Gazette].* www.resmigazete.gov.tr

Şenel, Muazzez and Şenel, A. Turhan. (1969). *Devlet Genel Güvenliği Ve Polis.* Ankara: Emniyet Genel Müdürlüğü.

Sezgin, Abdülkadir. (1996). *Alevilik Deyince.* İstanbul: Burak Yayınevi.

(2002). *Sosyolojik Açıdan Alevilik-Bektaşilik.* Ankara: Yeni Türkiye Yayınları.

(2012 [1990, 1991, 1995]). *Hacı Bektaş Veli ve Bektaşilik.* Ankara: Kültür Bakanlığı.

SP (Saadet Partisi [Felicity Party]). (3 November 2002). *Saadet Partisi Seçim Beyannamesi. Acil Onarım ve Atılım Programı* [Party Programme]. İstanbul: Alfa Menkul Değerler.

Subaşı, Necdet. (2006). *Diyanet İşleri Başkanlığı Üzerine Laik Bir Cumhuriyet'te Sürdürülebilir Din Politikaları.* Muğla Üniversitesi.

(2011). 'Yeni Anayasada Din Alanı'. *Stratejik Düşünce.*

Tankut, Hasan Reşit. (1937). *Dil Ve Irk Münasebetleri Hakkında.* İstanbul: Devlet Basimevi.

(1938). *Nusayriler Ve Nusayrilik Hakkında.* Ankara: Ulus Basımevi.

(2000). *Zazalar Üzerine Sosyolojik Tetkikler.* Ankara: Kalan Basım Yayın Dağıtım.

(2008). *Maraş Yollarında.* Kahramanmaraş: Ukde.

TBMM Gizli Celse Zabıtları (GCZ) [Secret Minutes of the Closed Sessions of the Grand National Assembly]. (1920–1924).

TBMM TDa (TBMM Tutanak Dergisi) [The Journal of the Grand National Assembly of Turkey]. (1946–1957).

[The Journal of Records of the Grand National Assembly of Turkey]. (1983–2014).

TC Devlet Bakanlığı. Alevi Çalıştayı [Alevi Opening Meeting Minutes].

TC MM (TC Millet Meclisi Tutanak Dergisi) [The Journal of the National Assembly Records]. (28 January 1965a [22.1.1962]). *Diyanet İşleri Başkanlığı Kuruluş Ve Görevleri Hakkında Kanun Teklifleri Geçici Komisyon Raporu.*

[The Journal of the National Assembly Records]. (28 January 1965b [24.1.1962]). *Diyanet İşleri Başkanlığı Kuruluş Ve Görevleri Hakkında Kanun, Hükümetin Teklîfi.*

TİTYEDF (Türkiye İlahiyat Tedrisatına Yardım Eden Dernekler Federasyonu) [Federation of Turkey Theology Educational Helpers Organisations]. (1962). *Diyanet İşleri Başkanlığı Teşkilatına Ait Kanun Tasarısı Hakkındaki Düşüncelerimiz.* Ankara: Türkiye İlahiyat Tedrisatına Yardım Eden Dernekler Federasyonu.

TM (TC Temsilciler Meclisi Tutanak Dergisi) [The Journal of the Representatives Assembly Records]. (6 January 1961–3 September 1961).

TOKI (Toplu Konut Idaresi [Mass Housing Administration]). www.toki.gov.tr/

TRT Haber. (15 November 2015). 'İslam Bu Tür Haydutlarin Tehdidi Altindadir'. *TRT Haber.* www.trthaber.com/haber/turkiye/islam-bu-tur-haydutlarin-tehdidi-altindadir-216151.html

Türk Anayasa Hukuku Sitesi [Portal of Turkish Constitutions]. www.Anayasa.Gen.Tr

Türk Diyanet Vakıf-Sen. (2008). *Diyanet İşleri Başkanlığı Tasarısı.* Ankara: Türk Diyanet Vakıf-Sen.

Türk Mühendis ve Mimar Odaları Birliği [Union of Chambers of Turkish Engineers and Architects, TMMOB].

Turkish Grand National Assembly of Turkey (Türkiye Büyük Millet Meclisi, TBMM). www.tbmm.gov.tr

Türkiye Büyük Millet Meclisi Başkanlığı Kütüphane ve Arşiv Başkanlığı [Grand National Assembly of Turkey Library and Archives]. www.tbmm.gov.tr/kutuphane/tutanak_sorgu.html

Türkiye Cumhuriyet Merkez Bankası [Central Bank of Turkey]. www.tcmb.gov.tr

Türkiye Diyanet Vakfı İslam Ansiklopedisi. www.islamansiklopedisi.info/ Türkiye Diyanet Vakfı Yayınları.

Turkish Statistical Institute (Türkiye İstatistik Kurumu, TUIK). www.turkstat.gov.tr

Türkiye Kömür İşletmeleri Kurumu [General Directorate of Turkish Coal, TKİ]. www.Tki.Gov.Tr

TÜSİAD (Türk Sanayicileri ve İş İnsanları Derneği) [Turkish Industry and Business Association]. www.tusiad.org

(2011). *Yeni Anayasa Yuvarlak Masa Toplantıları Dizisi: Yeni Anayasanın Beş Temel Boyutu.* TÜSİAD.

(2013). *Çalışma 2013 Raporu.* TÜSİAD.

Uluğ, Naşit Hakkı. (1975). *Halifeliğin Sonu.* İstanbul: Türkiye İş Bankası Yayınları.

(2007 [1939]). *Tunceli Medeniyete Açılıyor.* İstanbul: Kaynak Yayınları.

(2009). *Derebeyi ve Dersim.* İstanbul: Kaynak Yayınları.

Ünalan, Sıddık. (1997). XX. 'Yüzyıl Sivas Tarihi ve Günümüz İnanç Coğrafyası'. Tarih Eğitimi Anabilim Dalı. PhD thesis.

Üzüm, İlyas. (1997). *Günümüz Aleviliği.* İstanbul: Türkiye Diyanet Vakfı İslam Araştırmaları Merkezi (İSAM) Yayınları.

World Bank, Worldwide Governance Indicators, http://info.worldbank.org/governance/wgi/index.aspx#home.

Yarar, Erol. (1997). *A New Perspective of the World at the Threshold of the 21st Century*. İstanbul: MÜSİAD.

Yayınevi, Bedir. (1966). *Din Aleyhtarı TRT'ye İhtar*. İstanbul: Bedir Yayınevi.

Yazıcıoğlu, Said M. (2013). *Ne Yan Yana Ne Karşı Karşıya (Anılar)*. İstanbul: Alfa Yayıncılık.

Yıldırım, Tuğba. (2011). *Kürt Sorunu Ve Devlet, Tedip Ve Tenkil Politikaları 1925–1947*. İstanbul: Tarih Vakfı Yurt Yayınları/Necmeddin Sahir Sılan Arşivi [Necmeddin Sahir Sılan Archives].

ZC (TBMM Zabıt Ceridesi), [Records of the Grand National Assembly]. (29 October 1339 [1923]). Period 2, Vol. 8, Assembly 1, Session 43.

(3 March 1340 [1924]). Period 2, Vol. 7, Assembly 1, Session 2.

(20 March 1340 [1924]). Period 2, Vol. 7/1, Assembly 2, Session 17.

(5 February 1937). Period 5, Vol. 16, Assembly 2, Session 33.

Secondary sources

Abbott, Andrew. (1988). 'Transcending General Linear Reality'. *Sociological Theory*, 6(2): 169–186.

Abrams, Philip. (1988). 'Notes on the Difficulty of Studying the State'. *Journal of Historical Sociology*, 1(1): 58–89.

Açıkel, Fethi. (1996). '"Kutsal Mazlumluğun" Psikopatolojisi'. *Toplum ve Bilim*, 70: 153–198.

Adak, Sevgi. (November 2015). '"Yeni" Türkiye'nin "Yeni" Diyaneti'. *Birikim*, (319): 78–85.

(2016). 'Anti-Veiling Campaigns and Local Elites in Turkey of the 1930s: A View from the Periphery' in Stephanie Cronin (ed.). *Anti-Veiling Campaigns in the Muslim World: Gender, Modernism and the Politics of Dress*. London; New York: Routledge, pp. 59–85.

Ahmad, Feroz. (1988). 'Islamic Reassertion in Turkey'. *Third World Quarterly*, 10 (2): 750–769.

(1993). *The Making of Modern Turkey*. London: Routledge.

(2000). 'Ottoman Perceptions of the Capitulations 1800–1914'. *Journal of Islamic Studies*, 11(1): 1–20.

Akın, Rıdvan. (2001). *TBMM Devleti, 1920–1923: Birinci Meclis Döneminde Devlet Erkleri ve İdare*. İstanbul: İletişim.

Akın, Yiğit. (2007). 'Reconsidering State, Party, and Society in Early Republican Turkey: Politics of Petitioning'. *International Journal of Middle East Studies*, 39 (03): 435–457.

Akinci, Ugur. (1999). 'The Welfare Party's Municipal Track Record: Evaluating Islamist Municipal Activism in Turkey'. *The Middle East Journal*, 53(1): 75–94.

Akit. (1 August 2016). 'FETÖ'nün Alevi Fitnesi'. *Akit*. www.yeniakit.com.tr/ haber/fetonun-alevi-fitnesi-198427.html

Akman, Canan A. (2010). 'Beyond the Ballot Box: Turkish Democracy under Tension between Idealism and Populism'. Annual Conference of the Canadian Political Science Association.

Akşam. (20 February 2013). 'Diyanet'ten Kürtçe Vaaz Yorumu'. *Akşam.* www.aksam.com.tr/siyaset/diyanetten-kurtce-vaaz-yorumu/haber-170966

Aktar, Ayhan. (2000). *Varlık Vergisi ve 'Türkleştirme' Politikaları.* İstanbul: İletişim.

(2006). *Türk Milliyetçiliği, Gayrimüslimler ve Ekonomik Dönüşüm.* İstanbul: İletişim.

(2009). '"Turkification" Policies in the Early Republican Era'. In Catharina Duft (ed.), *Turkish Literature and Cultural Memory.* Wiesbaden: Harrassowitz Verlag.

Aktay, Yasin. (2000). *Türk Dininin Sosyolojik Imkanı.* İstanbul: İletişim.

(2003). 'Diaspora and Stability: Constitutive Elements in a Body of Knowledge.' In M. Hakan Yavuz and John L. Esposito (eds.), *Turkish Islam and the Secular State: The Gülen Movement.* Syracuse University Press, pp. 131–155.

(2015). 'Prof. Dr. Yasin Aktay'ın Değerlendirmesi.' In Hayrettin Karaman, *Bir Varmış Bir Yokmuş – Hayatım ve Hatıralarım 3.* İstanbul: İz Yayıncılık, pp. 377–406.

Aktürk, Şener. (2009). 'Persistence of the Islamic Millet as an Ottoman Legacy: Mono-Religious and Anti-Ethnic Definition of Turkish Nationhood'. *Middle Eastern Studies*, 45(6): 893–909.

(2012). *Regimes of Ethnicity and Nationhood in Germany, Russia, and Turkey.* Cambridge University Press.

(2015). 'Religion and Nationalism: Contradictions of Islamic Origins and Secular Nation-Building in Turkey, Algeria, and Pakistan'. *Social Science Quarterly*, 96(3): 778–806.

Akyol, Taha. (1998). *Medine'den Lozan'a.* İstanbul: Milliyet Yayınları.

(2008). *Ama Hangi Atatürk.* İstanbul: Doğan Kitap.

Albayrak, Sadık. (1977). *Şeriat'ten Laikliğe. Türkiye'de İslamcılık – Batıcılık Mücadelesi.* İstanbul: Sebil Yayınevi.

Alkan, Mehmet Ö. (2009). 'II. Meşrutiyet'te Eğitim, İttihad Ve Terakki Cemiyeti, Milliyetçilik, Militarizm Veya "Militer Türk-İslam Sentezi"' in Ferdan Ergut (ed.), *II. Meşrutiyeti Yeniden Düşünmek.* İstanbul: Tarih Vakfı Yurt Yayınları, pp. 57–85.

Altan, Mehmet. (29 April 2014). 'İç Savaşın Kanlı Cehenneminden Geçmeden'. *T24.* http://t24.com.tr/yazarlar/mehmet-altan/ic-savasin-kanli-cehennemin den-gecmeden,9141

Althusser, L. (2006). 'Ideology and Ideological State Apparatuses (Notes towards an Investigation)' in A. Sharma and A. Gupta (eds.), *The Anthropology of the State: A Reader.* Malden, MA; Oxford: Blackwell, pp. 86–111.

Al Jazeera. (8 September 2016). 'Cemaatler kayıt altına alınmalı'. *Al Jazeera.* www.aljazeera.com.tr/al-jazeera-ozel/cemaatler-kayit-altina-alinmali

Al Monitor, (12 December 2014). 'Erdogan Defends Brotherhood's Qaradawi after Arrest Warrant'. *Al Monitor.*

(12 April 2017). 'Turkey's Last Ergenekon Trial Ends as All Defendants Acquitted'. *Al Monitor.*

Anadolu Agency. (13 December 2014). '5. Din Şurası Kararları Açıklandı'. *Anadolu Agency.* http://aa.com.tr/tr/yasam/5-din-surasi-kararlari-aciklandi/92911

(2 April 2017). '47,155 Remanded in FETO Probe since July 2016 Coup Bid'. Anadolu Agency. www.aa.com.tr/en/july-15-coup-bid/47-155-remanded-in-feto-probe-since-july-2016-coup-bid/786527

Anderson, Benedict. (1991). *Imagined Communities: Reflections on the Origin and Spread of Nationalism*. New York: Verso Books.

Angrist, M. P. (2004). 'Party Systems and Regime Formation in the Modern Middle East: Explaining Turkish Exceptionalism'. *Comparative Politics*, 36(2): 229–249.

Antoun, Richard T. and Hegland, Mary Elaine (eds.). (1987). *Religious Resurgence: Contemporary Cases in Islam, Christianity, and Judaism*. Syracuse University Press.

Arai, Masami. (1992). *Turkish Nationalism in the Young Turk Era*. Vol. 43. Leiden: Brill.

Aras, Bülent. (1998). 'Turkish Islam's Moderate Face'. *Middle East Quarterly*, 5(3): 23–29.

Arat, Yeşim. (2010). 'Women's Rights and Islam in Turkish Politics: The Civil Code Amendment'. *The Middle East Journal*, 64(2): 235–251.

Asad, Talal. (1992). 'Religion and Politics: An Introduction'. *Social Research*, 59(1): 3–16.

(1999). 'Religion, Nation-State, Secularism' in Peter van der Veer, and Hartmut Lehmann (eds.), *Nation and Religion: Perspectives on Europe and Asia*. Princeton University Press, pp. 178–196.

(2003). *Formations of the Secular: Christianity, Islam, Modernity*. Stanford University Press.

(2009). *Genealogies of Religion: Discipline and Reasons of Power in Christianity and Islam*. Baltimore, MA; London: Johns Hopkins University Press.

Ata, Kelime. (2007). *Alevilerin İlk Siyasal Denemesi: (Türkiye) Birlik Partisi (1966–1980)*. Ankara: Kelime Yayınevi.

(29 December 2013). 'Aleviyse Fişlenir Elbet!' *Radikal*. www.radikal.com.tr/radikal2/aleviyse_fislenir_elbet-1168653

Atasoy, Yıldız. (2009). *Islam's Marriage with Neoliberalism: State Transformation in Turkey*. New York: Palgrave Macmillan.

Ateş, Kazım. (2006). 'Ulusal Kimlik İçinde Alevi-Yurttaş Ve Merkez-Çevre Eksenini Yeniden Düşünmek'. *Toplum ve Bilim*, 107: 259–275.

(2012). *Yurttaşlığın Kıyısında Aleviler*. Ankara: Phoenix Yayınevi.

Avcı, Hanefi. (2010). *Haliç'te Yaşayan Simonlar*. Ankara: Angora.

Axiarlis, E. (2014). *Political Islam and the Secular State in Turkey: Democracy, Reform and the Justice and Development Party*. London: IB Tauris.

Ayata, Sencer. (1996). 'Patronage, Party and the State: The Politicisation of Islam Turkey'. *Middle East Journal*, 50(1): 40–56.

Aydemir, Şevket Süreyya. (1976). *Tek Adam: Mustafa Kemal: 1922–1938*. Vol 2. İstanbul: Remzi Kitabevi.

Aydın, Ayhan. (16 July 2017). 'Balkanlar'da Aleviler- Bektaşiler Üzerinde Oynanan Oyunlar ve Yunanistan'daki Son Gelişmeler'. *Alevinet*. www.alevinet.com/2017/07/16/balkanlarda-aleviler-bektasiler-uzerinde-oynanan-oyunlar-ve-yunanistandaki-son-gelismeler/

Ayhan, Halis. (2000). 'Cumhuriyet Dönemi Din Eğitipıine Genel Bir Bakış: Atatürk'ün Islam Dini ve Din Eğitimi Hakkındaki Görüşleri'. *M.Ü. İlahiyat Fakültesi Dergisi*, 18(2000): 5–27.

Aytaç, S. Erdem and Öniş, Ziya. (2014). 'Varieties of Populism in a Changing Global Context: The Divergent Paths of Erdoğan and Kirchnerismo'. *Comparative Politics*, 47(10): 41–59.

Azak, Umut. (2010). *Islam and Secularism in Turkey: Kemalism, Religion and the Nation State*. London: IB Tauris.

Balcı, Bayram. (27 January 2014). 'Turkey's Religious Outreach in Central Asia and the Caucasus'. *Carnegie*. http://carnegieendowment.org/2014/01/27/ turkey-s-religious-outreach-in-central-asia-and-caucasus-pub-54357

Bali, Rıfat N. (2006). 'The Politics of Turkification during the Single Party period.' In Hans-Lukas Kieser (ed.), *Turkey beyond Nationalism: Towards Post-Nationalist Identities*. London: IB Tauris, pp. 43–49.

Balkan, Neşecan, Balkan, Erol and Öncü, Ahmet (eds.). (2015). *The Neoliberal Landscape and the Rise of Islamist Capital in Turkey*. New York; Oxford: Berghahn Books.

Bardakçı, Mehmet. (2013). 'Coup Plots and the Transformation of Civil–Military Relations in Turkey under AKP Rule.' *Turkish Studies*, 14(3): 411–428.

(2015). 'The Alevi Opening of the AKP Government in Turkey: Walking a Tightrope between Democracy and Identity'. *Turkish Studies*, 16(3): 349–370.

Barkey, H. J. (1990). *The State and the Industrialization Crisis in Turkey*. Boulder, CO: Westview Press.

Barkey, H. J. and Çongar, Y. (2007). 'Deciphering Turkey's Elections: The Making of a Revolution'. *World Policy Journal*, 24(3): 63–73.

Barkey, Karen. (2005). 'Islam and Toleration: Studying the Ottoman Imperial Model'. *International Journal of Politics, Culture, and Society*, 19(1–2): 5–19.

Barr, Michael D. and Govindasamy, Anantha Raman. (2010). 'The Islamisation of Malaysia: Religious Nationalism in the Service of Ethnonationalism'. *Australian Journal of International Affairs*, 64(3): 293–311.

Barth, Fredrik. (1969). *Ethnic Groups and Boundaries: The Social Organization of Culture Difference*. Bergen: Universitetsforlaget; London: Allen & Unwin.

Başbuğ, İlker. (2016). *15 Temmuz Öncesi ve Sonrası*. İstanbul: Doğan Kitap.

Başgil, Ali Fuat. (1960). *İlmin Işığında Günün Meseleleri*. İstanbul: Yağmur Yayınları.

Başkan, Filiz. (2004). 'The Political Economy of Islamic Finance in Turkey: The Role of Fethullah Gülen and Asya Finans'. In Clement M. Henry and Rodney Wilson (eds.), *The Politics of Islamic Finance*. Edinburgh University Press, pp. 216–239.

Bayar, Yeşim. (2009). 'The Dynamic Nature of Educational Policies and Turkish Nation Building: Where Does Religion Fit In?' *Comparative Studies of South Asia, Africa and the Middle East*, 29(3): 360–370.

(2016a). *Formation of the Turkish Nation-State, 1920–1938*. Basingstoke: Palgrave Macmillan.

(2016b). 'Constitution-Writing, Nationalism and the Turkish Experience'. *Nations and Nationalism*, 22(4): 725–743.

Bayat, Asef. (2007). *'Islam and Democracy: What Is the Real Question?' ISIM Papers*. Amsterdam University Press.

Bayır, Derya. (2016). *Minorities and Nationalism in Turkish Law*. London: Routledge.

Bayrak, Mehmet. (1997). *Alevilik ve Kürtler: İnceleme-araştırma ve Belgeler*. Ankara: Öz-Ge Yayınları.

(2004). *Kürdoloji Belgeleri-II*. Ankara: Öz-Ge Yayınları.

Bayramoğlu, Ali. (21 February 2012). 'AK Parti-cemaat ittifakı sona erdi'. *Habertürk*. www.haberturk.com/polemik/haber/718138-ak-parti-cemaat-itti faki-sona-erdi

BBC. (31 March 2014). 'Erdoğan'dan Balkan Mesajı: Bedelini Ödeyecekler'. BBC. www.bbc.com/turkce/haberler/2014/03/140330_turkiye_secimler

(3 April 2017). 'Kılıçdaroğlu: 15 Temmuz Kontrollü Darbe Girişimidir'. BBC. www.bbc.com/turkce/haberler-turkiye-39478777

(16 April 2017). 'YSK Başkanı Sadi Güven: Mühürsüz Zarf Kararı Bir İlk Değil'. BBC. www.bbc.com/turkce/haberler-turkiye-39616136

Bedirhanoğlu, Pınar and Yalman, Galip L. (2009). 'Neoliberal Küreselleşme Sürecinde Türkiye'de 'Yerel' Sermaye: Gaziantep, Denizli ve Eskişehir'den İzlenimler'. *Praksis*, 19: 241–266.

(2010). "State, Class and the Discourse: Reflections on the Neoliberal Transformation in Turkey." In Alfredo Saad-Filho and Galip L. Yalman (eds.), *Economic Transitions to Neoliberalism in Middle-Income Countries: Policy Dilemmas, Economic Crises, Forms of Resistance*. London/New York: Routledge, pp. 107–127.

Bein, Amit. (2006). 'Politics, Military Conscription, and Religious Education in the Late Ottoman Empire'. *International Journal of Middle East Studies*, 38(2): 283–301.

(2007). 'A "Young Turk" Islamic Intellectual: Filibeli Ahmed Hilmi and the Diverse Intellectual Legacies of the Late Ottoman Empire'. *International Journal of Middle East Studies*, 39(4): 607–625.

(2009). '"Ulama" and Political Activism in the Late Ottoman Empire: The Political Career of Şeyhülislàm Mustafa Sabri Efendi (1869–1954)' in Meir Hatina (ed.), *Guardians of Faith in Modern Times: 'Ulama' in the Middle East*. Leiden; Boston, MA: Brill, pp. 67–90.

(2011). *Ottoman Ulema, Turkish Republic: Agents of Change and Guardians of Tradition*. Stanford University Press.

Belge, Ceren. (2006). 'Friends of the Court: The Republican Alliance and Selective Activism of the Constitutional Court of Turkey'. *Law and Society Review*, 40(3): 653–692.

Berkes, Niyazi. (1964). *The Development of Secularism in Turkey*. Montreal: McGill University Press.

Berkey, Jonathan P. (2001). *Popular Preaching and Religious Authority in the Medieval Islamic Near East*. Seattle, WA: University of Washington Press.

Berland, Allison. (2017). 'When Do Religious Parties Moderate? Religious Party Moderation in Indonesia, Turkey, and India'. *SAIS Review of International Affairs*, 37(1): 131–143.

Bhargava, R. (2011). 'Rehabilitating Secularism' in Craig Calhoun, Mark Juergensmeyer and Jonathan VanAntwerpen (eds.), *Rethinking Secularism*. Oxford University Press, pp. 92–113.

Bilici, Mücahit. (2006). 'The Fethullah Gülen Movement and Its Politics of Representation in Turkey'. *The Muslim World*, 96(1): 1–20.

Billig, Michael. (1995). *Banal Nationalism*. London: Sage.

Birdoğan, Nejat. (1995). *İttihat-Terakki'nin Alevilik Bektaşilik Araştırması (Baha Sait Bey)*. İstanbul: Berfin Yayınevi.

Birelma, Alpkan. (September 2013). 'Antikapitalist Müslümanlar grubu üyeleriyle söyleşi'. *Birikim*, 293.

Birgün. (29 October 2016). 'İşte Gülenciler Sonrası Ülkeyi Saran Tarikat Ağları'. *Birgün*. www.birgun.net/haber-detay/iste-gulenciler-sonrasi-ulkeyi-saran-tarikat-aglari-133401.html

Bora, Tanıl. (2003a). 'Nationalist Discourses in Turkey'. *The South Atlantic Quarterly*, 102(2–3): 433–451.

(2003b). *Türk Sağının Üç Hali*. İstanbul: Birikim Yayınları.

(2013). 'Türkiye'de İslâmcılık Düşüncesi ve Hareketi Üzerine Birkaç Not' in *Türkiye'de İslamcılık Düşüncesi ve Hareketi Sempozyumu*. İstanbul: Zeytinburnu Belediyesi Kültür Yayını, pp. 514–537.

(2017). *Cereyanlar: Türkiye'de Siyasî İdeolojiler*. İstanbul: İletişim.

Bora, Tanıl and Gültekingil, Murat (eds). (2002). *Modern Türkiye'de Siyasi Düşünce Cilt 2-Kemalizm*. İstanbul: İletişim.

(eds). (2003). *Modern Türkiye'de Siyasi Düşünce Cilt 4-Milliyetçilik*. İstanbul: İletişim.

Boratav, Korkut. (2003). *Türkiye İktisat Tarihi*. Ankara: İmge Kitabevi.

Borovalı, Murat and Boyraz, Cemil. (2015). 'The Alevi Workshops: An Opening without an Outcome?' *Turkish Studies*, 16(2): 145–160.

Bose, Anuja. (2009). 'Hindutva and the Politicization of Religious Identity in India'. *Journal of Peace, Conflict and Development*, 13, 1–30. www.bradford.ac.uk/social-sciences/peace-conflict-and-development/issue-13/Issue-13-Article-8-formatted.pdf

Bose, Sumantra. (1997). '"Hindu Nationalism" and the Crisis of the Indian State: A Theoretical Perspective' in Sugata Bose and Ayesha Jalal (eds.), *Nationalism, Democracy and Development: State and Politics in India*. Oxford University Press, pp. 104–164.

(2013). *Transforming India: Challenges to the World's Largest Democracy*. Cambridge, MA: Harvard University Press.

Bourdieu, Pierre. (1977). *Outline of a Theory of Practice*. Cambridge University Press.

(1979). 'Symbolic Power'. *Critique of Anthropology*, 4(13–14): 77–85.

(1989). 'Social Space and Symbolic Power'. *Sociological Theory*, 7(1): 14–25.

Bourdieu, Pierre. (1994). 'Rethinking the State: Genesis and Structure of the Bureaucratic Field'. *Sociological Theory*, 12(1): 1–18.

(2013). 'Symbolic Capital and Social Classes'. *Journal of Classical Sociology*, 13 (2): 292–302.

Bowen, John R. (2016). *On British Islam: Religion, Law, and Everyday Practice in Shari'a Councils*. Princeton University Press.

Boyunsuz, Ş. Özsoy. (2016). 'The AKP'S Proposal for a "Turkish Type of Presidentialism" in Comparative Context'. *Turkish Studies*, 17(1): 68–90.

Bozan, İrfan. (2007). *Devlet ile Toplum Arasında*. İstanbul: TESEV Yayınları.

(20 July 2016). 'Kritik yıl 1986'. *Al Jazeera Türk*. www.aljazeera.com.tr/al-jazeera-ozel/kritik-yil-1986

(21 July 2016). 'Kaç 'Cemaat Subayı' Var?' *Al Jazeera Türk*. www.aljazeera.com.tr/al-jazeera-ozel/kac-cemaat-subayi-var-2

Bozarslan, Hamit. (2003). 'Alevism and the Myths of Research: The Need for a New Research Agenda' in Paul J. White and Joost Jongerden (eds.), *Turkey's Alevi Enigma: A Comprehensive Overview*. Leiden, the Netherlands: Brill, pp. 3–16.

Bozkurt, Gülnihal. (1998). 'The Reception of Western European Law in Turkey (From the Tanzimat to the Turkish Republic, 1839–1939)'. *Der Islam*, 75(2): 283–295.

(2010). *Batı Hukukunun Türkiye'de Benimsenmesi*. Ankara: Türk Tarih Kurumu Yayınları.

Bozkurt, Umut. (2013). 'Neoliberalism with a Human Face: Making Sense of the Justice and Development Party's Neoliberal Populism in Turkey'. *Science and Society*, 77(3): 372–396.

Brass, Paul R. (ed.). (1985). *Ethnic Groups and the State*. London: Croom Helm.

Brass, Paul. R. (1988). 'The Punjab Crisis and the Unity of India' in Atul Kohli (ed.), *India's Demoracy: An Analysis of Changing State-Society Relations*. Princeton University Press, pp. 169–213.

(1990). *The Politics of India since Independence*. Cambridge University Press.

(1991). *Ethnicity and Nationalism: Theory and Comparison*. New Delhi; Newbury Park, CA: Sage.

Braude, Benjamin. (1980). 'Foundation Myths of the Millet System' in Benjamin Braude and Bernard Lewis (eds.), *Christians and Jews in the Ottoman Empire: The Functioning of a Plural Society*. New York; London: Holmes and Meier, pp. 65–86.

Breen, M. J. and Reynolds, C. (2011). 'The Rise of Secularism and the Decline of Religiosity in Ireland: The Pattern of Religious Change in Europe'. *International Journal of Religion and Spirituality in Society*, 1(2): 195–212.

Brennan, Martin. (2008). 'Class, Politics and Race in Modern Malaysia'. *Journal of Contemporary Asia*, 12(2): 188–215.

Brown, Nathan J. (2012). *When Victory Is Not an Option: Islamist Movements in Arab Politics*. Ithaca, NY: Cornell University Press.

Brubaker, Rogers. (1985). 'Rethinking Classical Theory: The Sociological Vision of Pierre Bourdieu'. *Theory and Society*, 14(6): 745–775.

(1992). *Citizenship and Nationhood in France and Germany*. Cambridge, MA: Harvard University Press.

(1995). 'Aftermaths of Empire and the Unmixing of Peoples: Historical and Comparative Perspectives'. *Ethnic and Racial Studies*, 18(2): 189–218.

(1998). 'Myths and Misconceptions in the Study of Nationalism' in John A. Hall (ed.), *The State of the Nation: Ernest Gellner and the Theory of Nationalism*. Cambridge University Press, pp. 272–306.

(1999). 'The Manichean Myth: Rethinking the Distinction between "Civic" and "Ethnic" Nationalism' in H. Kriesi, K. Armington, H. Siegrist and A. Wimmer (eds.), *Nation and National Identity: The European Experience in Perspective*. Chur: Rüegger, pp. 55–71.

(2002). 'Ethnicity without Groups'. *European Journal of Sociology*, 43(02): 163–189.

(2011). 'Nationalizing States Revisited: Projects and Processes of Nationalization in Post-Soviet States'. *Ethnic and Racial Studies*, 34(11): 1785–1814.

(2012). 'Religion and Nationalism: Four Approaches'. *Nations and Nationalism*, 18(1): 2–20.

Brubaker, Rogers. and Cooper, Frederick. (2000). 'Beyond Identity'. *Theory and Society*, 29: 1–47.

Bruce, Steve. (2003). *Politics and Religion*. Cambridge: Polity Press.

Bruinessen, Martin van. (1991). 'Religion in Kurdistan'. *Kurdish Times*, 4(1–2): 5–27

Buğra, Ayşe. (1998). 'Class, Culture, and State: An Analysis of Interest Representation by Two Turkish Business Associations'. *International Journal of Middle East Studies*, 30(4): 521–539.

(2013). *Kapitalizm, Yoksulluk ve Türkiye'de Sosyal Politika*. İstanbul: İletişim.

Buğra, Ayşe and Candaş, Aysen. (2011). 'Change and Continuity under an Eclectic Social Security Regime: The Case of Turkey'. *Middle Eastern Studies*, 47(3): 515–528.

Buğra, Ayşe and Keyder, Çağlar. (2006). 'The Turkish Welfare Regime in Transformation'. *Journal of European Social Policy*, 16(3): 211–228.

Buğra, Ayşe and Savaşkan, Osman. (2010). 'Yerel Sanayi ve Bugünün Türkiye'-sinde İş Dünyası'. *Toplum ve Bilim*, 118.

(2012). 'Politics and Class: The Turkish Business Environment in the Neoliberal Age.' *New Perspectives on Turkey*, 46: 27–63.

(2014). *New Capitalism in Turkey: The Relationship between Politics, Religion and Business*. Cheltenham: Edward Elgar.

Bugün. (5 April 2014). 'Gökçek: En çok Oy Veren İlçeden Hizmete Başlayacağım'. *Bugün*.

Bulaç, Ali. (2008). *Din, Kent ve Cemaat: Fethullah Gülen Örneği*. İstanbul: Ufuk Kitap.

(12 April 2014). 'Ey Vicdan ve Akıl Sahipleri'. *Zaman Gazetesi*.

(22 December 2014). 'AK Parti Bir Proje Miydi?' *Zaman Gazetesi*.

Bulut, Faik. (2016). *Kim bu Fethullah Gülen: Dünü Bugünü Hedefi*. İstanbul: Berfin Yayınları.

Bulsara, Hament and Kissane, Bill. (2009). 'Lijphart and Irish Democracy'. *West European Politics*, 32(1): 172–195.

Burity, Joanildo. (2016). 'Minoritisation and Global Religious Activism: Pentecostals and Ecumenicals Confronting Inequality in Politics and Culture'. In Dawn Llewellyn and Sonya Sharma (eds.), *Religion, Equalities, and Inequalities*. London: Routledge, pp. 137–148.

Bursalı, Şebnem. (29 July 2016). 'Hedef İç Savaştı'. *Yeni Asır*. https://www .yeniasir.com.tr/yazarlar/sebnem_bursali/2016/07/29/hedef-ic-savasti

Çağaptay, Soner. (2002). 'Kemalist Dönemde Göç ve İskan Politikaları: Türk Kimliği Üzerine Bir Çalışma'. *Toplum ve Bilim*, 93: 218–241.

(2006). *Islam, Secularism and Nationalism in Modern Turkey: Who Is a Turk?* London: Routledge.

(2017). *The New Sultan: Erdogan and the Crisis of Modern Turkey*. London; New York: IB Tauris.

Çağatay, Neşet. (1972). *Türkiye'de Gerici Eylemler: 1923'ten bu Yana*. Ankara: Üniversitesi İlahiyat Fakültesi Yayınları.

Çakır, Ruşen. (1994). *Ne Şeriat Ne Demokrasi, Refah Partisi'ni Anlamak*. İstanbul: Metis Yayınevi.

(2002). *Ayet ve Slogan*. İstanbul; Metis Yayınları.

(26 August 2004). 'Bilimsel Fişleme'. *Vatan*. http://rusencakir.com/Bilimsel-fisleme/312

(2008). 'İsmail Kara: "Cemaat ve Tarikatlar Sivil Toplum Hareketi Değildir"'. *Vatan*. www.rusencakir.com/Ismail-Kara-Cemaat-ve-tarikatlar-sivil-toplum-hareketi-degildir/979

(23 July 2016). '28 Aralık 1986 Tarihli Nokta Dergisi Haberi: Orduya Sızan Dinci Grup: Fethullahçılar'. medyascope.tv/2016/07/23/28-aralik-1986-tar-ihli-nokta-dergisi-haberi-orduya-sizan-dinci-grup-fethullahcilar/

Çakır, Ruşen and Bozan, İrfan. (2005). *Sivil, Şeffaf ve Demokratik Bir Diyanet İşleri Başkanlığı Mümkün Mü?* İstanbul: TESEV.

Çakır, Ruşen, Bozan, İrfan and Talu, Balkan. (2004). *İmam Hatip Liseleri: Efsaneler ve Gerçekler*. İstanbul: TESEV Yayınları.

Çakmak, Diren. (2009). 'Pro-Islamic Public Education in Turkey: The Imam-Hatıp Schools'. *Middle Eastern Studies* 45(5): 825–846.

Calhoun, Craig J. (1993). 'Nationalism and Ethnicity'. *Annual Review of Sociology*, 19: 211–239.

(1997). *Nationalism*. Minneapolis: University of Minnesota Press.

Calhoun, C., Juergensmeyer, M. and Van Antwerpen, J. (eds.). (2011). *Rethinking Secularism*. Oxford University Press.

Can, Kemal and Bora, Tanıl. (2004). *Devlet, Ocak, Dergâh: 12 Eylül'den 1990'lara Ülkücü Hareket*. İstanbul: İletişim.

Çarkoğlu, Ali and Bilgili, Nazlı Çağın. (2011). 'A Precarious Relationship: The Alevi Minority, the Turkish State and the EU'. *South European Society and Politics*, 16(2), 351–364.

Çarkoğlu, Ali and Kalaycıoğlu, Ersin. (2009). *The Rising Tide of Conservatism in Turkey*. New York: Palgrave Macmillan.

Carneiro, Robert. L. (2000). 'The Transition from Quantity to Quality: A Neglected Causal Mechanism in Accounting for Social Evolution'. *Proceedings of the National Academy of Sciences*, 97(23): 12926–12931.

Carothers, Thomas. (2002). 'The End of the Transition Paradigm'. *Journal of Democracy*, 13(1): 5–21.

Casanova, José. (1994). *Public Religions in the Modern World*. University of Chicago Press.

(2011). 'The Secular, Secularizations, Secularisms' in Craig Calhoun, Mark Juergensmeyer and Jonathan Van Antwerpen (eds.), *Rethinking Secularism*. Oxford University Press, pp. 54–74.

Cederman, Lars-Erik. (2005). 'Computational Models of Social Forms: Advancing Generative Process Theory'. *American Journal of Sociology*, 110(4): 864–893.

Çem, Munzur. (2009). *Dersim Merkezli Kürt Aleviliği*. İstanbul: Vate Yayınevı.

Cengiz, Kurtuluş. (2013). *'Yav İşte Fabrikalaşak': Anadolu Sermayesi'nin Oluşumu: Kayseri Hacılar Örneği'*. İstanbul: İletişim.

Cesari, Joceylne. (2014). *The Awakening of Muslim Democracy: Religion, Modernity, and the State*. New York: Cambridge University Press.

Çetin, Muhammed. (2010). *The Gülen Movement: Civic Service without Borders*. New York: Blue Dome Press.

Çetinsaya, Gökhan. (1999). 'Rethinking Nationalism and Islam: Some Preliminary Notes on the Roots of "Turkish-Islamic Synthesis" in Modern Turkish Political Thought'. *The Muslim World*, 89(3–4): 350–376.

Challand, Benoît. (2008). 'A Nahḍa of Charitable Organizations? Health Service Provision and the Politics of Aid in Palestine'. *International Journal of Middle East Studies*, 40(02): 227–247.

Chambers, Richard L. (1972). 'The Ottoman Ulema and the Tanzimat' in N.R. Keddie (ed.), *Scholars, Saints, and Sufis: Muslim Religious Institutions in the Middle East since 1500*. Berkeley, CA: University of California Press, pp. 33–46.

Chatterjee, Partha. (1994). 'Secularism and Toleration'. *Economic and Political Weekly*, 29(28): 1768–1777.

Chaves, Mark. (1994). 'Secularization as Declining Religious Authority'. *Social Forces*, 72(3): 749–774.

Chiriyankandath, James. (2000). 'Creating a Secular State in a Religious Country: The Debate in the Indian Constituent Assembly'. *Journal of Commonwealth and Comparative Politics*, 38(2): 1–24.

Çiçek, Cuma. (2011). 'Elimination or Integration of Pro-Kurdish Politics: Limits of the AKP's Democratic Initiative'. *Turkish Studies*, 12(1): 15–26.

Çınar, Menderes. (2005). *Siyasal Bir Sorun Olarak İslamcılık*. Ankara: Dipnot Yayınları.

Çıtak, Zana. (2010). 'Between "Turkish Islam" and "French Islam": The Role of the Diyanet in the Conseil Français du Culte Musulman'. *Journal of Ethnic and Migration Studies*, 36(4): 619–634.

Cizre, Ümit. (2001). 'Turkey's Kurdish Problem: Borders, Identity, and Hegemony' in Brendan O'Leary, Ian S. Lustick and Thomas Callaghy (eds.), *Right-Sizing the State: The Politics of Moving Borders*. Oxford; Oxford University Press, pp. 222–252.

(ed). (2008). *Secular and Islamic Politics in Turkey: The Making of the Justice and Development Party*. London: Routledge.

(10 August 2016). 'Turkey in a Tailspin'. *MERIP*. www.merip.org/mero/mero081016#_2

(2017). *Fear and Loathing in Turkey: The Backstory to Erdoğan's Referendum*. MERIP. http://merip.org/mero/mero042617.

Cizre, Ümit and Çınar, Menderes. (2003). 'Turkey 2002: Kemalism, Islamism and Politics in the Light of the February 28 Process'. *The South Atlantic Quarterly*, 102(2): 309–332.

Cizre, Ümit and Walker, Joshua. (2010). 'Conceiving the New Turkey after Ergenekon'. *The International Spectator*, 45(1): 89–98.

Clark, Janine A.(2004a). 'Social Movement Theory and Patron-Clientelism: Islamic Social Institutions and the Middle Class in Egypt, Jordan, and Yemen'. *Comparative Political Studies*, 37(8): 941–968.

(2004b). *Islam, Charity and Activism: Middle-Class Networks and Social Welfare in Egypt, Jordan, and Yemen*. Bloomington, IN: Indiana University Press.

(2006). 'The Conditions of Islamist Moderation: Unpacking Cross-Ideological Cooperation in Jordan'. *International Journal of Middle East Studies*, 38(4): 539–560.

CNN-Türk. (3 September 2009). 'Diyanet'ten Kürtçe Vaaz ve Hutbeye Yeşil Işık'. CNN-Türk. www.cnnturk.com/2009/turkiye/09/03/diyanetten.kurtce.vaaz.ve.hutbeye.yesil.isik/542022.0/index.html.

(8 March 2016). 'Mehmet Görmez Özerk Diyanet Istedi'. CNN-Turk. www.cnnturk.com/turkiye/mehmet-gormez-ozerk-diyanet-istedi.

Çobanoğlu, Yavuz. (2012). *'Altın Nesil' in Peşinde*. İstanbul: İletişim.

Çokgezen, Murat. (2000). 'New Fragmentations and New Cooperations in the Turkish Bourgeoisie'. *Environment and Planning: Government and Policy*, 18(5): 525–544.

Conversi, Daniele. (1999). 'Nationalism, Boundaries, and Violence'. *Millennium: Journal of International Studies*, 28(3): 553–584.

Copeaux, Etienne. (2000). *Türk Tarih Tezinden Türk-İslam Sentezine*. İstanbul: Tarih Vakfı Yurt Yayınları.

Corbridge, Stuart. (2000). *Reinventing India: Liberalization, Hindu Nationalism and Popular Democracy*. Cambridge; Oxford; Malden, MA: Polity.

Cornell, Svante E. (19 October 2015). 'The Rise of Diyanet: The Politicization of Turkey's Directorate of Religious Affairs'. *The Centre for Security Studies*. https://isnblog.ethz.ch/government/the-rise-of-diyanet-the-politicization-of-turkeys-directorate-of-religious-affairs

(2017). 'A Religious Party Takes Hold: Turkey'. *SAIS Review of International Affairs*, 37(1): 21–38.

Cortell, Andrew P. and Peterson, Susan. (1999). 'Altered States: Explaining Domestic Institutional Change'. *British Journal of Political Science*, 29(1): 177–203.

Coskun, Ceren. (2005). 'The Directorate of Religious Affairs: State, Nation and Religion in Turkey in the 1990s'. Master's thesis.

Coşkun, Mustafa Kemal and Şentürk, Burcu. (2012). 'The Growth of Islamic Education in Turkey: The AKP's Policies toward Imam-Hatip Schools' in Kemal İnal and Güliz Akkaymak (eds.), *Neoliberal Transformation of Education in Turkey: Political and Ideological Analysis of Educational Reforms in the Age of the AKP*. New York; Basingstoke: Palgrave Macmillan, pp. 165–178.

Council of Europe Monitoring Committee. (12 December 2016). Council of Europe.

Craciun, Magdalena. (2017). *Islam, Faith, and Fashion: The Islamic Fashion Industry in Turkey*. London: Bloomsbury.

Cumhuriyet. (10 November 2010). 'Bardakoğlu'nun Veda Konuşması'. *Cumhuriyet*. www.cumhuriyet.com.tr/haber/diger/195110/Bardakoglu_nun_veda_konusmasi .html

(13 October 2014). 'İstanbul'da Korkutan Gelişme: Alevi Evleri İşaretlendi'. *Cumhuriyet*. www.cumhuriyet.com.tr/haber/turkiye/129705/istanbul_da_kor kutan_gelisme__Alevi_evleri_isaretlendi.html

(23 May 2015). 'Alevilerin Evleri Yine İşaretlendi'. *Cumhuriyet*. www .cumhuriyet.com.tr/haber/turkiye/283273/Alevilerin_evleri_yine_isaretlendi .html

(10 December 2016). 'From Forced Marriage to Forced Coup'. *Cumhuriyet*. www.cumhuriyet.com.tr/haber/english/643331/From_forced_marriage_to_ forced_coup.html

(27 February 2017). 'Cami-cemevi Projesi İçin 15 Yıl Hapis Talebi'. *Cumhuriyet*. www.cumhuriyet.com.tr/haber/turkiye/686854/Cami-cemevi_projesi_icin_15_ yil_hapis_talebi.html

(18 September 2017). 'Ali Erbaş Cübbesini Giydi . . . İşte İlk Sözleri: Seküler-izm Kıskacında Debelenen İnsanlık'. www.cumhuriyet.com.tr/haber/turkiye/ 826395/Ali_Erbas_cubbesini_giydi..._iste_ilk_sozleri__Sekulerizm_kiskacinda_ debelenen_insanlik...html

Daily Sabah. (15 June 2017). 'Turkey's Diyanet Foundation Educates Thousands Abroad'. www.dailysabah.com/education/2017/06/15/turkeys-diyanet-foun dation-educates-thousands-abroad

Davison, Andrew. (1995). 'Secularization and Modernization in Turkey: The Ideas of Ziya Gökalp'. *International Journal of Human Resource Management*, 24(2): 189–224.

(2003). 'Turkey, a Secular State?' *The South Atlantic Quarterly*, 102(2): 333–350.

Delibaş, Kayhan. (2015). *The Rise of Political Islam in Turkey: Urban Poverty, Grassroots Activism and Islamic Fundamentalism*. London: IB Tauris.

Demir, Fırat. (2005). 'Militarization of the Market and Rent-Seeking Coalitions in Turkey'. *Development and Change*, 36(4): 667–690.

Demir, Ö., Acar, M. and Toprak, M. (2004). 'Anatolian Tigers or Islamic Capital: Prospects and Challenges'. *Middle Eastern Studies*, 40(6): 166–188.

Demirpolat, Enver. (1997). XX. 'Yüzyıl Van İli Tarihi ve İnanç Coğrafyası'. Masters thesis.

Demiralp, Seda. (2009). 'The Rise of Islamic Capital and the Decline of Islamic Radicalism in Turkey'. *Comparative Politics*, 41(3): 315–335.

Demirel, Ahmet. (2010). *İlk Meclis'in Vekilleri: Millî Mücadele Döneminde Seçim-ler*. İstanbul: İletişim.

(2013). *Tek Partinin İktidarı*. İstanbul: İletişim.

Deringil, Selim. (1990). 'The Struggle against Shiism in Hamidian Iraq: A Study in Ottoman Counter-Propaganda'. *Die Welt des Islams*, 30(1/4): 45–62.

(1991). 'Legitimacy Structures in the Ottoman State: The Reign of Abdulha-mid II (1876–1909)'. *International Journal of Middle East Studies*, 23(3): 345–359.

(1993a). 'The Invention of Tradition as Public Image in the Late Ottoman Empire, 1808 to 1908'. *Comparative Studies in Society and History*, 35(1): 3–29.

(1993b). 'The Ottoman Origins of Kemalist Nationalism: Namik Kemal to Mustafa Kemal'. *European History Quarterly*, 23(2): 165–191.

(1998). *The Well-Protected Domains: Ideology and the Legitimation of Power in the Ottoman Empire, 1876–1909*. London: IB Tauris.

(2000). '"There Is No Compulsion in Religion": On Conversion and Apostasy in the Late Ottoman Empire: 1839–1856'. *Comparative Studies in Society and History*, 42(3): 547–575.

Deutsche Welle. (31 January 2018). 'Bozdağ: KHK'larla 110 bin 778 Kişi İhraç Edildi'. *Deutsche Welle*. www.dw.com/tr/bozda%C4%9F-khklarla-110-bin-778-ki%C5%9Fi-ihra%C3%A7-edildi/a-42378100

Diamond, Larry J. (2002). 'Thinking about Hybrid Regimes'. *Journal of Democracy*, 13(2): 21–35.

Dillon, Michele. (2002). 'Catholicism, Politics, and Culture in the Republic of Ireland' in T. G. Jelen and C. Wilcox (eds.), *Religion and Politics in Comparative Perspective: The One, the Few, and the Many*. Cambridge University Press, pp. 47–70.

Dinçer, Nahit. (1971). 'İmam Hatip Okulları Üzerine Bir İnceleme'. *Diyanet Dergisi*, (104–105): 53–58.

(1974). *1913'den Bugüne İmam Hatip Okulları Meselesi*. İstanbul: Yağmur Yayınevi.

Dinler, Zeynel. (1994). *Bölgesel İktisat*. Bursa: Ekin Kitabevi.

DİTİB Haber. (September 2015). *DİTİB Haber*. www.ditib.de/media/Image/bul ten/DiTiB_Haber_Eylul_2015.pdf

Doğan, Ali Ekber. (2007). *Eğreti Kamusallık*. İstanbul: İletişim.

(2009). 'İslamcı Sermayenin Gelişme Dinamikleri ve 28 Şubat Süreci' in İlhan Uzel and Bülent Duru (eds.), *AKP Kitabı: Bir Dönüşümün Bilançosu*. Ankara: Phoenix Yayınevi, pp. 283–306.

Doğanay, Ülkü. (2007). 'The Turkish Parliament on Democracy'. *Parliamentary Affairs*, 60(3): 388–408.

Domínguez, J. I. and Poiré, A. (eds.). (2013). *Toward Mexico's Democratization: Parties, Campaigns, Elections and Public Opinion*. New York; London: Routledge.

Dressler, M. (2015). 'Rereading Ziya Gökalp: Secularism and Reform of the Islamic State in the Late Young Turk Period'. *International Journal of Middle East Studies*, 47(03): 511–531.

Dressler, Markus. (2013). *Writing Religion: The Making of Turkish Alevi Islam*. New York: Oxford University Press.

Dündar, Fuat. (2011). *İttihat ve Terakki'nin Müslümanları İskân Politikası (1913–1918)*. İstanbul: İletişim.

Dunleavy, Patrick. (1985). 'Bureaucrats, Budgets and the Growth of the State: Reconstructing an Instrumental Model'. *British Journal of Political Science*, 15 (3): 299–328.

(1992). *Democracy, Bureaucracy and Public Choice: Economic Explanations in Political Science*. New York: Prentice Hall.

(2010). 'Rethinking Dominant Party Systems' in M. Bogaards and F. Boucek (eds.), *Dominant Political Parties and Democracy: Concepts, Measures, Cases and Comparisons*, Abingdon, Oxon, England; New York: Routledge, pp. 23–44.

Duran, B. and Yıldırım, E. (2005). 'Islamism, Trade Unionism and Civil Society: The Case of Hak-İş Labour Confederation in Turkey'. *Middle Eastern Studies*, 41(2): 227–247.

Duran, Burhanettin. (2004). 'Cumhuriyet Dönemi İslâmcılığı' in Yasin Aktay (ed.), *Türkiye'de Siyasi Düşünce Cilt 6/İslamcılık*. İstanbul: İletişim, pp. 129–156.

Duru, Bülent and Uzel, İlhan (eds.). (2009). *AKP Kitabı: Bir Dönüşümün Bilançosu*. Ankara: Phoenix Yayınevi.

Duvar. (12 April 2017). 'Hangi Cemaatler Evetçi Hangileri Hayırcı?' *Duvar*. www.gazeteduvar.com.tr/gundem/2017/04/12/hangi-cemaatler-evetci-hangi leri-hayirci/

Eder, Mine. (2010). 'Retreating State? Political Economy of Welfare Regime Change in Turkey'. *Middle East Law and Governance*, 2(2): 152–184.

Ehteshami, Anoushiravan. (2004). 'Islam, Muslim Polities and Democracy'. *Democratization*, 11(4): 90–110.

Eligür, Banu. (2010). *The Mobilization of Political Islam in Turkey*. Cambridge University Press.

Ercan, Fuat. (2003). 'Sınıftan Kaçış: Türkiye'de Kapitalizmin Analizinde Sınıf Gerçekliğinden Kaçış' in A. H. Köse, F. Şenses and E. Yeldan (eds.), *Korkut Boratav'a Armağan Küresel Düzen: Birikim, Devlet ve Sınıflar*. İstanbul: İletişim, pp. 611–669.

Erdem, Gazi. (2008). 'Religious Services in Turkey: From the Office of Şeyhülislâm to the Diyanet'. *The Muslim World*, 98(2-3): 199–215.

Erdemir, Aykan. (2005). 'Tradition and Modernity: Alevis' Ambiguous Terms and Turkey's Ambivalent Subjects'. *Middle Eastern Studies*, 41(6): 937–951.

Ergil, Doğu. (2000). 'Identity Crises and Political Instability in Turkey'. *Journal of International Affairs*, 54(1): 43–62.

Ergin, Sedat. (22 July 2016). 'O Albaylar Gitti Darbeciler Geldi'. *Hürriyet*. www.hurriyet.com.tr/yazarlar/sedat-ergin/o-albaylar-gitti-darbeciler-geldi-40164262

Ergül, F. Aslı. (2012). 'The Ottoman Identity: Turkish, Muslim or Rum?' *Middle Eastern Studies*, 48(4): 629–645.

Erşahin, Seyfettin. (2008). 'The Ottoman Foundation of the Turkish Republic's Diyanet: Ziya Gokalp's Diyanet Ishları Nazâratı'. *The Muslim World*, 98(2–3): 182–198.

Esen, Berk and Gümüşcü, Şebnem. (2016). 'Rising Competitive Authoritarianism in Turkey'. *Third World Quarterly*, 37(9): 1581–1606.

Eser, Turan. (12 November 2017). 'Yeni Rejim Kurulurken Diyanet'in Rolü'. *BirGün*. www.birgun.net/haber-detay/yeni-rejim-kurulurken-diyanet-in-rolu-189764.html

Esposito, John L. and Yavuz, M. Hakan (eds.). (2003). *Turkish Islam and the Secular State*. Syracuse University Press.

European Stability Initiative. (2005). *Islamic Calvinists: Change and Conservatism in Central Anatolia*. Berlin and İstanbul: European Stability Initiative.

Evrensel. (7 May 2013). 'Alevilere Yönelik Hak İhlalleri Artıyor'. *Evrensel.* www.evrensel.net/amp/56218/alevilere-yonelik-hak-ihlalleri-artiyor
(5 March 2014). 'Erdoğan "Tapeleri" Doğruladı, Dinleyenleri Suçladı'. *Evrensel.* www.evrensel.net/haber/79695/erdogan-tapeleri-dogruladi-dinleyenleri-sucladi
(22 November 2017). 'Malatya'da Alevilerin Evleri Kırmızı Boyayla İşaretlendi'. *Evrensel.* www.evrensel.net/haber/338665/malatyada-alevilerin-evleri-kirmizi-boyayla-isaretlendi
EY. (2015). *World Islamic Banking Competitiveness Report 2016.* EY. www.ey.com/Publication/vwLUAssets/ey-world-islamic-banking-competitiveness-report-2016/%24FILE/ey-world-islamic-banking-competitiveness-report-2016.pdf
Findley, Carter V. (2010). *Turkey, Islam, Nationalism, and Modernity: A History, 1789–2007.* New Haven: Yale University Press.
Flinders, M. (2005). 'Majoritarian Democracy in Britain: New Labour and the Constitution'. *West European Politics,* 28(1), 61–93.
Fortna, Benjamin. (2002). *Imperial Classroom. Islam, Education and the State in the Late Ottoman Empire.* Oxford University Press.
Fox, Jonathan. (2004). 'The Rise of Religious Nationalism and Conflict: Ethnic Conflict and Revolutionary Wars, 1945–2001'. *Journal of Peace Research,* 41(6): 715–731.
(2008). *A World Survey of Religion and the State.* Cambridge University Press.
Freedom House. https://freedomhouse.org/
Gallagher, Michael. (1991). 'Proportionality, Disproportionality and Electoral Systems'. *Electoral Studies,* 10(1): 33–51.
Gallagher, Michael, and Mitchell, Paul. (2008). *The Politics of Electoral Systems.* Oxford University Press.
Gandhi, J. and Lust-Okar, E. (2009). 'Elections under Authoritarianism'. *Annual Review of Political Science,* 12: 403–422.
Garvin Tom. (2004). *Preventing the Future: Why Was Ireland So Poor for So Long?* Dublin: Gill & Macmillan.
Geddes, Barbara. (1999). 'What Do We Know about Democratization after Twenty Years?' *Annual Review of Political Science,* 2(1): 115–144.
Geertz, Clifford. (1966). 'Religion as a Cultural System' in M. Banton (ed.), *Anthropological Approaches to the Study of Religion.* London: Tavistock, pp. 1–39.
Gellner, Ernest. (2008). *Nations and Nationalism.* Ithaca, NY: Cornell University Press.
Gençkaya, Ömer Faruk. (1999). 'Reforming Parliamentary Procedure in Turkey'. In Ömer Faruk Gençkaya, Ruşen Keleş and Yasushi Hazama (eds.), *Aspects of Democratization in Turkey.* Tokyo: Institute of Developing Economies, pp. 2–21.
Gerring, John. (2004). 'What Is a Case Study and What Is It Good For?' *American Political Science Review,* 98(02): 341–354.
Ghazzal, Zouhair. (2008). 'The Ulama: Status and Function' in Youssef M. Choueiri (ed.), *A Companion to the History of the Middle East.* Chichester; Malden, MA: Wiley-Blackwell, pp. 71–86.
Gibb, H. A. R. and Bowen, H. (1963). *Islamic Society and the West: A Study of the Impact of Western Civilization on Moslem Culture in the Near East.* London: Oxford University Press.

Gill, Anthony. (2001). 'Religion and Comparative Politics'. *Annual Review of Political Science*, 4(1): 117–138.

Giroux, H. A. (1981). 'Hegemony, Resistance, and the Paradox of Educational Reform'. *Interchange*, 12(2): 3–26.

Girvin, B. (1996). 'Church, State and the Irish Constitution: The Secularisation of Irish Politics?' *Parliamentary Affairs*, 49(4): 599–615.

Göçek, Fatma Müge. (1993). 'Ethnic Segmentation, Western Education, and Political Outcomes: Nineteenth-Century Ottoman Society'. *Poetics Today*, 14(3): 507–538.

(1996). *Rise of the Bourgeoisie, Demise of Empire: Ottoman Westernization and Social Change*. New York: Oxford University Press.

Göçmen, Ipek. (2014). 'Religion, Politics and Social Assistance in Turkey: The Rise of Religiously Motivated Associations'. *Journal of European Social Policy*, 24(1): 92–103.

Gökaçtı, Mehmet Ali. (2005). *Türkiye'de Din Eğitimi ve İmam Hatipler*. İstanbul: İletişim.

Göle, Nilüfer. (1997). 'Secularism and Islamism in Turkey: The Making of Elites and Counter Elites in Turkey'. *Middle East Journal*, 51(1): 46–58.

(ed.). (2000). *İslamın Yeni Kamusal Yüzleri*. İstanbul: Metis Yayıncılık.

(2012). 'Post-Secular Turkey'. *New Perspectives Quarterly*, 29(1): 7–11.

(2013). *The Forbidden Modern: Civilization and Veiling*. Ann Arbor: University of Michigan Press.

Gorski, P. S. and Altınordu, A. (2008). 'After Secularization?' *Annual Review of Sociology*, 34: 55–85.

Göymen, K. (2005). 'Türkiye'de Bölge Politikalarının Evrimi ve Bölgesel Kalkınma Ajansları'. http://research.sabanciuniv.edu/1373/1/KorelGoymenOrtaklik.pdf.

Gözaydın, İştar B. (2008). 'Diyanet and Politics'. *The Muslim World*, 98(2-3), 216–227.

(2009a). *Diyanet, Türkiye Cumhuriyeti'nde Dinin Tanzimi*. İstanbul: İletişim.

(2009b). 'The Fethullah Gülen Movement and Politics in Turkey: A Chance for Democratization or a Trojan Horse?' *Democratization*, 16(6): 1214–1236.

(2014). 'Management of Religion in Turkey: The Diyanet and Beyond' in Özgür Heval Çınar and Mine Yıldırım (eds.), *Freedom of Religion and Belief in Turkey*. Newcastle upon Tyne, England: Cambridge Scholars Publishing, pp. 10–35.

Grugel, Jean and Bishop, Matthew Louis. (2013). *Democratization: A Critical Introduction*. Houndmills, Basingstoke, Hampshire; New York: Palgrave Macmillan.

Gülalp, Haldun. (2001). 'Globalization and Political Islam: The Social Bases of Turkey's Welfare Party'. *International Journal of Middle East Studies*, 33(3): 433–448.

(2005). 'Enlightenment by Fiat: Secularization and Democracy in Turkey'. *Middle Eastern Studies*, 41(3): 351–372.

Gültekin, Ahmet Kerim and Yüksel, Işık. (2005). 'Dr. Ali Bardakoğlu'yla Söyleşi'. *Kırkbudak – Anadolu Halk İnançları Araştırmaları*, 1(3): 4–23.

Gümüşçü, Şebnem. (2008). 'Economic Liberalization, Devout Bourgeoisie, and Change in Political Islam: Comparing Turkey and Egypt'. *EUI Robert Schuman Center for Advanced Studies*.

———. (2010). 'Class, Status, and Party: The Changing Face of Political Islam in Turkey and Egypt.' *Comparative Political Studies*, 43(7): 835–861.

———. (2013). 'The Emerging Predominant Party System in Turkey'. *Government and Opposition*, 48(02): 223–244.

Günay, Ünver. (2006). 'Türkiye'de Toplumsal Değişme ve Tarikâtlar'. *İslâmiyât*, 5(4): 141–162.

Gündoğan, Cemil. (2012). 'Geleneğin Değersizleşmesi: Kürt Hareketinin 1970'lerde Gelenekselle İlişkisi Üzerine'. In Büşra Ersanlı, Günay G. Özdoğan and Nesrin Uçarlar (eds.), *Türkiye Siyasetinde Kürtler*. İstanbul: İletişim, pp. 93–150.

Gündoğdu, Cihangir and Genç, Vural. (2013). *Dersim'de Osmanlı Siyaseti*. İstanbul: Kitap Yayınevi.

Gündoğdu, İbrahim and Gough, Jamie. (2013). 'Class-Cleansing in Istanbul's World-City Project' in Libby Porter and Kate Shaw (eds.), *Whose Urban Renaissance? An International Comparison of Urban Regeneration Strategies*. London: Routledge, pp. 16–24.

Gunter, Michael. (2007). 'Turkey's Floundering EU Candidacy and Its Kurdish Problem'. *Middle East Policy*, 14(1): 117–123.

Gupta, Akhil. (1995). 'Blurred Boundaries: The Discourse of Corruption, the Culture of Politics and the Imagined State'. *American Ethnologist*, 22(2): 375–402.

Gupta, Dipankar. (1991). 'Communalism and Fundamentalism: Some Notes on the Nature of Ethnic Politics in India'. *Economic and Political Weekly*, 26(11/12): 573–582.

Gürakar, Esra. Ç. (2016). *Politics of Favoritism in Public Procurement in Turkey: Reconfigurations of Dependency Networks in the AKP Era*. New York: Springer.

Gürbey, Sinem. (2009). 'Islam, Nation-State, and the Military: A Discussion of Secularism in Turkey'. *Comparative Studies of South Asia, Africa and the Middle East*, 29(3): 371–380.

Gürsel, Kadri. (18 November 2013). 'AKP, Gulen Community in Open War'. *Al-Monitor*.

Gürsoy, Yaprak. (2011). 'The Impact of EU-Driven Reforms on the Political Autonomy of the Turkish Military'. *South European Society and Politics*, 16(2): 293–308.

Haber 7. (24 July 2013). 'Görmez: Diyanet Dini Bakımdan Özerk Olmalı'. *Haber 7*. www.haber7.com/guncel/haber/1053718-gormez-diyanet-dini-bakimdan-ozerk-olmali

Habertürk. (5 June 2007). 'Alevilerde MHP'ye Olan İlgi Giderek Artıyor'. *Habertürk*. www.haberturk.com/gundem/haber/25276-alevilerde-mhpye-olan-ilgi-giderek-artiyor

——— (25 October 2010). 'Diyanet'ten "Kürt Sorununa Bakışı Çalıştayı"'. *Habertürk*. www.haberturk.com/yasam/haber/564855-diyanetten-kurt-sorununa-bakisi-calistayi

(6 April 2012). 'Halka Anladığı Dilde Hitap Etmeliyiz'. *Habertürk*. www
.haberturk.com/gundem/haber/731773-halka-anladigi-dilde-hitap-etmeliyiz
(20 January 2014). 'Eksen kaymasıyla karşı karşıyayız'. *Habertürk*. www
.haberturk.com/gundem/haber/914190-eksen-kaymasiyla-karsi-karsiyayiz
(14 November 2016). 'Diyanet İşleri Başkanı Mehmet Görmez: "Din Eğiti-
minde Müfredat Yeniden Yapılandırılmalı"'. *Habertürk*. www.haberturk
.com/gundem/haber/1323475-diyanet-isleri-baskani-mehmet-gormez-din-
egitiminde-mufredat-yeniden-yapilandirilmali
(7 November 2017). 'Diyanet İşleri Başkanlığı Suriyeli 100 İmam İstihdam
Edecek'. www.haberturk.com/suriyeli-100-imam-istihdam-edilecek-1703025
Hale, Henry. E. (2005). 'Regime Cycles: Democracy, Autocracy, and Revolution
in Post-Soviet Eurasia'. *World Politics*, 58(01): 133–165.
Hale, William. (1994). *Turkish Politics and the Military*. London: Routledge.
Hale, William and Özbudun, Ergun. (2009). *Islamism, Democracy and Liberalism
in Turkey: The Case of the AKP*. New York: Routledge.
Hall, Peter A. and Taylor, Rosemary C. R. (1996). 'Political Science and the
Three New Institutionalisms'. Paper presented to MPIFG Scientific Advis-
ory Board.
(1998). 'The Potential of Historical Institutionalism: A Response to Hay and
Wincott'. *Political Studies*, 46(5): 958–962.
Halliday, Fred. (1995). 'The Politics of "Islam" – A Second Look'. *British Journal
of Political Science*, 25(3): 399–417.
(2000). *Nation and Religion in the Middle East*. London: Saqi Books.
Hamid, Ahmad F. A. (2007). 'Patterns of State Interaction with Islamic Move-
ments in Malaysia during the Formative Years of Islamic Resurgence'.
Southeast Asian Studies, 44(4): 444–465.
Hamid, Ahmad F. A. and Fauzi, Ahmad. (2009). 'The New Challenges of
Political Islam in Malaysia'. Working Paper 154. Murdoch University, Asia
Research Centre.
Hamid, Shadi. (2014). *Temptations of Power: Islamists and Illiberal Democracy in a
New Middle East*. Oxford University Press.
Hammond, Andrew. (2015). 'Salafism Infiltrates Turkish Religious Discourse'.
Middle East Institute. www.mei.edu/content/map/salafism-infiltrates-turkish-
religious-discourse
Hanioğlu, M. Şükrü. (1995). *The Young Turks in Opposition*. New York: Oxford
University Press.
(2010). *A Brief History of the Late Ottoman Empire*. Princeton, NJ: Princeton
University Press.
(2012). 'The Historical Roots of Kemalism' in A. Kuru and A. Stepan (eds.),
Democracy, Islam, & Secularism in Turkey. New York; Chichester: Columbia
University Press, pp. 32–60.
Hasan, Zoya. (1990). 'Changing Orientation of the State and the Emergence of
Majoritarianism in the 1980s'. *Social Scientist*, 18(8/9): 27–37.
Hassan, Mona. (2011). 'Women Preaching for the Secular State: Official Female
Preachers (bayan vaizler) in Contemporary Turkey'. *International Journal of
Middle East Studies*, 43(03): 451–473.

Hatina, Meir. (2003). 'Historical Legacy and the Challenge of Modernity in the Middle East: The Case of al-Azhar in Egypt'. *The Muslim World*, 93(1): 51–68.

    (2009a). 'The Clerics' Betrayal? Islamists, "Ulama" and the Polity' in Meir Hatina (ed.), *Guardians of Faith in Modern Times: 'Ulama' in the Middle East.* Leiden, the Netherlands: Brill, pp. 247–264.

    (ed.). (2009b). *Guardians of Faith in Modern Times: 'Ulama' in the Middle East.* Leiden, the Netherlands: Brill.

Hausner, J., Jessop, B. and Nielsen, K. (1995). *Strategic Choice and Path-Dependency in Post-Socialism: Institutional Dynamics in the Transformation Process.* Brookfield, VT: Edward Elgar.

Hay, Colin and Wincott, Daniel. (1998). 'Structure, Agency and Historical Institutionalism'. *Political Studies.* 46(5): 951–957.

Haynes, Jeffrey. (1995). 'Religion, Fundamentalism and Identity: A Global Perspective'. Discussion Paper No. 65. United Nations Research Institute for Social Development.

    (2009). *Routledge Handbook of Religion and Politics.* London; New York: Routledge.

Hechter, Michael. (2004). 'From Class to Culture'. *American Journal of Sociology*, 110(2): 400–445.

Hefner, R. W. (2010). 'Religious Resurgence in Contemporary Asia: Southeast Asian Perspectives on Capitalism, the State, and the New Piety'. *The Journal of Asian Studies*, 69(4): 1031–1047.

Hefner, R. W. and Zaman, M. Q. (2007). *Schooling Islam: The Culture and Politics of Modern Muslim Education.* Princeton University Press.

Hendrick, Joshua D. (2013). *Gülen: The Ambiguous Politics of Market Islam in Turkey and the World.* New York University Press.

Henry, Clement M. and Wilson, Rodney (eds). (2004). *The Politics of Islamic Finance.* Edinburgh University Press.

Heper, Metin. (1985). *The State Tradition in Turkey.* Beverley: Eothen Press.

    (2000). 'The Ottoman Legacy and Turkish Politics'. *Journal of International Affairs*, 54(1): 63–86.

    (2013). 'Islam, Conservatism, and Democracy in Turkey: Comparing Turgut Özal and Recep Tayyip Erdogan'. *Insight Turkey*, 15(2): 141–156.

Heper, Metin and Toktaş, Ş. (2003). 'Islam, Modernity, and Democracy in Contemporary Turkey: The Case of Recep Tayyip Erdoğan'. *The Muslim World*, 93(2): 157–185.

Heyd, Uriel. (1950). *Foundations of Turkish Nationalism: The Life and Teachings of Ziya Gökalp.* London: Luzac.

Hibbard, Scott W. (2010). *Religious Politics and Secular States: Egypt, India, and the United States.* Baltimore: Johns Hopkins University Press.

Hobsbawm, Eric. J. (1990). *Nations and Nationalism since 1780: Programme, Myth, Reality.* Cambridge University Press.

Hoşgör, Evren. (2011). 'Islamic Capital/Anatolian Tigers: Past and Present'. *Middle Eastern Studies*, 47(2): 343–360.

Human Rights Watch. (21 February 2014). 'Turkey: President Should Veto Judiciary Law'. *Human Rights Watch.* www.hrw.org/news/2014/02/21/turkey-president-should-veto-judiciary-law.

(2017). 'Turkey: Events of 2016'. *World Report 2017*. Human Rights Watch.

Hunter, Shireen. (2014). *Reformist Voices of Islam: Mediating Islam and Modernity*. Armonk, NY: M.E. Sharpe.

Huntington, Samuel P. (1991). *The Third Wave: Democratization in the Late Twentieth Century*. Norman; London: University of Oklahoma Press.

(1993). 'The Clash of Civilizations?' *Foreign Affairs*, 72(3): 22–49.

Hür, Ayşe. (24 October 2010). 'Türbanın 60 Yıllık Serüveni'. *Taraf*. www.taraf .com.tr/ayse-hur/makale-turbanin-60-yillik-seruveni.htm

Hurd, E. S. (2007). 'Theorizing Religious Resurgence'. *International Politics*, 44(6): 647–665.

(2011). 'A Suspension of (Dis)Belief: The Secular-Religious Binary and the Study of International Relations' in Craig Calhoun, Mark Juergensmeyer and Jonathan VanAntwerpen (eds.), *Rethinking Secularism*. Oxford University Press, pp. 166–184.

Hürriyet Daily News. (25 November 2013). '78 Percent of Gezi Park Protest Detainees Were Alevis: Report'. *Hurriyet Daily News*. http://www.hurriyetdailynews .com/78-percent-of-gezi-park-protest-detainees-were-alevis-report–58496

(1 October 2014). 'Turkey Aims to Open Islamic University: Top Religious Head'. *Hurriyet Daily News*. www.hurriyetdailynews.com/turkey-aims-to-open-islamic-university-top-religious-head-72418

(14 December 2015). 'Turkey's Top Cleric: Secularism Threw World Into Total War'. *Hurriyet Daily News*. www.hurriyetdailynews.com/turkeys-top-cleric-secularism-threw-world-into-total-war-92503

(2 January 2016). 'Legal Status to Alevi Worship Houses a "Red Line," Says Turkey's Religious Body Head'. *Hurriyet Daily News*. www.hurriyetdaily news.com/legal-status-to-alevi-worship-houses-a-red-line-says-turkeys-religious-body-head-93366

(13 December 2017). 'Turkey Claims Ahmet Şık "Not Arrested for Journalistic Activities" in ECHR Defense'. *Hurriyet Daily News*. www.hurriyetdaily news.com/turkey-claims-ahmet-sik-not-arrested-for-journalistic-activities-in-echr-defense-124044

Hürriyet. (4 January 2001). 'İmam Hatipler İçin Yetki Savaşı'. *Hürriyet*. http:// hurarsiv.hurriyet.com.tr/goster/ShowNew.aspx?id=-212834, 431.

(6 May 2001). 'Bostancıoğlu'nun, TÜDEV'le Savaşı Sürüyor'. *Hürriyet*. http:// hurarsiv.hurriyet.com.tr/goster/ShowNew.aspx?id=-241530

(12 December 2011). 'Diyanet'te 'Mele' Dönemi'. *Hürriyet*. www.hurriyet .com.tr/diyanet-te-mele-donemi-19443417

(27 March 2013). 'Görmez: "İzmir'in farklı bir dindarlığı var"'. *Hürriyet*. www.hurriyet.com.tr/gormez-izmirin-farkli-bir-dindarligi-var-22892652

(20 December 2013). '100 Milyar TL'lik İhale Devi Medyaya Girdi'. *Hürriyet*. www.hurriyet.com.tr/ekonomi/25409671.asp

(1 October 2014). 'Diyanet'ten İslam Üniversitesi'. www.hurriyet.com.tr/diya net-ten-islam-universitesi-27304749

(16 January 2015). 'AK Partili Vekil: "90 Yıllık Reklam Arası Sona Erdi"'. www.hurriyet.com.tr/ak-partili-vekil-90-yillik-reklam-arasi-sona-erdi-27972573

(21 December 2016). 'Suriyeli Öğrencilere 4 Milyon Ders Kitabı'. www.hurriyet.com.tr/suriyeli-ogrencilere-4-milyon-ders-kitabi-40313436

Hutchinson, John. (1994). *Modern Nationalism*. London: Fontana Press.

(2004a). 'Myth against Myth: The Nation as Ethnic Overlay'. *Nations and Nationalism*, 10(1–2): 109–123.

(2004b). *Nations as Zones of Conflict*. Thousand Oaks, CA; London: Sage.

İğde, İsrafil. (2010). 'Dini Mekanlar Dışında Sunulan Din Hizmetleri: Cezaevi Örneği'. Yunus Emre Camii Eğitim ve Kültür Derneği I. Ulusal Din Görevlileri Sempozyumu Tebliğleri.

Ignatius, David. (16 October 2013). 'David Ignatius: Turkey Blows Israel's Cover for Iranian Spy Ring'. *Washington Post*. www.washingtonpost.com/opinions/david-ignatius-turkey-blows-israels-cover-for-iranian-spy-ring/2013/10/16/7d9c1eb2-3686-11e3-be86-6aeaa439845b_story.html?utm_term=.d4ceea65b48e

İhvanlar. (4 November 2017). 'Cumhurbaşkanına İçerden Kurulan Büyük Tuzak'. www.ihvanlar.net/2017/11/04/cumhurbaskanina-icerden-kurulan-buyuk-tuzak/

Ikenberry, G. John. (1994). 'History's Heavy Hand: Institutions and the Politics of the State'. Working paper. https://scholar.princeton.edu/sites/default/files/HistorysHeavyHand_0.pdf

Imber, Colin. (2002). *The Ottoman Empire*. New York: Palgrave Macmillan.

Inglis, Tom. (2007). 'Catholic Identity in Contemporary Ireland: Belief and Belonging to Tradition'. *Journal of Contemporary Religion*, 22(2): 205–220.

İnal, İbrahim Hakkı and Alagöz, Muhammed Nurullah. (2016): '1970'ler Türkiye'sinde Dinde Reform Tartışmaları: Nesil Dergisi Çevresi Örneği'. *Harran Üniversitesi İlahiyat Fakültesi Dergisi*. 35(35): 28–52.

İnalcık, Halil. (2001). 'Kanunname'. *Türkiye Diyanet Vakfı İslâm Ansiklopedisi*. 24: 333–337. www.islamansiklopedisi.info/dia/ayrmetin.php?idno=240333

İnsel, Ahmet. (2003). 'The AKP and Normalizing Democracy in Turkey'. *The South Atlantic Quarterly*, 102(2): 293–308.

İrem, Nazım. (2002). 'Turkish Conservative Modernism: Birth of a Nationalist Quest for Cultural Renewal'. *International Journal of Middle East Studies*, 34(01): 87–112.

Jacobsohn, G. J. (2010). *Constitutional Identity*. Cambridge, MA: Harvard University Press.

Jacoby, Tim. (2003). 'For the People, of the People and by the Military: The Regime Structure of Modern Turkey'. *Political Studies*, 51(4): 669–685.

(2006). 'Agriculture, the State and Class Formation in Turkey's First Republic (1923–60)'. *The Journal of Peasant Studies*, 33(1): 34–60.

Jalal, Ayesha. (1995). *Democracy and Authoritarianism in South Asia: A Comparative and Historical Perspective*. Cambridge University Press.

(1998). 'Nation, Reason and Religion: Punjab's Role in the Partition of India'. *Economic and Political Weekly*, 33(32): 2183–2190.

Jenkins, Richard. (1994). 'Rethinking Ethnicity: Identity, Categorization and Power'. *Ethnic and Racial Studies*, 17(2): 197–223.

Jessop, Bob. (1990). *State Theory: Putting the Capitalist State in its Place*. Cambridge: Polity.

(2004). 'Institutional Re(turns) and the Strategic-Relational Approach' in D. Valler and A. Wood (eds.), *Governing Local and Regional Economic Development: Institutions, Politics and Economic Development*. Aldershot: Ashgate, pp. 23–56.

(2007). *State Power: A Strategic-Relational Approach*. Cambridge: Polity.

(2010). 'Constituting Another Foucault Effect: Foucault on States and State-craft' in U. Bröckling, S. Krasmann and T. Lemke (eds.), *Governmentality: Current Issues and Future Challenges*. New York: Routledge, pp. 56–73.

Juergensmeyer, Mark. (1993). *The New Cold War? Religious Nationalism Confronts the Secular State*. Berkeley, CA: University of California Press.

(2011). 'Rethinking the Secular and Religious Aspects of Violence' in Craig Calhoun, Mark Juergensmeyer and Jonathan Van Antwerpen (eds.), *Rethinking Secularism*. Oxford University Press, pp. 185–203.

Kadıoğlu, Ayşe. (1996). 'The Paradox of Turkish Nationalism and the Construction of Official Identity'. *Middle East Studies*, 32(2): 177–193.

Kahf, Monzer. (2004). 'Islamic Banks: The Rise of a New Power Alliance of Wealth and Shari'a Scholarship' in Clement M. Henry and Rodney Wilson (eds.), *The Politics of Islamic Finance*. Edinburgh University Press, pp. 17–36.

Kalaycıoğlu, Ersin. (2005). *Turkish Dynamics: Bridge across Troubled Lands*. London: Palgrave Macmillan.

(2007). 'Politics of Conservatism in Turkey'. *Turkish Studies*, 8(2): 233–252.

(2015). 'Turkish Popular Presidential Elections: Deepening Legitimacy Issues and Looming Regime Change'. *South European Society and Politics*, 20(2): 157–179.

Kale, Başak. (2014). 'Transforming an Empire: The Ottoman Empire's Immigration and Settlement Policies in the Nineteenth and Early Twentieth Centuries'. *Middle Eastern Studies*, 50(2): 252–271.

Kalyvas, Stathis N. (1996). *The Rise of Christian Democracy in Europe*. Ithaca, NY; London: Cornell University Press.

Kandiyoti, Deniz. (2009). 'Secularisms, Citizenship and Gender Equality: Contested Approaches'. Religion Revisited – Women's Rights and the Political Instrumentalisation of Religion Conference. Heinrich-Böll-Foundation and UNSRID.

(2012). 'The Travails of the Secular: Puzzle and Paradox in Turkey'. *Economy and Society*, 41(4): 513–531.

(2014). 'No Laughing Matter: Women and the New Populism in Turkey'. *Open Democracy*. www.opendemocracy.net/5050/deniz-kandiyoti/no-laughing-matter-women-and-new-populism-in-turkey.

(2016). 'The Mutation of the Turkish State: The Long View'. *The Middle East at SOAS*, 12 (5): 38–39.

Kandiyoti, Deniz and Emanet, Zühre. (2017). 'Education as Battleground: The Capture of Minds in Turkey'. *Globalizations*, 14(6): 869–876.

Kara, İsmail. (2000). *Kutuz Hoca'nın Hatıraları: Cumhuriyet Devrinde Bir Köy Hocası*. İstanbul: Dergâh Yayınları.

(2002). *Şeyhefendinin Rüyasındaki Türkiye*. İstanbul: Dergah Yayınları.

(2005). 'Turban and Fez: Ulema as Opposition' in E. Özdalga (ed.), *Late Ottoman Society: The Intellectual Legacy*. London: Routledge, pp. 162–200.

(2007). 'Müsavat mı Eşitsizlik mi?' in Murat Koraltürk, Tanıl Bora, and Mehmet Ö. Alkan (eds.), *Mete Tunçay'a Armağan*. İstanbul: İletişim.

(18 July 2010). 'Islamism versus Islam: An Interview with Professor Ismail Kara'. *The Majalla*. www.majalla.com/eng/2010/07/article5586374

(2012). *Cumhuriyet Türkiyesi'nde Bir Mesele Olarak İslam*. İstanbul: Dergah Yayınları.

(2013). 'Türkiye'de İslâmcılık Düşüncesi ve Hareketi Üzerine Birkaç Not' in *Türkiye'de İslamcılık Düşüncesi ve Hareketi Sempozyumu*. İstanbul: Zeytinburnu Belediyesi Kültür Yayını, pp. 15–45.

(2016). *Cumhuriyet Türkiyesi'nde Bir Mesele Olarak İslam 2*. İstanbul: Dergah Yayınları.

(April 2016). 'Bekir Topaloğlu Hoca İçin Rahmet Kayıtları'. *Derin Tarih*, 52–57.

Kara, Mustafa. (1992). 'II. Abdülhamid Dönemine Tasavvuf Tarihi Açısından Genel Bir Bakış' in *Abdülhamid ve Dönemi Sempozyum Bildirileri*. Istanbul: İlim Kültür ve Sanat Vakfı Tarih Enstitüsü, pp. 65–73.

Karagül, Ibrahim. (1 March 2013). 'Yüzyıllık Parantezi Kapatacağız'. *Yeni Şafak*. www.yenisafak.com/yazidizileri/yuzyillik-parantezi-kapatacagiz-494795

Karakaya-Stump, Ayfer. (16 March 2014). 'Alevizing Gezi.' *Jadaliyya*. www.jadaliyya.com/pages/index/17087/alevizing-gezi

(2018). 'The AKP, Sectarianism, and the Alevis' Struggle for Equal Rights in Turkey'. *National Identities*, 20(1): 53–67.

Karaman, Hayrettin. (13 April 2017). 'Neyi oyluyoruz?' *Yeni Şafak*. www.yenisafak.com/yazarlar/hayrettinkaraman/neyi-oyluyoruz-2037309

(30 July 2017). 'Müftülere Nikah Yetkisi'. *Yeni Şafak*. www.yenisafak.com/yazarlar/hayrettinkaraman/muftulere-nikah-yetkisi-2039274

Karpat, Kemal. (1959). *Turkey's Politics: The Transition to a Multi-Party System*. Princeton University Press.

(1972). 'The Transformation of the Ottoman State, 1789–1908'. *International Journal of Middle East Studies*, 3(3): 243–281.

(1982). 'Millets and Nationality: The Roots of the Incongruity of Nation and State in the Post-Ottoman Era' in Benjamin Braude and Bernard Lewis (eds.), *Christians and Jews in the Ottoman Empire: The Functioning of a Plural Society*. New York; London: Holmes & Meier, pp. 141–169.

(1985). *Ottoman Population 1830–1914: Demographic and Social Characteristics*. Madison, WI: University of Wisconsin Press.

(2001). *The Politicization of Islam: Reconstructing Identity, State, Faith, and Community in the Late Ottoman State*. Oxford University Press.

Kaufmann, E. (2008). 'The Lenses of Nationhood: An Optical Model of Identity'. *Nations and Nationalism*, 14(3): 449–477.

Kaufmann, E. and Haklai, O. (2008). 'Dominant Ethnicity: From Minority to Majority'. *Nations and Nationalism*, 14(4): 743–767.

Kaya, Ayhan. (2015). 'Islamisation of Turkey under the AKP Rule: Empowering Family, Faith and Charity'. *South European Society and Politics*, 20(1): 47–69.

Kayalı, Hasan. (1997). *Arabs and Young Turks: Ottomanism, Arabism, and Islamism in the Ottoman Empire, 1908–1918*. Berkeley, CA: University of California Press.

Keddie, Nikki R. (1966). 'The Pan-Islamic Appeal: Afghani and Abdülhamid II'. *Middle Eastern Studies*, 3(1): 46–67.

(ed.). (1972). *Scholars, Saints, and Sufis: Muslim Religious Institutions in the Middle East since 1500*. Berkeley, CA: University of California Press.

(1994). 'The Revolt of Islam, 1700 to 1993: Comparative Considerations and Relations to Imperialism'. *Comparative Studies in Society and History*, 36(3): 463–487.

(1998). 'The New Religious Politics: Where, When, and Why Do "Fundamentalisms" Appear?' *Comparative Studies in Society and History*, 40(4): 696–723.

Kehl-Bodrogi, Krisztina. (2003). 'Atatürk and the Alevis: A Holy Alliance?' in Paul J. White and Joost Jongerden (eds.), *Turkey's Alevi Enigma: A Comprehensive Overview*. Leiden, the Netherlands: Brill, pp. 53–70.

Kemal, Yahya. (1963). 'Ezansız Semtler'. *Sebilürreşad*, 15(352): 22–23.

Kenanoğlu, Ali. (11 April 2013). 'Olağan Haller'. *Evrensel*. www.evrensel.net/yazi/53975/olagan-haller

Kepel, G. (1994). *The Revenge of God: The Resurgence of Islam, Christianity and Judaism in the Modern World*. University Park, PA: Penn State University Press.

Ketchley, N. and Biggs, M. (2017). 'The Educational Contexts of Islamist Activism: Elite Students and Religious Institutions in Egypt'. *Mobilization*, 22(1): 57–76.

Keyder, Çağlar. (1987). *State and Class in Turkey*. London: Verso.

Kieser, Hans-Lukas. (2003). 'Alevis, Armenians and Kurds in Unionist-Kemalist Turkey (1908–1938)' in Paul J. White and Joost Jongerden (eds.), *Turkey's Alevi Enigma: A Comprehensive Overview*. Leiden, the Netherlands: Brill, pp. 177–196.

(ed.) (2006). *Turkey beyond Nationalism: Towards Post-Nationalist Identities*. London: IB Tauris.

Kirişci, Kemal. (2000). 'Disaggregating Turkish Citizenship and Immigration Practices'. *Middle Eastern Studies*, 36(3): 1–22.

Kissane, B. (2003). 'The Illusion of State Neutrality in a Secularising Ireland'. *West European Politics*, 26(1): 73–94.

Kissane, B. and Sitter, N. (2010a). 'The Marriage of State and Nation in European Constitutions'. *Nations and Nationalism*, 16(1): 49–67.

(2010b). 'National Identity and Constitutionalism in Europe: Introduction'. *Nations and Nationalism*, 16(1): 1–5.

Kitschelt, H. P. (ed.). (1999). *Post-Communist Party Systems: Competition, Representation, and Inter-party Cooperation*. Cambridge University Press.

Koçak, Cemil. (2005). 'Parliament Membership during the Single-Party System in Turkey (1925–1945)'. *European Journal of Turkish Studies*, 3.

Koçan, Gürcan and Öncü, Ahmet. (2004). 'Citizen Alevi in Turkey: Beyond Confirmation and Denial'. *Journal of Historical Sociology*, 17(4): 464–489.

Koelle, Peter. B. (2000). 'The Inevitability of the 1971 Turkish Military Intervention'. *Journal of South Asian and Middle Eastern Studies*, 24(1), 38–56.

Koinova, Maria. (2013). *Ethnonationalist Conflict in Postcommunist States: Varieties of Governance in Bulgaria, Macedonia, and Kosovo*. Philadelphia, PA: University of Pennsylvania Press.

Köker, Levent. (2007). 'Kemalizm ve 21. Yüzyıl Türkiye Demokrasisi' in Bora Tanıl (ed.), *Mete Tunçay'a Armağan*. İstanbul: İletişim, pp. 115–132.

Kolluoğlu, Biray. (2013). 'Excesses of Nationalism: Greco-Turkish Population Exchange'. *Nations and Nationalism*, 19(3): 532–550.

KONDA. (16 April 2014). *KONDA Yerel Seçimler Sonrası Sandık ve Seçmen Analizi*. www.konda.com.tr/tr/raporlar/KONDA_30Mart2014_YerelSecim Analizi.pdf

Köni, Hakan. (2012). 'Saudi Influence on Islamic Institutions in Turkey Beginning in the 1970s'. *The Middle East Journal*, 66(1): 97–110.

Koraltürk, Murat. (2011). *Erken Cumhuriyet Döneminde: Ekonominin Türkleştirilmesi*. İstanbul: İletişim.

Korkut, Şenol. (2010). 'The Diyanet of Turkey and Its Activities in Eurasia after the Cold War'. *Acta Slavica Iaponica*, 28(2010): 117–139.

Köse, Ahmet H. and Bahçe, Serdal. (2009). '"Hayırsever" Devletin Yükselişi: AKP Yönetiminde Gelir Dağılımı ve Yoksulluk' in İlhan Uzel and Bülent Duru (eds.), *AKP Kitabı: Bir Dönüşümün Bilançosu*. Ankara: Phoenix Yayınevi, pp. 492–509.

Koylu, Mustafa. (2005). 'Religious Education in Modern Turkey' in S. Gündüz and C. S. Yaran (eds.), *Change and Essence: Dialectical Relations between Change and Continuity in the Turkish Intellectual Tradition*. Washington, DC: Council for Research in Values and Philosophy, pp. 45–64.

Krasner, Stephen. D. (1984). 'Approaches to the State: Alternative Conceptions and Historical Dynamics'. *Comparative Politics*, 16(2): 223–246.

Küçük, Hülya. (2002). *The Role of the Bektashis in Turkey's National Struggle*. Leiden, the Netherlands: Brill.

Kuran, Timur. (2004). 'The Economic Ascent of the Middle East's Religious Minorities: The Role of Islamic Legal Pluralism'. *The Journal of Legal Studies*, 33(2): 475–515.

Kuru, Ahmet T. (2005). 'Globalization and Diversification of Islamic Movements: Three Turkish Cases'. *Political Science Quarterly*, 120(2): 253–274.

    (2007). 'Passive and Assertive Secularism: Historical Conditions, Ideological Struggles, and State Policies toward Religion'. *World Politics*, 59(4): 568–594.

    (2009). *Secularism and State Policies toward Religion: The United States, France, and Turkey*. Cambridge University Press.

    (December 2017). 'Islam and Democracy in Turkey: Analyzing the Failure'. *The Montréal Review*. www.themontrealreview.com/2009/Islam-And-Democracy-In-Turkey.php

Kuru, Ahmet T. and Stepan, Alfred. (eds). (2012). *Democracy, Islam, and Secularism in Turkey*. New York; Chichester: Columbia University Press.

Kuru, Zeynep A. and Kuru, Ahmet T. (2008). 'Apolitical Interpretation of Islam: Said Nursi's Faith-Based Activism in Comparison with Political Islamism and Sufism'. *Islam and Christian–Muslim Relations*, 19(1): 99–111.

Kushner, David. (1977). *The Rise of Turkish Nationalism, 1876–1908*. London; Totowa, NJ: Cass.

    (1987). 'The Place of the Ulema in the Ottoman Empire During the Age of Reform (1839–1918)'. *Turcica*, 19: 51–74.

Kutlay, Naci. (2015). *İttihat Terakki ve Kürtler*. Ankara: Dipnot Yayınları.

Laakso, Markku and Taagepera, Rein. (1979). 'Effective Number of Parties: A Measure with Application to West Europe'. *Comparative Political Studies*, 12(1), 3–27.

LaFranchi, Howard. (12 December 2012). 'For Newly Recognized Syrian Rebel Coalition, a First Dispute with US'. *Christian Science Monitor*. www.csmonitor .com/USA/Foreign-Policy/2012/1212/For-newly-recognized-Syrian-rebel-coalition-a-first-dispute-with-US

Landau, Jacob M. (1996). 'Muslim Opposition to Freemasonry'. *Welt des Islams*, 36: 186–203.

Lapidus, Ira M. (1997). 'Islamic Revival and Modernity: The Contemporary Movements and the Historical Paradigms'. *Journal of the Economic and Social History of the Orient*, 40(4): 444–460.

  (2001). 'Between Universalism and Particularism: The Historical Bases of Muslim Communal, National, and Global Identities'. *Global Networks*, 1(1): 37–55.

Lee, Raymond L. (1990). 'The State, Religious Nationalism, and Ethnic Rationalization in Malaysia'. *Ethnic and Racial Studies*, 13(4): 482–502.

Lerner, Hanna. (2013). 'Permissive Constitutions, Democracy, and Religious Freedom in India, Indonesia, Israel, and Turkey'. *World Politics*, 65(4): 609–655.

  (2014). 'Critical Junctures, Religion, and Personal Status Regulations in Israel and India'. *Law and Social Inquiry*, 39(2): 387–415.

Levitsky, Steven and Murillo, Maria V. (2013). 'Building Institutions on Weak Foundations'. *Journal of Democracy*, 24(2): 93–107.

Levitsky, Steven and Way, Lucan. (2002). 'The Rise of Competitive Authoritarianism'. *Journal of Democracy*, 13(2): 51–65.

  (2012). 'Beyond Patronage: Violent Struggle, Ruling Party Cohesion, and Authoritarian Durability'. *Perspectives on Politics*, 10(4): 869–889.

Lewis, Bernard. (1952). 'Islamic Revival in Turkey'. *International Affairs*, 28(1): 38–48.

  (1968). *The Emergence of Modern Turkey*. London: Oxford University Press.

Lieven, Dominic C.B. (2000). *Empire: The Russian Empire and Its Rivals*. London: John Murray.

Lijphart, Arend. (1999). *Patterns of Democracy*. New Haven, CT; London: Yale University Press.

Lord, Ceren. (2012). 'The Persistence of Turkey's Majoritarian System of Government'. *Government and Opposition*, 47(2): 228–255.

  (2016a). 'Between Islam and the Nation: Nation-Building, the Ulama and Alevi Identity in Turkey'. *Nations and Nationalism*, 23(1): 48–67.

  (2016b). 'Rethinking the Justice and Development Party's "Alevi openings"'. *Turkish Studies*, 18(2): 278–296.

  (2017). 'Situating Change under the AKP' in Meltem Ersoy and Esra Özyürek (eds.). *Contemporary Turkey at a Glance II: Turkey Transformed? Power, History, Culture*. Wiesbaden: Springer Fachmedien, pp. 7–24.

Lord , Ceren. (February 2018). 'The Story behind the Rise of Turkey's Ulema'. *MERIP*. www.merip.org/mero/mero020418

338   Bibliography

Loveman, Mara. (1999). 'Is "Race" Essential?' *American Sociological Review*, 64(6): 891–898.

Lüküslü, Demet. (2016). 'Creating a Pious Generation: Youth and Education Policies of the AKP in Turkey'. *Southeast European and Black Sea Studies*, 16(4): 637–649.

Madan, T. N. (1987). 'Secularism in Its Place'. *The Journal of Asian Studies*, 46(4): 747–759.

Maden, Fahri. (2016). 'En Uzun Yüzyılında Bektaşilik ve Bektaşiler' in İmran Gürtaş (Der.) and Yalçın Çakmak (eds.), *Kızılbaşlık, Alevilik, Bektaşilik*. İstanbul: İletişim, pp. 185–214.

Magaloni, Beatriz. (2008). 'Credible Power-Sharing and the Longevity of Authoritarian Rule'. *Comparative Political Studies*, 41(4–5): 715–741.

Mahoney, James (2000). 'Path Dependence in Historical Sociology'. *Theory and Society*, 29(4): 507–548.

Mahoney, James and Schensul, D. (2006). 'Historical Context and Path Dependence' in Robert E. Goodin and Charles Tilly (eds.), *The Oxford Handbook of Contextual Political Analysis*. Oxford University Press, pp. 454–471.

Mahoney, James and Thelen, Kathleen (eds.). (2009). *Explaining Institutional Change: Ambiguity, Agency, and Power*. Cambridge University Press.

Mandaville, Peter. (2014). *Islam and Politics*. London; New York: Routledge.

Mangi, L. C. (2009). 'Neoinstitutionalism and the Appropriation of Bourdieu's Work: A Critical Assessment'. *Revista de Administração de Empresas*, 49(3): 323–336.

Mann, Michael. (2003). *The Sources of Social Power, 2*. Cambridge University Press.

Mardin, Şerif. (1971). 'Ideology and Religion in the Turkish Revolution'. *International Journal of Middle East Studies*, 2(3): 197–211.

   (1973). 'Centre-Periphery Relations: A Key to Turkish Politics?' *Daedalus*, 102(1): 169–190.

   (1982). 'Turkey: Islam and Westernization' in Carlo Caldarola (ed.), *Religions and Societies: Asia and the Middle East*. Herndon, VA: Walter de Gruyter, pp. 171–198.

   (1989). *Religion and Social Change in Modern Turkey: The Case of Bediüzzaman Said Nursi*. Albany, NY: State University of New York Press.

Martin, David. (2007). 'What I Really Said about Secularisation'. *Dialog*, 46(2): 139–152.

Massicard, Elise. (2007). *Türkiye'den Avrupa'ya Alevi Hareketinin Siyasallaşması*. İstanbul: İletişim.

   (2013). *The Alevis in Turkey and Europe: Identity and Managing Territorial Diversity*. London: Routledge.

   (2016). 'Alevi Critique of the AK Party, Criticizing "Islamism" or the Turkish State?' in Umit Cizre (ed.), *The Turkish AK Party and Its Leader: Criticism, Opposition and Dissent*. New York: Routledge, pp. 75–102.

Masters, Bruce. (1992). 'The Sultan's Entrepreneurs: The Avrupa Tüccaris and the Hayriye Tüccaris in Syria'. *International Journal of Middle East Studies*, 24(4): 579–597.

MAZLUMDER. (2012). *II. Kürd Forumu*. Ankara: MAZLUMDER.

McPherson, Eve. (2011). 'Political History and Embodied Identity Discourse in the Turkish Call to Prayer'. *Music & Politics*, 5(1): 1–13.

Means, G. P. (1978). 'Public Policy toward Religion in Malaysia'. *Pacific Affairs*, 51(3): 384–405.

Mecham, R. Q. (2004). 'From the Ashes of Virtue, a Promise of Light: The Transformation of Political Islam in Turkey'. *Third World Quarterly*, 25(2): 339–358.

Melikoff, Irene. (1998). *Hacı Bektaş, Efsaneden Gerçeğe*. İstanbul: Cumhuriyet Kitapları.

Mert, Nuray. (2004). 'Türkiye İslâmcılığına Tarihsel Bir Bakış' in Yasin Aktay (ed.), *Türkiye'de Siyasi Düşünce Cilt 6/İslamcılık*. Istanbul: İletişim, pp. 411–419.

Meşe, Ertuğrul. (2017). *Komünizmle Mücadele Dernekleri*. İstanbul: İletişim.

Metcalf, Barbara Daly. (1982). *Islamic Revival in British India: Deoband, 1860–1900*. Princeton University Press.

Metiner, Mehmet. (5 September 2013). 'Çoğulculuk Mu, Azınlık Tahakkümü Mü?' *Yeni Şafak*. yenisafak.com.tr/yazarlar/MehmetMetiner/cogulculuk-mu-azinlik-tahakkumu-mu/39408

(10 October 2013). 'Cemevleri Terör Yuvası'. *Yeni Şafak*. www.yenisafak.com/yazarlar/ahmetunlu/maas-katsayisindaki-artislar-memur-sozlesmeli-ve-emek lilere-nasil-yansiyacak-2046371

Michaud-Emin, L. (2007). 'The Restructuring of the Military High Command in the Seventh Harmonization Package and Its Ramifications for Civil–Military Relations in Turkey'. *Turkish Studies*, 8(1): 25–42.

Migdal, J. S. (2001). *State in Society: Studying How States and Societies Transform and Constitute One Another*. Cambridge University Press.

Milli Düşünce, Merkezi. (7 March 2012). 'Çelebi Feyzullah Ulusoy'la Sohbet'. *Milli Düşünce Merkezi*. http://millidusunce.com/celebi-feyzullah-ulusoyla-sohbet/

Milli Çözüm. (29 January 2015). 'Dilipak'la Ali Bulaç'ın İtirafları ve Batili Merkezlerle İrtibatlari'. www.millicozum.com/mc/subat-2015/dilipakla-ali-bula cin-itiraflari-ve-batili-merkezlerle-irtibatlari.

Milli Gazete. (31 October 2017). 'İsmailağa'dan İhsan Şenocak Açıklaması'. *Milli Gazete*. www.milligazete.com.tr/haber/1281358/ismailagadan-ihsan-senocak-aciklamasi

(4 November 2017). 'İhsan Şenocak'tan 'Ehl-i Sünnet'i Temsil Açıklaması'. *Milli Gazete*. www.milligazete.com.tr/haber/1283947/ihsan-senocaktan-ehl-i-sunneti-temsil-aciklamasi

Milliyet. (24 July 1951). 'İskenderun Hadisesi'. *Milliyet*.

(1 August 1951). 'Hükümetten Şiddetle Hareket Bekliyoruz'. *Milliyet*.

(22 August 1977). 'Diyanet İşleri Başkanı'nın Cübbesi, Şeyhülislâmların Giydiği Cübbe Modeli Oluyor'. *Milliyet*.

(30 December 1978). 'Diyanet İşleri'. *Milliyet*.

(18 August 2001). 'Alevilerin İbadet Yeri Cami Olmalı'. *Milliyet*. www.milliyet.com.tr/alevilerin-ibadet-yeri-cami-olmali/guncel/haberdetayarsiv/18.08.2001/249045/default.htm

(11 November 2010). 'Bölücü Akımlara Karşı İrşat Ekipleri.' *Milliyet.* www.milliyet.com.tr/bolucu-akimlara-karsi-irsat-ekipleri-gundem-1313418/

(4 September 2014). 'Başbakan Davutoğlu'dan Önemli Açıklamalar'. *Milliyet.* www.milliyet.com.tr/basbakan-davutoglu-dan-onemli/siyaset/detay/1935619/default.htm

(4 April 2017). 'Fetö Projesi Cami-Cemevi, Sağlık Merkezine Dönüşüyor'. *Milliyet.*   www.milliyet.com.tr/feto-projesi-cami-cemevi-saglik-merkezine-ankara-yerelhaber-1953856/

Mitchell, Timothy. (1991). 'The Limits of the State: Beyond Statist Approaches and Their Critics'. *American Political Science Review,* 85(01): 77–96.

Mohamad, Maznah. (2009). 'The Authoritarian State and Political Islam in Muslim-Majority Malaysia'. In Johan Saravanamuttu (ed.). *Islam and Politics in Southeast Asia.* Abingdon; New York: Routledge, pp. 65–84.

Moore, C. H. (1990). 'Islamic Banks and Competitive Politics in the Arab World and Turkey'. *The Middle East Journal,* 44(2): 234–255.

Moustafa, Tamir. (2000). 'Conflict and Cooperation between the State and Religious Institutions in Contemporary Egypt'. *International Journal Middle East Studies,* 32(1): 3–22.

Müftüler-Baç, M. (2005). 'Turkey's Political Reforms and the Impact of the European Union'. *South European Society and Politics,* 10(1): 17–31.

Müftüler-Baç, Meltem and Keyman, Fuat E. (2012). 'The Era of Dominant-Party Politics.' *Journal of Democracy,* 23(1): 85–99

Mumcu, Özgür. (1 April 2017). 'Hayrettin Karaman Vesayeti'. *Cumhuriyet Gazetesi.* www.cumhuriyet.com.tr/koseyazisi/711308/Hayrettin_Karaman_vesayeti.html

(9 August 2017). 'Devlet Kurmak'. *Cumhuriyet Gazetesi.* www.cumhuriyet.com.tr/koseyazisi/799191/Devlet_kurmak.html

Mumcu, Uğur. (6 January 1987). 'Birader Vakıfları'. *Cumhuriyet.* www.guncelmeydan.com/pano/birader-vakiflari-ugur-mumcu-t33433.html

(1990). *Kazım Karabekir Anlatıyor.* Ankara: Tekin Yayınevi.

(1993). *Rabıta.* İstanbul: Tekin Yayınevi.

Musil, Pelin Ayan. (2015). 'Emergence of a Dominant Party System after Multi-partyism: Theoretical Implications from the Case of the AKP in Turkey'. *South European Society and Politics,* 20(1): 71–92.

Mynet Haber. (17 March 2013). 'Anayasanın Ruhunu Gömmek Lazım'. https://www.mynet.com/anayasanin-ruhunu-gommek-lazim-110100683958

Nandy, Ashis. (1988). 'The Politics of Secularism and the Recovery of Religious Tolerance'. *Alternatives: Global, Local, Political,* 13(2): 177–194.

Nasr, Vali. (2005). 'The Rise of "Muslim Democracy"'. *Journal of Democracy,* 16(2): 13–27.

Navaro-Yashin, Yael. (2002). *Faces of the State: Secularism and Public Life in Turkey.* Oxford: Princeton University Press.

New York Times. (3 January 2018). 'Banker from Turkey Is Convicted in U.S. Over Plot to Evade Iran Sanctions'. *New York Times.* www.nytimes.com/2018/01/03/world/europe/turkey-iran-sanctions-trial.html

North, Douglass C. (1991). 'Institutions'. *Journal of Economic Perspectives,* 5(1): 97–112.

Norton, J. D. (1988). 'The Turks and Islam' in Peter Clarke (ed.), *The World's Religions: Islam*. London: Routledge, pp. 84–101.

Nugent, David. (1994). 'Building the State, Making the Nation: The Bases and Limits of State Centralisation in "Modern" Peru'. *American Anthropologist*, 96(2): 333–369.

Ocak, Ahmet Yaşar. (1983). *Alevi ve Bektaşi İnançlarının İslam Öncesi Temelleri*. İstanbul: İletişim.

(1996). *Türk Sufiliğine Bakışlar*. İstanbul: İletişim.

(1998). *Osmanlı İmparatorluğu'nda Zındıklar ve Mülhidler*. İstanbul: Tarih Vakfı Yurt Yayınları.

Öcal, Mustafa. (2008). 'Türkiye'de Din Eğitimi Tarihi Literatürü'. *Türkiye Araştırmaları Literatür Dergisi*, 12: 399–430.

(2015). *Osmanlı'dan Günümüze Türkiye'de Din Eğitimi*. İstanbul: Dergah Yayınları.

Okur, Salih. (2011). *Ulemanın Gözüyle Bediüzzaman*. İstanbul: Kayıhan Yayınları.

Okutan, M. Çağatay. (2004). *Tek Parti Döneminde Azınlık Politikaları*. İstanbul: İstanbul Bilgi Üniversitesi.

Olson, Robert. (1989). *The Emergence of Kurdish Nationalism and the Sheikh Said Rebellion, 1880–1925*. Austin: University of Texas Press.

(2013). *The Emergence of Kurdish Nationalism and the Sheikh Said Rebellion, 1880–1925*. Austin: University of Texas Press.

Öniş, Ziya. (2009). 'Conservative Globalism at the Crossroads: The Justice and Development Party and the Thorny Path to Democratic Consolidation in Turkey'. *Mediterranean Politics*, 14(1): 21–40.

(2013). 'Sharing Power: Turkey's Democratization Challenge in the Age of the AKP Hegemony'. *Insight Turkey*, 15(2, 1013): 103–122.

(2014). 'Monopolizing the Center: The AKP and the Uncertain Path of Turkish Democracy'. *Available at SSRN* 2499213. http://papers.ssrn.com/sol3/papers.cfm?abstract_id=2499213

Oran, Baskın. (1999). *Atatürk Milliyetçiliği*. Ankara: Bilgi Yayınevi.

Ortaylı, İlber. (2001). *İmparatorluğun En Uzun Yüzyılı*. İstanbul: İletişim.

(2012). *Ottoman Studies*. İstanbul: Bilgi Üniversitesi Yayınları.

OSCE (Organization for Security and Co-operation). (17 April 2017). 'International Referendum Observation Mission, Republic of Turkey – Constitutional Referendum, 16 April 2017'. www.osce.org/odihr/elections/turkey/303681

Özbudun, Ergun. (1992). *1921 Anayasası*. Ankara: Atatürk Araştırma Merkezi/Yayınevi Genel Dizisi.

(2000). *Contemporary Turkish Politics: Challenges to Democratic Consolidation*. London: Lynne Rienner Publishers.

(2006). 'From Political Islam to Conservative Democracy: The Case of the Justice and Development Party in Turkey'. *South European Society and Politics*, 11(3–4): 543–557.

(2009). *Türk Anayasa Hukuku*. Ankara: Yetkin Yayınları.

(2011). *The Constitutional System of Turkey: 1876 to the Present*. New York: Palgrave Macmillan.

(2014). 'AKP at the Crossroads: Erdoğan's Majoritarian Drift'. *South European Society and Politics*, 19(2): 155–167.

(2015). 'Turkey's Judiciary and the Drift toward Competitive Authoritarianism'. *The International Spectator*, 50(2): 42–55.

Özbudun, Ergun and Gençkaya, Ömer Faruk. (2009). *Democratization and the Politics of Constitution-Making in Turkey*. Budapest: Central European University Press.

Özdalga, Elisabeth. (2000). 'Worldly Asceticism in Islamic Casting: Fethullah Gülen's Inspired Piety and Activism'. *Critique: Journal for Critical Studies of the Middle East*, 9(17): 83–104.

(2006). 'The Hidden Arab: A Critical Reading of the Notion of "Turkish Islam"'. *Middle Eastern Studies*, 42(4): 551–570.

Özgür, İren. (2012). *Islamic Schools in Modern Turkey: Faith, Politics, and Education*. Cambridge University Press.

Özkan, Behlül. (7 December 2016). 'The Failure of a Neo-Ottoman Foreign Policy'. *New York Times*. www.nytimes.com/2016/12/07/opinion/turkey-ottoman-foreign-policy-iraq-syria-failing.html

Özkırımlı, Umut. (2000). *Theories of Nationalism: A Critical Introduction*. Basingstoke: Palgrave.

Özman, Aylin and Dede, Kadir. (2016). 'Türk Sağı ve Masonluğun Söylemsel İnşası'. In İnci Özkan Kerestecioğlu and Güven Gürkan Öztan (eds.). *Türk Sağı: Mitler, Fetişler, Düşman İmgeleri*. İstanbul: İletişim Yayınları, pp. 169–202.

Öztürk, Ahmet Erdi. (2016). 'Turkey's Diyanet under AKP Rule: From Protector to Imposer of State Ideology?' *Southeast European and Black Sea Studies*, 16(4): 619–635.

Öztürk, Özgür. (2015). 'The Islamist Big Bourgeoisie in Turkey' in Neşecan Balkan, Erol Balkan, and Ahmet Öncü (eds.), *The Neoliberal Landscape and the Rise of Islamist Capital in Turkey*. New York; Oxford: Berghahn Books, pp. 117–141.

Öztürk, Veli. (2010). *Cumhuriyet Dönemi Milli Eğitim Şûralarında Din Ve Ahlak Eğitimi İle İlgili Olarak Alınan Kararlar Ve Tartışmalar*. İzmir: Tibyan Yayıncılık.

Pantham, T. (1997). 'Indian Secularism and its Critics: Some Reflections'. *The Review of Politics*, 59(3): 523–540.

Parkin, Frank. (1974). *The Social Analysis of Class Structure*. London: Routledge.

Parla, T. and Davison, A. (2004). *Corporatist Ideology in Kemalist Turkey: Progress or Order?* Syracuse University Press.

Patton, M. J. (2007). 'AKP Reform Fatigue in Turkey: What Has Happened to the EU Process?' *Mediterranean Politics*, 12(3): 339–358.

Peletz, M. G. (2002). *Islamic Modern: Religious Courts and Cultural Politics in Malaysia*. Princeton University Press.

PEN. (24 January 2018). 'Turkish Constitutional Court's Ruling Ignored as Mehmet Altan Remains in Detention'. https://pen.org/press-release/turkish-constitutional-courts-ruling-ignored-mehmet-altan-remains-detention/

Pew Research Religion and Public Life Project. www.pewforum.org

Pierret, Thomas. (May 2014). 'The Syrian Islamic Council'. *Carnegie*. http://carnegie-mec.org/diwan/55580

(25 May 2014). 'Profiles of Syrian Sunni Clerics in the Uprising'. *Carnegie.*
http://carnegie-mec.org/diwan/51284?lang=en

Pierret, Thomas and Selvik, K. (2009). 'Limits of "Authoritarian Upgrading" in Syria: Private Welfare, Islamic Charities, and the Rise of the Zayd Movement'. *International Journal of Middle East Studies*, 41(4): 595–614.

Pierson, P. and Skocpol, T. (2002). 'Historical Institutionalism in Contemporary Political Science' in Ira Katznelson and Helen V. Milner (eds.), *Political Science: The State of the Discipline.* New York: W.W. Norton & Company, pp. 693–721.

Pioppi, D. (2004). 'From Religious Charity to the Welfare State and Back. The Case of Islamic Endowments (waqfs) Revival in Egypt'. EUI Working Paper RSCAS 2004/34.

Poggi, Gianfranco. (1990). *The State: Its Nature, Development and Prospects.* Oxford: Polity Press.

Poulton, Hugh. (1997). *Top Hat, Grey Wolf and Crescent.* London: Hurst.

Poyraz, Bedriye. (2005). 'The Turkish State and Alevis: Changing Parameters of an Uneasy Relationship'. *Middle Eastern Studies*, 41(4): 503–516.

Price, D. E. (1999). *Islamic Political Culture, Democracy, and Human Rights: A Comparative Study.* Westport, CT; London: Praeger.

Przeworski, Adam and Sprague, John D. (1986). *Paper Stones: A History of Electoral Socialism.* University of Chicago Press.

Przeworski, Adam, Alvarez, Michael E., Cheibub, José Antonio and Limongi, Fernando. (2000). *Democracy and Development: Political Institutions and Well-Being in the World, 1950–1990.* Cambridge University Press.

Pupcenoks, Juris. (2012). 'Democratic Islamization in Pakistan and Turkey: Lessons for the Post-Arab Spring Muslim World'. *The Middle East Journal*, 66(2): 273–289.

Radikal. (31 October 2011). 'Kenan Evren'le Anlaşabiliyorduk Erbakan'la Uyuşamadık'. *Radikal.* www.radikal.com.tr/yazarlar/ezgi-basaran/kenan-evrenle-anlasabiliyorduk-erbakanla-uyusamadik-1068004/

(28 September 2012). 'Taksim'e 15 Bin Kazık'. www.radikal.com.tr/turkiye/taksime_15_bin_kazik-1101967

(26 October 2012). 'Darbeciler 5 Bin Çocuğu İmam Hatibe Sürdü'. *Radikal.* www.radikal.com.tr/turkiye/darbeciler-5-bin-cocugu-imam-hatibe-surdu-1105436/

(7 May 2013). 'Maltepe'de Alevilerin Evleri 'Ölüm'le İşaretlendi'. *Radikal.* www.radikal.com.tr/turkiye/maltepede-alevilerin-evleri-olumle-isaretlendi-1132546/

(11 July 2013). 'Asker, Alevileri İç Tehdit Saymış: "Aleviler Devlete Sızmaya Çalışıyor"'. *Radikal.* www.radikal.com.tr/turkiye/asker_alevileri_ic_tehdit_saymisaleviler_devlete_sizmaya_calisiyor-1141286

(8 October 2013). 'Mehmet Metiner: Cemevleri Terör Merkezi'. *Radikal.* www.radikal.com.tr/turkiye/mehmet_metiner_cemevleri_teror_merkezi-1154560

(14 May 2014). 'Kurtulmuş'tan SPK ve BDDK Mesajı'. *Radikal.* www.radikal.com.tr/ekonomi/kurtulmustan_spk_ve_bddk_mesaji-1192039

Rawls, John. (1987). 'The Idea of an Overlapping Consensus'. *Oxford Journal of Legal Studies*, 7(1): 1–25.

Reporters without Borders. World Press Freedom Index.

Reuter, O. J. and Turovsky, R. (2014). 'Dominant Party Rule and Legislative Leadership in Authoritarian Regimes'. *Party Politics*, 20(5): 663–674.

Robins, Philip. (2003). *Suits and Uniforms: Turkish Foreign Policy since the Cold War*. London: Hurst.

Rodrik, Dani. (30 July 2016). 'Is the U.S. behind Fethullah Gulen?' Dani Rodrik's weblog. http://rodrik.typepad.com/dani_rodriks_weblog/2016/07/is-the-us-behind-fethullah-gulen.html

Rokkan, Stein. (1999) (ed. Flora, P. with Kuhnle, S. and Urwin, D.) *State Formation, Nation-Building and Mass Politics in Europe: The Theory of Stein Rokkan*. Oxford University Press.

Rosenfeld, Michel. (1994). 'Identity of the Constitutional Subject'. *Cardozo Law Review*, 16: 1049–1109.

Roy, Olivier. (1994). *The Failure of Political Islam*. Cambridge, MA: Harvard University Press.

Rubin, Aviad. (2013). 'The Status of Religion in Emergent Political Regimes: Lessons from Turkey and Israel'. *Nations and Nationalism*, 19(3): 493–512.

Rueschemeyer, Dietrich, Huber, Evelyne and Stephens, John D. (1992). *Capitalist Development and Democracy*. Cambridge: Polity.

Rustow, Dankwart A. (1981). 'Atatürk as an Institution-Builder' in A. Kazancıgil and E. Özbudun (eds.), *Atatürk: Founder of a Modern State*. London: C. Hurst.

Sabah. (23 January 1997). 'Türkiye Müslümanlığı'. *Sabah*. https://fgulen.com/tr/turk-basininda-fethullah-gulen/fethullah-gulenle-gazete-roportajlari/sabahta-hulusi-turgutla/7885-Sabah-Turkiye-Muslumanligi

(1 March 1998). 'Diyanet'ten türbana "yeşil ışık"'. *Sabah*.

(29 February 2012). 'Adıyaman'da Alevi Evlerine İşaret'. *Sabah*. www.sabah.com.tr/gundem/2012/02/29/adiyamanda-alevi-evlerine-isaret

(5 February 2014). 'Paralel Yargının 2 Numarası'. *Sabah*. www.sabah.com.tr/Gundem/2014/02/05/paralel-yarginin-2-numarasi

Sahliyeh, E. F. (ed.). (1990). *Religious Resurgence and Politics in the Contemporary World*. Albany, NY: SUNY Press.

Said, Edward W. (4 October 2001). 'The Clash of Ignorance'. *The Nation*. www.thenation.com/article/clash-ignorance

(2003). *Orientalism*. London: Penguin.

Sakallıoğlu, Ümit Cizre. (1996). 'Parameters and Strategies of Islam–State Interaction in Republican Turkey'. *International Journal of Middle East Studies*, 28 (2): 231–251.

(1997). 'The Anatomy of the Turkish Military's Political Autonomy'. *Comparative Politics*, 29(2): 151–166.

Salamé, Ghassan (ed.). (1994). *Democracy without Democrats? The Renewal of Politics in the Muslim World*. New York: IB Tauris.

Sarıbay, Ali. Y. (1985). *Türkiye'de Modernleşme Din ve Parti Politikası*. İstanbul: Alan Yayıncılık.

Sartori, Giovanni. (2005). *Parties and Party Systems: A Framework for Analysis*. Colchester: ECPR Classics.

Savcı, Bahri. (1967). 'Diyanet İşleri Teşkilâtının Gelişmeleri'. *SBF Dergisi*, 20(3): 85–102.

Sayari, S. and Hasanov, A. (2008). 'The 2007 Elections and Parliamentary Elites in Turkey: The Emergence of a New Political Class?' *Turkish Studies*, 9(2): 345–361.

Sayari, Sabri. (2007). 'Towards a New Turkish Party System?' *Turkish Studies*, 8(2): 197–210.

(2011). 'Clientelism and Patronage in Turkish Politics and Society'. Sabanci University. http://research.sabanciuniv.edu/16988/

Schedler, A. (2006). 'The Logic of Electoral Authoritarianism' in Andreas Schedler (ed.), *Electoral Authoritarianism: The Dynamics of Unfree Competition*. Boulder, CO: Lynne Rienner, pp. 1–26.

Schumpeter, Joseph A. (1950). *Capitalism, Socialism, and Democracy*. New York: Harper.

(2007). *Imperialism and Social Classes*. New York: Meridian Books.

Schüler, Harald. (1999). *Particilik Hemşehrilik Alevilik*. İstanbul: İletişim Yayıncılık.

Schwedler, Jillian. (2006). *Faith in Moderation: Islamist Parties in Jordan and Yemen*. Cambridge University Press.

(2011). 'Can Islamists Become Moderates? Rethinking the Inclusion-Moderation Hypothesis'. *World Politics*, 63(2): 347–376.

Scott, Alev and Christie-Miller, Alexander. (2 December 2014). 'Isis Starts Recruiting in Istanbul's Vulnerable Suburbs'. *Newsweek*. www.newsweek.com/2014/09/19/exclusive-how-istanbul-became-recruiting-ground-islamic-state-269247.html

Sebilürreşad. (1948). 'Güzel Bir Gaye İçin Tutulan Yanlış bir Yol'. *Sebilürreşad*, 1(1): 12–16.

(1950). 'Diyanet Reisinin Mühim Beyanati'. *Sebilürreşad*, 4(86): 163–166.

(1961). 'Diyanet Riyaseti Teşkilatı Tasarısı Kakkında Gazetelerdeki Tenkidler'. *Sebilürreşad*, 14(348): 363–367.

Şen, Mustafa. (2010). 'Transformation of Turkish Islamism and the Rise of the Justice and Development Party'. *Turkish Studies*, 11(1): 59–84.

Şener, Cemal. (2003). *Alevilerin Etnik Kimliği*. İstanbul: Etik Yayınları.

Seufert, Günter. (2006). 'Religion: Nation-Building Instrument of the State or Factor of Civil Society? The AKP Between State- and Society-Centered Religious Politics' in Hans-Lukas Kieser (ed.), *Turkey Beyond Nationalism: Towards Post-Nationalist Identities*. London: IB Tauris, pp. 136–146.

(2014). 'Is the Fethullah Gülen Movement Overstretching Itself? A Turkish Religious Community as a National and International Player.' Berlin: SWP Research Paper 2/2014.

SGEU (Secretariat General for EU Affairs). (2010). *Law No 5982, Amending Certain Provisions of the Constitution*.

Shankland, David. (1999). *Islam and Society in Turkey*. Huntingdon: Eothen.

Sidel, J. T. (2007). 'On the "Anxiety of Incompleteness": A Post-Structuralist Approach to Religious Violence in Indonesia'. *South East Asia Research*, 15 (2): 133–212.

Şık, Ahmet. (2012). *İmamın Ordusu*. http://xeberler.files.wordpress.com/2011/04/51984426-dokunan-yanar.pdf

(2014). *Paralel Yürüdük Biz Bu Yollarda: AKP-Cemaat İttifakı Nasıl Dağıldı?* İstanbul: Postacı Yayınevi.

(17 August 2016). 'Ahmet Şık: 15 Temmuz Gecesi Ne Olduğu Tam Anlatılmıyor'. *Bianet.*

(10 November 2016). 'Yandaş Yazar İddiası: Hükümet Darbeyi Biliyordu'. *Cumhuriyet.* www.cumhuriyet.com.tr/haber/turkiye/628777/Yandas_yazar_iddiasi__Hukumet_darbeyi_biliyordu.html

(13 December 2016). '15 Temmuz'un Yanıtsız Soruları'. *Cumhuriyet.* https://bianet.org/bianet/siyaset/177836-ahmet-sik-15-temmuz-gecesi-ne-oldugu-tam-anlatilmiyor or www.cumhuriyet.com.tr/haber/turkiye/644907/15_Temmuz_un_yanitsiz_sorulari.html

Sil, R. and Katzenstein, P. J. (2010). *Beyond Paradigms: Analytic Eclecticism in the Study of World Politics.* New York: Palgrave Macmillan.

Sinclair-Webb, Emma. (2003). 'Sectarian Violence, the Alevi Minority and the Left: Kahramanmaraş 1978' in Paul J. White and Joost Jongerden (eds.), *Turkey's Alevi Enigma: A Comprehensive Overview.* Leiden, the Netherlands: Brill, pp. 215–236.

Skocpol, Theda. (1985). 'Bringing the State Back In: Strategies of Analysis in Current Research' in P.B. Evans, D. Rueschemeyer and T. Skocpol (eds.), *Bringing the State Back In.* Cambridge University Press, pp. 3–42.

Smith, Anthony D. (1986). *The Ethnic Origins of Nations.* Oxford: Basil Blackwell.

(1998). *Nationalism and Modernism.* London: Routledge.

(2003). *Chosen Peoples: Sacred Sources of National Identity.* Oxford University Press.

Smith, Benjamin. (2005). 'Life of the Party: The Origins of Regime Breakdown and Persistence under Single-Party Rule'. *World Politics,* 57(03): 421–451.

Smith, Kristin. (2004). 'The Kuwait Finance House and the Islamization of Public Life in Kuwait' in Clement M. Henry and Rodney Wilson (eds.), *The Politics of Islamic Finance.* Edinburgh University Press, pp. 168–190.

Sökefeld, Martin. (2008). *Struggling for Recognition: The Alevi Movement in Germany and in Transnational Space.* New York: Berghahn Books.

Somer, Murat. (2007). 'Moderate Islam and Secularist Opposition in Turkey: Implications for the World, Muslims and Secular Democracy'. *Third World Quarterly,* 28(7): 1271–1289.

(2011). 'Does it Take Democrats to Democratize? Lessons from Islamic and Secular Elite Values in Turkey'. *Comparative Political Studies,* 44(5): 511–545.

(2014). 'Moderation of Religious and Secular Politics: A Country's "Centre" and Democratization'. *Democratization,* 21(2): 244–267.

(2017). 'Conquering Versus Democratizing the State: Political Islamists and Fourth Wave Democratization in Turkey and Tunisia'. *Democratization,* 24(6): 1025–1043.

Soner, Bayram Ali and Toktaş, Şule. (2011). 'Alevis and Alevism in the Changing Context of Turkish Politics: The Justice and Development Party's Alevi Opening'. *Turkish Studies,* 12(3): 419–434.

Star Gazetesi. (19 July 2016). 'İran'ın Suriye'deki Milisleri Darbe Girişimini kutladı!' www.star.com.tr/dunya/iranin-suriyedeki-milisleri-darbe-girisimini-kutladi-haber-1126769/

Stark, R. and Bainbridge, W. S. (1980). 'Towards a Theory of Religion: Religious Commitment'. *Journal for the Scientific Study of Religion,* 19(2): 114–128.

Stark, Rodney. (1999). 'Secularization: RIP'. *Sociology of Religion*, 60(3): 249–273.

Stepan, Alfred. (2011). 'The Multiple Secularisms of Modern Democratic and Non-Democratic Regimes' in Craig Calhoun, Mark Juergensmeyer and Jonathan Van Antwerpen (eds.), *Rethinking Secularism*. Oxford University Press, pp. 114–144.

Sunar, İlkay. (2004). 'Populism and Patronage: The Demokrat Party and Its Legacy in Turkey' in İlkay Sunar (ed.). *State, Society and Democracy in Turkey*. İstanbul; Bahçeşehir University Publication, pp. 121–131.

Sunar, İlkay and Toprak, Binnaz. (1983). 'Islam in Politics: The Case of Turkey'. *Government and Opposition*, 18(4): 421–441.

Sunier, Thijl, and Landman, Nico. (2014). *Transnational Turkish Islam*. Basingstoke; New York: Palgrave Macmillan.

T24. (20 September 2010). 'Gülen Cemaati Hakkâri'yi Anlatıyor', *T24*. http://t24.com.tr/haber/arsiv,99542; http://t24.com.tr/haber/arsiv,99734

(10 June 2011). 'Erdoğan: Bazı Kitaplar Vardır ki Bombadan Daha Tesirlidir!' *T24*. http://t24.com.tr/haber/erdogan-bazi-kitaplar-vardir-ki-bombadan-daha-tesirlidir,150308

(25 November 2013). 'Emniyete Göre, Gezi Parkı Şüphelilerinin Yüzde 78'i Alevi!' http://t24.com.tr/haber/gezide-kac-eylem-gerceklesti-kac-kisi-gozal tina-alindi,244706

Taagepera, Rein. (2002). 'Implication of the Effective Number of Parties for Cabinet Formation'. *Party Politics*, 12(1), 3–27.

Taniyici, S. (2003). 'Transformation of Political Islam in Turkey Islamist Welfare Party's Pro-EU Turn'. *Party Politics*, 9(4): 463–483.

Tanör, Bülent. (1995). *Osmanlı-Türk Anayasal Gelişmeleri: 1789–1980*. İstanbul: Der Yayınları.

Tanyılmaz, Kurtar. (2015). 'The Deep Fracture in the Big Bourgeoisie of Turkey' in Neşecan Balkan, Erol Balkan and Ahmet Öncü (eds.), *The Neoliberal Landscape and the Rise of Islamist Capital in Turkey*. New York; Oxford: Berghahn Books, pp. 89–116.

Tarih ve Toplum. (29 March 2013). 'Muammer Aksoy Neden Öldürüldü?' https://toplumsaltarih.wordpress.com/2013/03/29/muammer-aksoy-neden-olduruldu/

Tarlo, Emma and Moors, Annelies (eds.). (2013). *Islamic Fashion and Anti-Fashion: New Perspectives from Europe and North America*. London: Bloomsbury Academic.

Taşkın, Yüksel. (2002). '12 Eylül Atatürkçülüğü ya da Bir Kemalist Restorasyon Teşebbüsü Olarak 12 Eylül' in Tanıl Bora and Murat Gültekingil (eds.), *Modern Türkiye'de Siyasi Düşünce Cilt 2-Kemalizm*. İstanbul: İletişim, pp. 574–583.

(2007). *Milliyetçi Muhafazakar Entelijansiya*. İstanbul: İletişim.

(2008). 'AKP's Move to "Conquer" the Center-Right: Its Prospects and Possible Impacts on the Democratization Process'. *Turkish Studies*, 9(1): 53–72.

Taşpınar, Ömer. (2004). *Kurdish Nationalism and Political Islam in Turkey: Kemalist Identity in Transition*. New York: Routledge.

(2014). 'The End of the Turkish Model'. *Survival*, 56(2): 49–64.

Taştan, Yahya Kemal. (2012). 'Kanonik Topraklardan Ulusal. Vatana: Balkan Savaşları ve Türk Ulusçuluğunun Doğusu'. *Journal of Turkish World Studies*, XI(2): 1–99.

Tastekin, Fehim. (20 January 2014). 'Turkish Intelligence Service Trucks Reveal Secrets'. *Al-Monitor*.

Taylor, Charles. (2011). 'Western Secularity' in Craig Calhoun, Mark Juergensmeyer and Jonathan Van Antwerpen (eds.), *Rethinking Secularism*. Oxford University Press, pp. 31–53.

Tehranian, Majid. (2007). 'Globalization and Religious Resurgence: An Historical Perspective'. *The Muslim World*, 97(3): 385–394.

Tejani, Shabnum. (2008). *Indian Secularism: A Social and Intellectual History, 1890–1950*. Bloomington, IN: Indiana University Press.

Tekeli, İlhan and Soral, Erdoğan. (1976). *Halk Sektörü Sorunu*. İstanbul: Gelişim Yayınları.

Tepe, Sultan. (2005). 'Turkey's AKP: A Model "Muslim-Democratic" Party?' *Journal of Democracy*, 16(3): 69–82.

  (2012). 'Moderation of Religious Parties: Electoral Constraints, Ideological Commitments, and the Democratic Capacities of Religious Parties in Israel and Turkey'. *Political Research Quarterly*, 65(3): 467–485.

Terzioğlu, Derin. (2013). 'How to Conceptualize Ottoman Sunnitization: A Historiographical Discussion'. *Turcica*, 44: 301–338.

Tezcür, Güneş Murat. (2010). 'The Moderation Theory Revisited: The Case of Islamic Political Actors'. *Party Politics*, 16(1): 69–88.

Tezcür, Güneş Murat and Çiftçi, Sabri. (2014). 'Radical Turks: Why Turkish Citizens Are Joining ISIS'. *Foreign Affairs*, www.foreignaffairs.com/articles/turkey/2014-11-11/radical-turks

Thelen, Kathleen. (1999). 'Historical Institutionalism in Comparative Politics'. *Annual Review of Political Science*, 2(1): 369–404.

Thelen, Kathleen and Steinmo, S. (1992). 'Historical Institutionalism in Comparative Politics' in S. Steinmo, K. Thelen and F. Longstreth (eds.), *Structuring Politics: Historical Institutionalism in Comparative Analysis*. Cambridge University Press, pp. 1–32.

Thomson Reuters Zawya. (2013). *Turkey Islamic Finance Report 2014*. Thomson Reuters.

Tibi, Bassam. (2001). *Islam between Culture and Politics*. New York: Palgrave.

  (2012). *Islamism and Islam*. New Haven, CT: Yale University Press.

The Times. (17 January 2017). 'Erdogan Plotted Purge before Coup, Say Brussels Spies'. *The Times*. www.thetimes.co.uk/article/erdogan-plotted-purge-before-coup-say-brussels-spies-2hh8mgx6h

Tittensor, David. (2014). *The House of Service: The Gulen Movement and Islam's Third Way*. Oxford University Press.

Topak, Oğuz. (2012). *Refah Devleti ve Kapitalizm*. İstanbul: İletişim.

Toprak, Binnaz. (1981). *Islam and Political Development in Turkey*. Leiden: Brill.

  (1990). 'Religion as State Ideology in a Secular Setting: The Turkish-Islamic Synthesis' in Malcolm Wagstaff (ed.), *Aspects of Religion in Secular Turkey*. Occasional Paper Series No. 40. University of Durham, Centre for Middle Eastern and Islamic Studies.

(2005). 'Islam and Democracy in Turkey'. *Turkish Studies*, 6(2): 167–186.
Toprak, Zafer. (1995). *Milli İktisat-Milli Burjuvazi*. İstanbul: Tarih Vakfı Yurt Yayınları.
Tremblay, Pınar. (25 July 2016). 'How Erdogan Used the Power of the Mosques against Coup Attempt.' *Al-Monitor*.
(12 April 2017). 'How Erdogan Uses Turkey's Mosques to Push "Yes" Vote'. *Al-Monitor*.
Tuğal, Cihan. (2002). 'Islamism in Turkey: Beyond Instrument and Meaning'. *Economy and Society*, 31(1): 85–111.
(2007). 'Nato's Islamists'. *New Left Review*, 44(5): 5–34.
(2009a). *Passive Revolution: Absorbing the Islamic Challenge to Capitalism*. Stanford University Press.
(2009b). 'Transforming Everyday Life: Islamism and Social Movement Theory'. *Theory and Society*, 38(5): 423–458.
(2016). *The Fall of the Turkish Model: How the Arab Uprisings Brought Down Islamic Liberalism*. Brooklyn, NY: Verso Books.
Tunaya, Tarık Zafer. (1952). *Türkiye'de Siyasi Partiler, 1859–1952*. Vol. 3. İstanbul: Doğan Kardeş Yayınları.
(1957). 'Türkiye Büyük Millet Meclisi Hükümetinin Kuruluşu ve Siyasi Karakteri', *İÜ Hukuk Fakültesi Mecmuası*, 23(3–4): 227–247.
(2007). *İslamcılık Akımı*. İstanbul: Bilgi Üniversitesi Yayınları.
Tunçay, Mete. (2005). *Türkiye Cumhuriyeti'nde Tek-Parti Yönetiminin Kurulması (1923–1931)*. İstanbul: Tarih Vakfı Yurt Yayınları.
Turam, Berna. (2007). *Between Islam and the State: The Politics of Engagement*. Stanford University Press.
(ed.). (2011). *Secular State and Religious Society: Two Forces in Play in Turkey*. New York: Palgrave Macmillan.
Türkeş, Mustafa. (2001). 'A Patriotic Leftist Development-Strategy Proposal in Turkey in the 1930s: The Case of the Kadro (Cadre) Movement.' *International Journal of Middle East Studies*, 33(1): 91–114.
Türkmen, Buket. (2009). 'A Transformed Kemalist Islam or a New Islamic Civic Morality? A Study of "Religious Culture and Morality" Textbooks in the Turkish High School Curricula'. *Comparative Studies of South Asia, Africa and the Middle East* 29(3): 381–397.
Türköne, Mümtaz'er. (16 January 2014). 'Hayrettin Hoca, Rüşvete Fetva Vermiş Oldu Mu?'
Tutar, Adem. (1997). XX. 'Yüzyıl Hatay Tarihi ve Günümüz İnanç Coğrafyası'. PhD thesis.
Ülger, Mustafa. (1997). XX. 'Yüzyil Eskişehir İli Tarihi Ve İnanç Coğrafyası'. Master's thesis.
Ulus, Özgür Mutlu. (2010). *The Army and the Radical Left in Turkey: Military Coups, Socialist Revolution and Kemalism*, Vol. 97). London: IB Tauris.
Ulutaş, Songül. (2012). 'Yüzyilin İlk Yarisinda Kapitalist Ticari İlişkilerdeki Dönüşümün Tarsus'taki Yansimalari (1839–1856)'. *Tarih İncelemeleri Dergisi*, XXVII(2): 499–525.
Ünal, Ali. (11 September 2011). 'Ustalık Dönemiyle İlgili Üç Endişe'. *Zaman*. https://fgulen.com/tr/turk-basininda-fethullah-gulen/fethullah-gulen-hakkinda-

kose-yazilari/2011-kose-yazilari/19655-Ali-Unal-Zaman-Ustalik-Donemiyle-Ilgili-Uc-Endise

Üngör, Ugur Ümit. (2012). *The Making of Modern Turkey: Nation and State in Eastern Anatolia, 1913–1950.* Oxford University Press.

Ünsür, Ahmet. (2000). *İmam-Hatip Liseleri.* İstanbul: Ensar Neşriyat.

Van der Veer, Peter. (1994). *Religious Nationalism: Hindus and Muslims in India.* Berkeley, CA: University of California Press.

(2011). 'Smash Temples, Burn Books: Comparing Secularist Projects in India and China' in Craig Calhoun, Mark Juergensmeyer and Jonathan VanAntwerpen (eds.), *Rethinking Secularism.* Oxford University Press, pp. 270–281.

Vanaik, A. (1992). 'Reflections on Communalism and Nationalism in India'. *New Left Review*, 196: 43–63.

Verdery, Katherine. (1993). 'Whither "Nation" and "Nationalism"?' *Daedalus*, 122(3): 37–46.

Vertigans, Stephen. (2003). *Islamic Roots and Resurgence in Turkey.* London: Praeger.

Voice of America. (25 September 2012). 'In Turkey, Religious Schools Gain a Foothold'. *Voice of America.* www.voanews.com/content/turkey-controver sial-education-reform-imam-hatip-schools/1514915.html

Voll, John O. (1987). 'Islamic Renewal and the "Failure of the West"' in Richard T. Antoun and Mary Elaine Hegland (eds), *Religious Resurgence: Contemporary Cases in Islam, Christianity, and Judaism.* Syracuse University Press, pp. 127–144.

Wacquant, Loîc. (2006). 'Pierre Bourdieu' in Rob Stones (ed.), *Key Contemporary Thinkers.* London and New York: Macmillan, pp. 261–277.

Wall Street Journal. (10 October 2013). 'Turkey's Spymaster Plots Own Course on Syria'. *Wall Street Journal.* www.wsj.com/articles/turkey8217s-spymaster-plots-own-course-on-syria-1381373295?tesla=y

Walzer, Michael. (1984). 'Liberalism and the Art of Separation'. *Political Theory*, 12(3): 315–330.

Warde, Ibrahim. (2004). 'Global Politics, Islamic Finance and Islamist Politics Before and After 11 September 2001' in Clement M. Henry and Rodney Wilson (eds.), *The Politics of Islamic Finance.* Edinburgh University Press, pp. 37–62.

Weber, Max. (1978). *Economy and Society: An Outline of Interpretive Sociology.* Berkeley, CA: University of California Press.

Weiker, Walter F. (1963). *The Turkish Revolution 1960–1961: Aspects of Military Politics.* Washington: Brookings Institution.

Wells, David. (1981). *Marxism and the Modern State: An Analysis of Fetishism in Capitalist Society.* Brighton: Harvester.

White, Benjamin T. (2011). *The Emergence of Minorities in the Middle East: The Politics of Community in French Mandate Syria.* Edinburgh University Press.

White, D. (2011). 'Dominant Party Systems: A Framework for Conceptualizing Opposition Strategies in Russia'. *Democratization*, 18(3): 655–681.

White, Jenny B. (2002). *Islamist Mobilization in Turkey: A Study in Vernacular Politics.* Seattle: University of Washington Press.

White, Paul J. and Jongerden, Joost (eds.). (2003). *Turkey's Alevi Enigma: A Comprehensive Overview*. Leiden, the Netherlands: Brill.

Wickham, Carrie R. (2004). 'The Path to Moderation: Strategy and Learning in the Formation of Egypt's Wasat Party'. *Comparative Politics*, 36(2): 205–228.

Wiktorowicz, Quintan (ed.). (2004). *Islamic Activism: A Social Movement Theory Approach*. Bloomington, IN: Indiana University Press.

Williams, Brackette F. (1989). 'A Class Act: Anthropology and the Race to Nation Across Ethnic Terrain'. *Annual Review of Anthropology*, 18: 401–444.

Wimmer, A. (1997). 'Who Owns the State? Understanding Ethnic Conflict in Post-Colonial Societies'. *Nations and Nationalism*, 3(4): 631–666.

    (2004). 'Does Ethnicity Matter? Everyday Group Formation in Three Swiss Immigrant Neighbourhoods'. *Ethnic and Racial Studies*, 27(1): 1–36.

    (2008). 'The Making and Unmaking of Ethnic Boundaries: A Multilevel Process Theory'. *American Journal of Sociology*, 113(4): 970–1022.

Wimmer, A. and Glick Schiller, N. (2002). 'Methodological Nationalism and Beyond: Nation-State Building, Migration and the Social Sciences'. *Global Networks*, 2(4): 301–334.

Wimmer, Andreas. (2002). *Nationalist Exclusion and Ethnic Conflict: Shadows of Modernity*. Cambridge University Press.

    (2013). *Ethnic Boundary Making: Institutions, Power, Networks*. New York: Oxford University Press.

Winter, Michael. (2009). '"Ulama" Between the State and Society in Pre-Modern Sunni Islam' in M. Hatina, (ed.). *Guardians of Faith in Modern Times: 'Ulama' in the Middle East*. Leiden, the Netherlands: Brill, pp. 21–46.

Yakut, Esra. (2005). *Şeyhülislamlık Yenileşme Döneminde Devlet ve Din*. İstanbul: Kitap Yayınevi.

Yalçınkaya, A. and Ecevitoğlu, P. (2013). *Aleviler Artık Burda Oturmuyor*. Ankara: Dipnot Yayınevi.

Yalçınkaya, Ayhan. (2009). 'Alevilik Hendeğinde AKP'nin Devesi: "Alevi Açılımı' Neyi 'Açıyor'" in İlhan Uzel and Bülent Duru (eds.), *AKP Kitabı: Bir Dönüşümün Bilançosu*. Ankara: Phoenix Yayınevi.

Yalman, Galip. (2002). 'Tarihsel Bir Perspektiften Türkiyede Devlet ve Burjuvazi: Rölativist bir Paradigma mı Hegemonya Stratejisi mi?' *Praxis*, 5: 7–23.

Yanardağ, Ayşe. (2012). 'Tevhid-İ Tedrisat Kanunu Uygulamasında Diyanet İşleri Başkanlığı'nın Rolü'. *Atatürk Yolu Dergisi*, 13(49): 241–264.

Yankaya, Dilek. (2012). '28 Subat, Yeni Islami Burjuvazinin Iktidari Yolunda Bir Milat'. *Birikim* (278–279): 29–37.

    (2014). *Yeni İslâmî Burjuvazi*. İstanbul: İletişim.

Yavuz, M. Hakan. (1997). 'Political Islam and the Welfare (Refah) Party in Turkey'. *Comparative Politics*. 30(1): 63–82.

    (2000). 'Cleansing Islam from the Public Sphere'. *Journal of International Affairs*, 54(1): 21–42.

    (2003). *Islamic Political Identity in Turkey*. New York: Oxford University Press.

    (2004a). 'Opportunity Spaces, Identity, and Islamic Meaning in Turkey' in Quintan Wiktorowicz (ed.), *Islamic Activism: A Social Movement Theory Approach*. Bloomington, IN; Indiana University Press, pp. 270–288.

    (2004b). 'Is There a Turkish Islam? The Emergence of Convergence and Consensus'. *Journal of Muslim Minority Affairs*, 24(2): 213–232.

Yavuz, M. Hakan. (ed.) (2006). *The Emergence of a New Turkey: Democracy and the AK Parti*. Salt Lake City, UT: University of Utah Press.

(2009). *Secularism and Muslim Democracy in Turkey*. Cambridge University Press.

Yavuz, M. Hakan. (2013). *Toward an Islamic Enlightenment: The Gülen Movement*. New York: Oxford University Press.

Yavuz, M. Hakan and Esposito, John L. (Eds). (2003). *Turkish Islam and the Secular State: The Gülen Movement*. Syracuse University Press.

Yeğen, Mesut. (1996). 'The Turkish State Discourse and the Exclusion of Kurdish Identity'. *Middle Eastern Studies*, 32(2): 216–229.

(2007). 'Turkish Nationalism and the Kurdish Question'. *Ethnic and Racial Studies*, 30(1): 119–151.

Yeni Akit. (21 May 2016). 'Diyanet'in Dev Projesine Alim Sabuni'den Destek'. *Yeni Akit*. www.yeniakit.com.tr/haber/diyanetin-dev-projesine-alim-sabuni den-destek-176279.html

(30 May 2016). 'Mehmet Görmez: Bin Alim Türkiye'de'. *Yeni Akit*. www .yeniakit.com.tr/haber/mehmet-gormez-bin-alim-turkiyede-179030.html

(26 November 2016). 'Diyanet 'Dini Yüksek İhtisas Merkezleri' Açıyor'. *Yeni Akit*. www.yeniakit.com.tr/haber/diyanet-dini-yuksek-ihtisas-merkezleri-aciyor-239199.html

Yenigün, Halil İbrahim. (2016). 'The Political and Theological Boundaries of Islamist Moderation after the Arab Spring'. *Third World Quarterly*, 37(12): 2304–2321.

Yeni Şafak. (29 December 2006). 'Diyanet TV 2007'de Yayında'. *Yeni Şafak*. www.yenisafak.com/gundem/diyanet-tv-2007de-yayinda-21965

Yeni Şafak. (22 July 2016). 'Darbeden Sonra Türkiye'yi İşgal Edeceklerdi: Plan İncirlik'te Yapıldı'. *Yeni Şafak*. www.yenisafak.com/gundem/darbeden-sonra-turkiyeyi-isgal-edeceklerdi-plan-incirlikte-yapildi-2498091

Yeşilada, Birol and Rubin, Barry (eds.). (2011). *Islamization of Turkey Under the AKP Rule*. London: Routledge.

Yetkin, Murat. (3 May 2014). 'Erdoğan Escalates Elimination of Gülenists from State'. *Hürriyet Daily News*. www.hurriyetdailynews.com/erdogan-escalates-elimination-of-gulenists-from-state.aspx?pageID=449andnID=65930andNews CatID=409

Yılmaz, Nail. (2004). 'Farklılaştıran ve Ayrıştıran Bir Mekanizma Olarak Kentle-şme'. *Sosyal Siyaset Konferansları Dergisi*, 38: 249–267.

Yılmaz, Zafer. (2017). 'The AKP and the Spirit of the "New" Turkey: Imagined Victim, Reactionary Mood, and Resentful Sovereign'. *Turkish Studies*, 18(3): 482–513.

Yücel, Hasan Ali. (1994). *Türkiye'de Orta Öğretim*. Ankara: TC Kültür Bakanlığı Başvuru Eserleri.

Zaman Gazetesi. (17 May 2003). 'Laikliğe En Uygun Din İslâm; Alevilik ise Ayrımcılıktır!' *Zaman Gazetesi*.

(26 February 2005). 'Diyanet Sünni Bir Kurum Değil'. *Zaman Gazetesi*.

(21 February 2010) 'Necdet Subaşı ile söyleşi'. *Zaman Gazetesi*.

Zaman, Muhammad Qasim. (2002). *The Ulama in Contemporary Islam: Custodians of Change*. Princeton University Press.

Zarcone, Thierry. (1993). 'Zulümden Yeniden Dini, Siyasi ve Toplumsal Mev-kiye Ulaşma (1925–1991)'. *Türkiye Günlüğü*, 23: 99–105.

Zeghal, Malika. (1999). 'Religion and Politics in Egypt: The Ulema of al-Azhar, Radical Islam, and the State (1952–94)'. *International Journal of Middle East Studies*, 31(3): 371–399.

Zilfi, Madeline C. (1983). 'Elite Circulation in the Ottoman Empire: Great Mollas of the Eighteenth Century'. *Journal of the Economic and Social History of the Orient/Journal de l'histoire economique et sociale de l'Orient*, 26(3): 318–364.

(2008). *Dindarlık Siyaseti Osmanlı Uleması*. Ankara: Birleşik Kitabevi.

Zimmer, O. (2003). 'Boundary Mechanisms and Symbolic Resources: Towards a Process-Oriented Approach to National Identity'. *Nations and Nationalism*, 9(2): 173–193.

Zırh, Besim Can. (2012a). 'Becoming Visible through Migration: Understanding the Relationships between the Alevi Revival, Migration and Funerary Practices through Europe and Turkey'. Unpublished PhD thesis.

(2012b). 'Following the Dead beyond the "Nation": A Map for Transnational Alevi Funerary Routes from Europe to Turkey'. *Ethnic and Racial Studies*, 35(10): 1758–1774.

Zubaida, Sami. (1992). 'Islam, the State and Democracy: Contrasting Conceptions of Society in Egypt'. *Middle East Report*, 179: 2–10.

(1993). *Islam, the People and the State*. London: IB Tauris.

(2011). *Beyond Islam: A New Understanding of the Middle East*. London; New York: IB Tauris.

Zucca, L. (2009). 'The Crisis of the Secular State: A Reply to Professor Sajó'. *International Journal of Constitutional Law*, 73(2): 130–149.

Zürcher, Erik J. (1984). *The Unionist Factor: The Role of the Committee of Union and Progress in the Turkish National Movement, 1905–1926*. Leiden, the Netherlands: Brill.

(1992). 'The Ottoman Legacy of the Turkish Republic: An Attempt at a New Periodization'. *Die Welt des Islams*, 32(2): 237–253.

(2002). 'Kemalist Düşüncenin Osmanlı Kaynakları' in Tanıl Bora and Murat Gültekingil (eds.), *Modern Türkiye'de Siyasi Düşünce Cilt 2-Kemalizm*. İstanbul: İletişim, pp. 44–55.

(2004). *Turkey: A Modern History*. London: I. B. Tauris.

(2010). *The Young Turk Legacy and Nation Building: From the Ottoman Empire to Atatürk's Turkey*. London: IB Tauris.

Index

Note: All political parties, organisations and institutions are indicated under their acronym. Locators in *italics* refer to figures. An 'n' after a locator refers to a footnote. A 't' after a locator refers to a table.

Books in the Series